Theory and Explanation in Geogra

# RGS-IBG Book Series

For further information about the series and a full list of published and forthcoming titles please visit www.rgsbookseries.com

# Theory and Explanation in Geography

Henry Wai-chung Yeung

WILEY

*Registered Offices*

John Wiley & Sons, Inc., 111 River Street, Hoboken, NJ 07030, USA

John Wiley & Sons Ltd, The Atrium, Southern Gate, Chichester, West Sussex, PO19 8SQ, UK

For details of our global editorial offices, customer services, and more information about Wiley products visit us at www.wiley.com.

Wiley also publishes its books in a variety of electronic formats and by print-on-demand. Some content that appears in standard print versions of this book may not be available in other formats.

A catalogue record for this book is available from the Library of Congress

Paperback ISBN: 9781119845508; Hardback ISBN: 9781119845492; ePub ISBN: 9781119845522; ePDF ISBN: 9781119845539; oBook ISBN: 9781119845515

Cover Design: Wiley

Cover Image: Wiley, © jimmyjamesbond/Getty Images

Set in 10/12pt PlantinStd by Integra Software Services Pvt. Ltd, Pondicherry, India

*For Li Mui Sheung, my late mother*

# Contents

# List of Tables

# List of Figures

# Preface and Acknowledgement

With a deep sense of us surviving the vicissitudes in life, let me state that this is emphatically a COVID-19 book – conceived, written, and published during the 2020–2023 pandemic. You might be able to gauge it from my *Squid Game*-symbolled cover. In light of good hygiene habits learnt during and thereafter the pandemic, let me preface the book with some 'health warnings' before saying something more personal and acknowledging several unrepayable intellectual debts and causal powers.

To begin, the book was conceived during my usual afternoon nap on 29 May 2020 – never underestimate the incredible power of power naps, my well-known little secret for research productivity! I felt strongly about something 'happening' in Geography that kept me awake. I just couldn't sleep over it – how can Geography contribute better to the understanding and explanation of all those life-changing disruptions (lockdowns everywhere), shortages (masks and toilet papers then), and everyday life and death occurring in the midst of this terrible COVID-19 pandemic? Can we do so by offering more reading 'against the grain' and incessant critiques from the perspectives of the various so-called critical 'theory'? Are these critical theories really theory as their names so pompously suggest? If so, in what sense and can it be explanatory? And so what? These were the unforgettable questions that I kept pondering over in that fateful hot afternoon (as often the case in tropical Singapore), and the rest is what you are reading, albeit with a fairly long delay over three years (blame it too on the pandemic and, as I've been saying to many old and new friends worldwide lately, TIE [see full spelling at the end])!

But what is this work *for* in terms of its audience, approach, and purpose/positionality? I hope the book is akin to some medication that presumably treats common symptoms and perhaps serious underlying conditions. On *audience*, this is an academic book written as a research monograph and thus comes with its highest scholarly intent and purpose. So it's not for the faint-hearted readers and don't bother to read it as an undergraduate text because it would be harder to survive my text than in *Squid Game* (only one out of 456 players emerged alive). To my best knowledge (and I've rechecked this with my dear colleague James Sidaway, himself a shrewd historian of our discipline), there is no recent authored academic book in Geography that goes into this kind of epistemological debates on theory and method. My favourite one though would be Derek Gregory's *Ideology, Science and Human Geography* published quite some decades ago. And yet such a statement beyond a typical textbook on contemporary geographical thought needs to be made to reinvigorate our collective sensibility on theory and explanation in Geography. I believe this monograph will provoke such serious reflections and (mis)givings among many practicing geographers and advanced students interested in the development of our collective thought and normative vision for society and space.

To ensure the book's performativity as a full-blown monograph, I have taken an open-ended *approach* of engaging with the original works of a strategic selection of critical theorists and (continental) philosophers and their well-known interlocutors in human geography. Nevertheless, I really don't like the arcane writing style of some of them and I want to spare you, my dear readers, from a similar agony of reading this work. I have therefore opted for an extensive engagement approach in my narratives and a writing style of citing some of them in the main text and putting in each chapter's endnotes the most tedious quotations, comprehensive literature grounding/long citations, and further elaborations on important debates. To me, this is a pragmatic and straightforward style of writing and theorizing – not too philosophical nor too convoluted. To the discerning readers, this is not quite like poststructuralist philosophers Gilles Deleuze and Félix Guattari's 'hallucinatory experiences' of writing in their *A Thousand Plateaus,* nor feminist philosopher Rosi Braidotti's nomadic habits of narration allowing for reading at random in her *Nomadic Theory* (note: only non-geographers like them are given 'titles' by way of introduction, a writing habit I have used throughout this book). Readers are thus advised to consider skipping these endnotes on the first pass and, if sufficiently impressed thereafter, to revisit them together with the main text on subsequent nomadic (re)readings and passes.

Still, the book is meant to be well grounded in the relevant literature, i.e. thorough enough by combining formative and contemporary work, and committed enough to following through such debates over theory with care and patience. In a reversal of critical urban scholar Ananya Roy's complaint about 'citationary alibis' in her field, I actually provide such alibis *for* critical theorists and their geographer interlocutors in my text. Nonetheless, instead of indemnifying them from any intellectual liabilities and granting any conceptual carte blanche to their theories, I do hope the book can be read as a rigorous interrogation of their key theories and concepts in geographical writing that comes with an acute awareness of the limits of these allegedly 'grand theories' in theory and practice. To render my approach more 'approachable', I also offer some personal reflections along the way to help readers contextualize different events and happenings in Geography at various times and places and my own theory development journey.

But why bother to write this book in the first place? In the larger scheme of things, losing an afternoon nap is really not a big deal. My *purpose* here, however, is indeed quite simple. Just like one very kind reviewer of my full manuscript has alluded, I too wished I had seen and perhaps read such a book during my Manchester PhD in the early 1990s (even though I did benefit much from reading and appreciating Gregory's *Ideology* in my undergraduate days just before going to England). I think my book is useful in making a clear(er) case for explanatory mid-range theory in Geography that might complement diverse accounts of 'weak theory' and other calls for grounded theory, dirty theory, minor theory, modest theory, and so on. Indeed, theory should be explanatory and geographical explanation should be grounded in theory. As you will find out from reading this book though, it is not a standard nor an authoritarian prescription for all theoretical efforts in Geography – doing so would likely shut down, rather than open up, possible avenues for new and meaningful theory work (my sincere thanks to Colin McFarlane for his persuasive reminder of this important point over a recent dinner in Singapore)! To borrow from Doreen Massey's *For Space*, my book is in itself a dynamic simultaneous multiplicity of (hopeful) becomings that must be open for a reimaginable and changeable future.

Let me clarify further my *positionality*. Despite my long-time training and practice in the subfield of economic geography and urban and regional studies, this book is not written for economic geographers per se, but rather for the entire discipline of Geography as a global knowledge enterprise. Since my PhD days (some details in Chapter 6), I have had a longstanding interest in, and quite some publications on, philosophical and epistemological debates in (economic) Geography. The book thus offers a broad engagement with various critical theories and approaches in social and cultural geography, feminist and postcolonial geographies, critical geopolitics, environmental studies, urban geography, economic geography, and so on. I hope readers from these and other subfields will take some cues from my approach here to reflect on their 'favourite' theories and explanations in all domains of geographical knowledge. While some of the key ideas in this book have been brewing and germinating for quite some time now, I have only been able to concretize and even materialize them in this form after a decade-long interregnum of producing several social science-oriented monographs on global production networks, developmental states in East Asia, and the interconnected worlds of electronics production! So, it's better late than never...

Ultimately, my goal is to stimulate more and better theorizing *and* explanatory work in our discipline and for the wider social sciences. If you get that message in this book, it will really make me happy, much like the late Doreen Massey in her personal note to me about her own happiness in reading my review of her *World City* (reproduced in my Chapter 4 endnotes). At the end of the day, that's what makes our scholarly work worth its salt.

On the more personal front, there were two life and death 'events' during the writing of this book – one real and another metaphorical – and I want to make sure these events and their influences are fully acknowledged here. First, I was caring for my late mother, who had moved to our home not too long after that sleepless afternoon nap, till her eventual passing at home in end June 2022 due to geriatric illness. This tragic event took place a couple of months after I had completed this book's first full draft (an experience similar to my dad's passing two years earlier just before I finished writing about 3 nanometre semiconductor chip-making in my previous book *Interconnected Worlds*). Her embodied presence always reminded me of the formidable bravery, fortitude, and strength of a 'golden tigress' in the Chinese zodiac. So, in loving memory, I dedicate this hopefully brave enough work to her.

Second, writing this book in the midst of living through a once-in-a-generation pandemic is quite a life and death experience. Many of us in academia are rather privileged to be able to get through it relatively unscathed. In particular, I feel very blessed with the opportunity to 'Think, Read, Write' almost on a daily basis during the pandemic. And yet one can also get rather bored doing it, though it might not be the kind of (political) boredom so well critiqued in Ben Anderson's work. Here, I thank various affective and eventful K-dramas, such as *Squid Game* launched in September 2021, for eventualizing life and death in such a dramatic and metaphorical way that kept me well focused in my own writing. Watching them during the pandemic and the book's writing could be both entertaining in a work-life balance sense and intriguing in an intensely intellectual manner. This is why I have chosen the three symbols in the melodrama to express my affect in/ towards theory and explanation – a tricky balancing act of theory (triangle) and explanation (square) much needed but also well supported in Geography (represented by the earth-shaded circle symbol!). I know very well that this choice might not convey the kind of aesthetic and scholarly sophistication expressed in the (famous) abstract artworks gracing the book covers of leading geographical treatises nor, as well guessed by my dear new colleague Dariusz Wójcik, in philosopher John McDowell's seesaw metaphor in his *Mind and World*. Nevertheless, I sincerely hope it does represent the kind of academic realism and intellectual honesty in my approach and purpose here.

Looking back, being able to write and express one's thought in this highly contested and geopoliticized world and feminist theorist Donna Haraway's Chthulucene is very much a privilege and luxury bestowed upon a few lucky authors. Located and at home in postcolonial Singapore, I feel even more lucky than these few counterparts. Having studied Geography ever since my early secondary school days in colonial Hong Kong during the 1980s and despite not getting distinction in the subject for my pre-university examination (I got C actually, and so did some very prominent British geographers whom I heard from!), I never thought I would be privileged enough to write a theoretical book of this nature *for* Geography – that reminds me of the late Doreen Massey's *For Space*. This book is therefore written with much gratitude and gratification. My gratitude comes from the affective feelings of both engagement with and acceptance in my scholarly community/communities. I don't take this privilege lightly but instead with a heavy dose of optimism, cruel or otherwise. Two anonymous reviewers, apparently senior figures in the discipline and non-economic geographers, have been most generous and constructive with their in-depth and spot-on comments that reaffirm my gratitude and provide key pointers for relatively minor revisions to make the book even better. Meanwhile, the studious act of writing this book also offers enormous gratification so much more than what I can ever hope for. After all, it is not often one gets to write and talk about one's own intellectual journey in such an unfettered and even playful manner (including this Preface!). Again, my sincere thanks to all parties for making this book happen.

Whereas the above paragraphs have elaborated on the context or conjuncture of this book's eventualizing, I now provide the concatenation of 'causal mechanisms' that complete my own explanation for this book's eventual becoming. Thanks to various journals and publishers for publishing my earlier conceptual work on critical realism and epistemological debates in (economic) Geography – these generative ideas underpin the origin of and my continual interest in this book's main tenets. While much of the actual writing in this monograph is new, some sections in later Chapters 4–6 have drawn on these earlier publications that are explicitly specified and acknowledged in relevant chapter endnotes. Several copyrighted figures are reproduced in this book and I acknowledge the kind permission granted by Cornell University Press, Oxford University Press, and Taylor and Francis.

Speaking of causality, I must acknowledge my university for the generous annual research grant support under my Distinguished Professorship (E-109-00-0008-01) that funds the acquisition of several hundred books *necessary* for this book's thinking, reading, and writing and many of my travel trips presenting some aspects of it to diverse audiences worldwide. Ideas in Chapter 6 were first presented in a session I co-organized with Kean Fan Lim at the RGS-IBG annual international conference in Newcastle in September 2022 and various in-person Geography seminars hosted by my alma mater, the University of Manchester, in November 2022, my good friend Jinn-yuh Hsu at the National Taiwan University in February 2023, my much-admired department at the University of British Columbia in March 2023, and more to come in Uppsala University and Melbourne University in May 2023, and so on.

I am most grateful for the wonderful comments and challenging questions from Kean Fan, James Sidaway, and Michael Webber (via Zoom) in Newcastle, Erik Swyngedouw and Jamie Doucette in Manchester, Crison Chien, Christopher Huang, Kuang-Chi Hung, Po-Yi Hung, and Regan Koch in Taipei, Rafi Arefin, Trevor Barnes, Juliet Lu, Priti Narayan, Jamie Peck, and Geraldine Pratt in Vancouver, and Anders Malmberg, Don Mitchell, and Gunnar Olsson in Uppsala. The relational theory chapter was earlier presented via Zoom to our department's Politics, Economies And Space (PEAS) research group in March 2022. Helpful comments were received from Dylan Brady, Neil Coe, Nathan Green, Avinash Gupta, Elaine Ho, Shaun Lin, Eugene McCann, Shaun Teo, Teo Yee Chin, and Josh Watkins. In end August 2023, an Author-Meets-Critics session for my book will be held at the annual international conference of the Royal Geographical Society in London. I am very thankful to Tim Cresswell, Colin McFarlane (again!), and Deborah Dixon for graciously serving as my book's critics. The endorsements from Tim Cresswell, Katharyne Mitchell, and Jamie Peck are much appreciated. Of course, the usual disclaimer applies and all errors and misreading in this book are mine.

Last but not certainly least, the causal powers for making this book happen must be given to (and derived from) the RGS-IBG Book Series' academic co-editors Ruth Cragg (for her superb handling of the entire editorial process) and my colleague Chih Yuan Woon (for his excellent advice and guidance along the way) and, at Wiley, Jacqueline Scott (former editor for Social Sciences and Humanities), Grace Ong (Publisher), and Radhika Sharma (Managing Editor) for their outstanding publisher support and editorial efficiency. Without all of your grit and unwavering commitment to this project, I won't get to write this Preface. So thank you very much indeed.

An equifinal causal condition of kinship must also be acknowledged before I end. Peter Dicken's fatherly advice and encouragement from a distance in Manchester are absolutely pivotal in bringing me and this book's writing into action. Back at home, my wife Weiyu has been most supportive throughout this difficult pandemic period and her steadfast care provides the crucial underlying mechanism to enable my thinking, reading, and writing. Kay and Lucas, our no-longer-young children, are never too tired of hearing me talking about 'process and mechanism' and 'theory and explanation'. And Kay is going to find her own T-cell mechanisms through PhD in immunology. I can never write a decent book without their familial interest. More importantly, their enthusiasm for *Squid Game* has clearly made it to my book cover!

On that closing note and before our parting (however temporary), I wish you well in reading this work and don't forget your TIE – Take It Easy, as life is too fragile and short...

Henry Wai-chung Yeung
Singapore
13 July 2023

# Chapter One
# Critical Human Geography Today: A Multitude of Approaches and Concepts?

Just over half a century ago, David Harvey (1969: p. 486) ended his *Explanation in Geography* with the grand statement that 'By our theories you shall know us'. As of the mid-2020s, it is not an exaggeration to claim that Geography is characterized by a multitude of (critical) approaches and concepts, but perhaps too few substantive theories explaining diverse geographical phenomena that can be and/or have been well adopted in the wider social and natural sciences. In critical human geography today, we are now better known for our nuanced interpretations and trenchant deconstructions of representations in all sorts of past and present discourses, texts, and images, our sophisticated understandings and accounts of diverse embodiment, intersectionality, practices, and encounters in everyday life, and our highly contextualized and place-based critiques of unequal and oppressive capitalist relations in society and space. In most of these critical geographical approaches well informed by different social theories and continental philosophies, however, it remains unclear what theory really means and if explanatory efficacy is important for theory and the theorizing process.

Indeed, the term 'theory' is often a misnomer or a 'placeholder' in these critical approaches grounded in specific social *theories*. For example, leading geographical proponents of poststructuralism (actor-network theory in Murdoch, 2006), postcolonialism (postcolonial theory in Jazeel, 2019), and new materialism (non-representational theory in Simpson, 2021) in Geography[1] have made clear that these approaches are not theory per se, but perhaps should be conceived more as methodology (or a 'method to describe' in Latour, 1996, 2005; and a 'style' of theorizing

*Theory and Explanation in Geography*, First Edition. Henry Wai-chung Yeung.

in Thrift, 1996, 2007; Anderson and Harrison, 2010a). To Jazeel (2019: pp. 14–15, 227; original italics), 'postcolonialism is best conceived not as a theory per se, but instead as *methodology*. If postcolonialism is opposed to information command, if much of its promise is in its persistent effort to unsettle the contours of power, it is indeed a contradictory exercise to map or survey postcolonialism as some*thing* as settled and authoritative as a "body of theory"'. While Nigel Thrift (1996: p. 30) describes in *Spatial Formations* his non-representational framework as a 'modest theory' and 'a theoretical synthesis… with a lighter touch', Simpson's (2021: p. 7) recent review of diverse geographical thoughts in non-representational theory notes that 'at the outset, much of the reference here was in the plural and was about "thinking" rather than a "theory." "NRT" really acts as an umbrella term for a wide range of ideas, concepts, theories, and approaches largely originating beyond the confines of geography which have in common concerns for practice'.

Despite Harvey's (1969) passionate call for 'our theories' emanating from Geography, there are now seemingly many different conceptions of what theory means in these critical approaches and/or 'isms' – universalistic, predictive, interpretive, explanatory, representational, non-representational, discursive, nomadic, and so on. If actor-network theory (and its variant in assemblage theory), postcolonial theory, non-representational theory, feminist theory, and the likes are not necessarily theory per se as their names suggest, what then is theory and how does it matter in Geography and beyond? How do we know a theory when we read or see someone's 'theoretical' thinking in words and textual representations? What might constitute the basic tenet(s) of theory and how might we go about practising theory development (i.e. the theorizing process)? What are the key considerations for such theorizing?

I believe these are important questions and reflexive issues for academic geographers, graduate students, and like-minded social scientists for/to whom this monograph is primarily written and speaks. But given the extensive theoretical and philosophical literature underpinning this work, the book is inevitably pitched at a fairly high scholarly level of abstraction that might not be suitable for undergraduate teaching. Instead, it represents a provocative effort in geographical scholarship to interrogate and complement the diverse calls in critical social science for grounded theory, weak theory, modest theory, dirty theory, minor theory, mid-range theory, and so on. To me, all these epistemological efforts necessitate a clearer sense of what theory (and explanation) actually means in our scholarly pursuit. Overall then, this monograph seeks to examine the nature of theory *and* explanation in contemporary geographical enquiry and to provide a potential focal point for rethinking theorizing in Geography. Its initial four chapters are grounded in a critically generous reading of different approaches in human geography and their diverse conceptions of theory (and explanation). In this sense, the book is written more for human geographers than peers and colleagues in physical geography, GIS, and remote sensing. This latter 'half' of Geography, however, can still benefit from reading this work in order to gauge a sense of *critical* theory development and broaden their epistemological apparatuses for causal theorizing that will go well beyond the conventional scientific approach to knowledge production.

Echoing the early Harvey, I maintain that theory is what defines an academic discipline and, in the grand scheme of things within academia, 'our theories' in Geography are currently perhaps still rather limited in number, scope, and impact. But this book's similarity with Harvey (1969) actually ends there. We now know Harvey's theories then were positivist explanations based on objective laws and empirical regularities – space and time were fixed, absolute, and independent of human conceptions. Contrary to this positivist Humean law-based approach (and those by other 'space cadets' of spatial science during the 1960s well described in Barnes, 2001, 2011), I have no intention at all to prescribe a common standard or model (i.e. what *all* geographical theories should be), nor a common explanatory framework (i.e. a specific geographical theory of some-*thing/event* in space and place). This seemingly 'authoritarian' goal is unrealistic and virtually impossible precisely because of the actually existing multitude of approaches and concepts in critical human geography today (to be discussed in depth in Chapter 2).

Since the 1970s, human geography has undergone many rounds of ontological and epistemological 'turns' so much so that theory and explanation mean rather different things to different geographers – even the concept 'difference' is still highly contentious today (Cockayne et al., 2017)! Despite these 'turns' (to be addressed in this book), the positivist norms of scientific approach remain fairly enduring in human geography and mostly dominant in physical geography, GIS, and remote sensing today. In certain subfields of human geography, research funding institutions often favour the quantitative testing of, and experimental approaches (e.g. randomized control trials) to, measurable variables as the proper 'scientific' explanations of socio-spatial outcomes. On the brighter side though, critical human geography is quite unique and exceptional in the wider social sciences wherein many larger disciplines, such as Economics, Political Science, and Sociology, have devoted specific subfields, faculty hiring, and even journals to *specializing* in 'theory development', i.e. economic theory (*Journal of Economic Theory*), political theory (*Political Theory*), and sociological theory (*Sociological Theory*). In Geography as a whole, we do not have such a ghettoized subfield, hiring practices, and journals known as 'Geographical Theory', except perhaps a few self-proclaimed theory books such as this one (and Harvey, 1969; Gregory, 1978). I believe this geographical exceptionalism is a good thing because it allows us to integrate theory and theory development into our everyday geographical research, scholarship, and practice.[2]

Still in these highly contested and sometimes overlapping turns in critical human geography, there is often a direct relationship between *ontology* (theorizing the nature of reality and existence in philosophy and metaphysics) and *epistemology* (our theory and knowledge of actually existing empirical worlds). Theory can exist in both domains of knowledges, though ontology tends to be much more philosophical and abstract. At this moment in the mid-2020s, 'What theory?' has ironically become a rather difficult question to answer. Geographers have engaged in all sorts of theorization, from ontological objects such as human subjectivity, mind and the body, political-economic structures, and more-than-human things and matter in general, to social constructions through representations and discourses, and experiential encounters and sensuous apprehension (e.g. affect, emotion, feelings, and so on). Amongst these many 'isms' representing different approaches to theorization in human geography, why and how do theory and explanation matter and/or work? This is the central focus of this book that advocates two things: first, theory and explanation as the *raison d'être* of human geography; and second, explanatory theories, one of the several possible kinds of theorizing, as its normative, context-specific, and practically adequate contributions to the social sciences.

More specifically, this book (re)examines why an explanatory theory might be useful in certain kind of geographical enquiry and how it can be better developed (i.e. theorizing) through *mechanism-based thinking* informed by critical realist and relational thought within Geography that has been recently revitalized in the broader social sciences. Avoiding what Jazeel (2019: p. 210; original italics) terms 'authoritarian theorization', my approach to theory and explanation – not as 'some-*thing* in which to specialize' but as a normative practice – might allow for more epistemological possibilities for crossing what Cox (2014: p. vii) describes as 'a highly fragmented field' in Geography characterized by 'a division by theory and method'. If well executed in the book, this approach can focus our attention on rethinking how we might better theorize and explain geographical realities. Defending sociologist Anthony Giddens' insistence on the importance of doing social theory in a particular way, Thrift (1996: p. 61) makes this point clearly by recognizing that 'theory is quite simply a way of clarifying one's ideas for emancipatory purposes. In other words, theory is limited, but it is still important'.

While many geographers tend to describe (and/or blame on!) different critical approaches and epistemologies as 'social theories', this book takes a more modest and specific conception of theory (and explanation). It does not seek or advocate social theory as such – these theories have much broader historical reach and societal coverage, from capitalism in Marxism to human-nature relations in poststructuralism (e.g. actor-network theory) and unequal power relations in feminist and postcolonial theories. While engaging with these approaches and their epistemologies, I focus on the explanatory nature of theory and develop a causal mechanism-based approach to theory and explanation in/for Geography, with the prospective view that it might enable our discipline's explanatory mission to be better accomplished in the next one to two decades. I believe this epistemological task is imperative and timely in the present turbulent world in which radical intellectual critiques seem to have lost some of their public appeal and trust in many democracies. Revisiting theory and explanation in Geography can be *one* way forward to rebuild better the analytical rigour and public relevance of our discipline. It can offer a strong(er) defence of the importance of critical scholarship in engendering the common good and our collective well-being against the sort of anti-intellectualism so eloquently critiqued in feminist historian Joan Scott's (2019) *Knowledge, Power, and Academic Freedom.*

While grounded more specifically in *some* of these critical approaches – relational thinking and realist philosophies,[3] this book does not seek to 'spatialize' these approaches by focusing on their conceptions of space and place. Instead, I draw upon these critical approaches to reorientate our attention to rethinking theory and explanation in/for Geography. Part of my purpose here is also driven by the lack of dedicated work on 'theory' and/or 'explanation' in recent human geography handbooks (e.g. Agnew and Livingstone, 2011; Lee et al., 2014; Aitkin and Valentine, 2015a). This lacuna is somewhat surprising since there are some relevant chapters in earlier collections for undergraduate teaching prior to 2010, e.g. 'theorizing' in Hubbard et al. (2002: ch. 1) and 'explaining' in Cloke et al. (2004: ch. 9).

## Main Argument and Approach

Before I delve more deeply into the book's key caveats and considerations in this chapter and contemporary geographical thought in Chapter 2, let me state my arguments more explicitly for the kind of theory and explanation to be pursued in this book. When we study a particular geographical phenomenon (e.g. place-based subject experience, inner-city decline, social movements, regional restructuring, or geopolitical conflicts), we can go about describing it in great detail and accuracy. In the more recent forms of geographical enquiry inspired by critical social theories since the late 1970s, we witness theory as uncovering social structures determining human action in structural Marxism and their trenchant critiques in the forms of poststructuralism, postmodernism, postcolonialism, and other thoughts (e.g. feminism, post-phenomenology, and posthumanism). In these critical 'post-' thoughts, theory is often abstract, discursive, and situated – spaces of social relations are discursively (de)constructed and contingently (re) framed through specific historical-geographical interrogations. Causal relations in these critical theories tend to be vague and indeterminant due to their 'flat ontologies' (Marston et al., 2005; Jones et al., 2007; Ash, 2020a) and/or commitment to heterogeneous associations and assemblages (Murdoch, 2006; Anderson et al., 2012a; Kinkaid, 2020).

Whatever one's epistemological position though, I believe a theory is likely built on existing or new concepts that necessarily abstract from material realities and/or social formations to form a set of meaningful and comprehensible statements. These theoretical statements can be interpretive, explanatory, or even normative. In a nutshell, all theories are an abstraction of the empirical world, but not all theories are explanatory of this actually existing world and even fewer are causal in their explanations. Just because a 'theory' – with the word 'theory' in its title – appears to be highly abstract and discursive does not necessarily mean it is an explanatory theory, and this is quite a commonly misunderstood syndrome in many critical approaches. While some of the above-named critical thoughts in human geography prefer a more open-ended and discursive approach to theorizing, this book argues for an *explanatory* kind of theory and theorizing. Here, I adopt sociologist Richard Swedberg's (2014: p. 17; emphasis omitted) simple definition of theory as 'a statement about the explanation of a phenomenon' and his view that '[a]n explanation represents the natural goal of theorizing and completes the process of building out the theory' (p. 98; see also Elster, 2015: p. 8). Theory, in short, is more than 'organized and patterned sets of ideas' (Cresswell, 2013: p. 7) and/or 'ways of knowing and being' (Aitken and Valentine, 2015b: p. 8); and explanation should go beyond interpreting, understanding, accounting, experiencing, making sense, critiquing, interrogating, (re)thinking, contextualizing, and so on of events, practices, and processes to uncover their causes that really make things happen in society and space.

The art of this explanatory theorizing, however, is a much more complicated and variegated thought process and practice. This book gestures towards a non-deterministic and yet mechanism-based approach to theory development and causal explanation in Geography. This kind of causal theory should be explanatory in nature, and its explanatory power depends on the identification and specification of mechanisms connecting cause and outcome within particular historical-geographical contexts. These causal mechanisms can be related to material processes, but also discursive practices or, as described in Jazeel (2019: p. 17), 'representational mechanics' – they clearly go beyond the primary idea of deterministic 'underlying structures' in the earlier Marxian thought that has been much critiqued and eschewed in poststructuralist and postcolonial approaches. In this sense, the book is as much an epistemological project as a normative one (see later section on 'key considerations'). In fact, I will argue that all epistemological debates and positions, whether in their empiricist, positivist, realist, poststructuralist, or feminist persuasions, are normative because they seek to justify or even normalize the importance, and sometimes the dominance, of a particular approach to situated knowledges and theory production (see also Agnew and Livingstone, 2011; Cox, 2014; Johnston and Sidaway, 2016).

In writing this book, I am fully aware that this mechanism-based conception of causal theory represents only *one* particular view of what (geographical) theory can be in an epistemological sense. I certainly do not pretend that this explanatory kind of theory represents the universe of all possible theories. Nor does the book provide a comprehensive ontology of the open-ended socio-spatial world for which this kind of theory can be developed. Nevertheless, I ground my argument for causal theory in relational thinking, critical realism and its more recent revitalization in speculative realism, and mechanism-based thought in the wider social sciences.[4] Engaging with these influential thoughts on mid-range theorizing and social mechanisms, this book aims to offer a clearer conception of causal mechanisms in order to speak to the kind of 'processual' or process-based theorization in the existing geographical literature and the wider social sciences.

Taken together, this book focuses on the relevance and usefulness of mid-range theories in geographical research and the importance of mechanism-based explanations in such causal theories. While the days of developing grand (social) theories for such complex geographies ranging from uneven global development to situated practices and embodied experiences in everyday life are perhaps over, we certainly still need less macro/planetary and more 'ordinary' theories that straddle capitalism's continuous reconfigurations and the changing dynamics of our everyday life and practices. These mid-range theories can focus on the more specific dimensions and unfoldings of these uneven developmental trajectories and embodied social practices such that they can be less 'essentialist' and 'reductionist'. Mid-range theories might also be a more productive way to theorize socio-spatial changes in an intellectual world of multiple and, often, conflicting approaches and in the post-pandemic world of far greater complexity and unpredictability. These theories can be helpful in uncovering causal mechanisms without the methodological commitment to theorizing the deep, deterministic, and totalizing structures of social relations, as manifested in certain extreme versions of geographical historical materialism.

While pushing for explanatory goals, these mid-range theories can also avoid the overzealous universalistic generalizations and acritical claims in positivism that, as argued by Cox (2014: p. 28), became the Achilles heel of the 'quantitative revolution' in human geography. Last but not least, mid-range theories might be more 'transferrable' across different social science disciplines due to their explanatory concern with specific domains of, and events/episodes in, society and space. This in turn provides new directions for Geography's future engagement with the wider social sciences and the development of relevant research agendas in geographical thought. Ultimately then, this book's examination of theory and explanation emphasizes the analytical significance of mid-range theories, contextualized explanations, and causal mechanisms in their variegated forms – from historical-material processes to discursive formations and social practices.

Before I pursue further this kind of mid-range theories and mechanism-based explanations in later chapters, this opening chapter, together with the next chapter on contemporary geographical thought, makes the case for revisiting theory and explanation in Geography by tracing its changing intellectual backdrop and context since Harvey (1969) and providing the necessary epistemological grounding in different critical approaches in human geography today. My primary focus in these two initial chapters is on critical human geography and its multitude of approaches and concepts since the 1990s in order to be more contemporary and to presage the kind of analytical geographies to be developed in later chapters. Taken together, both chapters situate the conceptions of theory and explanation in different epistemological approaches, such as structuralist, poststructuralist, posthumanist, feminist, and postcolonial geographies, and discuss the possible limitations of these approaches in relation to causal explanations and geographical theorizing. At the risk of caricaturing such diverse bodies of work and approaches within very limited space – some accounts here (e.g. feminist theory and postcolonial theory) are likely to be too thin and reductionist in the eyes of specialists and practitioners of these 'isms' and I ask for forbearance, these two chapters also serve as a framing template for later chapters that will revisit and identify the distinctive role of explanatory theories in Geography.[5]

To 'cramp' the enormous literature on these different approaches into the two opening chapters, I do not intend to go back too much to the original philosophers and critical theorists. Instead, I focus on their contemporary adoption in critical human geography.[6] This meta-narrative approach should serve the primary purpose of this book – engaging with existing approaches in human geography and yet highlighting possible gaps in their explanatory intentions and capabilities. This 'less philosophical' approach is similar to Simpson's (2021: p. 5; my emphasis) recent book on non-presentational theory in which he notes that '"NRT" is often felt to be difficult to grasp given the way that it mixes conceptual vocabularies, complex social theories, and references to seemingly *esoteric* continental philosophy; involves potentially unusual styles of research and writing; and, as there is often either a surprising empirical focus or as there isn't a clear empirical object of study at all'.

My narrative approach of relying on secondary texts on these critical social theorists and philosophers (except for critical realism, actor-network theory, assemblage theory, and feminist theory where key theorists and philosophers will be evoked) also reflects the fact that there are excellent texts and chapters written by geographers (for geographers) on each of these approaches that draw freely and sometimes very extensively on the original material – repeating such lengthy quotes might not be too productive for an audience in the 2020s and beyond.[7] Ironically, many of these original theorists and philosophers have less to say about theory and explanation per se, and much more about their conceptions of knowledge, language, mind, body, society, politics, space, time, and so on. This book thus focuses more on the contemporary work in the discipline on theory and explanation and its potential for future development. In this sense, the book is more an introspective piece about the discipline and its future, rather than one that covers the entire spectrum of critical social theories and philosophical traditions.[8]

As such, the first two chapters offer a critical examination of explanatory theorizing within the context of ongoing debates in diverse epistemologies in/for Geography. Drawing upon an 'old' theme of theory and explanation in human geography since Harvey (1969), I survey briefly how theory and explanation have been treated in various critical approaches and 'turns' and move swiftly across some of them to develop a more synthetic view of theory and explanation for future geographical enquiry. Overall then, the main text in this opening chapter and the ensuring book is meant to be more readable, less jargon-laden, and lightly referenced. Insofar as possible, I relegate relevant lengthy quotes, contextual material, and personal reflections to endnotes for advanced readers and paraphrase/weave their core messages into my narrative. Throughout the book's main text, only the most essential quotes are incorporated sparingly. I hope this different style of academic writing offers a more amenable level of abstraction – not too abstract beyond comprehension by the less well informed, and yet intellectually challenging enough to the experts.[9]

The remaining of this opening chapter is organized into three sections. In the next section, I elaborate on two important caveats on what the book is *not* about – neither the championing of a particular approach and/or an actual theory of the socio-spatial world, nor a philosophy in/for Geography and/or a new 'turn'. I then examine three key considerations *of*, and *for*, theory and explanation in Geography in terms of normative concerns in the politics of theorizing, the importance of socio-spatial contexts, and the yardstick of practical adequacy. The final section reiterates this book's synthetic approach that allows for greater epistemological possibilities for rethinking theory and explanation in geographical research. It also introduces the book's overall narrative, organization, and the ensuring chapters.

## Important Caveats: What This Book Is Not About

I start with two disclaimers to alleviate at the outset some possible concerns and/ or expectations from readers. These caveats require some elaboration beyond a simple statement, an important lesson from my close reading and reflecting on earlier influential works in human geography. Opening her *Hybrid Geographies* with a concise disclaimer of its non-philosophical tract and situated knowledge, Sarah Whatmore's (2002: p. 6) modest claim was subsequently critiqued by sympathetic reviewers as 'inconsistent or even hypocritical' and 'false modesty'. In response, Whatmore (2005: p. 843) conceded that she might have chosen her words 'too carefully in retrospect'.[10] In what follows, I reflect more openly on my book's positionality in relation to various critical approaches and philosophical/ ontological 'turns'.

First and foremost, this book does not advocate a particular critical *approach* nor an actual *theory* of the world and being. This non-deterministic gesture is perhaps more befitting in an intellectual world of Geography characterized by its leading historians (Cresswell, 2013; Cox, 2014; Johnston and Sidaway, 2016) as a fractured plurality of critical approaches and relatively peaceful co-existence of substantially fragmented communities – the idea of geographical exceptionalism in theory and practice noted at the beginning. I take a more catholic view towards integrating constructive ideas from across different approaches insofar as they are consistent with my key considerations of/for theory and explanation in Geography (see next section). While I have previously written about critical realism and, more recently, its relevance for distinguishing mechanism from process thinking in human geography (Yeung, 1997, 2019a), readers of this work will notice my discussion of theory and explanation may depart quite significantly from most critical realist thinkers and philosophers in terms of my epistemological claims and emphasis on mid-range theories, contextualized explanation, causal mechanisms in variegated 'material' forms – from narratives and representations (e.g. 'discursive formations' and 'affective atmospheres' in poststructuralist thought and 'representational mechanics' in postcolonialism) to material practices and assemblages (e.g. actor-network theory and assemblage thinking) and situated knowledges (feminist and postcolonial thought). In this sense, the book embraces *both* realist and social constructionist thought in its engaged-pluralistic epistemological orientation (cf. Hacking, 1999; Barad, 2007; Elder-Vass, 2012; Gabriel, 2015).[11]

More significantly, even realist thinking has substantially evolved from its more restrictive forms of transcendental realism in the 1970s (after Roy Bhaskar, 1975, 1979) and critical realism in the 1980s (Sayer, 1981, 1984; Allen, 1983, 1987; Bhaskar, 1986, 1989). It is now not exaggerating to claim that since the late 2000s, realist thinking has made a major return via the expanded and diversified work of critical realists, such as the late Roy Bhaskar and his followers (including their institutionalization of critical realism with its own journal, book series, country networks, and regular conferences; see Chapter 3 endnote 28), and another group of 'speculative' philosophers advocating 'the rise of realism' (DeLanda and Harman, 2017; see also Rutzou, 2017; Rutzou and Elder-Vass, 2019; Elder-Vass, 2022).[12] Where relevant, I will introduce this revitalized realist thinking in greater length in later chapters (2 to 4). Suffice to say here that in both critical realism and speculative realism, material objects exist and are not socially constructed, but social structures are because they depend for their existence on how we think about them and act in relation to their potential (but not deterministic) and conjunctural structuring effects.

Following this non-deterministic orientation towards critical approaches, *mechanism* in social science explanation cannot and should not be conceived as a machine-like mechanical or technical sequence of physical things, like some critics of mechanism-based realist thought have argued and some dismissive readings of this work as too macho-mechanical-technical might think. In actor-network theory terminology, such mechanism is not made up of non-humans or material things. Mechanism refers to the different but necessary steps for a 'social' cause in its broadest sense to produce empirical effect within specific contexts. Some of these steps can be recursive and thus a causal mechanism needs not be sequential in its action and practice. In social science explanation, a causal mechanism often refers to a discrete process embedded in social relations, rather than machines, matters, and things per se, as will be further conceptualized in later chapters (3 to 5).

Despite my epistemological claims of mid-range theories and causal explanations in context, this book does not offer an actual theory of the world/empirical reality/space/subjectivity-humanism. It does not develop a spatial theory of capitalism, the materiality of social relations, the meanings or conceptions of space and place, the spatiality of social life, nor a theory of geographical knowledge or key concepts in Geography per se. There is a fairly large and substantial literature in human geography on these theories and their analytical subjects.[13] Still, the search for an all-encompassing theory of space and spatiality remains elusive and perhaps impossible. As well recognized over a decade ago by humanistic geographer Yi-Fu Tuan in his 2010 panel discussion at the annual meeting of the American Association of Geographers,

> is a theory of space and spatiality possible? My answer is that I have my doubts, for space, to me, is a cultural and experiential construct, the meaning of which can vary widely from people to people, and from individual to individual... Isn't it strange that this should be the case when few of us fully grasp what our own theorists say about space and spatiality, even though they speak in prose and strive, as scholars of a scientific or philosophical bent, for maximum clarity? Suppose one theorist does come up with a theory or framework that grips the imagination and commands the respect of many. Can it be that its power lies not, as the theorist himself [*sic*] may believe, in its compelling logic, but rather in its hidden metaphors – its poetry? (Merriman et al., 2012: pp. 12–13).

Tuan's critical view on the Holy Grail of an all-encompassing geographical theory should serve us well in terms of not only his doubtfulness about such a venture, but also his suspicion towards the increasing role of poetical power rather than compelling logic in determining a theory's acceptance in Geography. Akin to realist philosopher Markus Gabriel's (2015) observation on scholars avoiding criticisms by evoking continental philosophy in ontological debates, hidden metaphors and poetical beliefs or parochial standards of justification are often deployed to prevent bad theory in human geography from being criticized by others from different critical approaches.[14]

This brings me to the second important caveat that the book is not about *philosophy* in/for Geography nor a new 'turn'. Unlike some influential geographers' works that draw heavily on original critical theorists and, indeed, 'continental' philosophers, this book attempts to be less poetical and more analytical logic-driven in order to avoid the general tendencies of such work to be overtly theoretical, textual, and representational.[15] Here, I take seriously critical realist Bhaskar's humble view that philosophy should serve as an underlabourer for knowledge production and projects of human emancipation by clearing away the 'philosophical rubbish' and obstacles to progress in social science, not as a dogmatic thought dictating its substantive content.[16] Another realist philosopher from the poststructuralist 'camp' also points to this underlabourer role of philosophy in clarifying ontological doubts for the (social) sciences. Introducing his Deleuzian ontology of assemblage theory, Manuel DeLanda (2006: p. 7) argues that cross-cultural comparisons, detailed analyses of social mechanisms, and historical vignettes in social science are worthy tasks that cannot be carried out within an impoverished ontological framework. To him, 'while philosophers cannot, and should not, pretend to do the work of social scientists for them, they can greatly contribute to the job of ontological clarification'.[17]

Still, I think the reverse trend in DeLanda's caution above might be taking place in contemporary human geography and critical social science. There is a real danger of geographers doing too much of this ontological work that resembles a form of 'philosophy envy' (or 'academic escapism', as coined by Häkli, 2020: p. 370).[18] Paraphrasing DeLanda, I argue that while geographers cannot, and should not, pretend to do the work of philosophers for them, we can greatly contribute to the job of theoretically grounded empirical knowledge production. In its extreme form, the current state of ontological contest and philosophical multiplication in human geography can be rather counterproductive when it becomes a form of asserting authority or, in Eric Sheppard's words, 'my ontology versus yours'.[19] To him, Geography as a discipline used to ground its respectability through its claim and rooting in science during the heydays of quantitative revolution. But instead of our 'physics/science envy' then, he wondered 'if we have now moved to try to claim respectability by rooting ourselves in philosophy... [W]hile geographers may spend a lot of time reading particular philosophers, do they actually sit down and debate with the philosophy profession about these issues and seek to learn from those debates' (Merriman et al., 2012: p. 16)?[20]

This raises an important issue of whether extensive import and quotes from philosophers of different (mostly 'continental') persuasions by geographers in their writings are often done to buttress one's discursive views and/or to burnish one's intellectual credentials and respectability? Sometimes, geographers practise 'reading against the grain' to draw out such traces of philosophical pointers just to import them into geographical writing and to offer their own re-readings that can perhaps lead to excessive regurgitation and, sometimes, the extremes of obscurity and befuddlement.[21]

In his recent book *Killer Cities*, Nigel Thrift (2021: p. xi) uses the term 'phiction' to describe these risky adventures into opaque philosophical writings akin to fiction.[22] Following Sheppard's reservation above, we might ask what is new and novel in these imports and (re)readings for Geography and for philosophy and how do they strengthen our existing or new theories and explanations? On their own, philosophical ideas cannot substitute for good geographical theories and explanations. As noted by Elden (2003: p. 239), we should not licentiously import and appropriate philosophical ideas through selective quotes unless one can appropriately explain 'their ideas in a way that might open them to a wider audience'.[23] Otherwise and to Simpson (2021: p. 221), such 'phictional' work in human geography may risk taking place within an echo chamber occupied by a select few well-read philosophical geographers. But even in philosophy, the endless dispute of human/mind versus world/reality can be equally debilitating as if its resolution were the magic key to all ontological secrets. As reflected by Graham Harman (2010: p. 174), a co-founder of speculative realism since the early 2000s, 'Whether we deny things-in-themselves outside the human/world correlate, or insist upon such extra-mental realities, this endless dispute [mostly in philosophy] orbits the single dismal pair of human and world. The relation between just these two terms is treated as the magic key that will unlock all the secrets of ontology if solved' (see also Sparrow, 2014: ch. 1).

More recently, Joronen and Häkli (2017: p. 562) caution the use of ontology in human geography as an assumed mandate and a quick pass to speak in the name of reality, rather than as a critical analytical step towards questioning it. The uncritical import of philosophical ideas on ontology runs a risk of turning theological, such that ontology becomes metaphysics or 'onto-theology' celebrating the endless becoming of entities. To them, this 'onto-theological lock-in easily turns into "theoretical path dependency," directing and circumscribing how the political is taken up' (Joronen and Häkli, 2017: p. 568). In Bhaskar's (2016) final work on realist philosophy, this form of 'onto-theological lock-in' is known as 'ontic fallacy', defined as our knowledge of the world being determined by the nature of the world itself. This fallacy overlooks the important role of epistemology in that our knowledge – like this very book – is an irreducibly social and changing product, and our access to knowledge and the world is always mediated by the research process (i.e. knowledge production). To Bhaskar (2016: p. 11; original italics), 'the ontic fallacy reduces the resulting knowledge to the world: it ontologises, hence naturalises or *eternalises* our knowledge and makes the social status quo seem permanent and ineluctable'. I will revisit this notion of ontic fallacy in my discussion of the various critical approaches throughout this book.

Avoiding too much dependence on such ontological registers from philosophers, my book takes a more catholic approach to ontology and different philosophies, as the starting point of knowledge production. But it focuses on *epistemology* – how do we go about producing knowledges – by arguing for the necessity of theory and explanation in empirical inquiry as 'the work of social scientists' in DeLanda's academic division of labour. One might contend that different ontologies may prescribe different epistemologies, from the deterministic ontology of Comtean positivism to the relativist claims of Jacques Derrida's postmodernist and poststructuralist thought. This book's epistemology eschews these philosophical extremes and argues for a pragmatist middle-ground that retains both causality and relationality in theory and explanation. I will develop these arguments much more explicitly in Chapters 3 and 4.

In short, a social ontology that claims reality as unknowable, impenetrable, and/ or always-becoming cannot support substantive epistemological effort towards theory and explanation because it will simply be a futile exercise in chasing after a moving target, i.e. 'explain' the un-explainable. It fails DeLanda's (2006: p. 7) job of ontological clarification prescribed for philosophers. Ironically, this danger is well recognized in poststructuralist philosophers Gilles Deleuze and Félix Guattari's (1987 [1980]) *A Thousand Plateaus*, often seen as a key poststructuralist referent in their celebrated flat ontology. In the concluding chapter laying out 'concrete rules and abstract machines' as a summary of their key concepts, they not only emphasize the importance of both the 'structuring' concepts of strata and stratification by starting with them first (before other more influential concepts such as 'assemblages' and 'rhizome'), but also caution against our urge towards disarticulation and destratification (or always-becoming).[24]

Conversely, a social ontology of reality as merely autonomous entities and fixed or transcendental structures renders theory and explanation rather dull, macho-mechanical, and over-deterministic. My project in this book is to gesture an epistemology that can be both meaningful and practical in empirical geographical research. Instead of thinking too incessantly the ontological question of what reality might be like (metaphysics), I would rather focus on how we might be able to understand and explain better the already existing world as it unfolds and takes place. In this sense, my project is less about *thinking* in terms of philosophical (mis)claims and much more about *doing* – the practice of knowledge production through developing novel theory and explanation. This pragmatic approach to ontology and epistemology is in line with recent efforts by sociologists Rutzou (2017), Decoteau (2018), and Rutzou and Elder-Vass (2019) in reconciling poststructuralist thought in assemblage theory with critical realism. As concluded by Rutzou and Elder-Vass (2019: p. 420),

> Good social research requires a social ontology that is both internally coherent and consistent with our experience of the world, including the evidence revealed by research. Just as many ontologists take a relaxed attitude to empirical research that allows them to cherry pick illustrations in service of the theory, many [social science] researchers take a relaxed attitude to ontology, allowing them to cherry pick concepts from different traditions. But where ontology is merely implicit, it risks inadvertent incoherence and logical irresponsibility. Where it is explicit let alone dogmatic, it risks discouraging or excluding attention to important aspects of social reality.

Overall then, readers will be pleased to know that this book is not proposing a new philosophical 'turn'! Human geography today has perhaps already suffered from premature 'turns' that have 'cancelled' far too much. As Cox (2014: p. vii) reflects critically, 'at each stage there has been an unnecessary rejection of too much. Ground has been vacated before it has been thoroughly turned over and cultivated. Each "turn" has reacted to what has gone immediately before it and, possibly to justify itself, has been too sweeping in its rejection'. In that sense, this book draws upon an 'old' theme of theory and explanation in Geography since Harvey (1969). But instead of surveying historically and genealogically how theory and explanation have been treated in these various critical approaches and 'turns', I move swiftly across some of them to find common grounds and to develop a more synthetic view of theory and explanation for future geographical enquiries and knowledge production. Going beyond the false dichotomous choice between explanation (as in positivism) and interpretation (as in hermeneutics) in the social sciences, this 'house-clearing' on theory and explanation might be in order *for* geographers who are confronted with a (looming) crisis of legitimacy: how can human geography thrive in the wider social sciences of the post-pandemic 2020s and beyond? My short answer is better theories and explanations! It is not just about better description and accounts – no matter how nuanced, but rather certainly more about realistic theories and explanations that can contribute to real-world understanding and interpretations necessary for a practically adequate social science. This manifesto brings me to some necessary considerations of, and for, theory and explanation in Geography.

## Key Considerations: Of/For Theory and Explanation

Despite a relatively large body of literature on the development of geographic thought and the geographies of geographical knowledge, we do not yet have a commonly recognized epistemology for theory and explanation. In this section, I consider and reaffirm three necessary criteria for theory development in relation to normative concerns, socio-spatial contexts, and practical adequacy. To be illustrated thoroughly throughout the book's chapters, these key considerations provide a critical guidance for adjudicating the kind of theory and the ways of theorizing that might be productively advanced in Geography and, in turn, the kind of geographical knowledge as our collective contribution to critical social science priorities and research agendas.

First, if we truly believe human geography should be critical and emancipatory, our theories and explanations must explicitly incorporate *normative concerns* and be sensitive to the *politics of theorizing*. The question of 'for what and on whose behalf' is imperative in theory development, even though its politics and geographical specificities (i.e. more practised in Anglo-American human geography) may be a dilemma for causal theorizing that needs remedy. My book does not advocate an 'anything goes' approach to theory characterized by epistemological relativism and radical contingency.[25] Rather, we need to be seriously concerned with the normative issues in theorizing and ask for what purpose and whom our theories might serve – I will offer some personal reflections on 'theorizing back' and my own theory development journey in economic geography in the penultimate Chapter 6. Here, I argue that critical theories are not the same as critical theorizing. As noted by Derek Gregory (1994: p. 62) in *Geographical Imaginations*, Habermas' (1972) notion of a critical theory with an emancipatory interest – both critical of real-world injustice and self-critical of its own 'politics of location' and its context of production (theorizing) – is particularly relevant in such a normative consideration; theory, in short, should be 'a sort of moving self-reflectivity' (Gregory, 1994: p. 86).[26]

In critical realist thought (e.g. Bhaskar, 2016), this notion of an immanent critique of one's own theory and its ontological foundation is also seen as a necessary practice for social science to demystify and enlighten common sense. In this reflexive thought, all knowledge is fallible, but not equally fallible. The adequacy of social knowledge can be established by practice through immanent critique and real-life applications. As such, we need to be cognizant of the inherent limits to our theories, such as the importance of open systems, contexts, and the politics of knowledge, and yet immanent critique requires us to specify clearly the kind of epistemological position(s) we are committed to and isolates any theory/practice inconsistency.[27]

As will be discussed in the next chapter, the multitude of critical approaches in human geography have rather different conceptions of theory and explanation. Broadly, we can distinguish between radical 'ideologically-oriented' and more 'open-ended' approaches to theory. Harney et al. (2016: pp. 323–324) refer to the former as normative theories in Marxism, feminism, critical race theory, and postcolonialism developed in the wake of post-positivism. The latter is often grounded in a process pragmatism premised on an ontology of anti-foundationalism that understands the world to be radically contingent and thus its open-ended epistemology and socially-embedded politics of inquiry (see also Popke, 2003; Shannon et al., 2021). And yet contrary to Harney et al.'s (2016) optimism in process pragmatism, these more open-ended approaches tend to exhibit normative 'blind-spots' that have recently been subject to significant critiques in human geography.[28]

In Tolia-Kelly's (2013: p. 154) earlier critique, human geography's recent surge towards new materialisms and material geographies is running a risk of doing/becoming 'surface geographies' that are merely recordings of matters at play on surface rather than critical evaluations of the politics and affects/effects of the interconnectivity and co-constitution of these materialities and their uneven geographies. To Sundberg (2014: p. 34), some of these posthumanist approaches might have committed 'the ontological violence authorized by Eurocentric epistemologies' that make and solidify universalizing claims about the socio-spatial world. Grounded in feminist and postcolonial thought, Mitchell and Elwood (2012: pp. 792–793) also take on the more open-ended approaches, such as non-representational theory in human geography, and contend that such a mode of theorizing individual bodily encounters and emotions tend to ignore normative concerns with social injustice and exploitation. More recently, Kinkaid (2020: p. 469) points further to the weak normative commitment in assemblage thinking and theorizing, despite its potential for explaining and intervening in uneven geographies.[29]

Indeed, such normative concerns with ethics and justice are particularly strong and prevalent in feminist scholarship and theorizing. Let me offer a brief example by way of a leading feminist theorist. In her performative theory of assembly, Judith Butler (2015a) argues strongly in favour of bodily enactments in public assemblies and demonstrations that are performative of the people's right to rights and transcend the binary claim of the public and private spaces of bodily appearance. Her 'ethics of cohabitation' call for the performativity of bodies in public not to be silenced, sequestered, or denied, for they are always there and here and never stop 'speaking'.[30] Irrespective of whether such a theory is merely performative or explanatory (and even causal) in its epistemological gesture – see more in Chapter 2 on feminist theory, there is no doubt that it offers a more explicitly normative take on how we *should* understand the politically difficult and shifting global connections of social movements (cf. McAdam et al., 2001; Abbott, 2016). In this spirit of theorizing, the value-laden nature of the social world makes it necessary for explicitly normative commitments in our theory production.

Second, our critical theories and explanations must be well grounded in different *socio-spatial contexts* precisely because of the contingency and specificity of place unique to Geography. To Gregory (1994: pp. 12–13), social theory is not only a critical discourse, but also a 'travelling theory' in relation to its contextual specificity.[31] As will be evident in Chapter 2, many of the more open-ended approaches in human geography are highly sensitive to context in their theoretical accounts of bodily encounters and affect, social identities and interactions, and broader community engagement. However, theories in the more radical ideologically-oriented approaches are often more concerned with unpacking the structural underpinnings and system-level injustice in capitalist societies. But as Doreen Massey (1984: p. 70) has argued some time ago in *Spatial Divisions of Labour*, there is no reason why such more structural theories cannot recognize contextual contingency and place-based specificity. To her, 'The challenge is to construct an approach which is neither detailed description and empiricism nor a "mechanistic Marxist" insensitivity. It is possible both to recognise specificity and to situate it within the grander historical movements of capitalist societies'.[32]

Irrespective of our critical approaches in human geography, the recognition of socio-spatial contexts is indispensable to the development of theory and explanation. I argue that this necessary sensitivity to context is particularly important for the development of causal theories informed by mechanism-based explanations in Geography and the wider social sciences. As well noted by philosopher of social science Daniel Little (2016), social beings are heterogeneous and changeable in different contexts, and the social world can never be like the natural world governed by Humean universal laws of nature. Indeed, such conceptions that social worlds are open systems characterized by both complexity and emergence and that mechanism-based explanations are context-dependent have already been well recognized in critical realist thought for over three decades (Bhaskar, 1986, 2016; Pozzoni and Kaidesoja, 2021; see also my Chapter 3).[33]

This insistence on theory and explanation in context can also be a useful strategy to avoid the sort of Cartesian desire for explanation, finality, and (accurate) representation that has been much critiqued in some critical approaches. Drawing extensively on Ludwig Wittgenstein's philosophy of language and meaning and 'uncertainty' of thought, Harrison (2002) offers a critical reading that questions the inherent difficulties of language and meaning in accounting for distinct objects, social conventions, and practices. This doubtful approach to scientific explanation is also central to Amoore's (2020a) work on algorithms and artificial intelligence grounded in poststructuralist and posthumanist thought in science and technology studies. In her call for the 'doubtfulness of partial perspectives', she examines critically the generative and emergent effects of algorithms in contemporary life and advocates a cloud ethics that explicitly instantiates a mode of doubtfulness to counter the grain of Cartesian thought. Taking an avowedly political-normative approach to cloud ethics, Amoore (2020a: p. 145) argues that 'It is precisely this mode of intuitive causality and embodied doubtfulness that I am seeking as a resistant and critical form of responsibility'.

Putting these arguments against rationalist explanation into this book's epistemological orientation, it seems quite clear that contextual contingencies and place-based specificities in the social world fundamentally disrupt the Humean theory of causal laws as constant empirical conjunctions or invariant regularities of events. And yet these contingencies and specificities do not necessarily invalidate the productive role of intuitive causality and mechanism-based explanation in theory development as long as good judgement and embodied doubtfulness are properly exercised. As such, theory and explanation *in context* can avoid the sort of transcendental finality in the Cartesian explanation of open systems (i.e. social worlds). Recognizing the importance of context and contingency in explanation also means that causal theory is always partial and its explanatory power is contingent on the operating context.

But this partiality of theory and contingency in explanation does not mean we should give up on explanatory theory and theorizing altogether and, instead, opt for descriptive accounts of unfolding, becoming, and eventalization that, in philosopher Michel Foucault's (2001: p. 227) argument against historiographic explanation in social analysis, serve as 'a way of lightening the weight of causality'. This is because the latter and more open-ended mode of understanding by leaving everything as it is and processual, termed 'witnessing' in Harrison (2002: p. 500), *can* also be as partial and incomplete.[34] I believe it is possible to conceive an iterative process of theorizing in which witnessing and (causal) explanation-in-context go hand in hand (more on this in Chapter 4). After all, there is no fundamental reason why one mode of knowledge production (i.e. processual understanding) must preclude another mode of knowledge production (i.e. causal explanation), however partial and doubtful each of them might be.[35] This brings me to the thorny consideration of how we know if theory is indeed useful.

Third, I advocate *practical adequacy* as a key criterion for adjudicating a theory's usefulness, irrespective of its normative stance and operational context. This consideration goes some way to address the 'so what' or 'why bother' question and to identify a theory's relevance for important real-world applications. In *Practising Human Geography*, Paul Cloke et al. (2004: p. 308; original italics) rightly note that scientific methods and positivist Geography fail to account for what it means to be human: as they put it cryptically, '*people are not rocks*' and human geography should be concerned with 'figuring out what spaces, places, environments and landscapes *mean* to people, or trying to understand the *meanings* that people in given situations acquire, elaborate, share and perhaps contest in relation to activities of geographical consequence'. I am concerned though that this approach to practising human geography might be taking a too human-centric view to the 'activities of geographical consequence'. What about those activities, things, and events of unintended geographical consequences that do not necessarily reflect the immediate consciousness of humans? Do these activities, things, and events in turn impinge on human consciousness that compel them to think and act in particular ways? Why and how do these particular ways work, practically? Can the understanding of meanings alone, no matter how well developed by means of empathy, intuition, or imagination, be practically sufficient in our explanatory goals? In philosopher Ian Hacking's (1999: pp. 20, 95) terms, we should unmask the underlying functions served by existing ideas and understandings in established order and raise our collective consciousness to make the world a better place.

This is where explanatory theories of such activities, things, and events are needed, *not just* nuanced understandings of humans and subjectivity in/around them. Eschewing theory and explanation just because 'people are not rocks' might seem a little premature and understating because these human-centric meanings and social constructions can perhaps be explained to arrive at even better understanding and practical outcomes. In short, we should not stop at just understanding meanings and experiences, but our theories need to engage with the practical adequacy of explanation for making possible our interventions and transformations in a material social world. Explanatory theories are necessary for human understandings and practices. But what counts as practical adequacy – a concept that might appear to be rather nebulous to some readers? Realist geographer Andrew Sayer (2015: p. 106) has made it easy to understand the practical adequacy of our theories and knowledge because 'the fact that we can successfully do so many things through our practical interventions in the world suggests that the knowledge informing those interventions has at least some "practical adequacy"'.[36] Similarly, practice philosopher Theodore Schatzki (2019) has argued that the value of a theory is akin to 'the proof is in the pudding' or its practical adequacy, not necessarily its conceptual elegance or sophistication.[37]

In brief then, a theory's practical adequacy refers to its analytical robustness in explaining empirical outcomes (being adequate to the researchers) and its usefulness to the practice of positive social change (being practical to both the researchers and the actors experiencing such change). Even though multiple good theories exist in different domains – ontological and epistemological – and we might simply have to live with this plurality, theory development remains a pragmatic matter and must be useful for researchers engaging in substantive empirical work and making real-world interventions.

In this context, even postcolonial theory/geographies, as one of the more ideologically-oriented critical approaches, has been critiqued for emphasizing too much on the deconstruction of colonial representations and the metaphorization of decolonization, and spending too little practical efforts in addressing the real-world issues of massive poverty, dispossession, inequality, abuses of human/ civil rights, and so on faced by many in the Global South (and, increasingly, in the Global North too!). Postcolonial feminist theorist Gayatri Chakravorty Spivak (1999: p. 142) thus argues in *A Critique of Postcolonial Reason* that 'We cannot "learn about" the subaltern only by reading literary texts, or, mutatis mutandis, sociohistorical documents… It is responsible to read books, but book learning is not responsibility'. As well recognized in Tariq Jazeel's (2019: p. 188) geographical text *Postcolonialism*, 'For many Indigenous communities, activists and scholars, decolonization is thus not (just) an injunction towards critical methodologies or theory work after and beyond Eurocentrism as Chakrabarty (2008 [2000]) might have it. It is about social and spatial justice. It is about addressing the continued fact of dispossession'.[38]

Taken together, practically adequate theories cannot be (just) about change in our mental constructs nor perceptual operations – that is a self-indulging kind of intellectual luxury in the ivory tower.[39] Equally important, these theories must also inform our understanding of the practical realities of conflicting interests and continual power struggles in an uneven social world characterized by interconnected structures of domination and discrimination. Positive social transformation needs more than reflexive change, but also much greater awareness of the power of causality and the practical adequacy of explanation.

## Chapter Outlines

Before venturing further in Chapter 2 to set the book's intellectual context by critically revisiting the role of theory and explanation in contemporary geographical thought, I now outline more explicitly the synthetic approach taken in this book. Grounded in and drawing on relevant debates on theory and explanation in various critical approaches to be discussed in the next chapter, this book focuses on the development of explanatory theory within a mechanism-based approach that takes seriously the above three key considerations of/for theory and explanation in Geography. And yet it occupies an epistemological position relatively free from the shackles of specific philosophical stances and ontological fixes (i.e. neither critical realism nor poststructuralism and postcolonialism). My approach seeks to explain enduring and/or changing *relations* between places that are constitutive of different spaces. As such, people (different gender, race, sexuality, culture, and identity), social groups, economic organizations, and political institutions are *critical agents* in diverse geographical phenomena at all spatial scales, from the individual (affects, emotions, and identities) and the regional (cultures, institutional thickness, and resilience) to the national and the global (change, growth, and development trajectories).

To reiterate two earlier caveats, my approach does not offer a new theory of society and space nor another (continental?) philosophical turn. Acutely aware of the inherent limits of grand social theories, it represents a coherent and yet rigorous effort to engage with what theory and theorizing entail in various critical approaches in human geography (Chapter 2) and to gesture towards and elaborate on a kind of explanatory theory underpinned by mid-range theorizing and causal mechanisms (Chapters 3–5) for critical geographical scholarship. While some readers might argue that this modest approach to theory and explanation is already quite evident in what many in Geography have been doing and/or at least striving for (e.g. relational thought and power dynamics in some Marxian, feminist, and postcolonial approaches in critical geographies), I contend that such doing (and striving for) in these various critical approaches can still be better consolidated and informed through mutual engagement with the kind of epistemological thought towards mechanism-based mid-range theorizing in this project. Nevertheless, my argument does not suggest that these highly influential approaches do not take theory seriously nor are short of explanations. But their focus on causal explanations and mechanisms of relationality and power dynamics might be better integrated and presented through a synthetic treatment offered in later chapters that address (1) mid-range theorizing; (2) relationality and causal powers in relational theory, and (3) theorizing mechanism and processual thought.

This synthetic project towards theory and explanation thus comprises these three interrelated steps to be elaborated more fully in Chapters 3–5. Taking the first step in Chapter 3, I discuss the kind of causal explanatory theory/theorizing that might be epistemologically realistic and practically adequate. To do so, I take up an *epistemological position* that views theory not only as abstract devices, but more importantly also as explanation of socio-spatial change. I elaborate on the importance of causal mechanism in such an explanatory kind of theory. This epistemology entails a different kind of normative position in human geography in which causal explanations are a necessary step towards critical geographical research. It contends that our socio-spatial interventions can be better developed if we have a clearer sense of why and how causal mechanisms interact with contingent contexts to produce specific socio-spatial events and outcomes.

I then discuss the relevance and usefulness of what might be termed *mid-range theories* in geographical research and the importance of mechanism-based explanations in such theories. My justification for mid-range theories is grounded specifically in some of the critical approaches, such as critical realist thought and relational thinking. Engaging with certain poststructuralist and postcolonial thought discussed in Chapter 2, I (re)introduce critical and speculative realism as a useful body of philosophical work for this mode of mechanism-based theorizing, though I am fully cognizant that it cannot substitute for other non-realist ontologies in the multiple trajectories of geographical scholarship (e.g. some open-ended approaches in poststructuralist, feminist, and postcolonial geographies). This section also draws upon the well-developed literature in analytical sociology, political science, and the philosophy of social science on mid-range theorizing and mechanism-based thinking.

My second step in Chapter 4 puts this epistemology of causal theory into the development of a *relational theory* through the reworking of relationality, power, and agency in the socio-spatial world that makes possible the search for causal mechanisms in explanatory theories. It takes stock of the analytical purchase of such relational thinking advanced by geographers grounded in poststructuralist, postcolonial, and institutionalist thought, such as the focus on the (un)folding of relations and co-relations in poststructuralist geography premised on actor-network theory and assemblage theory and its conceptions of power – heterogeneous associations and 'thing-power' – different from postcolonial theory and feminist thought discussed in Chapter 2. But Chapter 4 builds on the critical discussion of these relational thoughts and develops a theory of relationality to identify the underlying causal properties of actors, practices, and structures. This relational theory specifies the nature of relationality and the multiple ways through which power works itself out in what might be termed 'relational geometries', defined as the spatial configurations of heterogeneous power relations that are more than simply 'heterogeneous relations' in actor-network theory or 'processes of becoming' in non-representational theory and some feminist and postcolonial theories.

Drawing on the work on power by geographers (e.g. Allen, 2003, 2016) and others (e.g. sociologists, political scientists, and philosophers), I then conceptualize different forms of *power* in such relational geometries and their causal effects in producing concrete/spatial outcomes. This reconceptualization of relationality represents an important step towards explanatory theory building because some extreme variants of the 'relational turn' in human geography tend to move towards anti-essentialism (e.g. actor-network theory) and 'surface relations' (e.g. non-representational theory). My relational theory thus entails an analytical movement away from recognizing the de facto differences in relational geographies to theorizing the causal efficacy of difference. A relational geography, then, requires such a conceptual apparatus to explain why and how relationality and power relations matter in making things happen and explaining events and outcomes that take place in society and space.

Having set up the *raison d'être* for mechanism-based explanatory theory (Chapter 3) and the ontological basis of causal powers in more-than-heterogeneous relations (Chapter 4), I move on in Chapter 5 to the third step in my synthetic approach and demonstrate what a mechanism-based explanatory theory might look like. Here, I develop a *theory of mechanism* that draws upon and yet goes beyond critical realism and engages with the rapidly growing 'mechanism thought' in the wider social sciences during the past two decades. I illustrate how to theorize and explain socio-spatial practices and phenomena in a more robust manner on the basis of clearer conceptions of explanation through mechanism-based thinking. Engaging with the more open-ended approaches and processual thought in human geography discussed in Chapters 2 and 4, this theory of mechanism conceptualizes *process* as a contingent change in a general recurrent series of related actions/events and *mechanism* as a particular and necessary relation connecting initial causal conditions, such as actions and events, with concrete outcomes in specific contexts – a mechanism can be a particular kind of process, but it is distinct from general processes. This particularity in mechanism is premised on the time-space specificities of the empirical phenomenon in question. These specificities in turn refer to the unique context in which one or more necessary mechanisms can be specified for explaining a concrete outcome.

In doing so, I examine how mechanism-based analytical tools for causal explanation in geographical analysis might be distorted by the kind of processual or process-based thinking common in contemporary geographical thought (e.g. open-ended approaches in Chapters 2 and 4) and why conceptual rethinking is necessary. Ironically, this conceptual discussion of process and its distinction from mechanism is largely missing in critical realist thought and poststructuralist theories (e.g. actor-network theory, non-representational theory, and assemblage theory). I argue that there is a tendency in the geographical literature to conflate mechanism and process in different meso-level theories of socio-spatial change and encounters. This conflation, in turn, distorts the causal links in core concepts and reduces their explanatory efficacy in accounting for socio-spatial formations and uneven geographical outcomes.

Chapter 5 therefore links this process-mechanism discussion back to the processual thinking in Marxist geography on social relations of production and dialectics and poststructuralist approaches to practices, encounters, and assemblages. In a modest way, my (re)conceptualization of the process/mechanism distinction seeks to offer a focused discussion of the importance of causal explanations and to reconcile both process-based thinking (in relational thought discussed in Chapter 4) and mechanism-based explanation for future geographical analysis. A brief 'case study' of the geographical studies of neoliberalization is offered to illustrate this process/mechanism conflation and how a better process-mechanism distinction can enhance its analytical and explanatory validity. This choice of illustrative materials might mislead readers to think that the book is leaning towards my own subfield in economic geography and urban and regional studies, despite my broad engagement with various critical theories and approaches in feminist and postcolonial geographies, social/cultural geography, urban geography, and so on in various chapters.[40] But in a pragmatic sense, my familiarity with these materials does allow me to reflect better on their intellectual origins and geographical situatedness in relation to theory and explanation as the main tenet of this book. I presume other geographers from these subfields will take some cues from my approach here to reflect on their 'favourite' theories and explanations in other domains of geographical knowledge.

In the final two chapters, I offer a 'stress test' of the practical adequacy and normative stance of this synthetic approach to building mechanism-based explanatory theories in Geography.[41] This test entails two parts – from initial theory construction and interrogating the situatedness of theory to making such kind of geographical theory appealing to the broader social science and public communities. Taking its epistemological cues from previous chapters, Chapter 6 focuses on *theorizing globalization* as one key contemporary geographical phenomenon and its underlying political-economic organizational platform known as 'global production networks'. My basic premise is to illustrate how an explanatory theory comprising causal mechanisms can be, and has been, developed to examine this all-important and yet highly contested contemporary phenomenon and its multifarious geographical outcomes. This process of theorizing builds on and speaks to the kind of causal explanations, mid-range theories, and mechanism-based thinking expounded in Chapters 3–5. Extending my earlier conceptual work on globalization and the theory of global production networks, I reflect on how explanatory mid-range theories can be developed and why they are important for understanding complex geographical phenomena. More specifically, Chapter 6 examines critically the entire process of theory building rather than the nuts and bolts of the global production networks theory (see Coe and Yeung, 2015). While this examination of the development process of an explanatory theory might appear to be self-centred, retrospective, and post hoc in rationalization, the case study does make a contribution to theory development in human geography by showing what kind of mid-range theorizing works and how it can be done effectively.

As an indispensable part of this stress test, Chapter 6 also pays special attention to the normative stance of theory and its situatedness in particular epistemic contexts. Indeed, such interrogations of situated knowledges have been much explored in feminist and postcolonial geographies. Drawing on these thoughts, Chapter 6 makes a similar case that geographical theories are not contextually neutral nor devoid of value-ladenness. Rather, they almost always reflect the positionality of theorists and the historical-geographical contexts in which these theories are situated. Such geographic specificity in constructing theories in human geography and 'other geographies' or 'distant geographies' outside the Anglo-American context perhaps should not be surprising in light of the institutionalization of Geography as an academic discipline. This chapter not only offers an immanent critique of this situatedness and the geographical specificity of existing theories in human geography, but also argues for the kind of reverse discourses in order for geographical work outside the Anglo-American context to 'theorize back'. While this debate on the situatedness of knowledge and theories has been well developed in feminist and postcolonial work, there has been relatively less attempt to engage in this mode of *theorizing back* through which a new theory on/in the Global South not only 'can speak', but also can 'speak back' to mainstream Anglo-American Geography. Drawing on my earlier theory work and my situatedness as a human geographer based in East Asia, I illustrate how such theorizing back in human geography and the wider social sciences has taken place and become impactful in the context of developing new theories of state capitalism and global production networks that are empirically grounded in the transformative material realities of East Asia. This reflexive and personalized section represents my own account of situated theory development in economic geography.

The concluding Chapter 7 completes my stress test of explanatory theory by examining the practical adequacy of theory and offers a brief reprise of Geography's future role in social science. Constrained by severe word limit, this relatively shorter chapter returns to epistemology by arguing for a kind of *analytical geographies* that can engage broadly with the wider social sciences of the future. To date, few geographers have developed explanatory theories that can move and shape the social sciences.[42] Still, not many geographers have reflected critically on the place of Geography in the social sciences. In his final chapter on making space for human geography in the social sciences, Cox (2014: p. 201) complains that 'in their more abstract claims as opposed to their empirical work, it is true that the other social sciences have, and with some important qualifications, given human geography short shrift'. Parallel to my main claims in Chapter 6, I argue here that geographers should perhaps construct reverse discourses in Geography to theorize back at social science – there is no reason why Geography should remain short shrift as simply the producers of geographic data for the theory mills of other social sciences.

This final chapter starts by making the case for how current and future mid-range theories and mechanism-based explanations in human geography can make practically adequate contributions to broader social science priorities and agendas by going beyond the offering of common concepts in human geography (e.g. space, place, scale, location, landscape, settlement, territory, network, and so on) and our often self-assumed midwifery/husbandry role in the social sciences. While spatializing social science theories by inserting into them the disturbing effects of space and place might well be appropriate in earlier canonical works, I argue that geographers should now be at the forefront of new (social) theory development during their formative phase, *not* after they have already been made (by inserting space into them thereafter). Going beyond the kind of 'academic esotericism' in some geographical work discussed in earlier chapters, these mid-range explanatory theories should also be more relevant for public engagement and policy agendas in the post-pandemic world confronted with immense uncertainty and widespread disruptions. The book ends with the plea for a more pragmatic approach to theory and explanation in Geography and its knowledge production in the 2020s and beyond.

# Notes

1  Throughout this book, I will use 'Geography' (with a capital G) to denote the long-established academic discipline and 'human geography' (in small caps) to indicate the subdiscipline's more specific form of knowledge communities.

2  My sincere thanks to one reviewer for prompting me to note this geographical exceptionalism that I have personally noticed for quite some time whenever I speak to (and often tease!) economists, political scientists, and sociologists.

3  Some prominent authors in these approaches refer to relational thinkers among actor-network theorists (e.g. Michel Callon, Bruno Latour, and John Law) and their interlocutors in Geography (e.g. Nigel Thrift, Jonathan Murdoch, and Sarah Whatmore), 'relational' geographers (e.g. Doreen Massey, John Allen, Ash Amin, and others), and realist philosophers in the traditions of critical realism (e.g. Roy Bhaskar, Margaret Archer, Rom Harré, Andrew Sayer, and others), and, recently, speculative realism (e.g. Manuel DeLanda, Graham Harman, Markus Gabriel, Tom Sparrow, and others).

4  Influential authors advocating this mechanism-based approach to causal explanation come from analytical sociology (e.g. Peter Hedström, Richard Swedberg, Philip Gorski, Neil Gross, and Dave Elder-Vass), political science (e.g. Jon Elster, John Gerring, James Mahoney, and Charles Tilly), and the philosophy of social science (e.g. Daniel Little, Stuart Glennan, Arthur Stinchcombe, and James Woodward).

5  For example, more explicit discussion of relational thinking in some of these critical approaches is offered in Chapter 4 on relational theory. Chapter 5 on mechanism and process revisits processual theorizing in geographical political economy and poststructuralist geographies, such as actor-network theory and non-representational theory.

6  In doing so, I draw upon leading texts and collections on the development of geographical thought (e.g. Agnew and Livingstone, 2011; Cresswell, 2013; Cox, 2014; Aitken and Valentine, 2015a; Johnston and Sidaway, 2016) and specialized geography texts/handbooks on specific approaches, e.g. poststructuralism (e.g. Murdoch, 2006), feminism (e.g. Moss and Donovan, 2017; Oberhauser et al., 2018; Johnston, 2019; Datta et al., 2020), postcolonialism (e.g. Sharp, 2009; Jazeel, 2019), and non-representational theory (e.g. Thrift, 1996, 2007; Anderson and Harrison, 2010a; Simpson, 2021). Where appropriate, the discussion is supplemented by key articles grounded in these specific approaches and published in leading geography journals.

7  Some earlier works by geographers, who drew extensively selected quotes from original texts by the likes of Karl Marx, Jacques Derrida, Michel Foucault, Gilles Deleuze, Judith Butler, Bruno Latour, Edward Said, Homi Bhabha, and so on, sometimes border on the extremes of obscurity and abstraction – what Seamon (2015: p. 45) characterizes as 'the dense, cerebral hardheartedness of the current dominant geographies' or what Thrift (2007: p. 3) recognizes as the problem of 'a certain kind of over-theoretization at present'. Despite my pitch for a more advanced audience rather than undergraduate students, readers of this book are also not necessarily well versed in the original material. Extensive quotes from these original texts might be too demanding and esoteric. See more discussion on how I intend to handle this material in the next section on caveats.

8    Indeed, many existing 'ism' books in geographical thought do not cover the full spec-
     trum of social theorists and philosophers either – readers will not often find readings
     of Adam Smith, Max Weber, Karl Polanyi, Benedict Anderson, Clifford Geertz, An-
     thony Giddens, and so on in books on feminist or poststructuralist geographies, nor
     Bruno Latour, John Law, Arjun Appadurai, and so on in books on Marxist geography.
     Work in non-representational theory and postcolonial geographies hardly look into
     the original texts of critical realism and structuration theories.

9    My approach to writing in this book is similar to Aitken and Valentine's (2015b:
     pp. 1–2) style of approaching human geography: 'It is an attempt to lift the seemingly
     impenetrable veil that sometimes shrouds philosophical and theoretical issues, and to
     show how these issues are linked directly to methodologies and practices... The book
     avoids jargon-laden, impenetrable language and concepts while not sacrificing the
     rigour and complexity of the ideas that underlie geographic knowledge and the ways
     that it is conflicted and contested'. Moving long quotes and clusters of citations to
     endnotes also resembles the writing styles in political theorist Jane Bennett's (2010)
     *Vibrant Matter* and Oswin's (2020) recent article.

10   Whatmore (2002: p. 6) states that 'This book is not a lot of things. It does not espouse
     a particular philosophy, although its engagements and commitments position it phil-
     osophically. It is neither a complete "thesis" nor an assembly of "empirical" fragments,
     but rather an effort to germinate connections and openings that complicate this
     settlement. It is not a "geography of nature" – though natures and geographies are
     always in play. Doubtless this list will grow as the book travels...'. But her critics have
     picked on these modest claims. Demeritt (2005: pp. 820–822) indeed thinks *Hybrid
     Geographies* is 'first and foremost, a philosophical tract. ... [Its] epistemic modesty of
     claims about partial and situated knowledge is somewhat belied by some quite strong
     claims about how the world actually is... If that strikes you as inconsistent or even
     hypocritical, it is partly because the underlying notion of situated knowledge has
     become debased through careless and sloppy usage'. Another more sympathetic com-
     mentator Braun (2005: pp. 834–835) also notes the same: 'despite the author's claims
     otherwise – and this is a moment of false modesty – this book is a decidedly
     philosophical book, one that puts to work a coherent and consistent set of philosophical
     propositions and asks us to imagine the world through its terms'.

11   Despite his abandonment of Derridean postmodernist hermeneutics in the early
     1990s, realist philosopher Maurizio Ferraris (2014 [2012]: p. 52) remains committed
     to the value of careful deconstruction before realist reconstruction: 'That is why, in my
     opinion, the real deconstruction must commit to distinguishing between regions of
     being that are socially constructed and others that are not, to establishing for each
     region of being some specific modes of existence, and finally to ascribing individual
     objects to one of these regions of being, proceeding case by case'. Through these com-
     binatorial steps of deconstruction and reconstruction, he calls for 'a "treaty of
     perpetual peace" between the realist insight and the constructionist one. It is simply a
     matter of assigning each one to its field of competence' (p. 63).

12   This strand of speculative realism literature summarized in Harman (2018) includes
     Manuel DeLanda's (2006, 2016) assemblage theory, Graham Harman's (2010, 2016,
     2017) object-oriented ontology, and Maurizio Ferraris' (2014 [2012], 2015), Spar-
     row's (2014), and Markus Gabriel's (2015) new realism. As noted in their first

correspondence in January 2007, DeLanda said to Harman that 'for decades admitting that one was realist was equivalent to acknowledging one was a child molester' (Harman, 2008: p. 368, DeLanda and Harman, 2017: pp. 1–2)! DeLanda (2016: p. 138; also in DeLanda and Harman, 2017: p. 3) reflects that he was an unapologetic realist after his 1991 book on warfare; he is also recognized by Harman (2010: p. 171) as 'a realist with a straight face and without ironic tricks'. As discussed in DeLanda and Harman (2017: ch. 1), both of them began to write in a realist direction in 2002 and that year marks the beginning of a prominent realist current in continental philosophy. See also feminist physicist Karen Barad's (2007: ch. 4) work on what she terms 'agential realism' in *Meeting the Universe Halfway* that 'rejects the notion of a correspondence relation between words and things and offers in its stead a *causal explanation* of how discursive practices are related to material phenomena. It does so by shifting the focus from the nature of representations (scientific and other) to the nature of discursive practices (including technoscientific ones), leaving in its wake the entire irrelevant debate between traditional forms of realism and social constructivism' (Barad, 2007: pp. 44–45; my emphasis).

13   Some well-known examples are Harvey (1982, 1989) on the spatial logics of capitalism; Massey (1984) on spatial divisions of labour; Soja (1989) on socio-spatial dialectics; Thrift (1996, 2007) on spaces of practices; Massey (2005) and Murdoch (2006) on different conceptions of space as relational, co-constitutive, multiplicity, and heterogeneous, and their social and political effects; Simonsen and Koefoed (2020) on the spatiality of social life in 'new humanism'; and Clifford et al. (2009) and Agnew and Livingstone (2011) on key concepts and geographical knowledge.

14   In his preface to *Fields of Sense: A New Realist Ontology*, Markus Gabriel (2015: p. xii), a leading contemporary German philosopher in idealism and new realism, proclaims that 'If "analytic philosophy" means a commitment to clearly expressed arguments and the willingness to revise arguments and give up beliefs in light of better counter-arguments, all philosophy is analytic, and what is not is mere rhetoric or metaphor-mongering... If "continental" philosophy means "philosophy" as it is practiced in continental Europe, there is no continental philosophy, as philosophy in continental Europe is just like philosophy anywhere else: an attempt to deal with concepts fundamental to our self-description as rational animals under the condition that we are able to articulate them in more concise and coherent ways than they are often used loosely in everyday life and in the other sciences... In short, the categories of analytic and continental philosophy are often merely used in order to prevent bad philosophy from being criticised by people who do not belong to the group of those sharing a particular set of beliefs or parochial standards of justification'.

15   These geographical works can appear to be rather philosophical with excessive quotes from original texts by critical social theorists (from Karl Marx to Jacques Derrida, Gilles Deleuze, Michel Foucault, Pierre Bourdieu, Ernesto Laclau, Bruno Latour, Judith Butler, Donna Haraway, Gayatri Spivak, Edward Said, Homi Bhabha, and so on) and philosophers (from Friedrich Nietzsche to Martin Heidegger, Ludwig Wittgenstein, Edmund Husserl, Maurice Merleau-Ponty, Henri Bergson, Michel de Carteau, John Dewey, and so on).

16   This intellectual high ground of viewing philosophy as an underlabourer for the (social) sciences has been consistently found throughout Bhaskar's (1975, 1989, 2008

[1993], 2016) work over four decades. Bhaskar (2016: p. 2) reiterates his commitment of critical realist philosophy as an underlabourer for knowledge production right at the beginning of his very last (albeit most reader-friendly) book-length manuscript (re) introducing critical realism for the social sciences and written just before his untimely death in November 2014: Quoting the 18th century British empiricist philosopher John Locke's (1975 [1690]) notion that 'The commonwealth of learning is not at this time without master-builders... [but] it is ambition [*sic*] enough to be employed as an under-labourer in clearing the ground a little, and removing some of the rubbish that lies in the way to knowledge', Bhaskar (2016: p. 2) declares that 'Critical realism aspires to clear the ground a little, removing, in the first place, the philosophical rubbish that lies in the way of scientific knowledge, especially but not only in the domain of the social sciences; and in this way to underlabour for science and (partly in virtue of this, it argues) more generally for practices oriented to human well-being and flourishing. These philosophies have been inherited largely unthinkingly from the past. At one time they may have played a progressive role, but they have long since ceased to do so'.

17   Agreeing with DeLanda (2006), feminist philosopher Rosi Braidotti (2011: pp. 6, 271) also points to the role of philosophy in 'the production of pragmatic and localized tools of analysis for the power relations at work in society at large and more specifically within its own practice. The philosopher becomes no more than a provider of analytic services: a technician of knowledge'. In *The Incorporeal*, another influential feminist philosopher Elizabeth Grosz (2017: p. 4) makes a similar case of philosophers in service of ontological clarifications: 'While I do not consider what follows to be a critique of epistemology, I aim to bypass epistemological questions in favor of a focus on an ontology sensitive to and engaged with the realities of space and time, of events and becomings, not just things and their knowable, determinable relations'. In her case of reworking ideas from a number of continental philosophers – from the Stoics, Benedict de Spinoza, and Friedrich Nietzsche to Gilles Deleuze, Félix Guattari, Gilbert Simondon, and Raymond Ruyer, she addresses the mind-body dualism through the concept of 'the incorporeal' that incorporates 'the subsistence of the ideal *in* the material or corporeal' and thus 'the immanence of the ideal in the material and the material in ideality' (Grosz, 2017: p. 5; original italics).

18   In his commentary on Ash's (2020a) (re)take on flat ontologies in actor-network theory, assemblage theory, theories of affect, and object-oriented ontology, Häkli (2020: p. 370) ruminates that 'Who would have thought that one day the arid "philosophical study of being" would become a hot topic in human geography? Not many, I bet, but these days it is difficult to find a paper that does not mention ontology in some way, shape or form'! See also DeLanda and Harman (2017: pp. 85–88) for an exchange of their views on different kinds of flat ontologies.

19   In the same 2010 AAG panel as Yi-Fu Tuan, Eric Sheppard cautioned that 'if we are going to make an ontological claim at all I think it should be relatively modest, not deeply philosophical. It is that complex emerging spatialities, or spatiotemporalities, matter. And they matter because even though they are in part constructed by us through a series of socionatural processes in which humans participate, they nevertheless always already exist, always coming back to shape what happens' (Merriman et al., 2012: p. 8). In the same forum, Nigel Thrift observed that 'there are many different

ways that you can define ontologies. If I was doing it I would probably index the Humean sense of the term, as inferences about the world's connections, natural organizations, perceptions of experience and causation and of what therefore constitutes both existence and non-existence. So that would, if you like, be a very general definition. Going on from that, though, I think what is interesting about the current moment is there are a lot of people who are playing around with this notion with the result, of course, that it has become *extremely confused*' (Merriman et al., 2012: p. 14; my emphasis).

20  See also Holbraad and Pedersen (2017) for an in-depth analysis of the ontological turn in anthropology. They note that despite 'a much-debated "ontological turn" within the discipline of anthropology... there is little agreement, and often little clarity, as to what anthropology's turn to ontology is actually meant to be, and how it relates to other recent ontological orientations within cognate fields' (Holbraad and Pedersen, 2017: pp. 44–45). Commenting on the apparent confusion over anthropology's ontological turn and its lack of conceptual parsimony, their solution is to argue for more 'turning', including turning on itself! As they conclude, 'the concepts that emerge out of our ethnographic engagements tend to seem similar because they are somehow tainted or otherwise influenced by the very *manner* or *method* by which they are derived. Maybe the ontological turn itself is just too "noisy" or powerful, generating concepts from here, there and everywhere, but somehow, and perhaps only to a certain extent, in its *own image*... For the point is that what the ontological turn seeks for itself, constitutively, is to *keep turning*. And turning in its most thoroughgoing orientation, as we have seen throughout this book, is fundamentally a reflexive exercise – it is above all of a matter of a turn turning on itself' (Holbraad and Pedersen, 2017: pp. 279–280; original italics).

21  Some of these quotes from philosophers can be rather weird and dysfunctional, from a few words (risking out-of-context quotation) to long paragraphs (risking obfuscation). Some book examples of such heavy engagement with critical social theorists and continental philosophers are Harvey (1989); Thrift (1996, 2007); Doel (1999); Massey (2005); Murdoch (2006); and Simonsen and Koefoed (2020). While Simonsen and Koefoed (2020: p. 2) recognize 'of course a risk to read philosophers as a nonphilosopher, since we do not have the resources fully to locate them in the intellectual histories from which they emerge', their book is actually much heavier in such readings of philosophers and critical theorists, from Maurice Merleau-Ponty, Michel de Certeau, and Hannah Arendt to Henri Lefebvre, Edward Said, and Sarah Ahmed and many others, than in its empirical illustration of these dense philosophical ideas and concepts with interview and observational materials from their four projects on urban encounters and embodied experiences in Denmark. For journal articles, see recent examples of such writing style in Joronen and Häkli's (2017) critique of Geography's 'ontological turn' (drawing much on Martin Heidegger); Ash (2020a) on 'flat ontology'; Bridge (2021) on John Dewey's pragmatist philosophy; and Kinkaid's (2021) critique of post-phenomenology (drawing much on Maurice Merleau-Ponty). In Robinson's (2016: p. 16) recast of comparative tactics for a more global urban studies, the need to go back into Deleuze's abstract philosophy and, by her own admission, 'an incredibly complex formulation' to justify all over again the relevance of *difference* for comparative urban studies in the late 2010s and beyond might seem a

little excessive (see also Cockayne et al., 2017). To take one example from the much celebrated poststructuralist work *A Thousand Plateaus*, Deleuze and Guattari's (1987 [1980]: pp. 87–91) thought on assemblage is what his interlocutor and philosopher DeLanda (2006: p. 3) calls 'Deleuzian hermeneutics' or 'a preoccupation with what Deleuze "really meant"' because 'part of a definition may be in one book, extended somewhere else, and qualified later in some obscure essay. Even in those cases where conceptual definitions are easy to locate, they are usually not given in a style that allows for a straightforward interpretation'.

22  As Nigel Thrift (2021: p. xi) reflects on some social theory writing, 'I have read too much social theory which blithely asserts the primacy of its account of the world on the basis of not much except other social theoretical accounts and a kind of theoretical puritanism. Fine, but with this tendency comes the risk of writing "phiction"'. But John Agnew (2011) is much more critical in his damning view of how (British) geographers latch onto French theorists to legitimize their rediscovery of 'place' for Geography. In the context of a revival of scholarly interest in the mediating role of place in social relations and acquisition of meanings, Agnew (2011: p. 322) notes that 'The ransacking of the works of French philosophers (Deleuze, Foucault, Derrida, Latour, etc.) by some British geographers to find a quotation or two to justify their re-animation of place would be just as simple-minded a representation of an equally wide range of writing'. Paradoxically though, Deleuze and Guattari (1987 [1980]: p. 24) intentionally took a rhizomatic approach to what they term 'nomadic' writing about many different plateaus such that their work cannot be 'ransacked' and reduced to straightforward subjects and objects (see also such 'nomadic habits' of writing and reading in Braidotti, 2011: p. 9)!

23  Reviewing critically Marcus Doel's (1999) *Poststructuralist Geographies*, Elden (2003: p. 239; emphasis omitted) has 'grave doubts' about the book's 'approach, and certainly its style' because Doel's 'own rampant licentiousness makes this text a collage, a bricolage, a patchwork of quotations and disparate thinkers uncritically assimilated to the schizoproject. However supportive of his endeavour readers might be, they are likely to be put off by the awkwardness of its expression and its intangibility. Doel appropriates the ideas of many, and rather than explaining their ideas in a way that might open them to a wider audience, seems content to speak like them'. For someone well versed with 'continental' philosophy (see Elden, 2001, 2004, 2017), Elden's remarks and their implications for geographical writing should be taken seriously.

24  Deleuze and Guattari (1987 [1980]: p. 503; my emphasis) caution that 'How could unformed matter, anorganic life, nonhuman becoming be anything but chaos pure and simple? Every undertaking of destratification (for example, going beyond the organism, plunging into a becoming) must therefore observe *concrete rules of extreme caution*: a too-sudden destratification may be suicidal, or turn cancerous. In other words, it will sometimes end in chaos, the void and destruction, and sometimes lock us back into the strata, which become more rigid still, losing their degrees of diversity, differentiation, and mobility'.

25  I concur with feminist-socialist Donna Haraway's argument against relativism, even though I may not subscribe entirely to her alternative and perhaps rather utopian approach. In her work on situated knowledges engaging with Sandra Harding's (1986) *The Science Question in Feminism*, Haraway (1991: p. 191) argues that 'The alternative

to relativism is partial, locatable, critical knowledges sustaining the possibility of webs of connections called solidarity in politics and shared conversations in epistemology. Relativism is a way of being nowhere while claiming to be everywhere equally. The "equality" of positioning is a denial of responsibility and critical enquiry. Relativism is the perfect mirror twin of totalization in the ideologies of objectivity; both deny the stakes in location, embodiment, and partial perspective; both make it impossible to see well. Relativism and totalization are both "god-tricks" promising vision from everywhere and nowhere equally and fully' (see also Harding, 1991: ch. 6; pp. 152–153).

26  But such a normative stance is not easy in practice! In his first book on the ideology of science and critical theories in human geography, Gregory (1978: p. 170) argues for a critical geography that moves beyond the epistemological discourse of positivism. And yet he concludes reflexively that 'in effect, I have as yet failed to apply to the critical model [theory] the same order of interrogation that I deployed against the traditional model [positivism] and, in particular, I have said very little about the nature of the emancipatory interest which provides the touchstone of the critique and the very foundation of the critical model itself'. See also feminist Sara Ahmed's (1998: pp. 54–58) *Differences That Matter* for her reflections on the practical difficulty in defining the universal emancipatory values of mediating ethics by feminist politics.

27  To Bhaskar (2016: p. 38), 'all human societies always already possess a proto-scientific account of the world and any serious science or philosophy is always necessarily trying to transform this account into a more adequate account, that is, to demystify and enlighten common sense. The relevant questions will then be how far this realism is developed (whether so as to include causal laws or universals, for example) and in what form it is manifest (empirical, conceptual, and so on). This of course gives the imma-nent critic of some position adopted in practice a way in which explicitly to critique it. But by the same token it becomes important for us not just to identify lazily as a realist, but to specify exactly what kind of realism the position being advanced is committed to'. See also Maurizio Ferraris' (2014 [2012]: ch. 3) arguments for immanent critique and the need for not only postmodernist deconstruction, but more importantly also realist reconstruction. To him, realist philosophy is critical 'in the Kantian sense of judging what is real and what is not, and in the Marxian sense of transforming what is not right' (p. 45). Such a paradox in the relationship between critique and creative (re)construction has also been recognized by feminist philosopher Rosi Braidotti (2011: p. 267) as 'a problem that has confronted all activists and critical theorists: how to balance the creative potential of critical thought with the dose of negative criticism and oppositional consciousness that such a stance necessarily entails'. She argues for an affirmative politics that 'entails the creation of sustainable alternatives geared to the construction of social horizons of hope, while at the same time doing critical theory, which implies resistance to the present'.

28  See Barnett (1999, 2008); Tolia-Kelly (2006); Mitchell and Elwood (2012); Joronen and Häkli (2017); MacFarlane (2017); Doucette (2020); and Kinkaid (2020, 2021). Taking a radical contingent view, Ruez and Cockayne (2021) recently offer an am-bivalent-affective response to these critiques and yet leave us with their ambivalence about ambivalence as something to work with, not work through! Here, I share Wilkinson and Lim's (2021: p. 113) concern with the ambivalent 'who' who can benefit from their new affective dispositions and capacities for action, and Linz and

Secor's (2021: p. 109; original italics) response that 'We confess to being ambivalent about this ambivalence about ambivalence with which we are left. How does a tool that itself resists self-identity even work? How does it become ready-to-hand without any fixing of meaning or function? Can we use it *without* stopping it from slipping away – a tool of unmastery?'.

29   Citing key feminist and postcolonial thinkers such as Judith Butler (2006 [1990], 2011 [1993]) and Gayatri Spivak (1988), Mitchell and Elwood (2012: pp. 792–793) argue that 'In furthering theory and tackling injustice both scholars noted the difficult but vital importance of relying on (and constantly critiquing) a community of praxis rather than merely on individual observations, passions, or celebrations. This runs counter to the general mood of NRT [non-representational theory], which frowns on boring, "normative" concerns such as these and favors, instead, an attention to our personal bodily encounters and emotions'. Drawing on approaches in feminism, sexuality, indigenous, and critical race theory, Kinkaid (2020: p. 469) also points to the danger of missing gender, sexuality, and race in assemblage thinking and argues that 'in disavowing social categories, assemblage thinking may further obscure the operations of power and inequality... [Indeed], assemblage might provide a critical lexicon for better understanding and intervening in the uneven geographies of our world. Yet in order to activate these possibilities and avert these dangers assemblage geographies must conduct a serious accounting of its theoretical foundations and normative commitments'.

30   Following some of political theorist Hannah Arendt's arguments for cohabitation and equality, Butler (2015a: pp. 118–119) claims that our ethical responsibility and global obligation in unchosen cohabitation is expressed in the plurality of bodily life and thus our commitment to preserving the life of the other, as in the relational interdependency of our bodies 'up against' the distant suffering of other bodies on earth. To her, 'it is only when we understand that what happens there also happens here, and that "here" is already an elsewhere, and necessarily so, that we stand a chance of grasping the difficult and shifting global connections in ways that let us know the transport and the constraint of what we might still call ethics' (Butler, 2015a: p. 122). In *The Incorporeal*, Elizabeth Grosz (2017: p. 1) uses the term 'ontoethics' to describe this ontological approach to 'the question of how to act in the present and, primarily, how to bring about a future different from the present'.

31   In *Geographical Imaginations*, Gregory (1994: p. 12) argues that 'social theory does not come ready-made. As I have said, it provides a series of partial, often problematic and always situated knowledges that require constant reworking as they are made to engage with different positions and places. Conceived thus, social theory, like geography, is a "traveling discourse," marked by its various origins and moving from one site to another'.

32   Addressing problems of explanation in his book *Society and Economy*, prominent economic sociologist Mark Granovetter (2017: p. 14) takes a similar view of explaining human action in its necessary social context: 'A fruitful analysis of any human action, including economic action, requires us to avoid the atomization implicit in the theoretical extremes of under- and oversocialized views. Actors do not behave or decide as atoms outside a social context, nor do they adhere slavishly to a script written for them by the particular intersection of sociocultural categories they happen to

occupy. Their attempts at purposive action are instead embedded in concrete, ongoing systems of social relations'.

33    As cautioned specifically in Bhaskar (2016: p. 80), 'it will not in general be possible to specify how a mechanism operates independently of its context. Hence we must not only relate mechanisms back to explanatory or grounding structures, as in the theoretical natural sciences, but also to context or field of operation. This means that in the social field in principle we need always to think of a context-mechanism couple, C + M, and thus the trio of context, mechanism, outcome (CMO), or more fully the quartet composed of context, mechanism, structure and outcome (CMSO)'.

34    Harrison (2002: p. 489) argues that 'the value of Wittgenstein's work lies in how it may be used as a way of getting to another understanding or sense of explanation... For Wittgenstein, as for (especially the later) Foucault, practices and their performance are understood as sufficient in themselves'. But in *The Art of Social Theory*, sociologist Swedberg (2014: pp. 71–74, 182–183) has extensively engaged with Wittgenstein to buttress his argument *for* explanation as the necessary ingredient of social theory.

35    Thrift (1986; reproduced in 1996: p. 132; original italics) compares theories with accounts: 'A theory is concerned with taking a set of events that already existed prior to it and made one kind of sense and reshaping them to make quite another kind of sense. It is a cognitive operation. In contrast, an account is a perceptual operation, a more explicit description of what an action taking place with a particular everyday context actually *is*'. I see these two modes as compatible since a proper description or account of what is taking place does entail theory as some *a priori* explanation or sense-making of what such events might be and why they *can* take place.

36    As Bhaskar (2009 [1986]: p. 104) argues in his *Scientific Realism and Human Emancipation*, 'Emancipation depends upon explanation depends upon emergence. Given the phenomena of emergence, an emancipatory politics (or more generally transformative or therapeutic practice) depends upon a realist science. But, if and only if emergence is real, the development of both science and politics are up to us'. Critical realist work should therefore be practical in the sense that it is applicable to everyday life. Bhaskar (2016: p. 4) notes further in his last and most reader-friendly book that 'For since there is only one world, albeit there are very variant descriptions of it, the theories and principles of critical realist philosophy should also apply to our everyday lives. If they do not, then something is seriously wrong. This means that our theories and explanations should be tested in everyday life as well as in specialist research contexts'. Committed to the need for social theory with an emancipatory intent, realist sociologist Dave Elder-Vass (2010: pp. 11–12) echoes Bhaskar's sentiment and argues that 'I do believe that we cannot pursue an emancipatory politics without a good understanding of how the social world does work and how it could work differently. It is only if we can provide causal explanations of the social world that we can attempt to predict the consequences of a possible change. It is only if we are able to predict, at least in broad outlines, these consequences that we can assess whether that change offers progress in a normative sense. And it is only if we can do this that we can honestly advocate it as an emancipatory strategy'.

37    As argued in his recent book *Social Change in a Material World*, 'The ultimate criterion for the [practical] adequacy of theory and theoretical concepts is their usefulness in empirical analysis, the use that is and can be made of them to conceptualize, describe, explain, and understand social life and social phenomena (or to order these cognitive

achievements). Success at conceptualizing, describing, explaining, and understanding might make theories and theoretical ideas useful for intervening in, that is, impeding, instigating, or inflecting social affairs. Although it is intellectually defensible for any work of theory that upholds theses such as these to be a work of pure theoretical development and elaboration, pure theory contravenes the spirit of the thesis; it is also tactically inadvisable' (Schatzki, 2019: p. 18).

38  Jazeel's (2016, 2019) argument has drawn upon indigenous studies (e.g. Tuck and Yang, 2012) to critique the dominant focus on representation and its literary critiques in postcolonial theory and subaltern studies (see also geographical debates in Curley and Smith, 2020; Oswin, 2020). In an earlier text on postcolonial geographies, Sharp (2009: pp. 145–146) also laments that 'the ideas of postcolonialism have been generated from inside the west, inside academia, and from an analysis of texts rather than fieldwork. The clever ideas of postcolonial theory are sometimes challenged for being too caught up with producing critiques of the texts central to western thought (whether western philosophy, literature or art) and for not spending enough time considering the real issues being faced by people in the global south today. For instance, some would wonder as to what the cultural and theoretical bases of postcolonialism can tell us about poverty, inequality, racism, subjugation'.

39  As noted in Deleuze and Guattari's (1987 [1980]: p. 500) *A Thousand Plateaus*, change alone through a smooth space (of thought?) may not be enough to save us: 'Movements, speed and slowness, are sometimes enough to reconstruct a smooth space. Of course, smooth spaces are not in themselves liberatory. But the struggle is changed or displaced in them, and life reconstitutes its stakes, confronts new obstacles, invents new paces, switches adversaries. Never believe that a smooth space will suffice to save us'!

40  My similar choice of illustrative materials in different chapters may invite such a reading, e.g. the focus on Doreen Massey's spatial divisions of labour in Chapter 3, regional development in Chapter 4, neoliberalization in Chapter 5, and economic globalization and the theory of global production networks in Chapter 6.

41  This idea of 'stress testing' might have its origin in the post-2008 global financial crisis and subsequent banking restructuring. But my evocation of the idea is more metaphorical than institutional, as practised in then the stress-testing of banks (see Fligstein, 2021).

42  Some contemporary exceptions are David Harvey's (1989, 2005) Marxist rethinking of postmodernity and neoliberalism; Edward Soja's (1989) spatialization of postmodern theory; JK Gibson-Graham's (2006[1996]) feminist critique of political economy; Michael Storper's (1997) institutionalist theory of regional development; Tim Cresswell's (2006) interpretive framing of mobilities; and so on.

# Chapter Two
# Contemporary Geographical Thought: Theory and Explanation

This chapter takes a quick tour of the key conceptual priorities and their styles of theory and/or explanation in the various critical approaches since David Harvey's (1969) rendition of the positivist approach for Geography. I can only present a highly selective and condensed reading of these approaches in contemporary geographical thought. The chapter is necessarily brief and stylized in light of space constraints and its key purpose of grounding this book's synthetic approach to theory and explanation. It is also meant to be critically charitable in engagement with these diverse approaches in human geography. Indeed, these approaches – often treated as ontologies in the geographical literature – are not entirely self-contained and isolated from each other; many have emerged from one another and/or coevolved as critiques of each other.

Put succinctly in summary Table 2.1, starting from the search for objectivity, causality, and universal covering laws in *positivism* and the quantitative revolution during the 1960s, human geography has since the 1970s moved on to embrace:

1. *phenomenology* and *humanistic geography*: the uncovering and understanding of human experiences, being, meanings, and sense of place;
2. *Marxism*: the analytical practice of dialectics and historical materialism in explaining capitalist modes of production and underlying class-based structures of social relations;
3. *critical realism*: the explanation of reality through causal mechanisms and empirical contingency;

4. *postmodernism*: the critique and deconstruction of representations in narratives, texts, and discourses;

5. *poststructuralism* (including actor-network theory, non-representational theory, and, most recently, assemblage theory): the social construction and unfolding of subject-formation, embodied practices and affect, encounters, relationality, and more-than-human worlds;

6. *feminism*: describing and understanding the embodiment and performativity of subjects, difference, and intersectionality in identities (gender, sexuality, race, and so on) and the positionality and reflexivity of knowledge production;

7. *postcolonialism*: the critique and uncovering of othering in texts, images, and cultures, and the unequal politics of representations and knowledge production; and

8. *post-phenomenology* and *posthumanism* (a more recent outgrowth of poststructuralism): the worldly understanding of objects, materiality, affect, being, emotions, and more-than-humans.

In varying degrees, this multitude of critical approaches in human geography often demonstrates a direct relationship between ontology (theory of reality and existence) and epistemology (theory of our knowledge of reality and existence). As noted in Chapter 1, theory exists in both types of knowledges, though ontological 'theories' are mostly philosophical and abstract. In developing the art of social theory, Swedberg (2014: p. 15) notes that one of the problems with social theory today is what he terms 'abstract theory'. Citing social theorist Pierre Bourdieu (1988: p. 774), he argues that in these abstract social theories, 'Data are mainly used to illustrate the theory, and the analysis is about as nonempirical as it gets. This is a version of what has been called "theoretical theory," [by Bourdieu] and it has been described as a theory that basically deals only with other (theoretical) theories' (see also Schatzki, 2019: p. 24).

In Geography, Harrison (2015: p. 143) has argued that the apparent obscurity of some philosophical debates, such as poststructuralism, is not simply a matter of the 'latest fashion' or 'elitist jargon'. Still, he concedes that the 'more telling criticism of poststructuralist thought is that it can become overburdened by its historical self-consciousness such that all that is produced in its name are commentaries on its own canonical and marginal texts'. In this sense, those discursive commentaries on other (theoretical) theories constitute what Gregory (1994: p. 11) terms social theory as a discourse – the vast network of signs, symbols, and practices through which our world(s) is made meaningful to ourselves and to others. As such, theoretical theory or abstract theory is mostly found in ontological or philosophical debates.

This monograph argues for explanatory theory that operates at the epistemological realm, i.e. how our knowledge of the actually existing empirical world(s) can be produced and what kind of theory might be useful in this pursuit of knowledge production in Geography. At its core, the book represents more an

**Table 2.1** Contemporary geographical thought on theory and explanation.

| Contemporary thought | Key philosophers (P), theorists (T), and geographers (G) | Research foci and conceptual priorities | Styles of theory and/or explanation | Quotes from geographers or philosophers/theorists on theory and/or explanation |
|---|---|---|---|---|
| **Since the 1960s**<br>Positivism and quantitative revolution | P: Auguste Comte, David Hume, Immanuel Kant, Carl Hempel, Karl Popper<br>G: David Harvey, Brian Berry, Peter Haggett, Peter Gould, Michael Chisholm | Spatial structures: patterns and processes; spatial science | Universal covering laws based on empirical regularities; Scientific method | 'Explanatory theories may be regarded as the apex of the scientific pyramid' (Michael Chisholm, 1975: p. 122). |
| **Since the 1970s**<br>Phenomenology and humanistic geography | P: Martin Heidegger, Edmund Husserl<br>G: Yi-Fu Tuan, Anne Buttimer, Denis Cosgrove, Stephen Daniels, Peter Jackson, David Ley, John Pickles, Tim Cresswell | Human experiences, being, meanings, and sense of place | Intersubjective understanding, self-knowledges, and qualitative interpretation; Thick description rather than explanatory theory | '[I]s a theory of space and spatiality possible?... I have my doubts, for space, to me, is a cultural and experiential construct' (Yi-Fu Tuan, in Merriman et al., 2012: p. 12). |
| Marxism | T: Karl Marx, Friedrich Engels, Louis Althusser<br>G: David Harvey, Doreen Massey, Neil Smith, Kevin Cox, Richard Peet, Eric Sheppard, Richard Walker, Erik Swyngedouw, Michael Webber, Noel Castree, Brett Christophers | Capitalist modes of production, class struggles, and uneven structures of social relations | Marx's theory of capital and crisis of accumulation; Analytical practice of dialectics and historical materialism | 'If the primary contradictions are revealed, as Marx held, in the course of crises, then it is to crisis theory that we must turn to get a political handle on what long-term strategies to pursue' (David Harvey, 2006a [1982]: p. xxiii). |

| | | | |
|---|---|---|---|
| **Since the 1980s**<br>Critical realism | P: Roy Bhaskar, Margaret Archer, Andrew Collier, Rom Harré, Ruth Groff, Mervyn Hartwig<br>G: Andrew Sayer, John Allen, John Lovering, Jamie Peck, Andy Pratt, Henry Yeung | Reality constituted by emergent and underlying structures; human emancipation | Abstraction of causal mechanisms and their activation in empirical contingency; Practical adequacy of theory and explanation | Theories 'should also apply to our everyday lives. If they do not, then something is seriously wrong' (Roy Bhaskar, 2016: p. 4). |
| Postmodernism | P/T: Jacques Derrida, Fredric Jameson, Jean-François Lyotard<br>G: Edward Soja, Michael Dear | Meanings in narratives, texts, and discourses; linguistic utterances and speech acts as (re)signification | Critique and deconstruction of representations through meta-reflexivity; The Los Angeles School of postmodern geographies | 'More seriously, we still know too little about the descriptive grammar and syntax of human geographies, the phonemes and epistemes of spatial interpretation. We are constrained by language much more than we know' (Edward Soja, 1989: p. 247). |
| **Since the 1990s**<br>Poststructuralism | P/T: Gilles Deleuze, Michel Foucault, Félix Guattari, Bruno Latour, Michel Callon, John Law, Manuel DeLanda<br>G: Nigel Thrift, Jonathan Murdoch, Sarah Whatmore, John Paul Jones, Deborah Dixon, Sallie Marston, Stuart Elden, Chris Philo, Louise Amoore, Ben Anderson, John-David Dewsbury, Marcus Doel, Paul Harrison, John Wylie | Subject-formation, embodied practices and affect, encounters, relationality, and more-than-human worlds | Actor-network theory; Non-representational theory; Assemblage theory; Social construction, unfolding, and descriptive accounts of change in events and becomings | An account is 'a perceptual operation, a more explicit description of what an action taking place with a particular everyday context actually is' (Nigel Thrift, 1996: p. 132).<br>'The task of post-structuralist theorizing is to trace the resulting trajectories of change' (Jonathan Murdoch, 2006: p. 11). |

(Continued)

**Table 2.1** (Continued)

| Contemporary thought | Key philosophers (P), theorists (T), and geographers (G) | Research foci and conceptual priorities | Styles of theory and/or explanation | Quotes from geographers or philosophers/theorists on theory and/or explanation |
|---|---|---|---|---|
| Feminism | T: Judith Butler, Donna Haraway, bell hooks, Sara Ahmed, Rosi Braidotti, Bonnie Honig<br><br>G: Doreen Massey, Linda McDowell, Susan Hanson, Janice Monk, Gillian Rose, Catherine Nash, Liz Bondi, JK Gibson-Graham, Robyn Longhurst, Katherine McKittrick, Geraldine Pratt | Embodiment and performativity of subjects, difference, and intersectionality in identities (gender, sexuality, race, etc.) | Feminist theory; Describing and understanding of gender norms and subversion in relation to positionality and reflexivity of knowledge production | Geography's raison d'être 'is the explanation of difference and diversity' (Linda McDowell, 1995: p. 280).<br><br>'[E]xplaining phenomena like racism and sexism – how they are reproduced, how they keep being reproduced – is not something we can do simply by learning a new language' (Sara Ahmed, 2017: p. 9). |
| Postcolonialism | T: Edward Said, Gayatri Spivak, Homi Bhabha, Dipesh Chakrabarty, Wael Hallaq<br><br>G: Alison Blunt, Gillian Hart, Jane Jacobs, Tariq Jazeel, Cheryl McEwan, Steve Pile, Jennifer Robinson, Vinay Gidwani | Othering in texts, images, and cultures; Unequal politics of representations and knowledge production | Postcolonial theory; Critique and deconstruction of (Eurocentric) representations; Allowing the weak and the subaltern to speak (back) | 'This time round, the term "critical theory," often untheorized and unargued, is definitely the Other, an otherness that is insistently identified with the vagaries of the depoliticized Eurocentric critic' (Homi Bhabha, 2004 [1994]: p. 29). |
| **Since the 2000s**<br>Post-phenomenology and posthumanism | P/T: Jane Bennett, Tim Ingold, Donna Haraway; Harman Graham, Manuel DeLanda, Markus Gabriel<br><br>G: Derek McCormack, Kirsten Simonsen, James Ash, Tim Edensor, Tom Roberts, Paul Simpson; Maan Barua, Jamie Lorimer, Kathryn Yusoff | Objects, matter, materiality, affect, being, emotions, more-than-humans, multi-species, and the Anthropocene | Theories in poststructuralism and speculative realism; Describing, accounting, and understanding things and events | '[I]s it not a human subject who, after all, is articulating this theory of vibrant matter?' (Jane Bennett, 2010: p. ix).<br><br>'Post-phenomenology and its concern with objects allows us to move beyond curiosity or provocation to begin to think the aesthetic causalities of how objects relate to one another and explore what non-human things are and what they do' (James Ash and Paul Simpson, 2016: p. 63). |

epistemological intervention than a philosophical one. But if theory means quite different things to each of us, it seems that even 'explanation' may have many different meanings too. To feminist geographer Linda McDowell (1995: p. 280), the *raison d'être* of Geography 'is the explanation of difference and diversity'. But what sort of difference and diversity to be explained and how we do 'explanation' remains a highly contentious matter because it might require some epistemological consensus for us to adjudicate the politics of difference and theorizing explanation. Cresswell (2013: p. 185) thus raises 'the issue of whether there was any way to differentiate differences that matter from differences that don't. To put it crudely, why do we take the difference between classes or genders more seriously than, say, the differences between people who prefer Coke and people who prefer Pepsi? If we have no foundational bedrocks to allow us to judge between differences, why not take all differences equally seriously?' (see also Cockayne et al., 2017).

Reprised in *Practising Human Geography*, Paul Cloke et al. (2004: p. 285) acknowledge this fundamental importance of explanation and yet point to its immense complexity and difficulties in the actual practice of human geography. They examine different forms of explanations, from descriptive and developmental to causal, comparative, and predictive explanations in everyday usage, and conclude with an observation of the shift in Geography's explanatory focus due to its interaction with social theory/theorists. To Cloke et al. (2004: p. 305), 'this broadening of the geographical discourse through mutual discovery has had implications for the content, as well as the nature, of explanation. We have moved from a position where the prime object of human geographical research was to explain the geographies which were uncovered around us, to one where those geographies become part and parcel of the explanation of a range of other processes'. This variety of approaches to explanation is also a key concern in the philosophy of social science (see Little, 1991, 2016; Woodward, 2003; Manicas, 2006; Schatzki, 2019; see also fuller development in Chapter 3).

This 'double movement' in our conception of the diverse nature and forms of explanation vis-à-vis our interactions with social theory begs the crucial question of what do theory and explanation really mean in these social theories and critical approaches? This chapter attempts to answer this thorny question by taking a fairly selective tactic. The following discussion does *not* elaborate on each of the eight strands of geographical thought and critical approaches since positivism in Table 2.1; interested readers should consult the vast literature on the development of geographical thought (Cresswell, 2013; Cox, 2014; Aitken and Valentine, 2015a; Johnston and Sidaway, 2016).

Instead, I focus only more specifically on the critical approaches constitutive of social theories with 'theory' in their names. These *theory-named* approaches range from my brief presentation of Marx's well-known theory of capital in Marxism to more in-depth discussion of actor-network theory, non-representational theory, and assemblage theory in 'open-ended' approaches such as poststructuralism, post-phenomenology, and posthumanism, and 'ideologically-oriented' theories in feminism and postcolonialism (see also Harney et al., 2016). In each of these 'theories', I examine the nature of theory and, if any, explanation as epistemological considerations. Where appropriate, my discussion also relates these implicit or explicit epistemologies to the broader philosophical origins and ontological gestures of these critical approaches. To minimize misunderstanding, let me be clear that this chapter is not meant to compare and contrast these critical 'theories' and approaches because doing so would perhaps create the unintended consequence of ascribing equivalence to them and downplaying the vast achievements of some over others. My intention is to interrogate what theory and explanation are about in *each* of these 'theories' and approaches, despite my earlier acknowledgement that some of them have co-evolved and/or are mutually co-constitutive. While not problematizing these 'theories' and their potential limits – a much larger subject matter for many monographs (!), my exposé on theory and explanation in these approaches is necessary for demonstrating the merits and potential of my synthetic approach to be offered in the next three chapters.[1]

## Theory in Marxism

In social science, Marxism is the single most influential critical approach named after a social theorist – I cannot think of another founder-named critical theory of greater academic influence and societal impact (see also Table 2.1). Karl Marx's theory of capital offers a unique political economy approach to understanding societal transformation through the method of historical materialism and structural explanations based on the analytical practice of dialectics. Its rendition in human geography through the pioneer works of 'transformed' David Harvey (1973, 1982, 1989, 2017) and many others (e.g. Massey, 1984; Smith, 1984; Sheppard and Barnes, 1990; Peet, 1991; see Cox, 2021) has made possible and empowered successive generations of critical geographical analyses of capitalist uneven development at the local, urban, regional, national, and even global scales. By theorizing the underlying and yet unequal modes of production, the exploitative capital-labour class relations, and the extraction of surplus value in modern capitalism, Marx's theory of capital and its crisis of accumulation provides a broadly structural and, as termed by Gibson-Graham (2006 [1996]: pp. 6, 35), 'capitalocentric' approach to explaining capitalist accumulation, uneven development, imperialism, and political-economic outcomes in society, space, and nature (Table 2.1). As David Harvey, the foremost Marxist geographer, has reminded us in his formidable reworking and spatializing of Marx's theory of capital and crises in *The Limits to Capital*,

> if Marx taught us anything it was, surely, that the world of appearances deceives and that it is the task of science to penetrate beneath the appearances and identify the *forces at work beneath*. If Marx's theory is as robust as he claims, then it should provide us with the necessary basis to interpret the dramatic and very evident forms of organizational change that have occurred under capitalism over the past century or so (Harvey, 2006a [1982]: p. 138; my emphasis).

Revisiting my three key considerations of, and for, theory and explanation in Geography in Chapter 1 – normative concerns, socio-spatial contexts, and practical adequacy, Marx's theory of capital and its incredible uptakes in human geography – perhaps much more so than in all other social science disciplines – are clearly normative in their critique of capitalism and politics of theorizing. The theory's practical adequacy in tackling real-world issues of poverty, exploitation, and uneven development is also strong (e.g. the occurrence of transformative socialist revolutions in world history during the first half of the 20th century). But the theory and its explanatory 'applications' in human geography have been less sensitive to socio-spatial contexts and individual life-worlds, let alone embodied practices and identity politics. In this regard, critics of Marxist (excessive) focus on capital's logic in material production, value extraction, and overaccumulation point to its often totalizing and reductionist accounts of societal changes and its relative neglect of subject-formation and agency difference at the individual levels – the so-called History 1 (Marx) and History 2s (everyday local 'being-in-the-world' practices) that are well distinguished in postcolonial critic Dipesh Chakrabarty's (2008 [2000]: ch. 2) *Provincializing Europe*.[2]

Still, some sympathetic geographers have argued that even these modes of difference at the individual levels can be better explained through analytical attention to their intersection with broader social processes such as alienation and exploitation in Marxian conception of capitalism (Henderson and Sheppard, 2015: p. 75). Moreover and in contrast with this book's core argument, capitalocentric Marxist approaches are not well known for building mid-range theories capable of 'ordinary' or meso-level explanations that somewhat sit in between grand structuralist theories (as in Marxism) and agent-centric accounts in the more recent critical approaches (e.g. poststructuralism). While many Marxist geographers have strived for such less grand and structural interpretations of socio-spatial outcomes in empirical research, their eventual adherence to Marx's theory of capital and Harvey's capitalist 'forces at work beneath' remains a fundamental contradiction in frustrating such an epistemological move towards mid-range theories and causal explanations.

Even a more conjunctural approach to renewing Marxism taken up by Louis Althusser to theorize the over-determination of a contradiction due to its multiple causes and conditions of existence within the capitalist complex whole has not been contextually sensitive enough to highly differentiated socio-spatial formations below the structural level of capitalism itself (Resch, 1992; Harvey, 2014). But as will be discussed further in Chapter 3, such conjunctural co/over-determination approach to theorizing capitalism can inform a more contemporary rethinking of causal mechanisms and relational thought in mid-range theories in critical human geography. I believe such mid-range theories can offer appropriate meso-level explanations of those mutual intersections and multiple (co-)determination between capitalist structures and agent-centric processes of subject-formation.

## Theories in Poststructuralism and Post-Phenomenology/Posthumanism

Going against the grand theories and metanarratives in what came before, these 'post-' approaches place theoretical emphasis on the power and effect of languages and representations through narratives, texts, and knowledge production. Delineating and defining precisely these approaches and thoughts is never easy and straightforward (see Doel, 1999; Harrison, 2002, 2015; Popke, 2003; Philo, 2012). As Jonathan Murdoch (2006) points out painstakingly in *Post-Structuralist Geography*, all of these 'post-' thoughts are linked and defined in relation to what came before, i.e. modernism, structuralism, and colonialism. But the problem is that these earlier thoughts are themselves subject to immense debates and fragmentation in various scholarly communities. Attempts to define poststructuralism are often fraught with problems and paradoxes – how can something championing the open-ended and processual becomings be delimited by such a narrative apparatus known as definition? Murdoch (2006: p. 4) thus laments that 'the term "structuralism" is likely to be shrouded in as much mystery as "post-structuralism." Thus, in order to gain some basic understanding of post-structuralism, it is first necessary to say something about structuralism. We can then go on to show how and why post-structuralism emerged in the ways that it did and say something about the nature of its concerns'.

To some critical theorists, our worlds as narrated in texts, meanings, and cultures are subject to the social and discursive reframing of literary apparatus such as metaphors and rhetoric (e.g. in the philosophical works of Jacques Derrida, Jean-Luc Nancy, Gilles Deleuze, and Félix Guattari). Sceptical of the universality of truth and knowledge claims, these approaches are highly critical of the taken-for-granted categories and objects of inquiry. On the other hand, knowledge and discourses are powerful explanations of subject performance, biopolitics, and socio-spatial outcomes (e.g. Michel Foucault's governmentality approach focusing on discursively constituted, totalizing power, and his later work on lively bodies, unpredictable populations, and biopolitics).

In general, we can conceive these critical 'post-' approaches as radically anti-essentialist and anti-foundational in their theoretical constructs in which meaning and identity are relational effects rather than law-like causal regularities, and their open-ended ethical concerns are with radical otherness and difference. To Harrison (2015: p. 132), 'poststructuralism denies any short cuts to simple truths and the construction of accounts which would seek to reduce the phenomena under investigation to either ahistorical or aspatial causes or to simply the effect of context. In so doing, poststructuralism presents a relational and open movement of thought, one which is permanently under revision, undergoing "trial by space"'. In this poststructuralist spirit of an open movement of thought, I find Murdoch's (2006: pp. 9–11; my emphasis) 'definition' of poststructuralism most congenial and clear:

It refers, in the main, to the multiple meanings and modes of identification that emerge from the constitution of relations within texts and within cultures. In this respect, it differs sharply from structuralism's concern to discover *underlying truths* about texts and cultures. Yet, post-structuralism should not be seen simply as a clean break from structuralism... Post-structuralism, then, describes social and cultural systems that are open and dynamic, constantly in the process of 'becoming'. The task of post-structuralist theorizing is to *trace* the resulting trajectories of change.

In what follows, I trace in some detail three 'theories' under the broad philosophical umbrella of poststructuralism and its more recent incarnations in post-phenomenology and posthumanism: (1) actor-network theory; (2) non-representational theory; and (3) assemblage theory. While presented in a historical sequence relatively to their emergence in geographical consciousness, these 'theories' are both diverse and not monolithic, and their very significant influences in human geography have been mostly concurrent since the 1990s. As indicated in Table 2.1, this strand of poststructuralist thought in human geography is particularly associated with relationality and processual interactions in more-than-human worlds, affect and embodiment, and process-practice orientations that began to emerge only in the mid-1990s among human geographers, particularly those based in the United Kingdom (e.g. Doel, 1996, 1999; Thrift, 1996, 2007; Whatmore, 1997, 2002; Murdoch, 1997a, 2006). Up to the mid-2000s, this poststructuralist thought remained 'emerging', as observed by one of its protagonists: 'it appears that post-structuralism has had a profound impact on the discipline of geography. However, it should be noted that post-structuralist geography is still to be found some distance away from "mainstream" geography (although it is undoubtedly a lot closer to the centre of the discipline than it once was)' (Murdoch, 2006: p. 24). By the late 2010s, I believe this poststructuralist geography and its variants in post-phenomenology and posthumanism had more than emerged to become the dominant approaches in critical human geography. This mainstreaming of poststructuralist 'theories' in the 2020s human geography certainly demands a reflexive and yet critical (re) examination of its basis for theory and explanation.

## Actor-Network Theory

Actor-network theory (ANT) first emerged from the social studies of science and technology in the 1980s.[3] Although it is called a 'theory', ANT does not usually explain why a network takes the form that it does. Rather, ANT is a way of thoroughly exploring the relational ties and heterogenous associations within a network, which can comprise a multitude of many different things and objects known as actants. These actants can be humans and non-humans. Actor-network theorists reject the modernist separations between subject and object, nature and culture, and being and beings in favour of hybrids and quasi-objects and their translations that may generate traceable and yet heterogenous associations (Latour, 2005; also, Latour, 2013: pp. 5–12). To its key protagonists Bruno Latour (1996: p. 374, 2017: p. 182), Michel Callon (1999: p. 194), and Annemarie Mol (2010: p. 257), ANT is not an explanatory theory, but a methodology or a 'semiotic theory/turn' concerned with what another ANT theorist John Law (2009) calls 'material semiotics'.[4] This focus on material semiotics is most evident in the trenchant critique of Jacques Derrida's postmodernist meta-reflexivity and deconstruction of texts by Bruno Latour (1988: pp. 166–168), ANT's foremost influential proponent, who argues that the postmodernist view of the readers as naïve believers of a text fit for their normal consumption is in itself naïve, uncritical, and unreflexive in its explanatory gesture.[5]

As a semiotic 'theory' or 'turn', actor-network theory recognizes both meaning and things/objects, not just texts (as among semioticians and postmodernists). Latour (1996: p. 373, 2017: p. 181) lists three unrelated strands of preoccupations in actor-network analysis:

1.   a semiotic definition of entity building: an actor or actant is something that acts or to which an activity is granted by others in the network. This is a semiotic understanding of relatedness;
2.   a methodological framework to record the heterogeneity of such a building: focusing empirically on heterogenous associations and relationships in actor-networks; and
3.   an ontological claim on the 'networky' character of actants themselves: there are only networks and nothing outside or in between.

In his more recent work advocating a new mode of enquiry into existence, Latour (2013: pp. 64–65) summarizes the key conditions of what he terms 'the art of speaking well':

1.   to describe networks in the actor-network theory mode, even at the risk of shocking modernist practitioners who are not accustomed to speaking in this way;
2.   to verify with these same practitioners that the description about them is valid, but only in practice;
3.   to explore the reasons for the gap between what the description reveals and the account provided by the actors, using the concepts of network and preposition; and
4.   to propose a different formulation of the link between practice and theory that can possibly close the gap between them and to redesign institutions harbouring such modernists without crushing them – this is the riskiest requirement!

If actor-network theory is not really a theory but a methodology and an ontology, does it offer the kind of causal explanation to be developed later in my book (see also Elder-Vass, 2008, 2010: pp. 176–179)? In one of his most explicit elaborations on explanation and its politics, Latour (1988: pp. 158–159; original italics) 'explains' what explanation means in relation to description, correlation, and deduction on a conventional scale of explanatory power. To him, deduction in positivism has the maximum explanatory power and therefore it makes scientists most enthusiastic about this form of explanation. But he considers description as a kind of explanation that 'most often has the literary character of a *story*… and is often associated with the work of historians'. He goes further to define an alternative: his 'own policy of explanation' in which 'A strong explanation becomes necessary when someone wishes to *act at a distance*'. To him, if one is in the same context as the explananda A (i.e. elements or features to be explained), a weak form of explanation through practice and description (story-telling) should suffice. But if one is away from this explananda A's context and wishes to act on it, a stronger explanation is needed because one is outside both the context of explananda A and its explanans (i.e. elements explaining A). In short, explanation is defined as a measure of the distance between these contexts.

One crucial implication is the distinction between practice (action in the same context) and knowledge (explanation across settings). The more we need to mobilize knowledge in one context to act on another setting or many other settings, the stronger the explanation will be required: 'If you now wish, from the setting x, to hold not only $x$', but many other settings, $x$" and so on…, you start to need more and more powerful explanations' (Latour, 1988: p. 160). This requirement for stronger explanations is associated with the slow establishment of his well-known concept of 'centres of calculation' for acting at a distance, and this epistemological rendering refers to the practical activity of 'network-building' in (social) science and thus the key object in the social studies of science and technology.[6]

To me, this 'internalist' argument for stronger and more powerful explanations needed for 'acting at a distance' makes good sense since we cannot be *in situ* or in the same context/setting all the time, e.g. in most social science research. But instead of focusing only on the positivist extreme of deduction, I think Latour has somewhat avoided the issue of causal explanation. He seems to favour heterogenous associations *within* the network as the only explanation, as if no causal mechanisms can operate outside the network. This explanatory weakness in causally differentiating heterogeneity in associations is evident when Latour (1996, 2017) concludes his clarifications of actor-network theory.[7] As such, his associative approach to explanation might be too internalist if the network is too large to be fully internalized and described. It might also be a kind of truism in the sense that associative explanation is contingent on network stability – the assumptions are that all actants and their heterogeneous associations must be already made apparent and explicit, and nothing exists outside the network.

Such a poststructuralist way of thinking of explanation through description – however 'saturated' and 'complete' as in Latour (1990, 1991: pp. 129–130) – may well be myopic, i.e. far too constrained by the network itself and 'surface' relations that might conceal underlying, dare I say, 'casual' mechanisms not amenable to such straight-forward description.[8] There is also the question of how to define and delimit the network, with possibly very large number of entities, actants, and relations, in a way that makes description, let alone explanation, practically adequate (as discussed in my key consideration #3 in Chapter 1). Just imagine tracing the entire actor-network of an iPhone, as I have attempted in my own empirical research (Yeung, 2022). It is already so incredibly complex and multi-scalar to defy easy description! How then do we account for current and contemporary networks that are still in the process of being assembled and stabilized? Can these ongoing processes be explained?

As most geographical studies of society and space deal with socio-spatial real-ities that are 'at a distance', the spatially stretched nature of such phenomena makes Latour's 'strong' and 'more powerful' explanations even more necessary. But his conception of explanation does not really address the crucial matter of *causality*, i.e. causal explanation as a different class of explanation beyond his three categories of description, correlation, and deduction. Here, even 'strong' explanation through deduction does not necessary imply causation, but only logical correspondence of an apparent or surface correlation (see more on this Humean law-like 'mechanical' regularities in scientific explanation in my Chapter 3). And yet he believes in the strong rejection of arguments couched in terms of 'cause and effect', such as capitalism as a cause being turned into a 'cause célè-bre' (Latour, 1988: p. 161). To account for this cause, e.g. what explains capitalist development of the world economy, he believes in the heterogeneous association of a few elements and thus 'the network' in explaining capitalism as a cause![9] Ul-timately, he suggests that we should throw away (strong) explanations and go for 'weaker' and one-off explanations with tailor-made causes:

> The paradox is that we shall always look for weak explanations rather than for gen-eral stronger ones. Every time we deal with a new topic, with a new field, with a new object, the explanation should be wholly different. Instead of explaining everything with the same cause and framework, and instead of abstaining from explanation in fear of breaking the reflexive game, we shall provide a one-off explanation, using a tailor-made cause. I am all for throw-away causes and for one-off explanations (Latour, 1988: p. 174).

Before moving on to the next 'theory' (non-representational theory), I consider briefly the work on theory and explanation by another well-known proponent and also critic of actor-network theory. Annemarie Mol (2010) sums it up best when she explains that ANT does not seek a law of nature-culture, nor offers an overarching explanatory framework or even hunt for causes; ANT 'merely' aims to *trace* effects:

> ANT is not a theory. It does not give explanations, and neither does it offer a grid or a perspective. Since 'ANT' has become an academic brand name, many authors start their articles with the promise that they will 'use actor-network theory'. Let me disappoint them: this cannot be done. It is impossible to 'use ANT' as if it were a

microscope. 'ANT' does not offer a consistent perspective. The various studies that come out of the ANT-tradition go in different directions. They do different things… ANT is not a theory. It offers no causal explanations and no consistent method. It rather takes the form of a repertoire. If you link up with it you learn sensitising terms, ways of asking questions and techniques for turning issues inside out or upside down (Mol, 2010: p. 261).

To her, causality and causal explanation are too deterministic for ANT because 'that entities/actors depend on others around them does not mean that they are caused by their surroundings. Causality tends to take a determinist form. Causal explanations usually remove activity from what is "being caused." In a network, by contrast, actors, while being enacted by what is around them, are still active. The actorship implied is not a matter of freedom, of escaping from a causal force. Instead, actors are afforded by their very ability to act by what is around them. If the network in which they are embedded falters, the actors may falter too. If they are not being enacted, actors are no longer able to do all that much themselves. They stop "working"' (Mol, 2010: pp. 257–258).

I think Mol's (2010) conception of causality and causal explanation assumes too much of a positivist kind of Humean universal causality. Her concern with (social) activity being removed from causal explanations is likely an outcome of the poor (or lack of) specification of causal mechanism that necessarily elaborates on this 'activity' of 'causing' (see my conceptualization later in Chapters 3 and 4 on causal mechanisms and relationality). Her network-centric interpretation of actor enactment and 'working' seems to be a particular kind of what might be termed 'network mechanism', i.e. causality via networked relationality. However, some of her conditions enabling enacting by a particular actant are not necessarily causal, but more likely contextual, i.e. they can be substituted in another situation. Mol's (2010: p. 258) example of a leaking roof that makes it hard for most physics experiments to carry through is illustrative here. A leaking roof is likely a contextual factor, not a causal condition, for experiments. After all, there are numerous such possibilities or circumstances disenabling such experiments or 'making the network fall apart and fail', from the lack of funding to debilitating regulation, key lab technologists falling sick, and so on. But should we include all these actants in this infinitely large and diffuse network that also includes everything and every possible 'disenablers'?[10]

Indeed, many such examples of actants in actor-network studies tend to be natural or physical things/object or technologies and such studies of their success/ failure or 'ordering' in enacting reality often appear rather functionalist in analysis and descriptive in method, i.e. you need this and that actants to get something, such as experiments or harvesting or medical treatments, going and working. But in explaining social-spatial outcomes (e.g. spaces of exclusions, radical social movements, urban change, and uneven development), many causal mechanisms are 'social' in the sense that they are less about physical objects per se (no doubt

there are many of them, e.g. traffic lights for/against exclusions and social movements, and they can be important in their own right) and more about pre-existing
structures and ongoing relations established by humans and non-humans. The
different modes of ordering in actor-network theory may appear to be weak and
diffuse/decentered, as they are perhaps too-inclusive and indeterminant. As Mol
(2010: p. 265) recognizes, 'ANT is a theory of the kind that produces lists of
terms. The list that starts with "co-ordination" assembles terms that evoke, res-
onate, shift or stage "what it is to hang together." It is not closed, this list, but
open'. To me, this list may become too descriptive and lacking an (causal) analysis of the 'gel' that keeps things hanging together in a network. It seems easier
to proclaim openness in a relativist way and proceed to describe or list everything that might possibly be related in this open repository. But it is much harder
analytically and empirically to specify the causal relations and the gel that truly
matter in getting these objects hanging together and making things happen (see
more in Chapter 4 on relational theory).[11]

Ironically, in stating 'ANT is not a theory' so categorically and explicitly, Mol
(2010) seems to have turned actor-network theory's ontology into an epistemology of 'not-theory theory' (ANT is not a theory!). In doing so, Mol (2010: p. 262)
notes further that 'we may call ANT "a theory" after all. But this implies that in
good ANT fashion we radically alter the meaning of the term "a theory." For if
ANT is a theory, then a "a theory" is something that helps scholars to attune to
the world, to see and hear and feel and taste it. Indeed, to appreciate it. If ANT
is a theory, then a theory is a repository of terms and modes of engaging with
the world, a set of contrary methodological reflexes'. To me, this perceived methodological openness of ANT (tracing the network, all the way) is not necessarily matched by an ontological openness, but rather by an authoritative ontology
of openness in the service of its contrary methodological reflexes. Overall, it is
reasonable to conclude that actor-network theory is an ontology (worlds of relationality and heterogeneous associations) and a methodology (how to go about
studying it). It is as much a descriptive methodology for the study of humans and
non-humans in society and nature as a relational ontology of it – so much so that
ANT is at serious risk of being a flat ontology, sitting at the opposite end of Paul
Cloke et al.'s (2004) 'people are not rocks' polarity.[12] But actor-network theory is
indeed not a theory, nor an explanation grounded in such a (causal) theory. The
word 'theory' in ANT is a misnomer.

## Non-Representational Theory

In human geography, strong theoretical interest in relationality and processual interactions in more-than-human worlds has emerged since the early 1990s.
Particularly so in cultural geography and with significant influences in social,
political, urban, and environmental geography, this body of poststructuralist

geographical work recognizes the importance of context to experiential meanings and interpretations and focuses on such processual interactions of embodiment, emotions, affect, events, and becoming not as a priori spatial order and
formations, but as performative practices that cannot be readily 'represented'.
Grounded in geographer Nigel Thrift's (1996, 2007) non-representational theory
(NRT) and the related work by many of his former students at Bristol University in the UK (Simpson, 2021: pp. 28–32),[13] this enormous geographical literature moves away from the earlier focus in postmodernism on *words* as textual
in the so-called 'dead geography' (Thrift, 2000; Thrift and Dewsbury, 2000) to
*life* as embodied in practice, affect, and event. Despite his many affinities with
actor-network theory (e.g. in Thrift, 1996), Thrift (2000, 2007) points critically
to actor-network theory's devoid of human capacity in favour of a flat ontology
of all things relational and thus its 'champagne without fizz' approach to understanding human expressive powers and imaginations.[14] To Philo (2012: p. 499),
Thrift's evolving thought in NRT is also 'distancing' from another poststructuralist philosopher Michel Foucault's governmentality approach to knowledge and
discourses – 'Thrift's unease with Foucault: too many words, too little doing; too
much knowledge in books, too little knowledge-in-action'.

In their comprehensive collection of NRT work in human geography, Anderson and Harrison (2010b) note that NRT emerges as a poststructuralist thought
from its predecessor known as social constructivism that is preoccupied with
representation (e.g. the symbolic landscapes literature in humanistic geography
and 'new cultural geography' in Table 2.1[15]) and the separation of mind and body.
To them, NRT's style of thinking is not anti-representations per se, but rather
sees representations 'as performative presentations, not reflections of some *a priori* order waiting to be unveiled, decoded, or revealed' (Anderson and Harrison,
2010b: p. 19; original italics). At the risk of doing something 'representational'
and attempting at 'a largely thankless task', they conclude that:

> it seems fair to say that non-representational theories are a set of predominantly,
> although not exclusively, poststructuralist theories that share a number of questions
> or problems; how do sense and significance emerge from ongoing practical action?;
> how, given the contingency of orders, is practical action organised in more-than-hu-
> man configurations?; and how to attend to events – to the 'non' that may lead to the
> chance of something different or a modification of an existing ordering? (Anderson
> and Harrison, 2010b: pp. 23–24).

Geographical accounts grounded in NRT often take a practice and processual
approach to the social, the subject, and the world. Some of these can also be about
the ethics of openness and sensuality. McCormack's (2003: p. 489) earlier work thus
argues that NRT's styles of thinking and working can contribute to human geography by highlighting the ethical as always implicated in and emergent from diverse
embodiments, opening up the ethical to the relational spaces of more-than-human

worlds and drawing attention to such connective sensibilities as processually enactive and performative rather than as sets of codified rules. Drawing on Thrift (1996, 2007), Simpson's (2021) recent text on NRT summarizes its core themes as process, subjectification, embodiment, affect, and agency in human and non-humans (see also Whatmore, 2002) – the process and practice of embodiment (i.e. bodily action, perception, and praxis), for example, draws much from feminist theory and, as will be discussed further in Chapter 3, can be conceived as a kind of conjunctural causal mechanism intersecting with a concatenation of other mechanisms (e.g. intersectionality) to produce convergent effects in society and space.

One of NRT's central concept and key concern is *affect*, and there is now a very sizeable literature on affect in human geography (Thrift, 2004, 2007; Anderson, 2006, 2014; Wright, 2015; Ruez and Cockayne, 2021) and social theory (Massumi, 2002, 2015; Stewart, 2007; Manning, 2016; cf. Leys, 2017).[16] During the 2010s, geographical work on affect emerged as a dominant literature in human geography with some hundreds of papers published in leading journals.[17] Ironically and as recognized by Simpson (2021: p. 73), the concept is not an easy one to define. Referring to the pre-cognitive aspects of embodied life, affect comes from the shifts in the state of our bodies that impact upon our capacities to act, and can be experienced through intensities of emotions, embodied movements, and encounters. These affective practices and shifting capacities can be found in bodily encounters in cities (Simonsen, 2010; Simonsen and Koefoed, 2020), socio-political 'atmospheres' (Anderson, 2009, 2016), emergent becomings/belongings (Wright, 2015), and during the clash of what Steve Pile (2021) terms 'bodily regimes' in *Bodies, Affects, Politics*.[18] Pile (2021: pp. 174–178) thus argues that geographers should go beyond the politics of location in thinking the geographies of the body to embrace an alternative (re) thinking of bodies as multiples and overdetermined distributions of the sensible and the aesthetic unconscious of affective politics.

Drawing heavily on poststructuralist and NRT thought, Anderson (2006) outlines an explicit *theory* of affect, feeling, and emotion that is attuned to their multiple processes and modalities. Rethinking of/from hope for a theory of affect, he argues that hopefulness is a type of relation emergent from particular encounters that enable bodies to go on through a renewed feeling of possibility. To him, 'this is a translation into the body of the affects that move between people in processes of intersubjective transmission to make a "space of hope." Feeling hopeful, in this case, is characterized by a yearning to live and to experiment as part of the tendency without end that is set in motion' (Anderson, 2006: p. 744). Arguing for the affective as a realm of 'processual excess', he conceptualizes some of these processes of becoming (hopeful) as affective contagion/transmission, concrescence from being an absolute impossibility to being an outside of a body, resemblance and limitation, circulation, displacement, and qualification, and so on. Other geographers have also theorized the different movement and modalities of affect in propagating space via circulation, transmission, contagion, travel, and translation (Pile, 2010; Ash, 2015; Gallagher, 2016).

Despite their best efforts in theorizing affect in relation to human bodily practices and encounters, these (mostly cultural) geographers remain challenged by the conundrum of incorporating matter and materiality into the unfolding of embodied action and the affective processes of becoming. As argued in political theorist Jane Bennett's (2010: p. 61) *Vibrant Matter* and feminist philosopher Rosi Braidotti's (2011: ch. 2) *Nomadic Theory*, affect is not specific to humans, organisms, or even to bodies only, because affect can also be identified with material things such as technologies, winds, vegetables, and minerals. NRT's 'solution' of reimagining matter/materiality, as in Anderson and Tolia-Kelly (2004), Latham and McCormack (2004), and Anderson and Wylie (2009), has only limited success, since the basis of imagination (i.e. matter/materiality) for that reimagining has no common understanding among different scholars of affect. As summed up nicely in Simpson (2021: p. 105), 'Materializing is often equated to a form of grounding investigations in some kind of tangible "gritty" reality and, in turn, a step back from more abstract forms of thinking and analysis... However, matter means different things and is deployed in reference to different things across the work discussed above. There are a host of different "materialisms" at play here, and the immaterial is not always necessarily about the theoretical, representational, metaphysical, or transcendent'.

Given its rather open-ended ontology fixing on process and the practice of becoming and its fairly descriptive approach to empirical analysis, non-representational theory and its main variants on affect and bodily regimes do not appear to be a coherent body of theory nor explanation to me. To be fair though, Thrift (1996: p. 30; also 2004) explicitly develops NRT at the beginning of his *Spatial Formations* as a 'modest theory' and 'a theoretical synthesis... with a lighter touch'. Drawing upon different theories of practice in the philosophical works of Martin Heidegger, Ludwig Wittgenstein, Maurice Merleau-Ponty, Pierre Bourdieu, and Michel de Certeau, he notes that non-representational models of the world focus on the 'external' in which 'basic terms and objects are forged in a manifold of actions and interactions' (Thrift, 1996: p. 6). Still, of his six main tenets of such non-representational models, he lists (last) its concern with 'a rather different notion of "explanation" which is probably best likened to understanding a person, a phenomenalism of character which involves, more than other approaches, empathic and ethical components'. To him, NRT is more about 'understanding' of affect and living than 'about unearthing something of which we might previously have been ignorant, delving for deep principles or digging for rock-bottom, ultimate causes' (Thrift, 1996: pp. 7–8).

What started off as a modest theory (or epistemology?) for developing an empathic understanding of practice and interactions in our lifeworlds has seemingly been deployed by a wide range of geographers to produce quite diverse and often contradictory accounts of these lifeworlds. And yet it can be frustrating to find out what NRT is not, as in the prefix 'non'! Like actor-network theory, NRT is not a theory per se and thus the term 'theory' in its name is also quite a misnomer. Its epistemological focus on events and change (futurity) and their always-unfolding relations is perhaps a way 'out' for the term 'non' in NRT. As well recognized by Anderson and Harrison (2010b: p. 19; my emphasis):

> Perhaps though, and like actor-network theory, the promise of non-representational theory would have been betrayed by any name that enabled it to be easily summed up and reduced. We think there is something more in the name; a force to the prefix 'non' that hints to something vital to non-representational theories that is worth thinking with and affirming. The 'non' is *frustratingly elusive*, it cannot be thought as such. It leaves things incomplete. It manages to obscure what it affirms by studiously avoiding positive nomination.

At its best then, I think NRT 'represents' an ethos and a style of thinking about event, practice, and affect and, in it, theory is a 'modest yet enlivening and pragmatic supplement' focusing on and accounting for embodied practice, movements, and performance (McCormack, 2003: p. 489; also Harrison, 2002; Cresswell, 2013: pp. 227–235; Simpson, 2021: pp. 6–7). The 'theory' in NRT does not seek to explain such practices nor their affect that remain processual and seemingly beyond causal theories and explanations. To sociologist Celia Lury (2021: pp. 57–58), NRT's descriptive method resembles more a form of radical empiricism that does not aim to offer explanations over and beyond the description of diverse phenomena in everyday life.[19] But even as a method for empirical research, NRT's focus on the ephemeral and the noncognitive world of affect and performance tends to crowd out the *normative concern* with the politics of practice and the socio-structural conditions of power and constraints in our everyday life – the first of my three key considerations of/for theory and explanation discussed in Chapter 1. In short, its mode of theorizing and practice of radical empiricism invariably lead to an inversion of politics and a dissolution of political will into preconscious affective lifeworlds. In *The Ascent of Affect*, historian of thought Ruth Leys (2017: p. 343; my emphasis) puts this critique in the most succinct way:

> we might put it that what is at stake for the theorists whose turn to affect I have been analyzing is a 'logic' according to which attention to ideology or belief is replaced by a focus on bodily affects that are understood to be the outcome of subliminal, autonomic corporeal processes. Stressing bodies over ideas, affect over reason, the new affect theorists claim that what is crucial is not your beliefs and intentions but the affective processes that are said to produce them, with the result that political change becomes a matter *not* of persuading others of the truth of your ideas but of producing new ontologies or 'becomings,' new bodies, and new lives.[20]

## *Assemblage Theory*

While the key thinkers behind actor-network theory (e.g. Bruno Latour) and non-representational theory (e.g. Nigel Thrift) have been strongly influenced by prominent poststructuralist philosophers such as Gilles Deleuze and Félix Guattari, it is in assemblage theory – another poststructuralist thought with the name 'theory' in its title – that we find the strongest and most direct influence of Deleuze and Guattari's thought. In their most influential text *A Thousand Plateaus*, Deleuze and Guattari (1987 [1980]: pp. 87–91) conceive an assemblage as a flattened 'plane of consistency' relating not only to the production of goods such as tools and technologies, but more importantly also to the primacy of bodies in linguistic terms.[21] In their explicitly flat ontology, an assemblage does not have a base nor a deep structure. Described as 'Deleuzian hermeneutics' by their interlocutor and philosopher Manuel DeLanda (2006: p. 3), Deleuze and Guattari's thought on assemblage is often scattered and diffused throughout their influential books and obscure essays. Nevertheless, it is in DeLanda's (2006, 2016) reworking of assemblage thinking throughout the work of Deleuze and Guattari that a poststructuralist approach to assemblage theory has been fully articulated, known as 'neo-assemblage theory' or 'assemblage theory 2.0' in DeLanda (2006: p. 3).[22] But as noted earlier in Chapter 1 (endnote 12), DeLanda's assemblage theory is also linked to a broader philosophical movement since the early 2000s towards speculative realism that recognizes autonomous objects and independent constitution of more-than-humans reality (Harman, 2010, 2018; DeLanda and Harman, 2017; Shaviro, 2014; Sparrow, 2014).

In human geography, this assemblage thinking and speculative realism are recently associated with geographical work in post-phenomenology and posthumanism (Table 2.1; see also Sundberg, 2014; Ash and Simpson, 2016, 2019; McCormack, 2017, 2018; Roberts, 2019; Kinkaid, 2021; Roberts and Dewsbury, 2021). By the mid-2010s and together with actor-network theory, assemblage thinking has been described by Müller and Schurr (2016: p. 217) as among the most popular conceptual approaches in human geography today (see also Anderson et al., 2012a; Bridge, 2021; Woods et al., 2021). The interest of geographers in assemblage theory is also linked to the role of affect in Deleuze and Guattari's (1987 [1980]: p. 399) thinking of assemblages as passional and compositions of desire.[23] Not surprisingly, the interest of non-representational theory in affect discussed earlier has intersected with such poststructuralist thinking in assemblage theory.

Anderson et al.'s (2012a) critical review of assemblage thinking in human geography offers a helpful introduction to some of the key ideas in assemblage theory. To them, assemblage theory has been used in various ways in human geography: as a *descriptor* of order and classification; as a *concept* elaborating on processes of agencement (as in Deleuze's idea of assemblage in French); and as an *ethos* sensitive to difference, heterogeneity, and indeterminacy. Couched in what they call 'a properly postrelational ontology' (Anderson et al., 2012a: p. 183), assemblage theory is lauded for its insistence on the autonomy of parts and the exteriority of relations in assemblages. They outline four ways in which 'assemblage thinking' can serve as an alternative response to the problematic in the recent 'relational turn' in human geography (see more discussion of such relational thought in Chapter 4). Here, I summarize these four key responses before evaluating the role of causal explanation and the politics of theorizing in assemblage thinking:

1. assemblage theory represents an *experimental realism* orientated to the emergent processes of composition and formation by focusing empirically on 'how these spatial forms and processes are themselves assembled, are held in place, and work in different ways to open up or close down possibilities' (Anderson et al., 2012a: p. 172). This experimental orientation encapsulates an ethos of open-endedness, emergence, and engagement with the world. This ethos is consistent with the notions of social worlds as open systems characterized by both complexity and emergence in critical realism noted in Chapter 1 (Bhaskar, 1986, 2016; Elder-Vass, 2010; Allen, 2012) and to be developed further in Chapter 3.

2. assemblage thinking offers a theorization of a world of present relations and *relations of exteriority*. Anderson et al. (2012a: p. 172) argue that 'what is novel about assemblage is the claim that "relations are exterior" to their terms'. Drawing on Deleuze's (1991 [1953]) consideration of the heterogeneity of components as an important characteristic of assemblage, DeLanda (2006: p. 12, 2016: pp. 3, 12) conceives these relations of exteriority as contingently obligatory: relatively autonomous entities are affected by relations and by the other terms they are related to, but they are not fully determined by those relations/terms. This contingent conception of relations among components and entities has close parallels with actor-network theory discussed earlier. As noted by Anderson et al. (2012a: p. 178), 'Both Latour's actor-network theory and assemblage theory are framed by ambivalence toward the a priori reduction of social-spatial relations to any fixed form or set of fixed forms – the micro and macro forms of reductionism introduced above. And both invite us to be open to how social-spatial relations are patterned and structured'.

3. assemblage theory presents a rethinking of *agency* in distributed terms and *causality* in non-linear and immanent terms. To Anderson et al. (2012a: p. 180), 'assemblage thinking entails a focus not just on how agency produces resultant forms, but on how the agency of both the assemblage and its parts can transform both the parts and the whole. The implication of assemblage thinking is that causality is located not in a pre-given sovereign agent, but in interactive processes of assembly through which causality operates as a non-linear process'. Drawing on political theorist William Connolly's (2005) work, they contrast this 'immanent causality' with mechanical linearity in 'efficient causality' and discuss Bennett's (2010: ch. 3) case study of omega-3 producing unpredictable causal effects on different bodies (see a critique in Abrahamsson et al., 2015: pp. 5–6; Leys, 2017: pp. 346–349; also my discussion in Chapter 4).

4.  assemblage theory provides an analytical orientation to the expressive capacity of assembled orders as they are stabilized and change. This addresses the paradox of dealing with both *stability* and *change* at the heart of relational thinking in human geography. As noted in (1) to (3), an assemblage is constituted by relatively autonomous components and parts, but its emergent nature of composition works with relations of exteriority to produce change and dynamism. Through this emergent causality, assemblage theory offers a novel response to the paradox. As argued by Anderson et al. (2012a: p. 180), 'Rather than produce an essentialist account of the internal characteristics or make-up of this or that assemblage, assemblage thinking insists that that range of causal factors might have produced similar emergent forms, and in different conditions the same constituent parts might have produced different assemblages'.

Taken together, the above rendition of assemblage theory draws our attention to the role of *causal explanation* in this 'theory' and its politics of theorizing. The causality of autonomous components and relations of exteriority seems to matter much in the explanatory gesture of assemblage theory (cf. the internalist approach to heterogenous relations in actor-network theory discussed earlier). To support this important observation, I now examine very briefly such gestures in the original works of Gilles Deleuze and Manuel DeLanda. In his 'assemblage theory 2.0', DeLanda (2006: p. 11) builds on Deleuze's work and argues that the properties of autonomous components *per se* cannot explain an assemblage as a whole because some of the relations are exterior to its interactions. But the exercise of such components' properties may be the *cause* of changing relations in an assemblage:

> These relations imply, first of all, that a component part of an assemblage may be detached from it and plugged into a different assemblage in which its interactions are different. In other word, the exteriority of relations implies a certain autonomy for the terms they relate, or as Deleuze [Deleuze and Parnet, 2002 [1977]: p. 55] puts it, it implies that 'a relation may change without the terms changing'. Relations of exteriority also imply that the properties of the component parts can never explain the relations which constitute a whole, that is, 'relations do not have as their causes the properties of the [component parts] between which they are established...' [Deleuze, 1991 [1953]: p. 98] although they may be caused by the exercise on a component's capacities (DeLanda, 2006: p. 11; see also, DeLanda, 2016: p. 10).

This brings us to the intriguing question of causality in Deleuze's poststructuralist conception of assemblage. For brevity, let me offer two contrasting quotes from *A Thousand Plateaus* to showcase Deleuze and Guattari's (1987 [1980]) non-committal and indeterminant approach to causality. On the one hand, they express strong disbelief in causal explanation and prefer a descriptive mapping of a line of flight (deterritorialization) at a highly abstract level of causality in their discussion on drug assemblages and pharmacoanalysis:

> This problem of specific causality is an important one. Invoking causalities that are too general or are extrinsic (psychological or sociological) is as good as saying nothing. There is a discourse on drugs current today that does no more than dredge up generalities on pleasure and misfortune, on difficulties in communication, on causes that always come from somewhere else. The more incapable people are of grasping a specific causality in extension, the more they pretend to understand the phenomenon in question. There is no doubt that an assemblage never contains a causal infrastructure. It does have, however, and to the highest degree, an abstract line of creative or specific causality, its *line of flight or of deterritorialization*; this line can be effectuated only in connection with general causalities of another nature, but is in no way explained by them (Deleuze and Guattari, 1987 [1980]: p. 283; original italics).

On the other hand and later in their chapter on refrains, Deleuze and Guattari (1987 [1980]) evoke the notion of *causality* and *mechanism* (machine) in their discussion of opposing movements (territorialization vs. deterritorialization) and assemblages. Referring to cases of a vast movement of deterritorialization in biological and physical worlds, such as salmon's pilgrimages to the sources, the supernumerary assemblies of locusts or chaffinches, and the long marches of lobsters, they argue that

> Whatever the *causes* of each of these moments, it is clear that the nature of the movement is different. It is no longer adequate to say that there is interassemblage, passage from a territorial assemblage to another type of assemblage; rather we should say that one leaves all assemblages behind, that one exceeds the capacities of any possible assemblage, entering another plane. In effect, there is no longer a milieu movement or rhythm, nor a territorialized or territorializing movement or rhythm; there is something of the Cosmos in these more ample movements. The localization *mechanisms* are still extremely precise, but the localization has become cosmic. These are no longer territorialized forces bundled together as forces of the earth; they are the liberated or regained forces of a deterritorialized Cosmos (Deleuze and Guattari, 1987 [1980]: p. 326; my emphasis).

They argue further that such ontological distinction between matter and life in the Cosmos has a place for stratification and causalities that in turn enable the passage from one stratum to another and vice versa (i.e. destratification). In this highly abstract poststructuralist thought, topological thinking characterizes a single plane or plateau that flattens different dimensions in lifeworlds and through which different lines of flight can run.[24] Even though they conceive these lines as abstract lines of creative or specific causality, Deleuze and Guattari (1987 [1980]) stop short of elaborating on their 'causes' and '(localization) mechanisms', leaving behind some vague notions of 'forces' operating on particular 'planes' or surfaces in a writing style symptomatic of what DeLanda (2006: p. 3) calls 'Deleuzian hermeneutics'.[25]

In short, the flat ontology of assemblage in 'Deleuzian hermeneutics' seems to trump any stratified conception of reality that, in the critical realist thought of Roy Bhaskar (1989, 2016), comprises both intransitive dimension (stratified with causal structures and generative mechanisms) and transitive dimension (our conception of reality).[26] Indeed, Deleuze and Guattari (1987 [1980]) do not elaborate on the notion of synthetic or emergent properties in an assemblage as a whole either, leaving it to DeLanda's (2006: p. 3) 'assemblage theory 2.0' and DeLanda's (2016) further theoretical reinterpretation of Deleuzian philosophical works on assemblage – a classic case of abstract theory or 'theoretical' theory pointed out at the beginning of this chapter.[27]

In DeLanda's (2006, 2016) speculative realist thinking though, emergent causality and explanation are brought into the fore in assemblage theory. While realist geographer John Allen's (2012: p. 190) question 'what kind of realism works for assemblage thinking?' is never actually posed in Anderson et al. (2012a) nor fully answered in their response (Anderson et al., 2012b), there is now a sizeable literature reconciling and synthesizing realism and assemblage thinking (Harman, 2008; DeLanda and Harman, 2017; Rutzou, 2017; Decoteau, 2018; Rutzou and Elder-Vass, 2019; see also Chapter 3 later). In his extensive engagement with DeLanda's (2006) work on assemblage theory, realist philosopher Graham Harman (2008: p. 368; original italics) argues that DeLanda 'openly declares himself a *realist*, and though he is already a fashionable author in some quarters, realism remains out of style even among his admirers'. To Harman (2010), DeLanda's (2006) assemblage theory is linked to Deleuze's work, but his speculative realist conception of assemblage, its constitutive components, and relations of exteriority (i.e. the 'intransitive' dimension of reality) has even more in common with Bhaskar's (1986, 1989) critical realism:

> Whether DeLanda be judged as naïve or not, his realism does not resemble the dull commonsense realism of yesteryear. Instead of an arid landscape of solid physical bulks paired with a boring human *cogito* that has the special gift and burden of corresponding with them, DeLanda provides a realism in which realities are never fully actualized even in the physical realm, let alone in our minds. He links this model with Deleuze's 'virtual' and uses this term frequently. But it may have even more in common with the 'intransitive' realm of Roy Bhaskar, whose influence DeLanda freely admits (Harman, 2010: pp. 171–172; original italics).[28]

Grounded in Deleuzian poststructuralist thought,[29] DeLanda's (2006: pp. 2–3, 2016: ch. 6) speculative realist social ontology and assemblage theory are 'all about objective processes of assembly: a wide range of social entities, from persons to nation-states, will be treated as assemblages constructed through very specific historical processes, processes in which language plays an important but not a constitutive role. A theory of assemblages, and of the processes that create and stabilize their historical identity, was created by the philosopher Gilles Deleuze in the last decades of the 20th century. This theory was meant to apply to a wide variety of wholes constructed from heterogeneous parts'. Despite this affinity between DeLanda's speculative realist thought and critical realism, DeLanda's (2006, 2016) social ontology of assemblage does not fully develop nor explain how and why these 'objective processes of assembly' come about in relation to their generative mechanisms and causal powers. As Bhaskar (2016: p. 39) points out in his final book, 'the realism of the speculative realists has mainly concerned with the existence of things, not the operation of their causal powers; it is a realism about things rather than (also) about causality and hence the activity of things'. To claim a kind of *critical* realism, one must be concerned not only with the independent existence of things, but also their causal powers and operations through real but non-deterministic mechanisms and their implications for politics and practices in society and space (see further discussion in my Chapters 3 and 4).[30]

This weak approach to causality and generative mechanisms in DeLanda's assemblage theory is paradoxical since he explicitly recognizes the importance of causality and actual mechanisms. I think it has more to do with his infatuation with Deleuzian topological thinking and virtual philosophy that has turned into a form of 'onto-theological lock-in' (Joronen and Häkli, 2017: p. 568) or 'ontic fallacy' (Bhaskar, 2016: p. 11) discussed in Chapter 1. As DeLanda (2006: p. 32; original italics) puts it: 'analysis in assemblage theory is not conceptual but causal, concerned with the discovery of the *actual mechanisms* operating at a given spatial scale. On the other hand, the topological structure defining the diagram of an assemblage is not actual but *virtual and mechanism-independent*, capable of being realized in a variety of actual mechanisms, so it demands a different form of analysis'. In other words, it is not just causal, but also quasi-causal, another term familiar to readers of Deleuze (e.g. non-linear and immanent causality in Anderson et al., 2012a: p. 180). Quasi-cause is a rival to the Humean mechanistic theory of linear causation, which famously assumes that the same causes yield the same effects every time (see more on this in Chapter 3). Still, DeLanda (2006: p. 32) argues for focusing on causal (not quasi-causal) mechanisms, even though his work has not succeeded in unravelling them: 'Despite the complementarity of causal and quasi-causal forms of analysis, in this book I will emphasize the former. Indeed, although I will try to give examples of the inner workings of concrete assemblages whenever possible, no attempt will be made to describe every causal mechanism in detail'.

DeLanda's (2006: chs. 3–5) empirical chapters on persons and networks, organizations and government, and cities and nations do not offer much specification of those complex mechanisms behind the synthesis of emergent properties in assemblages. There is no sense of the actual crisis or outcome to be explained nor the elucidation of causal mechanisms as promised in his social ontology of assemblage theory. In fact, the conceptual term 'causal mechanism' has virtually completely dropped out in his empirical chapters, leaving only 'forces' and 'processes' to carry the ontological weight of his causal analysis. Much of the discussion is also rather descriptive, discursive, and typological by drawing on conceptual materials from different social scientists and sorting them into different descriptive definitions and types (e.g. being, individuals, communities, networks, organizations, nations, and so on). There is no empirical analysis and the historical analysis promised is absent, leaving the contingent contexts in which the missing causal mechanisms might operate completely out of the so-called 'causal analysis'.

Overall though, I think assemblage thinking has advanced over actor-network theory by recognizing the non-linear causality of both autonomous components/ parts and their relational interactions in the composition and formation of assemblages (see also Müller and Schurr, 2016).[31] But its specification of emergence and causality remains rather vague and fails to address several key questions. How do autonomous components/parts, as specific objects *constitutive* of an assemblage, 'unleash' their capacities to effect changes through this relational configuration known as assemblage? Are some relations or processes *more* causal than others in effecting real changes? Can these more emergent/immanent processes become causal mechanisms for specific changes? What are the contingent conditions for realizing their causality? I will return to these questions in Chapters 3 and 4. Indeed, this inadequacy in assemblage thinking has led to fellow speculative realist philosopher Harman's (2008) immanent critique of the missing theory of causal relations in a DeLandian universe by 2030![32] In addition to this inadequate elucidation of causality and generative mechanisms and the contradictory claims of its experimental realist thinking, I think there are two further unresolved weaknesses in assemblage thinking: descriptive social ontology and the missing politics of theorizing.

First, assemblage thinking is still much more concerned with describing and accounting for an assemblage (what it is and how it comes into being and becoming) than the politics of difference and contentious socio-spatial outcomes that might be produced and explained by the heterogenous processes of assembling assemblages. To Anderson et al. (2012b: p. 215), it is more 'a resource' for understanding the composition and formation of enduring assemblages.[33] In light of its ambivalent idea of social explanation and causality and its tendency to privilege description over explanation, I think assemblage 'theory' is not, and cannot be, a substantive theory for social science. It is best conceived as a social ontology for envisioning, rethinking, and describing the compositional multiplicity of relations and things in society and space.[34] Making concrete and explanatory theories out of such assemblage thinking requires us to be attuned to causal powers in the emergent configurations of relations and entities that might be better grounded in critical realist and relational thought (see more in Chapters 3 and 4). Allen (2012: p. 192) thus calls for 'a kind of realism that works for assemblage thinking. It has nothing to do with adding things together in a mindless descriptive exercise, yet everything to do with the careful conceptualization of entities and their powers in relation; that is, in the tangle of relations and things that comprise an assemblage'.

Second, the politics of theorizing in assemblage thinking remains insensitive to difference. As one key consideration of/for theory and explanation in Geography in Chapter 1 (socio-spatial context and practical adequacy are two other considerations), this criterion imposes a serious challenge to assemblage theory (and some other poststructuralist approaches). In her feminist critique of assemblage thinking, Kinkaid (2020: p. 458) provocatively asks 'Can assemblage think difference?' and claims that assemblage geographies 'remain remarkably aloof from feminist thought. I argue that assemblage geographies are seriously limited in their descriptive, conceptual, and ethico-political potential by ignoring feminist concerns, including social difference, power, positionality, and related epistemological problems'.[35] She points to important missing feminist 'matters' in each of the three dimensions of assemblage thinking in Anderson et al. (2012a): (1) *descriptor*: its missing 'traditional' social categories of gender, sexuality, and race and their identity formation; (2) *concept*: its apolitical 'flat ontology' and missing feminist relational analytic in terms of the production of social and symbolic difference and their co-constitution with the material; and (3) *ethos*: its missing feminist ethics concerning with the (re)production of relations of symbolic-material inequality (see also Oswin, 2008, 2020; Adey, 2012; Doucette, 2020).[36]

## Post-Phenomenology and Posthumanism

Before we move on to examine theory and explanation in the more ideologically-oriented approaches since the 1990s (i.e. feminism and postcolonialism), it is useful to update the above discussion of the three poststructuralist 'theories' and their respective ontological thoughts in relation to recent theoretical and philosophical thinking in human geography since the 2000s (see Table 2.1). In what might be known as *post-phenomenology* (Ash and Simpson, 2016, 2019; McCormack, 2017; Roberts, 2019; Ash, 2020b; Engelmann and McCormack, 2021; Kinkaid, 2021) and *posthumanism* (Lorimer, 2012, 2020; Yusoff, 2013, 2018; Sundberg, 2014; Barua, 2021; Roberts and Dewsbury, 2021), geographers have moved beyond the focus on subject/human experience, embodiment, and practice in non-representational theory to (re)embrace objects, elements, matters, materiality, multi-species, and the Anthropocene. Unlike poststructuralism in human geography, this newer literature is still emerging and relatively diverse in its claims. Kinkaid's (2021: p. 299) most recent review thus notes that 'as a relatively new paradigm... post-phenomenology, like any subfield, is internally diverse, draws on numerous reference points and traditions, and emphasizes various theoretical and methodological aims'.

In general, we can identify at least three distinctive features in the theoretical claims in such geographical work grounded in post-phenomenology and/or post-humanism: (1) focus on objects in human life; (2) vitality of things in more-than-human worlds; and (3) distinctive 'styles' of thinking and writing.[37] First, there is a strong (re)turn to *objects* and their materiality as the 'stuff' of human life or what Engelmann and McCormack (2021) term 'elemental worlds' and their affective relations with bodies and life. In *The Incorporeal*, feminist philosopher Elizabeth Grosz (2017: p. 16) even laments that 'Today just about everyone is a materialist. Not only within the discipline of philosophy, but throughout the humanities and sciences'! To Ash and Simpson (2016: p. 49), 'post-phenomenological work is not straightforwardly post-structural in emphasis, argumentation, or scope. Instead it places a greater emphasis on objects/materiality as opposed to textuality'. Drawing on Graham Harman's (2010, 2017) and Tristan Garcia's (2014) object-oriented ontology in speculative realism,[38] they argue that the specific qualities of objects matter much to the understanding of a social world of dynamic change and emergence (à la assemblage theory). In many of the poststructuralist theories above (e.g. non-representational theory and assemblage theory), such objects and their real properties may actually disappear in these theories' ontological priorities placed on processes, relations, and relationality. Without paying sufficient attention to the 'aesthetic causalities' of these objects and matters, Ash and Simpson (2016: p. 63) believe that it will be hard to account for why people do certain things or why events unfold in particular ways:

> Post-phenomenology and its concern with objects allows us to move beyond curiosity or provocation to begin to think the aesthetic causalities of how objects relate to one another and explore what non-human things are and what they do in ways that attend to these things as objects, rather than relations or processes.

In *The Ontological Turn*, anthropologists Martin Holbraad and Morten Pedersen (2017: p. 200; original italics) argue that this focus on objects as things in their own right with their own reflexivity in post-phenomenology and posthumanism is akin to other human-centric conceptualization of subject reflexivity: 'Allowing things, that is, to make a difference *as things* to the way we may think of them – to help to dictate their own terms of engagement, becoming, so to speak, their own "thing-theorists" – by virtue of the characteristics that make them most thing-like, namely what, entirely crudely for now, we may call their "material properties"'. In short, taking things seriously as 'the things themselves' can complement those practice-oriented and processual approaches that take seriously the people for whom things and objects may matter.

Second, posthumanism conceives the vitality of things in the more-than-human worlds, particularly in the current Anthropocene. It draws our analytical attention away from the hybrid associations of humans and things in such collectives as networks and assemblages in actor-network theory and assemblage theory that tend to gloss over the inherent qualities of these humans and things. This posthumanist critique assigns agency or capacity to humans or things rather than their heterogenous associations. In *Vibrant Matter*, Bennett (2010: p. viii) argues that vitality refers to 'the capacity of things – edibles, commodities, storms, metals – not only to impede or block the will and designs of humans but also to act as quasi agents or forces with trajectories, propensities, or tendencies of their own. My aspiration is to articulate a vibrant materiality that runs alongside and inside humans to see how analyses of political events might change if we gave the force of things more due'. In her posthumanist gestures of vital materialism, the material agency or effectivity of nonhuman or not-quite-human things can be seen as exposing a wider distribution of agency and reshaping conceptions of self/humans in the more-than-human worlds.[39]

Third and à la non-representational theory and assemblage theory, geographical work in post-phenomenology and posthumanism claims to offer new 'styles' for thinking about the (non)human both in terms of conceptualizing and writing about objects and a concern for those objects' style. To Ash and Simpson (2019), this style of analysis acknowledges the co-constitutive nature of our being in the world. As such, they argue that 'we can define a postphenomenological style as a matter of learning to explicitly attend to the various shifting expressions of objects and how those expressions contribute to how a situation works. In other words, postphenomenology's style is characterized by a mode of analysis that seeks to understand what objects express, what can influence this expression, and how this expression might go on to prime what happens' (Ash and Simpson, 2019: p. 144). In empirical terms, descriptive accounting and understanding of our lifeworlds and encounters seem paramount in most geographical studies grounded in post-phenomenology and critical phenomenology (e.g. Wilson, 2017; Ash, 2020b; Simonsen and Koefoed, 2020; cf. Hepach, 2021; Kinkaid, 2021). To Roberts and Dewsbury (2021), these renewed uptakes of vitalist concepts in posthumanism signal a style of philosophical aspiration in our attitudes towards thought that goes beyond merely radical empiricism (e.g. in non-representational theory). As an aspirational attitude towards thought, its productive push for life compels us to think more about each new encounter.

Overall, this analytical shift in the recent work in post-phenomenology and posthumanism away from the excessive emphasis on textuality, hybridity, and relationality in earlier poststructuralist 'theories' is a welcome one. Its (re)turn to agency in objects and things and their material properties adds much to our broader understanding of events and challenges in the more-than-human worlds. Not surprisingly though, there are some important blind-spots in terms of theory and the politics of theorizing (i.e. normative concerns). To begin, this emerging geographical literature on post-phenomenology and posthumanism seems to have little say about what theory and explanation are vis-à-vis subjects, objects, and their relations and how explanatory research should be conducted in an epistemological sense (i.e. the why and so what questions). This perhaps reflects their implicit or explicit premise on the ontological and philosophical explication of subjects/subjectivity, objects, matters, relations, and materiality, rather than the development of concrete theories and causal explanation *of* them, i.e. more about the what and how questions than the why and so what concerns.[40]

This lack of substantive theories for explaining the sort of 'aesthetic causalities' in objects and matters (Ash and Simpson, 2016: p. 63) is partly attributed to the writing style and an excessive ontological dependency in post-phenomenology and posthumanism. I offer a few brief examples here. While Ash and Simpson (2019: p. 145) argue for the need of creating (new) languages and vocabularies as new ways of thinking, seeing, and feeling things and objects, their analysis remains mostly descriptive and interpretive.[41] In Ash (2020a), the empirical case is 'bump stocks' (for guns) as things/entities whose relationship with machine guns (another entity) and trigger pulls (action) become co-constitutive by their material forms. In some national contexts such as the United States, the political and normative implications can be very significant in terms of the legality of owning a bump stock rifle and events emerging from its (il)legal usage, such as mass shooting.

But Ash's (2020a: p. 351) reliance on the alleged flat ontological approaches in speculative realism and object-oriented philosophy to work through his politics of rifle-machine gun differentiation does not offer a mechanism-based theory of machine guns. Instead, his analysis appears to be a form of empirical realism that merely focuses on the surface forms of objects and things without realizing the existence and significance of enduring causal mechanisms underlying such surface phenomena and events.[42] In his response to critics, Ash (2020c: p. 378; my emphasis) qualifies his surface form analysis through de-determination as a method as only the starting point of a theory!

> It is important to be clear here that the method of de-determination offered in the article cannot, on its own, provide an account of events, temporality, space, causality or many other things. This is because, for me, a flat ontology is not a complete system of thought. Rather, flat ontology is a *starting* or orientating point, where basic presuppositions are made that go on to (de)limit the kind of further analysis that is possible.

Defending his abstract flat ontology, Ash (2020c: p. 380) further argues for the 'missing middle' of his beginnings and ends of things, i.e. their generative mechanisms of how entities come into being, to be theorized *later on*. From a critical realist perspective, I think it is precisely these missing middles of generative mechanisms and causality that matter much in theory and explanation in social science. While Ash (2020a: p. 358) concludes by noting that he 'has not suggested that there is a "correct" type of flat ontology that geographers should or must use', I echo McCormack's (2020: p. 369; my emphasis) critique: 'But how to understand what ontological orientations are *better* in particular circumstances?

This is a theoretical and speculative question. It is also an empirical one, not least because it requires us to think about the form of the relation between propositions and examples'. In short, I believe theories and empirics matter much in the (in)comprehension of these differences in flat ontologies. Re-description couched in 'theoretical' theories cannot substitute for substantive (and explanatory?) theory development situated in specific epistemic system. As another critic Häkli (2020: p. 371) puts it, 'what is it about this definitional issue that an improved flat ontology might help us resolve? Various news sources indicate that the difference between a bump stock rifle and a machine gun has for long been a politically contested issue… One wonders, then, what the legislator might have learned from Ash's [ontological] take on the definition of a machine gun'.

This brings me to the politics of theorizing as a key consideration of/for theory (again!). Here, much geographical work in post-phenomenology and posthumanism has offered new takes of the phenomenal worlds of humans and multi-species in different and alternative theoretical terms and conceptual grammars through their ontological styles of writing. But their highly philosophical arguments and descriptive approaches cannot substitute for contestable theories and explanations of such empirical phenomena that can add much value to our understanding of the politics of contestation in these social and more-than-human worlds. Their reliance on flat ontologies of different philosophical origins, such as poststructuralism and speculative realism, may also miss out important considerations of emergence through causal properties at a higher level (e.g. social structures) that cannot be reduced to the same as individual components (or 'vibrant matter' in Bennett's 2010 examples). These higher-level structures and entities are also compositional in nature and cannot be conveniently understood through their constitutive 'matter' alone.

Resembling a form of onto-theological 'lock-in', as termed by Joronen and Häkli (2017: p. 569) and discussed in Chapter 1, this ontological foundation of post-phenomenology and posthumanism in equal potentiality and emergence in everything non-human might eliminate the agential possibility of humans imposing structure and meaning on this contingency. Put differently, politics and practice in changing the world need human subjects, irrespective of our ontological commitments and ethics of responsibilities. It is not difficult to agree with Kirsten Simonsen and Lasse Koefoed's (2020: p. 132; my emphasis) argument in *Geographies of Embodiment* that 'critical phenomenology is a philosophical/theoretical practice, but even more importantly, it is at the same time a *political practice* of restructuring the world in order to generate new and liberatory possibilities for meaningful experiences and existence… And it is rooted in an ethic of responsibilities that can perhaps open up for a "new humanism" and for the hope that the world can be recreated through common political action'.[43] But as argued strongly in Kinkaid's (2021: pp. 305, 309) recent review, post-phenomenology offers a far too decentred view of the (human) subject and therefore runs the risk of focusing too much on subjectivity as emergent, based on encounters and events. Its flat ontologies also perpetuate a too contingent view of critical social categories, such as gender, race, and sexuality, as products of these encounters and events. This open-ended view runs the risk of denying the existential continuity, structure, and systematicity of these critical and yet signifying social categories in socio-spatial life.

Summing up this full section on poststructuralist 'theories' and recent work in post-phenomenology and posthumanism, I question if every*thing* – humans and non-humans – is and/or becomes vital and political, what then becomes possible in human agency? The term 'political' may become so generic and therefore meaningless, much like 'neoliberalism' or 'globalization' (see my discussion respectively in Chapters 5 and 6). Even in a posthumanist world of multi-species and vital things, we still need humans, as subjects, and their cognitive capacity to exercise this posthumanist practice and to engage intentionally in the contentious politics of change to resolve current and future real-world problems. The ontological turn towards the production of difference or alterity in these open-ended approaches and 'theoretical' theories might be politically sounding. But clever words alone do not make politics, and more textual gymnastics on difference do not tease out the politics of real struggles by people and non-humans in this more-than-humans world. Such pragmatic interventions and change require clear-headed explanations of why and how they are necessary and possible in these open-ended worlds. In their rush to deny any foundationalist and essentialist thought, these open-ended approaches have paradoxically disavowed the prospect for any explanatory theory-building in the name of their own 'theories' of ontological openness and the multiplicities of being and becoming. This normative concern with the politics of theorizing brings me next to two ideologically-oriented critical approaches to subjects and their struggles that have emerged in human geography since the 1990s – feminism and postcolonialism.

## Theories in Feminism and Postcolonialism

While discussed separately in this section, these two critical approaches – feminist theory and postcolonial theory – have developed concurrently with and influenced mutually the above more open-ended approaches in human geography since the 1990s. As examined more closely below, each of the two approaches has its own conceptual predispositions and epistemological priorities (Table 2.1). And yet they also intersect much with each other, as evident in Blunt and Rose's (1994) early integrated discussion of feminist and postcolonial approaches in human geography. Since then, these two approaches continue to intersect much with other critical epistemologies in sexuality, Indigenous, disability, and Black studies, and critical race theory (Oswin, 2008; Price, 2010; Mollett and Faria, 2018). Despite these seemingly productive efforts in building normative intellectual agendas and engaging in collective efforts towards emancipatory goals during the past three decades, the actually existing presence and impact of these epistemologies in Geography can still be disappointing to some. In her recent critique, Oswin (2020: p. 10) laments that in human geography and geographical writing:

> rarely is there an overarching commitment to think through how patriarchy, colonialism, homophobia, transphobia, gender norms, racism, ableism and more – either individually or, even less often, in mutual constitution – take and shape place. This disciplinary state of affairs is disappointing, frustrating and the cause of significant harm and discomfort to many individuals. It is also a failure of the critical capacities of the discipline in the face of its own collectively accumulated evidence.

While I concur sympathetically with Oswin's (2020) observation above, I think this frustrating and perhaps even harmful state of affairs in Geography might have something to do with the excess of philosophical critiques and the nature of theory/explanation in these more ideologically-oriented approaches. Even though reflexivity and politics of theorizing are clearly well embedded in the situated knowledges of these often highly contextualized approaches, the *practical adequacy* of analysing difference and advocating change through explanatory theories, or what McDowell (1995: p. 280) calls 'explanation of difference and diversity', has not been fully accomplished (cf. Cockayne et al., 2017). This partial accomplishment of my third consideration of/for theory remains inadequate in light of feminist-socialist Donna Haraway's (1991: p. 131) and feminist-philosopher Sandra Harding's (1991: ch. 5) call over three decades ago for feminist theory and practice to *explain* and *change* such unequal systems of difference as a permanent fracture in society and space.[44]

As argued recently by Rosi Braidotti (2011: p. 172) in *Nomadic Theory*, such a processual view of becomings is critical because 'nomadic theory stresses difference as the principle of not-one, so as to remind us that difference is not a concept but a process. It, moreover, is not a simple additive, or something you can join, but rather a permanent fracture'. But how to theorize and explain such difference as a permanent fracture remains a continuous project in feminist theory. In *Living a Feminist Life*, Sara Ahmed (2017: p. 9; my emphasis) thus aptly reminds us the importance of taking feminist theory home and for such explanatory theory to be more than just about a new language:

> I think that the more difficult questions, the harder questions, are posed by those feminists concerned with *explaining* violence, inequality, injustice. The empirical work, the world that exists, is for me where the difficulties and thus the challenges reside. Critical theory is like any language; you can learn it, and when you learn it, you begin to move around in it. Of course it can be difficult, when you do not have the orientation tools to navigate your way around a new landscape. But *explaining* phenomena like racism and sexism – how they are reproduced, how they keep being reproduced – is not something we can do simply by learning a new language.

In particular, the politics of representation and knowledge production in these two approaches tend to focus on the contested formation of subjects and their different voices and identities. Situatedness and positionality matter much in theory development and thus analytical interpretations and accounts are almost always partial. Such partial explanations of subject differences in experience and encounters are often attributed to gender, race, sexuality, class, and other intersectional relations. The idea of 'othering' or individual subject-formation and identities is also critical to explaining oppression and subordination in gender, race, and ethnic relations. Taken together, it seems that both critical approaches tend to place their analytical foci on either macro-/societal or micro/individual-level accounts. In the following two subsections, I focus more closely on what 'theory' means in these two critical approaches defined by their practitioners through rallying around what might generally be termed 'feminist theory' and 'postcolonial theory'.

At the risk of a too-thin re-presentation (or even caricaturing) of these 'theories' – here I seek readers' forbearance, let me qualify that my primary intention is to interrogate the idea of theory and explanation in a small number of canonical works. Due to space limit and the central theme of my book (on theory and explanation), I cannot realistically survey the substantive matters and empirical concerns in these two approaches that, by the early 2020s, have evolved to produce a very large body of knowledge both in the humanities and the social sciences. Even within critical human geography, such an unrealistic task of adequately re-presenting and surveying this diverse literature in feminist and postcolonial geographies cannot be easily accomplished even by recently published books (e.g. Oberhauser et al., 2018; Jazeel, 2019; Johnston, 2019), handbooks (e.g. Moss and Donovan, 2017; Jazeel and Legg, 2019; Datta et al., 2020), and field-specific journal special issues (e.g. *Gender, Place and Culture*) and journal papers (e.g. Amoore, 2020b; MacLeavy et al., 2021). Having consulted these geographical sources in detail, my discussion below follows the same *modus operandi* of my earlier section on poststructuralism and post-phenomenology and re-examine critically what theory means to some of the original theorists in both feminist and postcolonial studies and their adaptation in critical human geography.

## Feminist Theory

After some four waves of feminist revolution in the humanities and the social sciences, it is not surprising at all that the literature on feminism is enormous and internally diverse.[45] Even a cursory review of this literature goes well beyond the remit of this book. Here, I can only take a particular epistemological approach to examine very selectively, through a small set of readings, what theory means in key feminist theory. Following the earlier section on poststructuralism and its related 'theories', it is useful to acknowledge that poststructuralism has also influenced some quarters of feminist thought in human geography (Dixon and Jones, 2015; Amoore, 2020b; MacLeavy et al., 2021). While acknowledging internal differences among feminists, Sharp (2011: p. 436) notes that 'Poststructural feminists regard the establishment of boundaries as a fundamentally masculinist move, a will to power through the defining and delimiting of an essence into something known. Feminism is always in excess, always escaping categorisation and limitation, always more than can be known and thus always subversive of accepted ways of knowing'.

This acknowledged connection to the more open-ended approaches and social ontologies has some serious implications for theory and epistemology. First, the always-in-excess and more-than-can-be-known in these poststructuralist feminist gestures has made explanatory theory practically difficult, if not impossible. This is because any form of defining a phenomenon to be explained and any delimiting of the causal explanation(s) of such 'something known' might be viewed as a gendered move and an exercise of a will to power by the dominant (masculinist?) epistemologies. To grapple with these challenging theoretical predispositions towards the open, the unknown, the undetermined, the undecidable, and the subversive, any theory in feminism might well have to be 'performative' rather than explanatory in its epistemological orientation. As will be examined shortly, Judith Butler's (1988, 2006 [1990], 2015a) work in theorizing performativity is perhaps most persuasive when taking on these epistemological challenges (cf. a critique in Elder-Vass, 2012: ch. 10). Her brand of feminist theory is also one of the most influential in feminist geography (see Kinkaid and Nelson, 2020).

Second, the closest poststructuralist account in line with these open-ended feminist gestures is perhaps non-representational theory in human geography. Despite her useful critique of the gender-blindness of most poststructuralist theories, Colls (2012) has offered a feminist account of the subject in non-representational theory. Ironically though, even non-representational theory recognizes representations and discourses and their performative role in practices and affect (Dewsbury et al., 2002; Anderson, 2019). As noted in Simpson (2021: p. 5), such representations can be significant for understanding the unfolding of (gendered) practices precisely because of their capacities to enter into relations and to affect and effect. In short, gendered representations and discursive practices are performative insofar as they are affective in (re)shaping social life through the unfolding of subject actions and interactions. Drawing on poststructuralist Gilles Deleuze's (1994 [1968]) ontology of difference-in-itself, Cockayne et al. (2017: p. 591) thus make the case for rethinking difference in gendered identities and representations not merely as existing empirical-political categories, but more as difference-in-itself beyond their own terms.

To examine what theory is and how theory 'performs' in feminist theory, I now turn to the theory work of two well-known feminist theorists: Judith Butler and Bonnie Honig (chosen for her most recent literary work). The idea of performativity comes from Butler's (1988, 2006 [1990]) highly influential work on a theory of gender performativity. As thoroughly surveyed by Kinkaid and Nelson (2020: p. 94),

> Butler's concept of performativity has been widely engaged in a range of geographical scholarship because it provides powerful ways to conceptualize the embodied and continual re-enactment of identity by a subject constituted by – not separate from– wider power relations and discourses. In bringing performativity into geographic debates, both the subject matter of performativity has shifted (from gender to a larger consideration of space and social relations) and the philosophical 'subject' of performativity has been revised with a finer attention to how space and the subject are performatively co-constituted.

Given this very significant influence of Butler's *concept* of performativity in feminist geography, it is useful to unpack further what her theory of performativity actually entails and the extent to which the 'theory' espoused is explanatory in nature. On gender identity, Butler's (1988, 2006 [1990]) theory of gender performativity and subject construction has enormously influenced feminist geography – the idea that certain performative acts by individuals would or could have a subversive effect on gender norms and subjectivity. These acts are often related to language and linguistics through the power of discourses or speech acts. As Butler (2015a: p. 28) wrote in *Notes Toward a Performative Theory of Assembly*, 'Performativity characterizes first and foremost that characteristic of linguistic utterances that in the moment of making the utterance makes something happen or brings some phenomenon into being'. As noted further by Bonnie Honig (2021: p. 138) in *A Feminist Theory of Refusal*, the concept of performativity actually began life as 'operativity', 'right at the heart of practices of resignification central to the last thirty years of feminist and queer scholarship, pitched not on the verge but in the mix'.

In this conception of performativity, the explanatory chain seems to start with discourses or speech acts that go beyond one's control. These acts 'perform' their psychosocial imposition and norm inculcation by (re)shaping the lived modes of embodiment over time. When a person acts and lives in accordance with such norms and expectations, the performative acts would have produced the new and subversive subject and made something happen, so to speak (no pun intended!). In the case of gender identity, Butler (2015a: p. 29) elaborates further on this process of performativity:

> those primary inscriptions and interpellations come with the expectations and fantasies of others that affect us in ways that are at first uncontrollable: this is the psychosocial imposition and slow inculcation of norms. They arrive when we can scarcely expect them, and they make their way with us, animating and structuring our own forms of responsiveness. Such norms are not simply imprinted on us, marking and branding us like so many passive recipients of a culture machine. They also 'produce' us, but not in the sense of bringing us into being, nor in the sense of strictly determining who we are. Rather, they inform the lived modes of embodiment we acquire

over time, and those very modes of embodiment can prove to be ways of contesting those norms, even breaking with them.

Despite its strong association with 'linguistic utterances' and signification, performativity goes beyond simply discourses to produce effects on gender norms in dual dimensions: (1) the processes of being acted on and (2) the conditions of 'being affected' and the possibilities for acting. While speech acts tend to take place in the first dimension, gender formation is also about bodily acts that are performative of those linguistic utterances. In this second dimension, Butler (2015a) argues for the practice of a performative theory that opposes the unliveable conditions in which gender and sexual minorities live. In this realm of 'being affected', she theorizes that the inadvertent and the unexpected can indeed happen such that 'gender can emerge in ways that break with, or deviate from, mechanical patterns of repetition, resignifying and sometimes quite emphatically breaking those citational chains [the term after Jacques Derrida's account of the speech act as citational] of gender normativity, making room for new forms of gendered life' (Butler, 2015a: p. 64; see also, 2011 [1993]: pp. xxi, 172). Unlike some of the poststructuralist 'theories' reviewed earlier, this feminist theory of gender performativity makes an explicitly normative claim of what the world should be – one that safeguards radical breaks with gender normativity and offers support and affirmation for those making such breaks.

But similar to some of these poststructuralist 'theories', Butler's (1988, 2006 [1990]) theory of gender performativity seems to be concerned with social ontology and ontological being (the mode of gender). In short, it theorizes the nature of social category (subjects) and the mode of being (performativity) in order to enable the discursive (re)enactment of the gendered bodies. Butler (2015a: p. 61) thus reflects more recently that 'When, long ago, I said that gender is performative, that meant that it is a certain kind of enactment, which means that one is not first one's gender and then later on decides how and when to enact it. The enactment is part of its very ontology, is a way of rethinking the ontological mode of gender, and so it matters how and when and with what consequences that enactment takes place, because all that changes the very gender that one "is". This ontological conception of enactment as performing gender is not too different from the idea of embodied practices and affect in non-representational theory examined earlier. Building on Haraway's (1991) work on bodily existence as dependent on systems of support that are both human and nonhumans, Butler's (2015a: p. 130) conception of the body as a living set of relations rather than an autonomous entity also represents an ontological claim of the body in the social worlds such that the body can only live and act in relation to its dependency on such infrastructural structures and environmental conditions.

From her influential theory of gender performativity in *Gender Trouble* to her recent *performative theory* of (public) assembly, Butler's theoretical concerns seemingly remain ontological in gesture and performative in practice. Her theories are neither explanatory nor causal in their analytical focus. Instead, her theories are more about what and how these social categories and modes of being *should be* understood ontologically – as bodily enactments and plural performativity.[46] In turn and as noted in Kinkaid and Nelson's (2020: p. 94) quote earlier and by other feminist geographers (Johnston, 2019; Datta et al., 2020), these key concepts in Butler's 'theories' provide the crucial ontological underpinnings for feminist geographers to shift the *what* of their subject matter (to gender and spaces of social relations) and to rework the *how* of their conceptual priority (co-constitution of the subject and space).

In her recent work, feminist political theorist Bonnie Honig (2021) takes a different and more epistemological approach to theory development. Instead of following Butler's ontological gestures in theorizing performativity and bodily enactments, Honig builds a *feminist theory of refusal* based on three known concepts and illustrates this theory and its politics of refusal by re-reading and re-interpreting a famous Greek tragedy play *The Bacchae*. Her method of theory is primarily interpretive and imaginative, but not explanatory nor causal in its epistemological orientation.[47] This feminist theory of refusal refers to different moments in what Honig (2021) terms 'the arc of refusal' in Euripides' play *The Bacchae*. She explores the politics of refusal by the women bacchants in *The Bacchae* to work at their shuttles and looms, to leave the relaxing and fun mountain range (Cithaeron), and eventually to return to their native city (Thebes). The play's tragedy was about the three daughters of Cadmus, founder of Thebes, who left the city for fun, relaxation, and hunting on Cithaeron as their refusal to work and, later on, unknowingly killed Pentheus, the king of Thebes and the son of one of them (Agave), who had tracked down and found them on Cithaeron. Honig's 'arc of refusal', as seen through the agon between these women bacchants and their king and other men in Thebes, can be summed up as:

> leave, suspend use in festival, hide out, rehearse some new moves, corporealize different habits, intensify use, try out a new world, imagine it, make it real, join up with others, fight with each other, care for each other, come back and claim your right to the city, too. You have the right to leave, the right to build elsewhere, but you also have an obligation to return because we are all depending on each other. We may succeed or fail. But we are in it together. This commitment is not for everyone all the time. But it is part of the promise of refusal as a world-building practice (Honig, 2021: p. 104).

Honig (2021) then connects these different moments in the arc of refusal with three key refusal concepts of *inoperativity* (after Giorgio Agamben), *inclination* (after Adriana Cavarero), and *fabulation* (after Saidiya Hartman) into a feminist theory of refusal. To her, the bacchants' refusal to work represents a form of 'inoperativity' through the suspension of the use of their bodies and/or the re-purposing of these bodies to a new and intensive use, whereas their partying and having fun on Cithaeron as their refuge from Thebes corresponds to 'inclination' as a disposition and a way to rethink or recover use as care and mutuality such that they can establish a new moral geometry or heterotopia of sorority (sisterhood) and relationality away from their native city and the patriarchal authority of their king (Pentheus). Offering her normative take for political action (cf. right to assembly in Butler, 2015a), Honig (2021: p. 71) writes that her theory, 'born in part of reading the *Bacchae* as a feminist parable of refusal, inoperativity, and inclinational care, is that when they succeed for a time, heterotopias valuably serve as spaces or times of rehearsal where alternative forms of life can be tried out and explored. They may inspire others who cannot envision change without the actualization of empirical inspiration and the reassurance of possibility'.

By offering these counter-narration (of the play), conceptual critique, and recovery (of the three key refusal concepts), Honig's theory focuses on how refusal is remembered or erased in women's life and how feminist agencies can be (re)interpreted and resurrected. But what sort of theory is it? In all fairness, I believe this feminist theory of refusal offers an *interpretive* apparatus or framework in the sense that different concepts related to refusal are brought together as conceptual lenses within the 'theory' to help her interpret or (re)read different scenes and events in literary work (e.g. *The Bacchae*), social movements (e.g. La Furiosa in 2019), and media representations (e.g. the film *The Fits* in 2015). As an interpretive or even imaginative 'theory', it represents a conceptualization of gendered relations and resistance *through* the critique and recovery of known concepts and vocabularies in the context of (re)interpreting literary and media work (see also similar moves in postcolonial theory to be discussed later).

But at its core, this interpretive apparatus does not theorize the relative explanatory power of each concept nor their specific analytical pathways in effecting dynamic changes in gendered relations or resistance. This feminist theory of refusal thus clearly differs from the sort of causal and explanatory theory in social science that seek to account for specific empirical effects or outcomes – whether in a drama (Greek tragedy) or in the contemporary world today. As Honig (2021: p. 12; my emphasis) states, her theory deploys all three concepts of inoperativity, inclination, and fabulation and considers 'what it would mean to see the women's violence as, in some way, deliberate and free: a refusal. This means approaching Euripides' play as an *imaginative exploration* of what is needed to render patriarchy inoperative, to engage it agonistically with inclination, and to demand or propose the fabulations that record it and support the effort to move past it'.

In practice, the above two *kinds* of 'theories' – Butler's performative feminist theory and Honig's interpretive/imaginative feminist theory – have heavily influenced feminist geography since the 1990s. Such interpretive and textual (re)readings *for* (queer) bodily matters and posthuman embodiment in feminist and queer theory are also enacted respectively in Butler's (2011 [1993]: chs. 4–6) earlier work, *Bodies That Matter*, Katherine Hayles' (1999: chs. 5 and 7) *How We Became Posthuman*, and Jasbir Puar's (2017: chs. 2–4, 2017: chs. 2–3) *Terrorist Assemblages* and *The Right to Maim*. There are also many other feminist 'theories' that have been adapted into, and emanating from, feminist geographical scholarship, and I am unable to survey them all here. My overall point though is that most of these theories tend to be interpretive, exploratory, imaginative or even speculative in their orientations towards theory. Some have even made explicit claims of *not* offering any epistemological correctives in their service of normative ontological ideals.[48]

Over the past several decades, many feminist geographers have similarly eschewed the earlier and more causally explanatory feminist-Marxist approach in the 1980s and the early 1990s to embrace the ontological contingency of performativity and identity politics as the key conceptual pillar in understanding gender roles and relational spaces (see Table 2.1). In their review of half a century of feminist geography since the 1970s, L. Johnston et al. (2020) have pointed to much accomplishment in rethinking class, work, development, migration, mobility, methodologies, and knowledge, and, more recently since the 2000s, bodies, home, emotion and affect, political ecology, sexuality and space, indigenous, and transgender and gender-variant geographies (also Oberhauser et al., 2018; Johnston, 2019). In another earlier and fairly exhaustive review of feminist geography covering the same time period, Johnston and Sidaway (2016: p. 305) note that 'while one of the key insights of feminist geography has been to bring home (so to speak) the social and cultural contingency of gender relations, it was challenging to negotiate the global range of these (given different expectations and norms of gender roles – and of gendered spaces – in different sites around the world)'.

Following the above brief review of feminist theory by two key thinkers, I think one such challenge is the unresolved epistemological link between theory and context. While there are many excellent critiques and conceptualizations of gender performativity and gendered spaces of social relations in feminist geography, geographers' accounts of *why* and *how* such difference and diversity in gendered geographies takes place tend to err on the side of contextual contingency and interpretations. Few feminist geographers are committed to providing the sort of explanation of difference and diversity advocated by McDowell (1995: p. 280) as the raison d'être of Geography. Even fewer are keen in theorizing the causal mechanisms associated with the gendered categorization of modernity and the politics of subject identities and experiences. This might be an inadvertent outcome of feminist geography's emphasis on situated knowledge (Harding, 1986, 1991; Haraway, 1988, 1991; Rose, 1993, 1997) and intimate writing (Moss and Donovan, 2017) that renders feminist theory and accounts much more contingent on their specific bodily and intellectual contexts. Taking much further this performative orientation to the politics of theorizing and situated knowledge, Katz (1996, 2017) advocates a kind of 'minor theory' to rework feminist marginality by decomposing major theories of some academic 'big boys' and refusing their hegemonic mastery in the academy and research practices. In a similar vein, Gibson-Graham (2008: p. 619) and Wright (2015) argue for a 'weak theory' approach to see multiple openings and to create space for other worlds – they refuse to extend explanation too widely and too deeply (i.e. too causally?).

In turn, this predicament of developing explanatory theory in feminist geography perhaps explains MacLeavy et al.'s (2021) shrewd observation that was raised earlier in Amoore's (2020b: pp. 4–5) concern with feminist geographic theories being annexed as 'merely feminist' in her introduction to feminist thought in human geography from 1993 to 2018:

> despite the uptake of feminist vocabularies, experiences and practices within the discipline, there is a continued annexing of feminist and gender-sensitive scholarship in mainstream human geography, which risks foreclosing the inherently political possibilities to know, act and inhabit space and social networks differently (MacLeavy et al., 2021: p. 1558).

While I agree with Dixon and Jones' (2015: p. 58) earlier and more upbeat conclusion that 'We have reached a point now where feminist geography has become so established a part of the discipline as to demand a review of past achievements and a companion text, as well as anticipatory forays',[49] I think it may be useful to demand such a critical review of whether an overemphasis on contingency and situatedness can be unfavourable to theory development in feminist geography. It may also help address Oswin's (2020) serious concern with human geography's disappointing state of affairs – the lack of an overarching commitment to think through and intervene in social and political discriminations in relation to gender, sexuality, race, disability, indigenous people, and so on. One anticipatory foray then is perhaps to go beyond the sort of ontological gestures, such as in Butler's conceptions of bodily enactments and plural performativity and Honig's arc of refusal as interpretive epistemology, to build new meso-level explanatory theories of difference and diversity that are less planetary in reach and more 'ordinary' in analytical range and practical adequacy. To me, there are no good epistemological reasons why key feminist concepts, such as embodiment and intersectionality, cannot be (re)developed into conjunctural causal mechanisms that help theorize and explain certain convergent effects of gendered relations in society and space (cf. the concepts of over-determination in Marxism earlier and representational mechanics in postcolonialism below). In the next two chapters, I will revisit this potential epistemological foray in the form of mid-range theories in relational thinking (some of which is derived from feminist geography). Before that, it is useful to examine one more 'theory' in critical geographies – postcolonial theory.

## *Postcolonial Theory*

Similar to feminism and feminist geography, politics of representation and knowledge production are central to and strongly featured in postcolonialism and postcolonial geography (Sharp, 2009; Jazeel, 2019). In *Geographies of Postcolonialism*, Joanne Sharp (2009: p. 5) notes that postcolonialism 'represents a shift from a form of analysis based solely around politics and economics (again the conventional way of understanding the impacts of colonialism) to consider instead the importance of the cultural products of colonialism, particularly the ways of knowing the world that emerged'. As a critical approach to analysing colonialism and seeking alternative accounts of the world, postcolonial thought has its origin in *literary theory* in the 1970s, in particular, Edward Said's (2003 [1978]) enormously influential work *Orientalism* (cf. a recent critique in Hallaq, 2018). Like feminist thought, it has gone through different 'waves' of new thinking, from the original critique of imaginary representations in the likes of Said (2003 [1978]) to the newer foci on cultural and identity politics (Bhabha, 2004 [1994]), intellectual interventions into knowledge production (Spivak, 1988, 1999; Chakrabarty, 2008 [2000]; Hallaq, 2018), and living with difference and universalism (Spivak, 2012). But postcolonialism is also an inherently geographical intellectual enterprise and has made significant and identifiable influence in Geography since the mid-1990s (see an early assessment in Sidaway, 2000). As well documented in Tariq Jazeel's (2019) recent text *Postcolonialism*, this influence has shifted from *how* others are represented in colonial discourses to *who* is able to bring themselves into representation on their own terms and the nature of theory as representation and its impossibility (e.g. in subaltern studies).[50]

Among all of the critical approaches reviewed in this chapter, postcolonial thought has paid the foremost attention to the epistemology of theory and the politics of theorizing (my first consideration of/for theory and explanation in Chapter 1 – context and practical adequacy being two other considerations). Here, theory is viewed as a critique and deconstruction of representations in colonial texts, images, cultures, and material forms (e.g. architecture and buildings) that are intimately linked to the identity of their authors/producers. These representations are not just forms of knowledge and coded things, but more importantly also sources for translation into oppressive practices and unjust sociospatial outcomes in different places around the world. As Jazeel (2019: p. 48) notes, 'Orientalist discourse is never far from power. It was precisely the ability of European science, art and literature to authoritatively represent the peoples and places of the East as at one and the same time passive, exotic, undeveloped, barbaric and alluring, that laid the foundation for contact, dispossession and colonial rule by imperial powers'.

This questioning of the claims of authenticity in colonial representations is particularly urgent because many of these practices and outcomes are highly political and contested in the postcolonial era we live in. As argued by Barnett (2015: pp. 172–173; original italics), 'The thrust of the postcolonial critique of representation is to throw into question the modes of authority through which particular styles, forms or voices come to be taken as representative of whole traditions, communities or experiences. When thought of in political terms, there is an important distinction between thinking of representation as *speaking for* and *speaking as'*. Through such critiques and deconstructions, postcolonial thought has argued for the dismantling and reopening of the taken-for-granted geographical knowledges intimately connected to the Eurocentrism of colonial power and Empire (see Livingstone, 1992; Gregory, 1994, 2004; Driver, 2001; Agnew and Livingstone, 2011). This in turn produces a radically open-ended intellectual space for rethinking geographical difference and the plurality of spaces of social relations that are as significant to feminism and some poststructuralist 'theories' reviewed earlier. It offers a more pluralist and embodied understanding of the different modes of authority (see also Brigstocke et al., 2021 and my reflections on 'theorizing back' in Chapter 6).

Despite its focus on unravelling the intimate relationship between representation as a process of knowing and representation as a set of practising dominant forms of authority and power, postcolonial thought does not seem to offer a *coherent theory* to explain those other voices and practices, multiple trajectories, and socio-spatial outcomes that might be directly linked to these representations in colonial texts and things.[51] Such explanatory theory requires the specification and unpacking of these very authoritative representations and their workings as causal mechanisms if we were to deploy them as explanations of coloniality, its unjust practices, and their socio-spatial effects. Colonial discourses can indeed be conceived as causal mechanisms and discursive formation can serve as mechanisms of change because human reasoning, while not material in nature, can be explanatory. There are no fundamental reasons why the (cultural) politics of representations (in texts or images or other forms) cannot be a kind of causal mechanisms of empirical changes and events – narratives and 'representational mechanics', as described in Jazeel (2019: p. 17), have causal powers and they can hurt, seriously! Equally, it is problematic if one goes to the extremes of the postmodernist advocacy of deconstruction alone as 'there is no outside-text'.[52] What matters perhaps is the practical adequacy of explaining events and happenings in these different conceptions of causal mechanisms.

I give one brief example from *Orientalism* in which Said (2003 [1978]: pp. 153–156) reminds us of the omnicompetent power of these 'representational mechanics' with a shrewd exposition of Karl Marx's 'non-Orientalist' representation of the Asiatic economic system as the solid foundation of Oriental despotism in his 1853 analysis of British rule in India. To overcome this dominant discourse about the Orient from both Orientalists (e.g. Silvestre de Sacy, Ernest Renan, and Edward Lane) and non-Orientalists (such as Marx) that made the colonized Orient unequal with the West, Said asks us to specify better, and indeed take to task, such formidable kind of representational *mechanisms*:

> In using Marx as the case by which a non-Orientalist's human engagements were first dissolved, then usurped by Orientalist generalizations, we find ourselves having to consider the process of lexicographical and institutional consolidation peculiar to

Orientalism. What was this operation, by which whenever you discussed the Orient a formidable mechanism of omnicompetent definitions would present itself as the only one having suitable validity for your discussion? And since we must also show how this mechanism operated specifically (and effectively) upon personal human experiences that otherwise contradicted it, we must also show where *they* went and what forms *they* took, while they lasted (Said, 2003 [1978]: p. 156; original italics).[53]

Clearly and as acknowledged by Said, this is not an easy operation and requires 'specifying the kinds of experiences that Orientalism typically employed for its own ends and represented for its wider-than-professional audience' (p. 156). This complex and yet difficult operation is necessary precisely because, as he explains later in the book, Orientalist representations are discursive formations that are purposeful and effective much of the time and capable of accomplishing one or many tasks (p. 273).[54] I will return to this epistemological need for better mecha-nism-specification in Chapter 5 in order to theorize how narratives or 'represen-tational mechanics' can have causal powers through exercising such purposeful and effective tasks.

Still and as emphasized repeatedly throughout Jazeel's (2019) text, postcolo-nialism is not a theory, but rather a methodology attuned to the politics of repre-sentation and difference. Given its epistemological orientation towards critique and unsettling the power of authority (i.e. speaking for), postcolonial thought cannot be conceived as a theory because postcolonial theory is itself contradic-tory of its very own disdain of representation and theory as settled and authorita-tive. Indeed in *The Location of Culture*, postcolonial literary theorist Homi Bhabha (2004 [1994]: pp. 255–257) emphasizes repeatedly in his rather abstract writings that postcolonial theory is about the 'enunciative present' – a liberatory discursive strategy focusing on the historical contingency, indeterminism, and ambivalence of cultural formations. For all its theoretical sophistication and abstract vocabu-laries, postcolonial thought offers a set of conceptual strategies and methodologi-cal toolkits to question pre-existing theories and knowledges. In doing so, it helps open up new possibilities for rethinking what we know and how we *should* know in the wake of colonialism and its contemporary iterations.

In lieu of a concluding section, I now sum up my main observations in this chapter that has navigated, albeit selectively and briefly, the complex terrain of different critical approaches and their key theories as practiced in contemporary geographical thought (see also Table 2.1). Revisiting my key considerations of/for theory and explanation in Geography in Chapter 1, it is clear that we can learn from some of these approaches the vital importance of taking seriously normative concerns and the politics of theorizing in theory development. Equally, we can recognize the inherent dangers of too much ontological lock-ins or abstract theo-rization in certain philosophical quarters underpinning these approaches. Much like Holbraad and Pedersen's (2017: p. 30) proclamation that ontology or meta-physics is the current zeitgeist in anthropology, this chapter's exposé of 'new ontologies' abound in human geography tells a similar story and happening in human geography – the creation of a multitude of conceptual vocabularies and aesthetics of thought, such as networks, affects, assemblages, multiplicities; multi-species and the Anthropocene, new materialism; emergence, vibrancy, intra-action; performativity, intersectionality, colonial present, and mimicry; and so on.[55]

Instead of clearing away the 'philosophical rubbish' and obstacles for social scientists to do their work – as discussed in my caveats in Chapter 1, some of these ontological lock-ins might have become too dogmatic in dictating the substantive content of critical social science. In short, an ontic fallacy occurs when our conception of the world(s) determines our knowledge of it. To some, this ontic fallacy can exhibit a form of academic inferiority and 'philosophy envy'. As Doreen Massey (2001: p. 13) dreads in her *Progress in Human Geography* annual lecture 2000, critical geographers have spent far too much time importing and retailing ontological claims and their theorists in the name of 'theories' and offered too little in return by reworking them into geographical theories proper![56] Similarly in his postscript to *Making Human Geography*, Kevin Cox (2014: p. 256) laments that

> The hegemonic position in human geography is now occupied by something that is called 'critical human geography'… Critical human geography is a highly eclectic mix, drawing variably on some soft critique of capitalism and bits and pieces of 'post' thinking that may be no more profound than the use of ideas of identity, social construction, and discourse. It is energized by social oppressions of an economic and cultural sort: the maldistribution of resources and of recognition, therefore. The oppressions of gender, race, ethnicity, development, and poverty attract special attention. The logic and language of class is barely visible. A pluralization of processes rules.

On the other hand, most critical approaches seem to place some epistemological emphasis on contingency and contextuality that tackles quite well my second key consideration of/for theory and explanation. But in some 'theories', over-emphasis on openness and contingency might lead to excessive indeterminacy and radical empiricism in a kind of relativist-gestured research that relies primarily on rhetorical accounts and descriptive interpretations couched in abstract vocabularies and ever-novel philosophical 'thinking'.[57] Indeed, even practitioners of abstract writing in such 'post-' approaches claim that we need to go beyond the contingent present and move into what Bhabha (2004 [1994]: p. 6) calls 'an expanded and ex-centric site of experience and empowerment'.[58] There is of course no easy solution to any of these ontological and epistemological challenges. But equally there is no fundamental reason, unless one is truly dogmatic and feeling inferior about it, why any of these approaches cannot take explanatory theories and causal mechanisms more seriously in their intellectual endeavours. Causal explanations and interpretive accounts should not be a hackneyed choice in critical human geography concerning with *why* social actors do *what* they do and *how* their individual and collective action or 'doings' in relation to the more-than-humans make a difference in society and space.

To practice philosopher Schatzki (2019: p. 118), all explanations of social change in a material world are causal explanations on a sufficiently broad sense of the causal, i.e. the efficient causality – one of philosopher Aristotle's four types of cause – of 'what brings that event about'. This is a productive-relational view of cause that 'produces' or generates effect. These causal explanations, with their attendant mechanisms (specified from general processes) and contexts (observed from empirical contingency), can go a long way beyond the description of the everyday life(worlds) of most people and yet become indispensable to critical social science. Grounded in this chapter's critical engagement with contemporary geographical thought, the next three chapters take a more synthetic approach and explain why and how the development of this kind of explanatory theory/ theorizing in, and for, Geography might be epistemologically realistic and practically adequate.

# Notes

1   I thank one reviewer for raising this important issue for clarification.
2   Chakrabarty (2008 [2000]: p. 254) concludes his influential book by revisiting the critique of Marx's abstract and universalistic view of capital in History 1: 'On one side is the indispensable and universal narrative of capital – History 1, as I have called it. This [Marxist] narrative both gives us a critique of capitalist imperialism and affords elusive but necessarily energizing glimpses of the Enlightenment promise of an abstract, universal but never-to-be-realized humanity. Without such elusive glimpses, as I have said before, there is no political modernity'. Much of his work though focuses on History 2s in the context of diverse struggles for subject identity, nationalism, and (family) belonging among the Bengalis in colonial (and postcolonial) India. See more on postcolonial theory later in this chapter.
3   As its key proponent Bruno Latour (2013: p. 5) reflects in his *An Enquiry into Modes of Existence,* 'in its early days, in the 1980s, this field was perceived by many scientists as a critique of scientific Certainty – which it was – but also of reliable knowledge – which it most certainly was not. We wanted to understand how – with what instruments, what machinery, what material, historical, anthropological conditions – it was possible to produce objectivity'.
4   In Donald MacKenzie's (2009, 2021: pp. 10–23) work grounded in actor-network theory, the material politics of market-making remains a central focus in what he terms 'material markets' and 'material political economy'. See also feminist literary critic Katherine Hayles' (2017: ch. 6) *Unthought* for a humanist take on the complex ecologies of human-algorithm interactions in such material markets as high-frequency trading in finance capital.
5   Taking on a leading postmodern philosopher Jacques Derrida's meta-reflexivity in deconstructing text, Latour (1988: p. 167; original italics) critiques that 'In terms of

reflexivity, translation, cunning and cleverness, I am not convinced that the post-modern deconstructionists are any match for the Evangelists and Fathers of the Church. In comparison they play with very few tools. Their meta-reflexivity is obtained by *adding* specific parts about the way texts or discourses should or should not be written (as I am doing now). This is what is usually called methodology. In the end the only way of writing a text that does not run the risk of being naively believed is to write methodologically. The dire result of such a tack is visible in the prose of Derrida... If the prose was just unreadable, not much harm would be done. But there is something worse in it; worse, that is, from their own reflexive point of view... Derrida really believes that by all his tricks, cunning and entrapments, the texts he writes are more deconstructed than the column of a *New York Times* journalist writing about the latest plane crash'. In *Sciences from Below*, feminist science studies scholar Sandra Harding (2008: ch. 1) offers an in-depth discussion of Latour's eschewing of postmodernism and his 'principled refusal' (p. 43) to engage with feminist and postcolonial studies.

6   As Latour (1990, 1991: p. 121; original italics) notes in his account of the chain of associations and translation movements in technological innovation such as George Eastman's Kodak cameras, 'explanation does not follow from description; it is description *taken that much further*. We do not look for a stabilized and simplified description before we begin to propose an explanation. On the contrary, we use what they do to an innovation or a statement to define the actors, and it is from them and them alone that we extract any "cause" we might need. Paradoxically our explanation are [sic] "internalist" in the sense that they all come from the inherent topography of specific networks'.

7   In his conclusion, Latour (1996: p. 380, 2017) argues that 'ANT is a powerful tool to destroy spheres and domains, to regain the sense of heterogeneity, and to bring interobjectivity back into the centre of attention (Latour, 1994). Yet it is an extremely bad tool for differentiating associations. It gives a black and white picture, not a coloured and contrasted one. Thus it is necessary, after having traced the actor-networks, to specify the types of trajectories that are obtained by highly different mediations. This is a different task, and the one that will make ANT scholars busy for a number of years to come'.

8   As critiqued pointedly by realist philosopher Roy Bhaskar (2010: pp. 141–142), 'if you take a specific ideology like that of poststructuralism, its position that there are no grounds, no deep structures, is a kind of oblivion – alethic untruth – of the fundamental facts of our societal existence, which remain under the dominance of the deep structures of capitalism. Poststructuralism is there as an accompanying ideology: capitalism does not exist, nor does the pulse of freedom. What exists is the surface, what you have really got, and since that is all that exists, it will always be there in one form or another. This is rather like assuming that you yourself as an embodied being are going to be immortal. That is the kind of thing the problems of philosophy point to'.

9   To Latour (1988: p. 162; original italics), 'You cannot explain the development of the world economy by invoking a force of some sort (for instance, capitalism) because this cause is itself helpless as long as centres do not exist which are able to capitalize, on a larger scale, on whatever is produced and sold. The heterogeneous association of many elements (which was supposed to be explained) is precisely what, *in the end*, gives strength to this capitalism which was supposed to offer an explanation. In more philosophical terms, it means that a cause (factor, determinant, pattern, or correlate) is the outcome of a trial of responsibility through which a few elements of the network are taken to be the impetus behind the whole business'.

10   Philosopher of science James Woodward (2003: p. 226) makes the case that this kind of explanation involving omissions is rather unsatisfying: 'it seems clear that there are purported explanations meeting this condition that (at the very least) strike us as unsatisfying. Some purported explanations involving omissions are cases in point... It is also true that if a large meteor had struck my office just as I was typing these words, I would not have typed them, but again, we are reluctant to accept the failure of the meteor to strike as part of the explanation for my writing what I did'. See also Glennan (2017: pp. 196–197) for a discussion of this problem of non-productive causation by omission and/or prevention. See fuller discussion of causality in my Chapter 3.

11   This social constructivist thought on an open reality as multiplicity in actor-network theory is also echoed in Thrift's (2021: pp. 4–5) recent work in which he declares that 'we try to construct a subjectivity which can live in the world as an open multiplicity, one which has no origin and no goal and no centre. This is to understand the world as a continual opening without closure, as a perpetual disequilibrium, in which we must never explain too much, as Deleuze put it, or we lose the ability to multiply the world and to appreciate that multiplication. This is a genuine risk society'. The most difficult issue here is that what is 'explain too much' varies enormously across different critical approaches and social science disciplines.

12   I thank another reviewer for bringing this question on ANT's flat ontology to my attention. As pointed out by geographers Müller and Schurr (2016: p. 221; original italics) though, 'ANT has produced many studies in which those concepts are developed and applied, and which can serve as a useful guide for further empirical work. But perhaps more important is the analytical advantage: while ANT still *starts* from description, it *arrives* at explanation through description'.

13   This British-centric orientation in NRT work and influence is not lost on Philo (2012: p. 498) who gestures in his review of NRT and Thrift's (1996) reluctance to invite French philosopher Michel Foucault along when exploring 'the strange country': 'it is sometimes objected, not unjustifiably, that the influence of his non-representationalist agenda has been picked up more fully by British academics than by their colleagues elsewhere'. In critical urban studies, Hubbard (2011: p. 560) also stresses that 'the principal advocates of a non-representational geography are all based in UK geography departments. Beyond the UK, urban geographers continue to work productively within their own fields of enquiry, studying important questions about what is going on in cities'. Let me offer a personal anecdote here, as I almost went to Bristol to do my PhD with Nigel Thrift in October 1992 and thereafter became a direct descendant of his Bristol diaspora during the 1990s. But I did have the great pleasure and fortune to have Nigel as the external examiner of my PhD at Manchester in 1995. With Adam Tickell as my internal examiner, he graciously passed my rather 'representational' thesis grounded in then critical realism (published as Yeung, 1998a)! In fact, this Manchester-Bristol 'network' started in 1992 when Nigel passed Adam Tickell's PhD at Manchester and, with our PhD supervisor Peter Dicken, brought economic sociologist Mark Granovetter's (1985) influential concept of embeddedness into the central optic of economic geography (Dicken and Thrift, 1992; see also Thrift, 2003; Yeung and, Peck, 2003; Hess, 2004).

14   To Thrift (2000: pp. 214–215, 2007: pp. 110–111), 'actor-network theory is much more able to describe steely accumulation than lightning strikes, sustained longings

and strategies rather than the sharp movements that may also pierce our dreams. Actor-network theory is good at describing certain intermediated kinds of effectivity, but, even though fleet Hermes is one of its avatars, dies a little when confronted with the flash of the unexpected and the unrequited... In their surely correct insistence that action is a property of the whole association, actor-network theorists tend to recoil with horror from any accusation of humanism. Quite rightly, they fear the taint of a centred human subject establishing an exact dominion over all. But the result of their fear is that actor-network theory has tended to neglect specifically human capacities of expression, powers of invention, of fabulation, which cannot be simply gainsaid, in favour of a kind of flattened cohabitation of all things. But human expressive powers seem especially important in understanding what is possible to associate, in particular the power of imagination'. Guilty as charged – Latour (1988: p. 173) indeed calls for a more direct engagement with the world's objects and things as they are rather than merely with words, language, and self-reference (as in postmodernism and the 'reflexivists'): 'there is more reflexivity in one account that makes the world alive than in one hundred self-reference loops that return the boring thinking mind to the stage... Down with Kant! Down with the Critique! Let us go back to the world, still unknown and despised. If you sneer at this claim and say "this is going back to realism," yes it is. A little relativism takes one away from realism; a lot brings one back'.

15  See this early literature in Ley and Samuels (1978); Cosgrove (1984); Cosgrove and Jackson (1987); Cosgrove and Daniels (1988); and later efforts in Jackson (2000) and Cresswell (2010).

16  See also Roberts (2014) and Wilson (2017) on how difference (respectively in experimental art and bodies) emerges from events and encounters. Philosopher Brian Massumi (2002, 2015) has argued that encounters are adventures of relation and speaking of affect means venturing into the political dimension of relational encounters and their emergent politics. Ruez and Cockayne (2021) recently argue for an affective approach to ambivalence in reconciling the opposing politics of critique and affirmation.

17  In his introductory review text, Simpson (2021: p. 102; original italics) observes that 'While affect has come to be bound up with both the development of NRTs and its more contentious contribution to the conduct of cultural geography, affect *has* come to be accepted as a significant feature of the geographies of everyday experiences of space and place. A glance at the contents pages of a range of mainstream human geography journals will regularly show a range of papers with affect in the title or as a keyword. From 2008 to 2018, over 120 articles were published in the journals *Transactions of the Institute of British Geographers, Environment and Planning A* and *D, Social and Cultural Geography,* and *Cultural Geographies* alone with "affect" as a keyword. And that doesn't necessarily capture those articles where affect is something engaged with as part of a broader account of individuals' or collectives' experiences in relation to a host of topics'. See also feminist Sara Ahmed's (2015 [2004]: pp. 205–211) 'Afterword' in the second edition of *Cultural Politics of Emotion* for the discussion of affect and emotion in feminist and queer studies that predates the so-called 'affective turn' since the beginning of the 2000s. Historian of thought Ruth Leys (2017) offers a genealogy and trenchant critique of affect research in the social sciences and humanities and concludes that despite all psychological research since the 1960s, no consensus on the nature of emotion and affect could be achieved even by the mid-2010s (p. 25)!

18  Some of these works on affect are grounded quite deeply in different philosophies, such as Maurice Merleau-Ponty's critical phenomenology (Simonsen and Koefoed, 2020); Gilles Deleuze's virtual philosophy; Michel Foucault's biopolitics (Anderson, 2006, 2009, 2016); and Jacques Rancière's political philosophy (Pile, 2021). See also recent critical reviews in Doucette (2020) and Kinkaid (2021).

19  In *Problem Spaces*, Lury (2021: pp. 57–58) notes that 'Radical empiricism is a move beyond sense- or observation-based empiricism, employing instead a focus on the processes and practices by which events or occasions come into being. Methods are said to be performative, to be understood in terms of play and experimentation. In place of (symbolic) representation as the primary epistemological vehicle, non-representational theory is concerned with presentations, practices, showings, tellings, happenings and manifestations of everyday life. Rather than aiming to develop explanations that claim to go behind or beyond the phenomena described, the aim is to present descriptions that are infused with fidelity to what they describe'. See also Bridge's (2021: p. 419) pragmatist take on radical empiricism in NRT, actor-network theory, and assemblage theory that 'points to a radically contingent and empirical (rather than transcendental) form of hyper-relational space, but one that situates (in a profound sense of that word) human experience and human reason, even allowing for human experience being relativised as just one component of the assembly/network within those spatial networks and assemblages'.

20  In the context of children geographies, Mitchell and Elwood (2012: p. 789; original italics) critique that 'We acknowledge the validity of NRT as a philosophical intervention but deplore its increasing use as method in empirical research. In the work of many (but not all) proponents of NRT we see not an opening of the entrenched battle lines of what constitutes the political but rather, through the elision of geographical methods which elicit social interrelations and historical patterns, an inversion of politics – the extension of a mode of thought that we believe to be profoundly *de*politicizing'. Evaluating NRT scholars from a political will approach, Doucette (2020: p. 318) also argues that 'Underlying their attention to the contingency of the political – its indeterminacy, potentiality, and emergent properties – is a hyper-determined sense of the biological properties of affect, emotion, and volition that limits its usefulness for an emancipatory understanding of political will. This hyper-determination is most visible in their strong view of affect that disregards concerted, willful action as largely an illusion'.

21  This paragraph from Deleuze and Guattari (1987 [1980]: p. 90) best summarizes their thought on assemblages: 'We think the material or machinic aspect of an assemblage relates not to the production of goods but rather to a precise state of intermingling of bodies in a society, including all the attractions and repulsions, sympathies and antipathies, alterations, amalgamations, penetrations, and expansions that affect bodies of all kinds in their relations to one another... Similarly, the semiotic or collective aspect of an assemblage relates not to a productivity of language but to regimes of signs, to a machine of expression whose variables determine the usage of language elements. These elements do not stand on their own any more than tools do. There is a primacy of the machinic assemblage of bodies over tools and goods, a primacy of the collective assemblage of enunciation over language and words. The articulation of the two aspects of the assemblage is effected by the movements of deterritorialization that quantify

their forms. That is why a social field is defined less by its conflicts and contradictions than by the lines of flight running through it. An assemblage has neither base nor superstructure, neither deep structure nor superficial structure; it flattens all of its dimensions onto a single plane of consistency upon which reciprocal presuppositions and mutual insertions play themselves out'.

22  In the true spirit of assemblage, DeLanda's (2006) book serves to 'assemble' the rudiments of Deleuze's assemblage theory dispersed throughout his many writings and develops it further into his 'assemblage theory 2.0' with his own definitions, arguments, and use of entirely different theoretical resources: 'It may be objected, however, that the relatively few pages dedicated to assemblage theory in the work of Deleuze (much of it in partnership with Félix Guattari) hardly amount to a fully-fledged theory. And this is, in fact, correct. But the concepts used to specify the characteristics of assemblages in those few pages (concepts such as "expression" or "territorialization") are highly elaborated and connected to yet other concepts throughout Deleuze's work. Taking into account the entire network of ideas within which the concept of "assemblage" performs its conceptual duties, we do have at least the rudiments of a theory' (DeLanda, 2006: p. 3).

23  To Deleuze and Guattari (1987 [1980]: p. 399), 'Assemblages are passional, they are compositions of desire. Desire has nothing to do with a natural or spontaneous determination; there is no desire but assembling, assembled, desire. The rationality, the efficiency, of an assemblage does not exist without the passions the assemblage brings into play, without the desires that constitute it as much as it constitutes them'.

24  Practice philosopher Schatzki (2019: p. 187; my emphasis) recently offers a cogent critique of such topological thinking as a betrayal of the poverty of specific categories: 'social and cultural theorists who write about topology or topological space too often fall back simply on calling interesting types of relations or relational spaces "topological"... This practice betrays a poverty of categories: conceptions of relational space well pre-exist the first stirrings of topology as a branch of mathematics in the 19th century and its subsequent emergence in the 20th. This practice also empties the term "topology" of its specificity. Topology does, in fact, emphasize relations, but these are relations of a *particular* type, namely, relations among features of surfaces that are preserved through continuous transformations of those surfaces. This characteristic of topology does not justify calling *any* relational space of interest "topological"'.

25  Indeed, Doreen Massey (2001: p. 15) believes that geographers should challenge such postmodernist and poststructuralist imaginations of space as a surface: 'This too is played into by some current social science theorizing. The depthlessness deplored by Jameson, enjoyed by Baudrillard. The smooth space of Deleuze which, in spite of disclaimers, is constantly prioritized over striated. The fascination with the desert, most particularly as "timeless space." The persistent horizontality of deconstruction's textualism. It is as though there has been a flipping around of the imaginative eye'.

26  As argued by philosopher Daniel Little (2016: p. 90), 'the parsimonious social theory associated with a flat ontology does not work. It forces us to overlook explanatory factors that are important for explaining social outcomes. And, it unreasonably asks us to ignore important features of the social world of which we have reasonably good understanding. In fact, the flat ontology is not far removed from the ontology associated with some versions of methodological individualism'. See also realist philosophers

Manuel DeLanda and Graham Harman (2017: pp. 85–88) for an exchange of their views on different kinds of flat ontologies and Markus Gabriel (2015: ch. 9) for a realist no-world-view assessment of how 'flat' flat ontologies can be! While opposing to a hierarchical ontology in his *Fields of Sense*, Gabriel (2015: p. 255) notes that 'Against flat ontology we need to have in view that it is impossible for there to only be a unified level (a plane of immanence, as it were, to misuse Deleuze's metaphor) of equal objects that happen to differ from each other in one way or other (most likely by their properties). Without the functional difference between fields of sense and objects neither objects nor fields could exist. The difference is functional in that something is both an object in some field and a field in which some object appears depending on the functional specification'.

27   In his 2016 'revision' of Deleuzian assemblage theory, DeLanda (2016) offers a new version of the concept of assemblage that seems to include virtually everything. Explaining his changes to the expanded concept of assemblage following Deleuze and Guattari's work, DeLanda (2016: pp. 6–7; my emphasis) notes that 'The other change, conceiving of the *components* of an assemblage as themselves assemblages, is also harmless, as is the idea that the *environment* of an assemblage is itself an assemblage'. To me, this idea that components and environment *of* an assemblage are also assemblages is seemingly tautological – if an entity's component or environment is already an assemblage, how can the entity not be an assemblage as well since it is both constituted by assemblages (components) within ever more assemblages (environment)? My critique in turn explains why assemblage theory has become more rhetorical and diffuse over time in its different interpretations and versions by DeLanda (2006, 2016) and others who build on Deleuze and Guattari (1987 [1980]) and their other works. Indeed, much of DeLanda's (2016) recent book is devoted to theoretical (re) interpreting Deleuze's philosophical ideas on assemblages, particularly those in *A Thousand Plateaus*, in various chapters on human history, languages, wars, scientific practice, virtual diagrams, and real entities in astrophysics and biology. Most of the book's examples are drawn from Deleuze and Guaratti and in the natural sciences, such as physics, chemistry, biology, and mathematics.

28   Opening his 2006 book on assemblage theory, DeLanda (2006: p. 1) makes very explicit his realist ontology and termed it 'social realism': 'Hence, a realist approach to social ontology must assert the autonomy of social entities from the conceptions we have of them. To say that social entities have a reality that is conception-independent is simply to assert that the theories, models and classifications we use to study them may be objectively wrong, that is, that they may fail to capture the real history and internal dynamics of those entities'. This realist ontological distinction between concept and assemblage is reiterated again in DeLanda (2016: p. 138; original italics): 'The concept itself is a product of our minds and would not exist without them, but concrete assemblages must be considered to be fully *independent of our minds*. This statement must be qualified, because in the case of social assemblages like communities, organisations, and cities, the assemblages would cease to exist if our minds disappeared. So in this case we should say that social assemblages are *independent of the content of our minds*, that is, independent of the way in which communities, organisations, and cities are conceived. This is just another way of saying that assemblage theory operates within a realist ontology'. The irony though is that in both books,

DeLanda (2006, 2016) relies on Bhaskar's (1975) foundational work on transcendental realism for science and does not incorporate any of Bhaskar's (1986, 1989, 2008 [1993], 2010) important later works on *critical* realism for social science (see more discussion of critical realism in my Chapter 3).

29    On Deleuze's own 'realist' moment, one can examine his penchant for creating new concepts in his works, e.g. *A Thousand Plateaus*. As Harman (2010: p. 34; my emphasis) wrote in 1997 comparing Deleuze with the phenomenologist Martin Heidegger, 'it is Deleuze who defines philosophy (interestingly enough) as a "creation of concepts," and then correctly describes these concepts as *independent forces* traversing and apportioning reality'. In DeLanda and Harman (2017: p. 30), DeLanda further claims that Deleuze is 'a rare case of a contemporary continental realist'!

30    In his commentary on Anderson et al. (2012a), Allen (2012: p. 191; my emphasis) questions assemblage theory's focus on the relations of exteriority because 'it is not relations per se that are at issue, but those that set themselves up as internal relations and, on that basis, claim prior knowledge of what the powers of a particular object or entity can necessarily do'. To him, this focus is contradictory with critical realism that 'works with *both* internally and externally related phenomena, where, broadly speaking, the former account for the powers of a particular entity, their tendencies and potential, and the latter make up the empirical realm of the contingent where entities interact and tendencies are realized, if at all. On this view, powers may exist unexercised and unrealized, and what happened in the past does not exhaust what is possible in the future. So, outcomes are open-ended and never fully determined'.

31    Müller and Schurr (2016: p. 217) compare the similarities or conjunctions between assemblage thinking and actor-network theory and note that 'The similarities between assemblage thinking and ANT are striking. Both have a relational view of the world, in which action results from linking together initially disparate elements. Both emphasise emergence, where the whole is more than the sum of its parts. Both have a topological view of space, in which distance is a function of the intensity of a relation. And both underscore the importance of the socio-material, i.e. that the world is made up of associations of human and non-human elements'. See also Bridge's (2021) recent attempt to bring John Dewey's pragmatism into actor-network theory and assemblage thinking.

32    In his hyperbolic assessment of Delanda's assemblage theory as the 'hegemonic philosophy' of the 2030s when 'Delanda has now replaced analytic philosophy as the very embodiment of the philosophical mainstream – perhaps containing splinter factions (the Harvard and Oxford DeLandians) but not facing much real dissent' (p. 381), Harman (2008: pp. 381–382) questions that 'one of the remaining empty rooms in philosophy in the year 2030 would be causation. What I would most miss in a De-Landian universe is an adequate theory of causal relations'.

33    In their response to critics, Anderson et al. (2012b: p. 215; original italics) conclude that 'we prefer to think of assemblage as a resource consisting of a multiple set of interrelated dispositions, concepts and methods that can be variously drawn upon in understanding how assemblages form and endure: as an *ethos*; a set of *conceptual frames*; and a range of *methodological stances*. By focusing on the qualities of composition and durability across difference assemblage theory therefore helps us to see and attend to the immanent capacities of assembled orders, and how they might be recomposed'.

34  Philosopher Little (2016: p. 13; my emphasis) thus notes that 'I think we do best to understand assemblage theory as a high-level and abstract ontological framework, an abstract description of the nature of the social world. It is, as DeLanda says, a "new philosophy of society." It highlights the pervasive fact of the heterogeneous nature of phenomena in the social world. But it is not a concrete sociological theory. It does not provide a substantive theory of what those component threads are; this is for concrete sociological theory to work out... So, assemblage theory is not a substantive social theory. It does not prescribe any specific ideas about the specific nature of the components, layers, laminations, or threads out of which social phenomena are composed. Instead, it offers a *vision* of how we should think of all such constructions in the social world'.

35  In *Volatile Bodies*, feminist philosopher Elizabeth Grosz (1994: ch. 7) engages quite extensively with Deleuze and Guattari's assemblage thinking and wonders if there might be a possibility for a 'Deleuzian feminism' focusing on becoming-woman and becoming-incorporeal (cf. critique in Ahmed, 1998: pp. 69–79; see also Braidotti, 2011: pp. 36–43).

36  Kinkaid (2020: p. 464; original italics) quotes critical theorist Elizabeth Povinelli's (2016: p. 91) argument from the viewpoint of minority and colonized subjects that 'the world of objects and subjects is not flat. It must be viewed from the unequal forces redrawing and demanding certain formations as the condition for an object's endurance, extension, and domination of interest' and argues further that: 'Without attending to how bodies have been invested with ontological difference, and how these symbolic economies operate *through* categories of social difference, assemblage thinking fails to render visible the operations of power and is poorly equipped to address the question of how symbolic-material differentials are maintained and endure'. In an earlier commentary on Anderson et al. (2012a), Adey (2012: pp. 198, 199; original italics) also finds that the use of ethos to describe assemblage thinking 'is left slightly underdone' and 'appears rather a bit vaguer... Ethos then provokes some centrally important questions for how one addresses theory and practice and engagement itself. We could be concerned that ethos too easily becomes a kind of misnomer for styles of conceptual and methodological engagement or maybe something *before* the formalized use of these sorts of terms and identifiers... How might ethos be divorced from, for instance, an *approach*, or a collection of theories and practices of concepts, terms and methods, etc? To a certain extent ethos appears to say nothing, while saying everything'.

37  See also posthumanism thought and new materialism in anthropology's 'ontological turn' in Holbraad and Pedersen (2017: pp. 199–241): 'thing theory' (thinking-through-things) and things as concepts in debate about material culture in anthropology.

38  Graham Harman first used the term 'object-oriented philosophy' to title his 1999 conference lecture at Brunel University, England (reproduced in Harman, 2010: ch. 6) when he raised some serious questions for philosophy at the end of the last millennium. He called for going beyond the concern with language, being, and social construction in 20th century philosophy that had missed out much on material objects. This object-oriented philosophy would later form the core of his 'speculative realism' movement since the early 2000s (see my Chapter 1 endnote 12) and his object-oriented ontology (Harman, 2017; also Garcia, 2014; Sparrow, 2014).

39   See Roberts and Dewsbury (2021) for a reassertion of the significance of vitalism as a philosophical aspiration for (post)human geography and Barua (2021) for a recent rethinking of the more-than-humans through a 'wider ontology' of infrastructure and the agency of animals. Interestingly, this vitalist ontology has been described as realist in its philosophical gestures. In *The End of Phenomenology*, Tom Sparrow (2014: pp. xv, 146), a philosopher of new realism, puts Jane Bennett, together with Levi Bryant, Ian Bogost, Timothy Morton, in his list of 'established figures of the second wave of speculative realism'. Another influential posthumanist in science studies, Karen Barad (2007: p. 136), also views her ontological venture as 'agential realism' that 'allows matter its due as an active participant in the world's becoming, in its ongoing intra-activity'. See also feminist philosopher Rosi Braidotti's (2011: pp. 132–138, 196) vitalist approach of 'matter-realism' as radical immanence and perpetual becoming in *Nomadic Theory*.

40   This ontological orientation towards more-than-human materiality and non-reductive materialism is also evident in Jane Bennett's (2010) *Vibrant Matter*, Elizabeth Grosz's (2017) *The Incorporeal*, and Katherine Hayles' (2017) call for a planetary cognitive ecology in *Unthought*.

41   Ash and Simpson (2019) offer two examples of writing about style in terms of allure and resonance through analysing a life-action children TV programme – *In the Night Garden* on BBC's CBeebies channel in the UK. The selection of this case is largely circumstantial (or even self-referential) as one of the authors watched it routinely with his two-year old daughter. Ironically, there is very little voice from the subjects (i.e. children) whose own feedbacks and interactions with the objects in the TV programme, from visuals to songs and music, remain muted in the mostly descriptive analysis. Such a post-phenomenological analysis seems almost entirely written from the realm and style of the adult researcher(s), rather than through inter-subjective understanding of the very subjects themselves (e.g. children).

42   Paradoxically, Ash (2020a: pp. 353–354) introduces the object-oriented ontology (OOO) of a speculative realist Tristan Garcia (2014) to resolve his ontological 'difficulty' of differentiating a rifle and a machine gun by focusing on their *surface forms* through a process of de-determination, defined as a matter of removing from our perception of its relation with other objects. But Garcia's (2014) own flat ontology is rather strange as it is negative of/about every*thing*: As Garcia (2014: p. 76) puts it: 'the world is precisely what is not something. The world has no other determination; it is neither material nor spiritual, neither logical nor symbolic, neither metaphysical nor sensible. The world is not something, full stop'.

43   See also Amoore's (2020a) argument for what she terms 'cloud ethics' based on her work on algorithms and artificial intelligence grounded in poststructuralist and posthumanist thought. Adopting a 'fabulatory method', Amoore (2020a: p. 158) argues that 'a cloud ethics engages fabulation in that it does not anchor narrative in the authorial source but rather "digs under stories, cracking them open," so that the reader might enter into the space of the becoming-political of the algorithm. What this means is that one cannot stand outside the algorithm to judge its morality, its role in doing good or evil. Instead, one must begin from the iterative writing that is itself generative of fungible thresholds of the good and the bad'.

44   Writing an entry on *Geschlecht* or sex/gender system for a Marxist dictionary in German, Haraway (1991: p. 131) notes that 'Gender is a concept developed to contest

the naturalization of sexual difference in multiple arenas of struggle. Feminist theory and practice around gender seek to explain and change historical systems of sexual difference, whereby "men" and "women" are socially constituted and positioned in relations of hierarchy and antagonism'.

45  In her early work on dominance and primate studies published in *Signs* in 1978 and reproduced in *Simians, Cyborgs, and Women*, Haraway (1991: p. 23) refers to *feminism* as 'a political position about love and power… [that] can draw from a basic insight of critical theory', from Marx to the Frankfurt school and others. Over four decades later and to Bonnie Honig (2021: p. 3), the term *feminist* 'refers to the project of enacting sex-gender equality, which includes pluralizing sex-gender practices and identities, in the face of governing powers that insist on gender binarism, heteronormative sphere separatism, patriarchal kinship, and the instrumentalities and inequalities they secure'. See also Amoore (2020b) and MacLeavy et al. (2021) for recent reviews of different and overlapping waves of work in feminist geography, including the most recent fourth wave of post-feminism. MacLeavy et al. (2021: p. 1561) note their discomfort with this 'wave-way' of describing feminism's history that comes at a cost of containing feminist scholarship to particular spaces and moments and limiting a more emergent and open-ended futurity of feminist thought and politics.

46  See Elder-Vass (2012: pp. 194–200) for a critique from a realist perspective that accepts the social construction of some aspects of our subjectivity and yet argues for 'a process in which the actors are material human beings with a capacity for agency that arises from their physical nature, and in which those actors are causally influenced by norm circles' (p. 203). In his recent work *Restating Orientalism*, postcolonial critic and Islamic law scholar Wael Hallaq (2018: p. 22) also cautions us the danger of giving language such a kind of metaphysical power that might turn into the totalization of narrative. To him, Edward Said's (2003 [1978]) *Orientalism* has 'effectively subscribed to a theory of discursive formations that gave performativity a metaphysical power. But performativity, today taken to extremes in academic discourse, and used in confusingly different ways, is not a license to accord language an absolute power'. See also Sara Ahmed's (2017: p. 9) caution against 'something we can do simply by learning a new language' quoted earlier.

47  A similar textual interpretive approach was taken by Donna Haraway (1991: ch. 6) when she 'read' Nigerian Buchi Emecheta's novels for 'women's experience'. In her endnotes to the chapter, Haraway (1991: p. 239) points out the usefulness of this kind of speculative reading strategy for feminist theorizing: 'The "particular" in feminist movement is not about liberal individualism nor a despairing isolation of endless differences, much less about rejecting the hope for collective movement. But the means and processes of collective movement must be imagined and acted out in new geometries. That is why I find the reading and writing strategies of SF (speculative fiction, science fiction, science fantasy, speculative feminism) so useful for feminist theorizing'. See also Haraway (2016) for her more recent application of this SF writing strategy to explaining how to live in the Chthulucene (in lieu of the Anthropocene).

48  One such example is Jasbir Puar's (2017) *The Right to Maim* that offers a speculative reimagining of the ontological multiplicity in affirmative becomings such as disability, trans, and racialized debility. Even though Puar builds on Karen Barad's (2007) 'ontological realism' discussed earlier in endnote 39, her poststructuralist reading of

theory and explanation continues to operate primarily at the ontological realm and offers no correctives to the politics of theorizing: 'The focus here is not on epistemological correctives but on ontological irreducibilities that transform the fantasy of discreteness of categories not through their disruption but, rather, through their dissolution via multiplicity. Rather than produce conceptual interventions that map onto the political or produce a differently political rendering of its conceptual moorings, reflected in the debate regarding transnormativity and trans of color conceivability, I wish to offer a generative, speculative reimagining of what can be signaled by the political' (Puar, 2017: p. 36).

49   This reading contrasts rather sharply with MacLeavy et al.'s (2021: pp. 1562, 1573) pessimistic concern with some apocalyptic pronouncements that feminism is yesterday's scholarship and yesterday's politics.

50   This intersection of postcolonial thought in geographical scholarship and 'other' geographies is also evident in Black geographies (Roy et al., 2020; Noxolo, 2022). Through trans-Atlantic epistemological ties between geographers in the UK and North America and the Caribbeans, postcolonial concerns with discursive representations and power relations are animated with black geographers' interest in the unjust origins and continual imprints of slavery, racialized power differentials, and anti-Black policies and practices in contemporary landscapes (e.g. McKittrick, 2006; McKittrick and Woods, 2007; Yusoff, 2018). See also Gilmore (2002), Allen et al. (2019), and Bledsoe (2021) for conceptual and methodological work on Black geographies and, similarly, Weheliye (2014) in Black studies.

51   On postcolonial thought's critique through the deconstruction of colonial texts and palimpsests, Doreen Massey (2005: p. 110) argues in *For Space* that 'while this deconstructive strategy may enable critique of colonial discourses and a pointing towards other voices, other stories for the moment suppressed, its imagery is not one which easily provides resources for bringing those voices to life... The gaps in representation (the erasures, the blind spots) are not the same as the discontinuities of the multiplicity in contemporaneous space; the latter are the mark of the coexistence of the coeval. Deconstruction in this guise seems hampered by its primary focus on "text," however broadly imagined. To picture this argument through the figure of the palimpsest is to stay within the imagination of surfaces – it fails to bring alive the trajectories which co-form this space'.

52   As noted further by Massey (2005), postmodern philosopher Derrida's work on textuality and spatiality as 'the world is like a text' betrays excessive 'horizontalities of deconstruction' such that texts become two-dimensional structures and their horizontal coherence/integrity can be disrupted through deconstruction. To Massey (2005: p. 51; original italics), 'It seems, therefore, ironic – if not downright churlish – to raise any objection. Yet perhaps there is in this formulation (this mind's eye imagination of the intellectual task at hand) *too much* emphasis on the purely horizontal and too little recognition of the multiple trajectories of which that "horizontality" is the momentary, passing, result'. See also a similar critique of Derrida by Bruno Latour (1988) in endnote 5 earlier and by two realist philosophers – DeLanda and Harman (2017: pp. 32–33).

53   See also Gayatri Spivak's (1999: pp. 71–99) deconstruction of Marx's writing on the Asiatic mode of production systems in her *A Critique of Postcolonial Reason*.

54  But as critiqued in Hallaq's (2018: ch. 1) *Restating Orientalism,* there are not only significant historical and geographical confusions in Said's *Orientalism,* but also a serious lack of clear demonstration of how these 'tasks' of the representational mechanism actually work on the colonized Other (e.g. in his ch. 2 'case studies' of how the structure of colonial thought dominated in French Algeria, British India, and Dutch Indonesia). The discursive and material relationships between the Orientalist text and the colonized ground remain underexplored in such postcolonial literary readings of the text rather than due consideration of its relationships with 'worldliness'. In his endnote, Hallaq (2018: endnote 33, p. 275) becomes even more critical of Said's work: 'In fact, *Orientalism*'s Orientals never emerge as real human beings, as mothers, friends, children, laborers, scholars, "organic" intellectuals, peasants, banished and dispossessed communities, or prisoners of various forms of colonial imprisonment… Judging it from the stark reality of colonized space, *Orientalism* may easily come across as an elitist academic work whose concern for the oppressed is driven by the hem and haw of a bourgeois ethic'.

55  To Holbraad and Pedersen (2017: p. 32), 'much of this writing takes the form of ever-novel metaphysical stories about what the world is and how it works – relations replacing entities, processes swallowing up essences, assemblages and networks co-opting subjects and objects, flows and stoppages usurping the metaphysics of presence, only to be trumped by objects that retire into themselves, and so on, in speculative recalibrations of the conceptual armoury of metaphysical thought'.

56  Commenting on the dismal state of (importing) theories in British geography, Massey (2001: p. 13; original italics) loathes that 'in spite of human geography's apparent academic significance in the UK at the moment, and the centrality of debates about space, place, positionality and so forth, an inordinate amount of time is currently spent by research practitioners in the discipline simply importing and retailing authors and approaches from elsewhere… Too little effort is put into thinking through what these theories/theorists have to say to geography specifically and – even more important – what difference it makes *to those theories* to work them through as *geographers.* Of course, some work is being done, but not enough. And this flavour of so much current work both is an index of a (probably unrecognized) feeling of academic inferiority and is – simply – too easy'.

57  I end with an example from postcolonialism. While Sharp (2009: p. 110) has already noted that postcolonial theory 'has a reputation for being very difficult', Tariq Jazeel (2019: p. 131; my emphasis) takes us much further with his confession on reading and teaching postcolonial literary theorist Homi Bhabha's (2004 [1994]) work: 'There is nothing straightforward about this passage (from Bhabha, 2004 [1994]). In fact, I confess that in the years I have been reading and teaching Homi Bhabha's work, the precise meaning of this passage, along with *countless* others in *The Location of Culture,* remain a mystery to me!'. For a British born and educated geographer like Jazeel, this confession from a native English speaker of Sri Lankan ancestry can be quite surprising – much more so than Sidaway's (2000: p. 598) earlier complaint that 'Bhabha's work is notoriously dense – and it does not make for an easy read'. The paragraph in Bhabha (2004 [1994]: p. 129; original italics) refers to his idea on the ambivalence of mimicry (or 'doubling', p. 107): 'Mimicry does not merely destroy narcissistic authority through the repetitious slippage of difference and desire. It is the process of *fixation*

of the colonial as a form of cross classificatory, discriminatory knowledge within an interdictory discourse, and therefore necessarily raises the question of the *authorization* of colonial representations; a question of authority that goes beyond the subject's lack of priority (castration) to a historical crisis in the conceptuality of colonial man [*sic*] as an *object* of regulatory power, as the subject of racial, cultural, national representation'. Somewhat paradoxically, Jazeel (2019: pp. 131–132) later qualifies his reading of Bhabha's work on mimicry as both textual and performative in that it is a form of mimicry and therefore 'a text that undermines the authority of Western philosophy because at times it can appear so complex as to be meaningless… Confusion, befuddlement and frustration at reading Bhabha can very well help us to grasp his thesis'! Having read *The Location of Culture* cover to cover, I am much less sure about it. As a non-English native speaker and a former 'subject' of British colonialism (growing up in colonial Hong Kong and learning ABC at 11 years old after arriving from Guangzhou, China, in 1979), I can only wish you agree with Jazeel's befuddlement and read my book in a similar fashion in order to grasp my thesis! See also my reflection on this matter of linguistic privilege in Chapter 6 endnote 18 and British literary scholar Terry Eagleton's (1996, 2004) critique of the disappearance of politics in many postmodernist and poststructuralist claims. Thanks to one reviewer for pointing out Terry Eagleton's work.

58 To Bhabha (2004 [1994]: p. 6; original italics), 'If the jargon of our times – postmodernity, postcoloniality, postfeminism – has any meaning at all, it does not lie in the popular use of the "post" to indicate sequentiality – *after*-feminism; or polarity – *anti*-modernism. These terms that insistently gesture to the beyond, only embody its restless and revisionary energy if they transform the present into an expanded and ex-centric site of experience and empowerment. For instance, if the interest in postmodernism is limited to a celebration of the fragmentation of the "grand narratives" of postenlightenment rationalism then, for all its intellectual excitement, it remains a profoundly parochial enterprise'.

# Chapter Three
# What Kind of Theory for What Kind of Human Geography?

This chapter represents the first move in my three-step synthetic project towards theory and explanation introduced in Chapter 1 and defines more explicitly the scope of this book – a critical examination of the nature of explanatory theory and why it matters in human geography today. Grounded in Chapter 2's critically generous reading of different approaches in human geography and their diverse conceptions of theory, this chapter argues for a particular kind of theory *and* explanation in contemporary geographical enquiry that might serve as a potential focal point for rethinking theorizing in Geography and our contributions to theory in social science. Avoiding excessive ontological lock-ins and overemphasis on openness and contingency in certain philosophical thoughts underpinning these approaches, I expand on an epistemological position that views theory not only as an abstract representational device or a rhetorical-descriptive apparatus, but more importantly also as a causal explanation of socio-spatial change and outcome. Here, I emphasize the importance of causal mechanism in such a kind of *explanatory theory* because broadly speaking, all explanations of social change in a material world can be causal explanations (Schatzki, 2019: p. 118). This productive-relational view of causality requires causal explanations to specify their attendant mechanisms in relation to general processes *and* the operating contexts of these mechanisms in relation to historical and geographical contingency.

In the chapter's first section, my epistemology for what might be termed 'analytical geographies' entails a normative position in which causal explanations are viewed as the necessary step towards socially relevant geographical research. It contends

*Theory and Explanation in Geography*, First Edition. Henry Wai-chung Yeung.

that socio-spatial interventions can be better served if we have a clearer sense of *why* and *how* causal mechanisms interact with contingent contexts to produce heterogeneous events and uneven outcomes in society and space. Without this explanatory clarity of causal mechanisms at work, how do we know if our advocacy for difference and change on behalf of the marginalized, the underprivileged, and the exploited can lead to meaningful societal outcomes and better futures for us all?[1] I am not entirely convinced that unpacking theoretical categories and understanding their epistemological positionalities and constitutions in some critical approaches discussed in Chapter 2 can go beyond immanent or even ambivalent critiques and self-reflexivity to offer concrete explanations of socio-spatial change and outcomes. While it is useful to think about, contextualize, situate, explore, interrogate, examine, and empathize with specific subjects, subjectivities, and socio-spatial phenomena, these analytical procedures are ultimately insufficient and practically inadequate in explaining and changing uneven and unjust socio-spatial realities.

Arguing for a normative (re)turn in social theory, Sayer and Storper (1997: p. 6; my emphasis) thus remark that 'Workers may not need Marx to know they are exploited and women may not need feminism to know that they are subordinated, but we are likely to need theory to know *how* and *why* these things come about'. As noted in Chapter 2 earlier and to be fair to both Marxism and feminist theory, there is no reason why their key concepts, such as over-determination, embodiment, and intersectionality, cannot be couched in terms of conjunctural causal mechanisms within an explanatory theory to account for how and why female workers are so badly exploited and subordinated in the context of highly variegated capitalisms and patriarchies differentiated by place-specific attributes (e.g. in the Global South). Moving away from their ontological straightjackets, such a pragmatic epistemological approach to theory and explanation should allow geographers to fulfil all three key considerations introduced in Chapter 1: normative theorizing, context-specificity, and practical adequacy.

While my analytical procedure may be necessary but not sufficient in its own right towards achieving positive social change, it can complement other productive modes of critical enquiries, such as critiques, (re)thinking, and descriptive accounts. Taking cues from my recent work (Yeung, 2019a, 2019b) and some sympathetic critics (e.g. Strauss, 2019; Whiteside, 2019), this chapter's second section discusses the practical adequacy of *mid-range theories* in this epistemology for analytical geographies that compels us to revisit some of the earlier philosophical thoughts in critical realism, speculative realism, poststructuralism, and post-phenomenology (see Table 2.1). While these thoughts are not mutually commensurable in terms of their ontologies, they do have varying things to say about this mode of mechanism-based theorizing and relational thinking.

Drawing upon the well-developed literature in sociology, political science, and the philosophy of social science on mechanism-based thinking, I explain why and how mid-range theories can accommodate both causal explanations and interpretive accounts advocated in those seemingly incompatible philosophical tracts and critical approaches. Without committing to the hackneyed choice of either explanation or description in our critical interpretations of empirical events in different socio-spatial worlds, I believe such mid-range theorizing based on causal explanations can enable the kind of critical human geography that understands and explains better individual experiences and collective action (re)shaping social formations in different places and across diverse spaces. As pointed out in Chapter 1's last section on chapter outlines, this gesturing towards modest theory and explanation is not new and has been at least implicitly practised by many geographers. This epistemological work in Geography also should not be left to 'theory-heads' in our discipline because it would otherwise contradict the kind of geographical exceptionalism among different social science disciplines (see Chapter 1 introduction). Geographers should indeed integrate our theory work with regular methodological and empirical investigations in different subfields. What the following sections do is to integrate this existing practice by such geographers with cutting-edge work done by other social scientists on mid-range theorizing and mechanism-based causal explanations. This consolidation in turn allows for a clearer and more consistent epistemology towards modest theory and explanation in the practice of analytical geographies.

## Analytical Geographies: Theory and Explanation in Geography

I opened this book with David Harvey's (1969) positivist conception of theory and echoed his overall argument that Geography is defined by our theories. When we study a particular geographical phenomenon, we can describe it in detail and with much empirical accuracy, much like the heydays of regional geography prior to the so-called 'quantitative revolution' in the 1960s (Barnes and Farish, 2006; Barnes, 2011; see also Table 2.1). Theory was not the core concern then in regional geography; accurate and comprehensive description was. Equally, we can re-present the pattern(s) and process(es) of this geographical phenomenon in stylized models and theories that abstract their essence from the empirical details or 'mess', much like what the young Harvey (1969: p. 486) was advocating as 'controlled, consistent, and rational, explanation of events'. In these positivist models and formal theories, causal explanations are often couched in terms of *sequential occurrence* such that for A (initial condition) to be a logical explanation of B (specific outcome), it must precede B in empirical events. To Harvey (1969: pp. 46–47), this a priori reduction of explanation to variation in the Humean laws of mechanics is a 'mechanical' or 'mechanistic' explanation.

My epistemological approach towards analytical geographies is certainly very different from young Harvey's Comtean positivist law-based epistemology that championed the so-called deductive-nomological or universal 'covering law' model of *scientific explanation* made famous by philosophers of science such as Carl Hempel (1942, 1965).[2] In this kind of analytical geographies, causal explanation is both necessary and important for understanding *why* and *how* socio-spatial phenomena take place. But such explanation cannot be based on Humean law-like 'mechanical' regularities in empirical events and sequences as often found in scientific explanation. Explanation in analytical geographies must be based on carefully theorized causal mechanism(s) that specifies both the *agency* and *pathway*(s) for 'making things happen' in these socio-spatial events and phenomena – the causal powers of agency generate answers to the 'why' question and the pathways or mechanisms through which these powers produce outcomes help address the 'how' question. The empirical operation of this analytical explanation must also be grounded in contextual contingencies and place-based specificities in a social world characterized by complexity, multiplicity, and emergence.[3]

This more 'open systems' view of explanation in analytical geographies fundamentally disrupts and deviates from the above covering law model of explanation based on constant empirical conjunctions or invariant regularities of events. Analytical geographies demands a kind of mechanism-based explanation in socio-spatial context that is inherently different from Harvey's (1969) regularity-based 'mechanical' explanation derived from Humean theory of causal laws. This rethinking of explanation in analytical geographies also echoes a similar call for new directions in the philosophy of social science. As philosopher Daniel Little (2018: pp. 420–421) reflects recently on Hempel's deductive-nomological model of scientific explanation,

> Seventy years after Hempel's, 1942 classic article, the covering-law theory is now generally regarded as a fundamentally wrong-headed way of thinking about historical (and social) explanation. Logical positivism is not a convenient lens through which to examine the social and historical sciences. There is too much contingency in the social world. Rather than being the result of law-governed processes, social outcomes proceed from the contingent and historically variable features of the actors and situations who make them. So the attention of many researchers interested in specifying the nature of historical and social explanation has focused on social mechanisms constituted and driven by common features of agency. This results in a different kind of explanation: accounts of particular episodes that shed light on the causal processes that appear to have been involved in their production, but no general accounts of large-scale historical patterns or outcomes.

In Chapter 2, I briefly reviewed how different critical approaches since structural Marxism have considered agency, relationality, process, and contingency in their ontological accounts in the name of 'theory'. Some of these 'theories' have also placed some emphasis on causality (e.g. assemblage theory and post-phenomenology), whereas others are less oriented towards explanation and more in favour of descriptive and/or interpretive accounts (e.g. actor-network theory, non-representational theory, feminist theory, and postcolonial theory). Overall, causality in these critical approaches tends to be vague and indeterminant due to their flat ontologies and/or commitment to heterogeneous associations and multiplicities in subject relations and identity formations. Many of these processual 'theories' are also not explanatory enough because they often merely describe empirical events or happenings without giving credence to the underlying reasons why and how these events take place in society and space – representing a form of radical empiricism (Bridge, 2021; Lury, 2021).

Despite my recognition of multiplicities and heterogeneity in these 'open-ended' approaches, I do not accept their explicit or implicit denial of the importance of explanation in theory. Echoing sociologist Richard Swedberg's (2014: pp. 17, 98) vision for the art of social theory and political theorist Jon Elster's (2015: p. 8) causal conception of social science explanation, I argue for a kind of analytical geographies committed to developing theory *and* explanation (and thus the title of this book). In this normative stance, theory should be explanatory and should identify mechanisms at work within specific contexts or open systems in the social world. As made clear by realist philosopher Roy Bhaskar (2016: p. 50; my emphasis) in *Enlightened Common Sense*, theory of our socio-spatial world is meant to be explanatory and not predictive as in the natural sciences:

> Closed systems cannot be established artificially in the human world [unlike laboratories in science]. But this does not mean that one cannot identify generative mechanisms at work in specific contexts or construct theoretical generalisations for them; or that there are no criteria for theory choice or development, or that there are no empirical controls on theory. Rather, it follows from the absence of closed systems that criteria for choice and development of theory will be *explanatory*, not predictive, and that empirical controls will turn on the extent to which events indicate or reveal the presence of structures.[4]

Nevertheless, I do not intend this kind of explanatory theory to represent the universe of all possible theories – that would suffer from 'Hume's guillotine' or the severing of 'is' from 'ought' in epistemology described in Whiteside (2019: p. 267). My approach to theory and explanation also inadvertently has less to say about discursive (de)constructions, identity politics, and subjective representations that are much better addressed in some of those critical approaches in human geography. But my mechanism-based conception of causality and explanatory theory does address a key epistemological blind-spot in these critical 'theories' that presumably survive 'Hume's guillotine' not by challenging it, but by denying the social reality in which the Humean positivist execution takes place, i.e. the dominance of such unquestionable 'science thinking' in today's uneven world. In the following two sub-sections, I elaborate further the nature of developing theory in relation to concepts and the nature of explanation arising from such theory development.

## *From Concepts to Theories*

In the social sciences and humanities, concepts are the basic building blocks of all theories, irrespective of whether we conceive of theory as simply a statement explaining a phenomenon (Swedberg, 2014: p. 17), an organized and patterned set of ideas (Cresswell, 2013: p. 7), or a way of knowing and being (Aitken and Valentine, 2015b: p. 8).[5] Table 3.1 offers a summary of these differences between concept and theory. Concepts are necessary to theory development, but in themselves insufficient in constituting a theory. Through a coherent set of statements, a theory elaborates on the necessary relationships between its constitutive concepts and the phenomenon for which the theory is developed. This theoretical elaboration can be descriptive, interpretive, explanatory, normative, and even predictive. In an explanatory theory, these necessary relationships are often couched in *causal* terms such that its underlying concept(s) contributes to explaining the causal pathway(s) or mechanism(s) for a likely outcome and phenomenon occurring in society and space. But most importantly, it is the theory that does the causal explanation, not its constitutive concept(s). Even if a theory is not explanatory in its gestures, such as those descriptive or interpretive 'theories' reviewed in Chapter 2, it is still constituted by some necessary concepts to make it 'theoretical' and abstract in prose and appearance.

**Table 3.1** Concepts and theories in analytical geographies.

| | Concept | Theory |
|---|---|---|
| Definition | An abstraction in thought | A set of explanatory statements comprising one or more concepts |
| Nature | A linguistic shorthand – sometimes value-laden – for observable or unobservable social entities and empirical reality | Elaboration of causal pathways and necessary relationships between constitutive concepts and empirical phenomenon |
| Purpose | Descriptive representation of a more complex phenomenon | (Partial) Understanding of why and how empirical events or phenomena take place |
| Components | Keywords, but not necessarily simple nor easy | Concepts, causal mechanisms, analytical pathways |
| Common appearance | One or more keywords (but less than five!) | A few paragraphs or pages devoted to something with 'theory' in its name (suspicious if it becomes a whole book or multiple books!) |
| Examples | *Observable concept*: cluster, family, market, racism, the body, the state, social network<br>*Unobservable concept*: affect, assemblage, embeddedness, globalization, homonationalism, lifeworld, patriarchy, bodily regime, class consciousness, institutional thickness, relational geometry, strategic coupling, accumulation by dispossession, line of flight, spatial division of labour | Wanted! Mid-range theories to be developed... (see Chapter 6 for an example of the theory of global production networks) |

Simply put then, concepts are abstractions of observable and, more often, unobservable social entities and/or phenomena of sufficient significance to theory construction and everyday life. As abstractive devices often in no more than just a few words, they are linguistic terms representational of these social entities and phenomena in order to render them intelligible to human understanding. Since concepts are developed by humans who invest time and resources to 'conceptualize' diverse entities and phenomena in society and space, they are both linguistic and value-laden in nature; they can sometimes be for laughs too that might come with hallucinatory experiences and make for a good 'nomadic' read![6] The descriptive meanings of concepts can vary in relation to the different contexts and locales in which they are developed, utilized, and understood. Some well-known concepts of observable social entities and/or phenomena are labour, family, firm, cluster (or agglomeration), terrain, or civil war. But affect, gender, intersectionality, belonging, embeddedness, territory, democracy, globalization, or even capitalism are much less observable, except that we can empirically observe their imprints and/or embodiment in our everyday experience and practice.

In short, a concept is derived through representational abstraction, but it does not explain in its own right; that explanatory role/power is fulfilled by a particular kind of theory known as *explanatory theory*. Given the central role of concepts in the development of all kinds of theories, it seems critical and imperative that a concept should be good. But what is a good concept and how do we know if we find or 'meet' one? This apparently simple question is actually rather difficult to answer. To some, a good concept is one that seems scholarly, abstract, or even dressed up in jargon-laden terminology. To others, a concept is good insofar as it is practically adequate for theory development and/or empirical research.[7] In *Living a Feminist Life*, feminist Sara Ahmed (2017: pp. 12–13) notes that concepts can even be 'sweaty' because of their usefulness for describing an unfolding situation and their being-in-the-worlds we are in, i.e. their connections with our embodied (sweaty) experiences.

In human geography, Andrew Sayer (1992: p. 138, 2010 [1992/1984]: p. 93) has made the most explicit and useful distinction of a good concept from a 'chaotic' concept. To him, the 'goodness' of a concept depends critically on its necessary relation with the phenomenon under investigation and its representation for descriptive, interpretive, or explanatory purposes. A chaotic conception happens when a bad or incoherent abstraction takes place by dividing an indivisible entity or conflating different and separable entities in a phenomenon. What appears to be a seemingly 'good' concept because of its abstract and jargon-laden terminology can still be a chaotic or a 'fuzzy' concept if its necessary relation with the referential phenomenon is missing or mis-specified.[8] Conversely, a good concept needs not be difficult or esoteric; it can be simple and straightforward in its analytical necessity vis-à-vis the entities of a phenomenon in society and space. As well argued by feminist philosopher Martha Nussbaum (2000: p. 23) in *Women and Human Development*, theory 'involves the systematization and critical scrutiny of thoughts and perceptions that in daily life are frequently jumbled and unexamined. For this task theory needs overarching analytical concepts that may not be familiar in daily conversation, although the theorist should be able to show that they correspond to reality and help us scrutinize it'.

Moving on from concepts to theories, we can distinguish different theories in relation to their composition of key concepts and their necessary or even causal relationships with the same or different socio-spatial phenomena. In his text on geographical thought, Tim Cresswell (2013) prefers a rather broad and all-inclusive conception of theory as a 'lens' to interpret messy reality. While I support his argument that theory should not be just spur-of-the-moment thoughts, I do find difficulty in his reference to theory throughout the text as almost any set of organized ideas and knowledge about the world by geographers – from Strabo of Amasia (64 BC–AD 23) and Ptolomy to all sorts of critical approaches and his own journey with developing theory as a kind of 'toolbox' for understanding place and mobility.[9] Without some sensible yardsticks, how do we tell if one set of organized ideas is helpful and good? In Chapter 1, I introduced the idea of practical adequacy as a key consideration of/for theory. Here, I argue further that a theory's constitutive concept(s) also matters much to its practical adequacy. Organized ideas might not be good concepts if their necessary relationships with empirical phenomena are not well conceptualized and specified. Just because some ideas are organized as a set of thought and knowledge does not mean they are good concepts nor theories. These ideas may be chaotic and their ensuring organized set or 'theory' may also be practically inadequate in addressing major societal challenges.

While it is not realist(ic) to expect this book to resolve the much larger 'unresolvable problem' of ontological incompatibilities in critical human geography identified in Chapter 2, I believe explanatory power, i.e. how well does a theory explain empirical outcomes?, can still be a useful way to evaluate a theory's practical adequacy. This concern with theory's explanatory power means that theory cannot simply be a kind of toolbox wherein we find particular sets of ideas for understanding the social world, defined by Cresswell (2013: p. 196) as the 'more pragmatic, approach [that] appears to be the main way of doing theory in twenty-first-century geography'. Although understanding the richness of individual experience is important and can be achieved through certain geographical approaches (e.g. humanistic geography,[10] non-representational theory, post-phenomenology, and posthumanism in Table 2.1 and Chapter 2), I wonder if these approaches to understanding everyday life and meanings necessarily precludes the possibility for such experiences as meanings, feelings, senses, emotions, affect, and performativity, to be *explained* – why and how do individuals and subjects feel and experience in particular ways?

I am also sceptical of the counter-argument that such explanation will always be reductionist, essentializing, or even generalizing. Indeed, any form of abstraction through concept-formation and theory development inevitably leads to the reduction of the richness of individual experiences. Explaining human feelings and experiences in an explanatory theory entails a reasonably 'causal' approach, i.e. what causes such feelings/experiences by individuals and groups in society and space. But such a reductionist presumption should not be an excuse or a blanket ontological cover for a kind of descriptive empiricism paying no heed whatsoever to any normative, conceptual, ideological, or practical obligations that might make us better human beings because of that explanatory understanding (see earlier discussion of such key considerations in Chapter 1).

Taken together, critical human geography must go beyond radical empiricism and descriptive interpretations to develop theory for the causal analysis of human action and practices that matter not only in our everyday life(worlds) and understanding, but also in (re)producing more equal and more just social-spatial consequences. In this kind of analytical geographies, theory development needs to be grounded in good concepts that are causally necessary to explaining human practices and social-spatial outcomes. While never meant to be fully universal nor grand and comprehensive enough to be a strong 'theory of everything', explanatory theory is more than the sort of 'modest theory' with a lighter touch in non-representational theory,[11] 'weak theory' in conceptualizing affect and emotions,[12] or descriptive 'theory' not intended for explanation, as in actor-network theory (cf. Elder-Vass, 2008, 2010). Striving for practical adequacy, this kind of theory is also necessarily concerned with causal powers in explanation, perhaps much more so than the epistemological interests of such ideologically-oriented approaches as feminist theory in unpacking gender performativity and postcolonial theory in the politics of representation.[13]

## From Theory to Explanation in Geography

To some critics, this pathway to theory might be construed as not engaging due to its perceived irreconcilablility with those social constructivist and ideologically-oriented approaches reviewed in Chapter 2. But how can such an engagement, pluralistic or otherwise, be possible if this irreconcilablility has been assumed a priori? This view does not seem to be a fair and reciprocal demand for constructive engagement. Echoing realist philosopher Markus Gabriel's (2015: ch. 12) call in *Fields of Sense* for epistemological pluralism (note: not epistemological relativism),[14] I remain committed to the call for more constructive dialogues and the plea for a diverse set of ideas and practices for theory if geographers were to advance our socially relevant agenda. Indeed, explanatory theory is never meant to be the *only* set of ideas and practices. Rather, it serves as an underlabourer for geographers interested in causal explanations and, hopefully, sheds some light on what might work better in such an endeavour.

To me, explanatory theory represents a modest epistemological contribution and a pragmatic form of immanent critique towards analytical geographies. Revisiting

*Explanation in Geography*, this explicitly explanatory and yet contextualized kind of theory seeks to address Harvey's (1969: p. 481; original italics) warning of geographers 'spiralling off into heady abstraction only to land with an uncomfortable thud on the *terra firma* of geographical reality'. Indeed, this heady abstraction devoid of the richness of geographical reality is as prevalent in *some* quarters of today's critical human geography as in the heydays of positivist formal models then – their practitioners often did not exercise adequate control of the sort of 'intellectual trampoline' offered by Harvey and others. So his warning of an uncomfortable thud of hard handing on *terra firma* remains as valid today! Despite the inherent limits to our knowledge production, my sense is that we need more robust causal explanations of an ever more complex and uneven geographical reality. Such explanatory theory represents only one critical step towards the lofty goal of accounting for the enormous complexities of uneven and unjust socio-spatial outcomes. As pointed out by Doreen Massey (1995: p. 323; original italics) sometime ago in her reflections on debates over a decade since her 1984 *Spatial Divisions of Labour*, 'It *is* possible to unearth by in-depth analysis key causal relations, including combinations, which may be replicated, even dominant, in numbers of situations. It is perhaps this approach, rather than a formulation of rules, which will be most productive'.[15]

In practice, developing a kind of theory that is explanatory requires us to pay far greater attention to the *varieties of explanation* in our epistemologies. Indeed, explanation has a long history of being debated within philosophical writings, let alone other works on method in science and social science. But as noted by philosopher of science Richard Fumerton (2018: p. 65), it is not easy to figure out what an explanation is![16] It ranges from interpretive explanation to correlational or statistical explanation and causal explanation (Little, 1991, 2016; Hedström, 2005; Glennan, 2017). To me, analytical geographies requires theories that provide causal explanations in context. This search for causal explanation is also well supported by recent work in the philosophy of science and social science. In *Inference to the Best Explanation*, philosopher of science Peter Lipton (2004 [1991]) outlines five popular accounts of explanation – reason, familiarity, deduction, unification, and necessity, and concludes that a sixth account – his causal view of explanation – is most promising (see also Manicas, 2006; Schatzki, 2019: pp. 119–121).[17]

Still, I reject the kind of blanket 'explanationism' in scientific method and scientific realism that does not allow for sceptical challenges to its basic notion that explanatory reasoning is fundamentally more justifying than other forms of reasoning, such as description, deduction, and prediction, by the so-called 'inference to the best explanation' (see McCain and Poston, 2018). For Lipton (2004 [1991]: p. 1), such inferential practices of inductive reasoning refer to the idea that 'our explanatory considerations guide our inferences. Beginning with the evidence available to us, we infer what would, if true, provide the best explanation of that evidence'. To him, several attributes can increase what he terms 'loveliness' or the 'potential explanatoriness' of an explanation: simplicity, unification, scope, precision, and the giving of a mechanism.[18] In analytical geographies, I see the last attribute 'the giving of a mechanism' as an important and critical step in developing *social* explanations of both *observable* and, often, *unobservable* phenomena that need not necessarily be termed 'the best' explanations as in scientific method. I concur with Lipton's 'loveliness' argument for mechanism-based causal explanation that might be relevant for a contrastive and comparative approach in analytical geographies.

While I will examine the nature of such causal mechanisms in the next section, suffice to reiterate here practice philosopher Theodore Schatzki's (2019: p. 118) argument in *Social Change in A Material World* that all explanations are causal explanations on a sufficiently broad sense of 'causal', following Aristotle's efficient causality of 'what brings that event about'.[19] Taking this notion of an 'efficient cause' further in *Assemblage Theory*, realist philosopher Manuel DeLanda (2016; also DeLanda and Harman, 2017: pp. 18–20) argues in his Deleuzian assemblage theory grounded in a realist ontology that singularities can characterize efficient causes as varying from one phenomenon to the next because

> singularities define a tendency in *mechanism-independent* terms, but we also need to specify the causal mechanisms that implement those tendencies in actual cases, and these will vary from case to case. This divergent relation between problems and their solutions also has epistemological consequences: if the same singularity can be actualised as a tendency in two very different phenomena, then it may also become actual as a tendency in the behaviour of solutions to an equation (DeLanda, 2016: pp. 179-180; original italics).

Simply put, explanation needs causal connections as its necessary condition of explanatory loveliness and practical adequacy. To realist philosopher Peter Manicas (2006: p. 20; original italics), 'Explanation, like understanding, requires that there is a "real connection," a generative mechanism or causal nexus that produced or brought about the event (or pattern) to be explained. A causal relation presupposes a *nomic* and *necessary* connection. We need not balk at this'.[20] Echoing philosophers of science and social science's arguments for causal explanation in Woodward (2003), Glennan (2017), and Schatzki (2019), this book supports the kind of causal explanation that is neither too general as all-embracing (i.e. grand theories) nor too descriptive (i.e. lacking causality) because such causal explanation is necessary for theory building. In this case, philosopher of science James Woodward's (2003: p. 5) notion that generality in explanation is not always a virtue makes good sense.[21]

In *Making Things Happen*, Woodward (2003: pp. 6–7) theorizes causal explanations as those in which the underlying relationships (the value of 'variables' in his term or 'causal mechanisms' in my view) can be subject to manipulation and control. To him, this 'manipulationist' conception of causal explanation has the advantages of:

1.  fitting a wide range of contexts especially those in the social and behavioural sciences;

2.  exhibiting an intuitively appealing underlying rationale or goal for explanation and the discovery of causal relationships because of their potentially exploitability through manipulation and control; and

3.  differentiating from correlationist accounts of causality, i.e. claims about correlations in causal relationships that do not reflect their direct causal connections (see also my further discussion of 'correlationism' in Chapter 4).

Causal explanations allow us to do things with them and, in doing so, 'making things happen' through our interventions in politics and practices (cf. the 'so what' question often raised in relation to other kinds of explanations and accounts in critical approaches reviewed in Chapter 2). But to ensure the validity of causal explanations, the underlying necessary causal relationships should be manipulatable such that their absence or alternations *might* (not 'must' in the sense of Humean generalized laws in the natural sciences) lead to different outcomes in diverse contexts. This 'might' in causality refers to the possibility of counterfactuality in answering the what-if-things-had-been-different question and thus the possibility of these causal relationships rendered knowable through such counterfactual thinking and explanations.

While causal relationships (might) exist in nature and society, 'discovering' them is a human-manipulative practice and *explanation* that is causal in nature requires distinctive epistemic interventions such as the kind of theorizing and empirical research examined in this book. But why should we be bothered with causal explanation and knowledge? To both philosophers of science James Woodward (2003: p. 30) and Stuart Glennan (2017: ch. 8), these causal explanations offer practical payoffs because more normative interventions are possible with such explanatory knowledges. But prediction is not what causal explanations are about – predicting future outcomes are not the inherent value of causal explanations nor causal theories. Prediction can be done via knowledge of Bayesian probability-based correlations alone without causal enquiry. As such, we do not need to know *why* certain things happen in order to predict *when* they will happen again – a good artificial intelligence-driven model can do so quite easily nowadays! But we do need causal explanations of these happenings to make sure they will not likely happen again or they will happen differently again. This is only possible if we exploit our causal knowledge to intervene successfully in the underlying relationships of these happenings.

Clearly, the search for good theories by inference to the best explanation remains elusive even in the natural sciences. To me, explanatory reasoning in the social sciences is but one form, albeit a very important one, of abductive and inductive accounts of human beliefs, activities and events, and socio-spatial changes. In analytical geographies, there is no fundamental truth and transcendental reality to be explained. Rather, there are pragmatic and realistic explanations of particular happenings and events in society and space – they might not be the 'best' and the most unfalsifiable in a scientific epistemological sense (e.g. rationalism and logic thinking), but they are practically adequate, and perhaps even partial, in normative terms (see Chapter 1's discussion of key considerations). This sort of explanation I seek is similar to philosophers of science Kareem Khalifa et al.'s (2018: p. 84) notion of 'explanatory pluralism' through what they term 'thick bundles' of relations, some of which are not necessarily explanatory (e.g. representation, prediction, analogy, and embedding). In the next section, I will examine a particular kind of theory – mid-range theories – that might help advance analytical geographies through mechanism-based causal explanations.

## Mid-Range Theories: Critical Realism, Causal Mechanisms, and Relational Thinking

I have so far argued for the importance of theory and explanation in analytical geographies. This kind of mechanism-based causal theory of the social world does not necessitate the sort of scientific empirical objectivity and closed systems to operate insofar as we are not aiming for universal laws and predictive models. Appreciating the importance of open systems and contingent contexts, I recognize a certain degree of uncertainty in our causal explanations, and yet an interpretation by the researcher (not necessarily objective due to one's situated knowledge and positionality!) can be judged on the basis of its practical adequacy, i.e. better than existing explanations in the service of positive social change. This pragmatic approach to theory and explanation is likely more adequate than the processual thinking in several critical approaches reviewed in Chapter 2. Whereas these approaches are often as, if not more, sensitive to geographical variations and historical contexts in their theorization of the diverse processes of socio-spatial practices and change at multiple scales, many of them take theorizing processes and relations as their starting *and* ending points and proceed to identify a plethora of influences, conditions, multiplicities, and interactions. Most of them do not entail detailed specification of causal mechanisms to make these processes and their relationality 'work' genuinely in effecting socio-spatial changes, leading to vague explanations comprising fuzzy or even chaotic concepts. This missing 'work-out' of processes and relationality in turn explains why mechanism-based explanations in theory development are both necessary and complementary to such processual and/or relational thinking in critical human geography (see more discussion in Chapter 4; also Ylikoski and Kuorikoski, 2010; Pozzoni and Kaidesoja, 2021).

Avoiding the unrealistic search for grand theories and all-inclusive explanations of social worlds, this section argues for a kind of *mid-range theories* that are more amenable to this renewed effort towards contextualized causal explanations in critical human geography. The idea of mid-range theory has its early origin in sociologist Robert Merton's (1968 [1949]) influential work on the nature of social theory. In *Social Theory and Social Structure*, Merton (1968 [1949]: p. 39) argues that mid-range theories (or what he calls 'middle-range theory') are 'theories that lie between the minor but necessary working hypotheses that evolve in abundance during day-to-day research and the all-inclusive systematic efforts to develop a unified theory that will explain all the observed uniformities of social behavior, social organization and social change'.[22] In Chapter 2, Marx's theory of capital is a unified theory of whole social systems (see more examples in Little, 2016: pp. 186–190). One may reasonably consider some of the critical 'theories', such as actor-network theory and assemblage theory, as such unified theories if they were actually theories rather than methods.

More recently in *Society and Economy*, sociologist Mark Granovetter (2017: pp. 14–15) similarly advocates a meso-level framework for explaining human action embedded in concrete and ongoing systems of social relations because these 'networks of relations constitute a crucial meso level lying conceptually between individual action and social institutions and cultures, and the way these micro and macro levels are linked through this meso level is a central focus of interest here'. In his theoretical analysis of social norms as elements in larger conceptual constructions, Granovetter argues that meso-level conceptions can serve as critical mechanisms mediating small-scale regularities (e.g. norms) and large-scale patterns (e.g. social change). Without a careful analysis of these mediating mechanisms, he notes further, we face the most difficult analytical problem of understanding how social constructions influence individual behaviour and action in social systems.

In analytical geographies concerned with mechanism-based causal explanations, unified and all-inclusive theories simply do not make sense because causal mechanisms can only be particular to the phenomena in hand and their operations are efficacious in specific socio-spatial contexts. There are thus no such things as universal or all-inclusive causal mechanisms. Mid-range theories addressing specific empirical phenomena and yet broad enough to apply across a wide range of socio-spatial settings are most preferred and practically adequate for my purpose of key considerations of/for theory in Chapter 1. Going beyond micro-level accounts of individual action, affect, event, or practice, these mid-range theories are constitutive of meso-level causation and explanations of recurring events or changes in social groups and institutions that can be theoretically specified and empirical validated (see more in Chapters 4 and 5). Over time, our core theoretical knowledge comprises a heterogeneous collection of causal mechanism schemas that can be adapted to particular situations and explanatory tasks.[23] I believe the development of a growing collection of mutually compatible causal mechanisms and mid-range theories of socio-spatial phenomena can help counter the excessive fragmentation in contemporary human geography and its multitude of approaches and concepts examined in Chapter 2. It can also better enable geographers to connect with, and contribute to, the development of social-scientific knowledge.[24]

As noted in Chapter 1 on important caveats (and endnote 12), causality and mechanisms are of most interest to realist thought and their related critical approaches in Table 2.1, whether it is the earlier philosophy of critical realism (and Marxism) since the mid-1970s or the more recent iteration in speculative realism (and assemblage theory) since the early 2000s. Despite recent interest in such realist thought in critical human geography (Allen, 2012; Cox, 2013a; Sayer, 2015; Yeung, 2019a), I certainly do not advocate a blanket return to critical realism as the guiding philosophy for human geography nor its reinvigoration as the only way forward in resolving Geography's alleged legitimation crisis. In a more modest way, this section draws upon realist thought to buttress my theory of mechanism as necessary relations for empirical outcomes and my call for explanatory theory in analytical geographies. As noted in Chapter 1 (and endnote 16), the role of (realist) philosophy is to serve as an underlabourer and an occasional midwife to social science. The precise practice of social scientific enquiry, including theory development, rests with social scientists. It is therefore important to acknowledge that realist thought appreciates the possibility of philosophical discourses contingent upon the actuality of social practices. While it does not tell us the precise form of mechanisms for a given empirical phenomenon, critical realism does recognize that some *real* mechanisms must exist for our explanatory theory development to be possible and relevant for making a difference in real-world changes.[25] The following two subsections specify the kind of realist thought most productive for the development of causal theory before examining what causal mechanisms might look like in mid-range theories.

## *What Realism – Critical and/or Speculative?*

Ever since the major works by Roy Bhaskar (1975, 1986, 1989), Andrew Sayer (1984, 1992), and others in the 1980s and thereafter, critical realism has emerged as an influential philosophy *for* the social sciences.[26] Human geography is no exception, with many geographers explicitly or implicitly practising realist research in their work (see geographical reviews in Pratt, 1995, 2009; Yeung, 1997; Roberts, 2001; Mäki et al., 2004; Cox, 2013a; Sayer, 2015, 2018). Many early 'adopters' of critical realism named in Cox's (2013a) reprise remain as the most influential human geographers today. Even though they no longer make explicit reference to critical realism in their current work, I argue that their thought has often implicitly internalized some realist ontological claims (e.g. existence of reality independent of human ideas) and certain elements of realist methodology (e.g. abstraction and intensive research). This continual relevance of realist thought will be more evident in the next two chapters when I examine relational theory and causal explanation in human geography.

Since its heyday during the 1980s and the early 1990s, however, critical realism has seemingly gone out of favour in human geography during the 21st century, to the extent that Cox (2013a: p. 3) declares 'In human geography today one hears very little about critical realism' – a silence much akin to Manuel DeLanda's 'child molester' metaphor for any self-acknowledged realist (quoted in Chapter 1 endnote 12)! This might be attributed to the rise of the 'cultural turn' in human geography in general (Thrift and Olds, 1996; Barnett, 1998; Castree, 2002; Allen, 2012), represented in Chapter 2 by a multitude of ontological and epistemological shifts *towards* relationally understanding and critically interrogating the discursive (de)constructions and performativity of subject identities, positionalities, and representations in the (co)constitution of society and space, and *away* from critical realists' preoccupation with uncovering causal mechanisms for explaining empirical phenomena.[27]

Pratt (2013: p. 28) further attributes this (cultural) turn – away from critical realism – to the 'faddishness' of human geography and the ever-increasing turnover in the 'market in ideas' in search of the next 'big idea'. Departing from radical Marxist geography in which critical realism exerted its greatest influence during the 1980s and through to the mid-1990s, the debate in human geography has since moved on to engage with trenchant critiques from poststructuralist, feminist, and postcolonial interventions discussed in Chapter 2 (cf. Sayer, 2001; Storper, 2001). In geographical debates on urban and regional economies, for example, critical realist geographers have switched gear to focus more on institutional approaches (Amin, 2001a; Peck and Tickell, 2002; Cox, 2004; Storper, 2009), relational analyses (Bathelt and Glückler, 2003, 2014; Yeung, 2005, 2009b, 2016; cf. Sunley, 2008), and evolutionary conceptions (Martin and Sunley, 2006; Grabher, 2009) of urban and regional economic change. Nevertheless, the influence of realist thought and methodology on these geographers remains significant, particularly among those concerned with causal explanations of urban and regional change. Against the backdrop of those faddish turns, certain elements of realist thought continue to be taken explicitly or implicitly in their empirical research. In the wider social sciences though, critical realism has gone in the opposite direction. It has actually grown its presence since the 2000s in several disciplines, such as analytical sociology, heterodox economics, and political science, and become more institutionalized as a leading philosophy of social science.[28]

While the enormous corpus of realist work since the 1970s cannot be easily reconciled and integrated, Table 3.2 summarizes three key strands of realist thought in natural science, social science, and the humanities. Here, I focus on *critical realism* and *speculative realism* that was first introduced in Chapter 1 (section on important caveats) and further elaborated in Chapter 2 (assemblage theory and post-phenomenology). Developed further from his transcendental realism in *A Realist Theory of Science* in 1975, Roy Bhaskar's version of critical realism can be succinctly summarized as a social-scientific philosophy that recognizes the existence of material reality independent of human consciousness (realist ontology), ascribes causal powers to properties/potential in objects

**Table 3.2** Realist thought in the sciences, social sciences, and humanities.

|  | Transcendental realism | Critical realism | Speculative realism |
|---|---|---|---|
| Domain | Natural sciences since the mid-1970s | Social sciences since the early 1980s | Social sciences and humanities since the early 2000s |
| Key thinkers | Roy Bhaskar, Rom Harré | Roy Bhaskar, Margaret Archer, Andrew Collier, Derek Layer, Andrew Sayer | Graham Harman, Manuel DeLanda, Markus Gabriel, Tristan Garcia, Maurizio Ferraris |
| Origin | 1. Rejection of Humean empiricism and Comtean positivism<br>2. A synthesis of the Copernican revolution | 1. Rejection of positivist account of methodological individualism<br>2. Rejection of empiricism, positivism, structuralism, and hermeneutics<br>3. Search for the possibility of naturalism | 1. Rejection of positivism, structuralism, hermeneutics, and naturalism<br>2. Poststructuralist philosophy and post-phenomenology<br>3. Object-oriented philosophy<br>4. New realism |
| Ontology | 1. Things and materials possess *causal powers* independent of human agency: their realization is contingent<br>2. *Intransitive* dimension of science: stratification of the world into different levels of 'ontological depth'<br>3. The existence of *natural necessity*: secretion of causal powers through generative mechanisms and enduring tendencies<br>4. *Closed systems*: possible regular conjunctions of events and outcomes | 1. *Pre-existence* of social structures: transformed and reproduced by social actors<br>2. Human agency with *intentions*: reasons as real causes<br>3. Continuous process of *structuration* between structures and agency<br>4. *generative mechanisms*: emergent properties and causal powers<br>5. *Open systems*: no regular conjunctions of social events and outcomes | 1. Autonomy and existence of *objects* and *entities* from human thought<br>2. Emergent properties of *assemblage* and *relations*<br>3. Distinction between *actual* and *virtual mechanisms*: non-linear causality<br>4. Different *fields of sense* for objects and entities: from natural to social and ideal objects<br>5. *Open systems*: compositional multiplicities and heterogeneity of reality |
| Epistemology | 1. Science is an *ongoing* process<br>2. *Transitive* dimension of science: social (re)production of knowledge<br>3. Search for *causal laws* in science: explanation but not prediction | 1. Possibility of *naturalism*<br>2. *Subject matter*: internal (necessary) and external (contingent) relations between objects and events<br>3. *Ethos*: a material perspective of knowledge<br>4. *Practice*: immanent critique, enlightened common sense, and human emancipation | 1. *Concepts* as independent forces traversing reality<br>2. *Subject matter*: causal analysis of processes and relations of exteriority as surface phenomena<br>3. *Ethos*: both material and discursive approaches to pluralistic knowledge<br>4. *Practice*: radical empiricism and descriptive accounts |

*(Continued)*

**Table 3.2**    *(Continued)*

|  | *Transcendental realism* | *Critical realism* | *Speculative realism* |
|---|---|---|---|
| Methodology | 1. Process of *retroduction*: a posteriori reasoning<br>2. Possibility of *experimentation*<br>3. Use of postulated entities and analogies<br>4. *Practice*: theoretical and empirical research | 1. Processes of *abstraction*, *retroduction*, and *abduction*<br>2. Impossibility of natural experimentation<br>3. Possibility of *direct awareness* of structures and mechanisms<br>4. *Practice*: causal-theoretical (abstract) and empirical (concrete) research | 1. Conceptualizing, interpretive (re)thinking, and 'nomadic' writing<br>2. Creation of *concepts*: use of metaphors and analogies<br>3. *Practice*: philosophical theorizing and empirical description |

Sources: Rebuilt from Yeung (1997: Table 1, p. 53) based on Bhaskar (1975, 1979, 1986, 1989, 2008 [1993]) and Sayer (1984, 1992), with updates from Bhaskar (2010, 2016); Harman (2008, 2010, 2018); DeLanda (2006, 2016); Ferraris (2014 [2012]), Gabriel (2015); and Delanda and Harman (2017).

and human reasons and their activation through generative mechanisms such as enduring social structures (realist ontology), rejects relativism in social and scientific discourses (realist epistemology), and re-orientates the social sciences towards its critical goals (realist epistemology). This version of critical realism makes its strongest claims at the ontological level (Bhaskar's vision of philosophy as an underlabourer clearing the 'philosophical rubbish' for social scientists): the independent existence of reality and causal powers ascribed to objects/human reasons and their activation through generative mechanisms that strengthen the possibility of reclaiming reality through a critical social science.[29]

In critical realism, mechanism occupies an important epistemological role through its conception of the world as being structured, differentiated, and changing. Realist ontology recognizes the existence of causal powers and their activation through generative mechanisms that produce differentiated social or physical phenomena in nature. To Bhaskar (1989: p. 18, 2016: pp. 5–7), these mechanisms are the *intransitive* objects of inquiry because without their existence to activate and transmit causal powers, explanations and subsequently social change are simply unknowable and impossible. But to develop social knowledge, the concept of mechanism serves an epistemological role in that the identification of mechanisms and their connection to other intransitive objects can form an important basis for theory construction and knowledge production. In short, mechanism has an intransitive dimension at the ontological level (its existence) and a transitive role in epistemology (our knowledge of its connection to an actual phenomenon in society and space). One key aim of substantive social science is to theorize and investigate the mechanisms at work that generate empirical events and discourses (see also Table 3.1). In contrast to poststructuralist and postcolonial thought in Chapter 2 and as noted further by Bhaskar (1989: p. 2) in *Reclaiming Reality*, these generative mechanisms and social structures 'are irreducible to the patterns of events and discourses alike. These structures are not spontaneously apparent in the observable pattern of events; they can only be identified through the practical and theoretical work of the social sciences' (see also Elder-Vass, 2012).

The operation or realization of generative mechanisms, however, is a contingent matter subject to specific *time-space contexts*. This is critical realism's strongest claim against Humean empiricist search for universal laws as the goal of explanatory (social) science. Ironically, this realist distinction between the necessity of mechanism and the contingency of its realization has been misunderstood by its radical critics who argue that critical realism's 'insistence' on both mechanisms and contingency leaves little room for political intervention. As Doreen Massey (2005: p. 198) argues cogently in *For Space*,

> this was anyway a misunderstanding of the meaning of 'contingency'. 'Contingent' in critical realism simply means not within the chain of causality currently under investigation. A contingency occurs when a number of such lines interact in some way to affect each other. All may be lines of 'necessity' in themselves. It is their interaction which is contingent. Given this, it is quite wrong to see a 'contingent' influence in an explanation as somehow indicating a subordination of that influence.[30]

Indeed, this idea of the contingent as a different 'line' of investigation is much more developed in another, and more recent, kind of realist thought – *speculative realism* (see Table 3.2). In the philosophical works after Graham Harman, Manuel DeLanda, Markus Gabriel, and others since the 2000s, the ideas of emergence and emergent properties, the autonomy of objects and entities, and the existence of assemblage as relations of exteriority with its constitutive components have more in common with critical realist thought.[31] Commenting on DeLanda's (2006) assemblage theory based on Gilles Deleuze's poststructuralist work, Graham Harman (2010: p. 179) notes in *Towards Speculative Realism* that 'The tacit move away from a two-storied house of virtual and actual [in Deleuze's work] toward a multilayered structure of differently scaled assemblies suggests a drift in DeLanda's inspiration from Deleuze toward Roy Bhaskar, founder of the popular Critical Realism movement, and a kindred spirit whose influence DeLanda openly celebrates' (see also Chapter 2's discussion of assemblage theory; DeLanda and Harman, 2017). In Figure 3.1, I re-present Daniel Little's (2016) thematic integration of critical realist thought with assemblage theory and analytical sociology (to be discussed in the next subsection). Similar to the key themes summarized in Table 3.2, all of these strands of thought are concerned with emergence and complexity in the social world(s) as open systems. But assemblage theory differs from critical realism and analytical sociology in its poststructuralist conception of the virtual and the compositional multiplicities of reality as surface phenomena.

By virtue of its recognition of the emergent properties in assemblages and the possibility of historical analysis, DeLanda's (2006, 2016) assemblage theory 2.0 might also resolve the problem of the missing link between the micro-and the

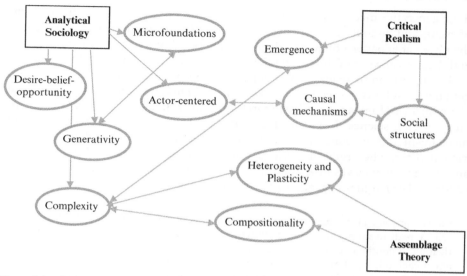

**Figure 3.1**  Critical realism, assemblage theory, and analytical sociology.
Source: Adapted and redrawn from Little (2016: Figure I.1, p. xix).

macro-levels of social reality. Table 3.3 offers a brief summary of different types of assemblages in relation to critical realist, speculative realist, and poststructuralist thought. Clearly both types of realist thought are more concerned with relatively unique configurations and stable wholes that come together to produce specific events in society and space. Sociologists Rutzou and Elder-Vass' (2019: p. 416) productive synthesis recognizes that all three types can shade into each other in practice (see also Decoteau, 2018). As argued in Rutzou's (2017: p. 409) careful comparison, Deleuze's poststructuralist ontology is not too incompatible with Bhaskar's realist ontology:

**Table 3.3**  Types of assemblages and realist thought.

| Assemblage | Definition | Philosophical thought | Examples |
|---|---|---|---|
| Conjunctural assemblage | Unique configurations of forces that come together to produce a given event | Critical realism; Bruno Latour | The causes of the French Revolution |
| Ephemeral assemblage | Transient and unstable wholes | Gilles Deleuze and Félix Guattari | Clouds, protests |
| Persistent assemblage | Relatively stable wholes that may have a tendency to recur in similar forms | Speculative realism: Manuel DeLanda and Graham Harman; critical realism | Atoms, bicycles, bureaucracies |

Source: Rutzou and Elder-Vass (2019: Table 1, p. 416). With permission of SAGE Publications.

The resonances with Bhaskar's distinction between closed systems and open systems, the critique of laws, and the advocacy of causation as 'conjunctural' is quite striking. Indeed, both Deleuze and Bhaskar stake their ontology of open systems in the natural and social world on similar ground, the critique of accounts grounded in repetition (Deleuze) or constant conjunction (Bhaskar). Both appeal to a language of production (Deleuze) or generation (Bhaskar) characterized by assemblages (Deleuze) or conjunctural causation (Bhaskar). Where Bhaskar uses the language of generative mechanisms and overdetermination, Deleuze favours the language of machines, yet both concepts play a similar role.

This quote reminds us vividly again that several key concepts from Marxism and feminist theory, such as over-determination, embodiment, and intersectionality, can certainly illuminate such conjunctural causation through a realist mechanism-based approach to theory development. These concepts can help theorize how different causal mechanisms converge and come together to produce tangible effects that explain empirical outcomes.

In the spirit of this section's argument for mid-range theories then, can assemblage theory be considered as such a meso-level theory? DeLanda (2006) seems to think so when he argues for the importance of *emergence* as a conceptual key in assemblage theory and the relevance of *causal mechanisms* as a solution to the recalcitrant micro-/macro-problem in social theory. As he argues in *A New Philosophy of Society*,

> it is important to define how these mechanisms should be properly conceptualized, particularly those mechanisms through which social wholes emerge from the interactions between their parts. The question of mechanisms of emergence has major consequences for social theory because it impinges directly on the problem of the *linkages between the micro and the macro*. This recalcitrant problem has resisted solution for decades because it has been consistently badly posed. Assemblage theory can help to frame the problem correctly, thus clearing the way for its eventual solution – a solution that will involve giving the details of every mechanism involved' (DeLanda, 2006: p. 32; original italics).

Taking cues from both critical and speculative realist thought, there are seemingly no inherent ontological objections nor epistemological obstacles to the development of mid-range theories that take seriously the emergent properties of agents and their relationality and the mechanisms of the causal nexus responsible for events and outcomes in social life and material worlds. Similarly, practice philosopher Schatzki (2019: pp. 139–140) argues for a realist position and the use of 'overviews', not universal generalizations, to handle the task of explaining complex social phenomena and change in such material worlds. These overviews are meant to convey the most significant and salient features of a field of social entities in reality. I concur with his realist view of the causal nexus as independent of human judgement. One productive way to 'unpack' its complexity is to develop mid-range theories of its different facets and constitutive relations that may in turn help people's (better) grasp of it and offer more robust explanatory outcomes for their eventual sense-making (e.g. self-knowledge and reflexivity). Before we move on to the nature of such relational theory development in the next two chapters (4 and 5), it is useful to explain a little further the importance of causal mechanisms in mid-range theories.

## Causal Mechanisms and Relational Thinking in Mid-Range Theories

If theory is indeed necessary and important to Geography's identity and legitimacy within the social sciences, a more explanatory kind of theory can be developed at the analytical level between the structuralist grand theories of capitalist formations and uneven development and the poststructuralist, feminist, and postcolonial theories of social beings and subject identities reviewed in Chapter 2. These mid-range theories draw upon meso-level concepts and analyses to intermediate between system-level all-inclusive generalizations and pure description and story-telling at the individual level in radical empiricism. But mid-range theories need causal mechanisms as explanatory tools for unravelling necessary (causal) relations and their operations in specific socio-spatial contexts (contingency). The key message here is the search for causal explanation in context that explicitly recognizes causality and yet rejects causal determinism. Mid-range theories are therefore causal but not deterministic in gesture; they are neither grand and universal in scope nor relativist in their epistemological uptake. Instead of taking on relativist claims that nothing can be 'represented' or explained because of the openness and becoming of things and reality, mid-range theories focus on causal explanation in context and provide a minimal epistemic infrastructure for the practice of immanent critique and contrastive analysis (see more on this in Chapter 6).

In mid-range explanatory theories, the causal mechanisms of empirical events or phenomena in society and space are more likely to be specified from general processes to account for social action and emergent powers connecting abstract causes and their concrete outcomes within particular historical-geographical contexts. While Chapters 4 and 5 will examine in depth respectively the nature of causal powers and the conceptual distinction between general process and particular mechanism, it is useful here to note the wider conceptual development in the social sciences during the past two decades that has witnessed the rapidly growing significance of *mechanism thought*.[32] As a substantial epistemological movement in the social sciences, this strong interest in mechanism represents a concerted effort to develop a more robust and explanatory form of contemporary social science to which human geography can, and should, make meaningful contributions.[33]

As noted in Chapter 1, mechanism in social science explanation cannot be a machine-like sequence of physical things. This serious misunderstanding has been wrongly argued by some critics of mechanism-based thought. Contrary to actor-network theory and posthumanist thought (Chapter 2), such mechanism cannot be made up of non-humans alone. Mechanism refers to the different but necessary steps for a 'social' cause in its broadest sense to produce empirical effect within specific context. Given the recursive nature of some of these 'working' steps, causal mechanism needs not be sequential in its explanatory pathway. In such social science explanation, causal mechanism often refers to discrete process embedded in social relations, rather than non-humans such as machines, tools, and things. This human agent-centric view of mechanism in social explanation differs from the 'physical' use of causal mechanism in the philosophy of science (Woodward, 2003; Glennan, 2017), such as renowned philosopher of science Wesley Salmon's (1984, 1989, 1998) causal-mechanical model of scientific explanation that is far too 'mechanical' and deductive for the social sciences (cf. Harvey, 1969: pp. 46–47). In this causal-mechanical model for the natural sciences, a causal process is a physical process capable of transmitting continuously a mark – defined as a local modification to a structure through the transfer of energy or momentum. Causal processes also interact that in turn modifies the structure of both processes. A scientific explanation of an event in the natural world thus entails tracing both causal processes and their physical interactions leading up to it.

This scientific approach is clearly too mechanical for social explanations because social mechanisms are not necessarily physical nor linear in nature. It also does not theorize well the specific workings of causal processes that turn them into mechanisms. To Woodward (2003: p. 357; my emphasis), this mechanical theory of explanation 'does not adequately deal with the problem of causal or explanatory relevance described above. That is, we still face the problem that the feature that makes a process causal (transmission of some conserved quantity or other) tells us *nothing* about which features of the process are causally or explanatorily relevant to the outcome we want to explain' (see also Glennan, 2017: p. 168). In short, we cannot deduce causality from sheer mechanical conceptions of causal processes. In the social world, such a deductive approach to causal explanation is even more problematic precisely because social mechanisms cannot be theorized a priori, but should rather be conceptualized *in relation* to the specific socio-spatial phenomenon in hand. Unlike most physical sciences, there is no 'natural' world out there for social scientists to abstract from, as our social world is always evolving and becoming *as* we theorize about it and change it (see also Table 3.2). Human agents and practices are more likely than physical things to serve as causes and, consequently, their constitutive social mechanisms as agent-generated causal mechanisms.

While poststructuralist assemblage thinking theorizes the 'exteriority of relations' and the non-linear causality of autonomous components in constituting assemblages (DeLanda, 2006, 2016; Anderson et al., 2012a; see also Chapter 2), it is less concerned with the specification of causation and causal mechanisms, as advocated in critical realism (Table 3.2). As noted by Rutzou and Elder-Vass (2019: pp. 408, 410),

Both philosophies are concerned with the concrete analysis of concrete situations and focus on how diverse elements interact to produce a given outcome. Both are grounded in a rejection of [Humean] causal laws. Both try to avoid reductionism and emphasize the necessity of a 'dialectical' and 'relational' approach to social ontology. Both stake their claims on an ontology of open systems... Critical realism's [CR] account of causation not only resembles that of assemblage theory but also provides an important corrective. CR offers a robust theory of causation that promises an explanation of both the contingency and recurrence of phenomena in the natural and social world and clarifies the relationship between actual and virtual that remains ambiguous within assemblage theory.[34]

Causal mechanisms in this kind of mid-range theories, however, differ from the *macro-causal structures* that determine, constraint, and interact with human agency in society and space.[35] In her commentary on my recent effort of (re) asserting causal mechanisms in relational-processual thinking in human geography (Yeung, 2019a), Whiteside (2019: p. 268) invokes one central element of the late Doreen Massey's 'philosophical blueprint'. Arguing for the importance of understanding 'causal structures in which processes intersect to impact upon each other, to influence/encourage/restrain/mould the operation of each other' (Massey, 1995: p. 316), this blueprint emerges from Massey's reflection on a decade of debate since the first edition of her *Spatial Divisions of Labour* in 1984 that was situated in then an era of heated structure vs. agency debate in British geography (Gregory and Urry, 1985). Massey's theory of spatial divisions of labour was firmly grounded in a Marxist analysis of the class structure of capital (after sociologist Erik Wright) and its social relations of production. In this majestic work, Massey (1984: p. 6, 1995: p. 6) argues for a more particularistic mode of *explanation* that

tries to break with the dichotomy between formal models and empirical description. It recognises underlying causal processes, but recognises, too, that such processes never operate in isolation. For it is precisely their operation in varying combinations which produces variety and uniqueness.

Taking a more explicitly relational view a decade later and thereafter, Massey (1995: p. 4) reflects that in her 1984 work, 'particular "causal relations" are seen as enabling rather than as determinate in their effects, and forever liable to be altered in their implications, or even nullified, by other sets of relations existing in the particularity of their occurrence at that precise point in time-space'.

In retrospect, Massey's discipline-shaping *theory* of spatial divisions of labour clearly has causal explanation in mind.[36] But it differs from the kind of mid-range theory in this book in terms of its apparent conflation of mechanism with process and its contingent view of causality and causal relations. First and foremost, the process-mechanism distinction in her original theory and her revisit a decade on is not clearly articulated. There is a sense that 'underlying causal structures/relations/processes' are used interchangeably and referred to as the same as underlying causal mechanisms in a critical realist sense.[37] In her 1995 edition, Massey (1995: pp. 297–298) reprises her book's central arguments in relation to 'the mechanisms of a specifically capitalist economy and society. It is important to be precise about what this statement means'. Despite this plea for precision, she proceeded to deploy different terminologies to describe causal mechanisms, such as 'economic mechanisms/causal processes' (p.298), 'capitalist accumulation' as 'mechanisms at work' (p.298), 'causal processes immanent in capitalist relations' (p.305), and process as 'necessary' and within 'causal structures' (p.316). In Chapter 5, I will return in greater detail to this critical issue of process/mechanism conflation in contemporary human geography.

Second, the necessary relation between causal mechanism and empirical events is perhaps too contingently defined in Massey (1995: p. 4) such that causal relations or causal processes are more 'enabling' and therefore can be 'altered' or 'nullified' by other sets of causal relations. The necessity of causal powers in these structures/relations/processes is at best unclear. Indeed, if these causal relations can be nullified by other relations at the time of their realization or occurrence, these relations are unlikely to be causal mechanisms since their *necessary* relations with specific empirical outcomes are not guaranteed, i.e. *not* necessary. Contrary to my call for mid-range theories, causal relations in spatial divisions of labour may appear to be too 'macro' in conjunction with the capitalist class structure in Marxism (see Table 2.1). These social relations of production are closer to the system-level generalizations expounded in Marxist geography then – a case of conjunctural causation derived from the Marxian notion of over-determination? It is hard to see how these macro-causal relations might be meso-level concepts amenable to further development into mid-range theories. Instead, these causal relations are more likely tendencies within the general capitalist processes (e.g. capital accumulation) shaping empirical outcomes in society and space.

How then does/can a mid-range theory work? While I will offer a more concrete example of such a mid-range theory in Chapter 6 (theorizing globalization through the theory of global production networks), let me conclude this chapter by reiterating its core message of the importance of explanatory theory in critical human geography and the relevance of mid-range theories in the kind of analytical geographies grounded in a realist understanding of causal mechanisms (critical realism) and emergent properties of relations among autonomous objects and entities (speculative realism and relational thinking). Realist philosopher Tuukka Kaidesoja (2019a: p. 28, 2019b: p. 1475) has decomposed a mid-range theory into three evolving components, each of which performs a different epistemic function in social science research:

1.  A conceptual framework about social phenomena: a set of interrelated concepts – existing and/or new – developed in relation to the empirical phenomenon;

2. A theoretical schema of causal mechanism(s): an abstract and yet incomplete description of interacting entities, actors, activities, and relations in causal mechanism(s); and
3. A cluster of mechanism-based explanations: all explanations based on causal mechanism(s) constitutive of the mid-range theory.

Taken together, I view mid-range theories of socio-spatial phenomena as fundamentally explanatory in nature; their explanations of such phenomena are grounded in specific concepts and causal mechanisms that are theorized and framed within certain domains of empirical research in Geography. The mid-range nature of these theories is specific to those research domains that are neither too macro in coverage nor too micro in specificity. The operations of such mechanism-based explanations, however, are dependent on the relational 'workings' of causal powers and their appropriate contexts and contingencies. I will return to these two important issues in the next two chapters – causal powers in Chapter 4 and context in Chapter 5. In human geography, a mid-range theory can be about processes and relations among social entities at different spatial scales precisely because it is not analytically tied to a particular scale in theorizing and specifying these processes into causal mechanisms for explanatory theory development. There are two distinct advantages to this multi-scalar conception of mid-range theories. First, a mid-range theory may afford greater possibility for multi-scalarity in its empirical application, from the body all the way to the global. This scalar flexibility allows it to build better connections with, and contribute more productively to, other mid-range theories in the wider social sciences (see more in my concluding Chapter 7). It can also address potential concern with the 'blackboxing' of mid-range concepts from higher-order/scale abstractions (e.g. global capitalism and planetary development).

Second, a mid-range theory tends to be theoretically coherent and empirically relevant because its analytical targets are phenomenon-specific and practically adequate. A good mid-range theory can tell us more about the causal properties of social forces and entities and help discover similar processes recurring in a variety of historical circumstances and spatial settings. In this sense, a mid-range theory might work better in addressing human agency and actor-specific roles in (co)shaping practices, events, and change within the broader social relations of our uneven and unjust world. A grand theory focusing on the class structure of capitalism may close off significant insights into actor-specific practices and strategies as embodied subjects shaping uneven geographical development. But a micro-level 'theory' of individual experiences, identities, and accounts may also close off the possibilities of analysing and explaining broader processes of change and transformation that matter much in human development and social change. Echoing Massey's (2001: p. 10) warning against excessive discursive turn(s) in human geography and her loathing of offering ever more metaphors to 10 Downing Street,[38] I believe that non-existent or totally unknown metaphors, stories, or imaginations of our extra-discursive reality will not likely achieve our normative goals. Instead, we need more mid-range theories to reconcile these apparent contradictions in both deterministic grand theories and descriptive 'local' accounts grounded in discursive metaphors and/or radical empiricism. In doing so, we might arrive at a modest kind of explanatory theories that can better inform us the practical realities of our uneven social world and some possible strategies in making it more just and ethical.

## Notes

1 Here, I share sociologist Petri Ylikoski's (2011: p. 167; original italics) argument for mechanism-based explanation in the social sciences: 'It is plausible to think that our contrastive explanatory preferences stem from our nature as active interveners in natural, psychological and social processes. We desire to know where to intervene to produce the changes we want, and this knowledge often presupposes answers to some *why* and *how* questions. Without this knowledge one would not know when the circumstances are suitable for an intervention and one would not be able to predict the results of the intervention'.

2 See also discussion of scientific explanation in the philosophy of science and social science, such as Harré (1970, 1985 [1972]); Little (1991, 2016); Bunge (1996); Woodward (2003); Lipton (2004 [1991]); Manicas (2006); and Glennan (2017). For an early geographical critique of this ideology of positivism, see Gregory (1978) and his examination of three explanatory approaches in human geography: structural, reflexive, and committed explanations (see also his social theory-inflected reflections on these approaches in Gregory, 1994: pp. 75–77).

3 As will be discussed in the second section, this conception of social worlds as open systems characterized by complexity, multiplicity, and emergence has been well recognized in critical realism for over three decades since realist philosopher Roy Bhaskar's pioneering work (Bhaskar, 1986, 2016; see also Elder-Vass, 2005, 2010; Ylikoski and Kuorikoski, 2010; Pozzoni and Kaidesoja, 2021). While this critical realist approach to explanation (and theory) is causal in nature (i.e. the intransitive dimension of reality), it also accepts fundamentally contingency as part of the transitive dimension of social reality, i.e. things and events are not always the same in different contexts.

4 Not all scientists believe that laboratories are 'closed systems' devoid of interferences and entanglements. In *Meeting the Universe Halfway*, feminist physicist Karen Barad (2007: ch. 7) meticulously shows that even in (quantum) physics, the principle of indeterminacy due to the problem of measurement and the entanglement of objects and observers in scientific experiments has been empirically validated.

5 As explained by Daniel Little (2016: p. 34) in *New Directions in the Philosophy of Social Science*, 'Concepts are of course essential to social knowledge. The heart of social inquiry has to do with coming up with concepts that allow us to better understand social reality: for example, racism, patterns of behavior, free market, class consciousness, and ethnic identities. Theory formation in the social sciences largely consists of the task of constructing concepts and categories that capture groups of social phenomena for the purpose of analysis'. See also Danermark et al. (2019: ch. 6).

6   Such an open-ended approach to concept creation seems particularly rampant in post-structuralism. In *A Thousand Plateaus*, poststructuralist philosophers Gilles Deleuze and Félix Guattari (1987 [1980]: p. 22; my emphasis) intentionally take a 'nomadic' approach and a rhizomatic writing style to create as many concepts or 'plateaus' in words: 'We are writing this book as a rhizome. It is composed of plateaus. We have given it a circular form, but *only for laughs*. Each morning we would wake up, and each of us would ask himself what plateau he was going to tackle, writing five lines here, ten there. We had *hallucinatory experiences*, we watched lines leave one plateau and proceed to another like columns of tiny ants. We made circles of convergence. Each plateau can be read starting anywhere and can be related to any other plateau... We just used words that in turn function for us as plateaus. RHIZOMATICS = SCHIZOANALYSIS = STRATO-ANALYSIS = PRAGMATICS = MICROPOLITICS. These words are concepts, but concepts are lines, which is to say, number systems attached to a particular dimension of the multiplicities (strata, molecular chains, lines of flight or rupture, circles of convergence, etc.). Nowhere do we claim for our concepts the title of a science. We are no more familiar with scientificity than we are with ideology; all we know are assemblages' (see also Grosz, 2017: pp. 142–148 for a critical discussion of Deleuze and Guattari's concept creation and preference for 'conceptual personae'). Such 'nomadic habits' of conceptual creativity and writing are also extensively practiced in feminist philosopher Rosi Braidotti's (2011) *Nomadic Theory* with which 'readers may open the book at any one point and be able to start reading it almost at random, in keeping with nomadic habits' (p.9)!

7   Pushing for his unified framework in *Social Science Methodology*, political scientist John Gerring (2012: pp. 116–117) argues rather broadly for four elements of an empirical concept (linguistic term, defining attributes, empirical indicators, and referential phenomena) and seven criteria of a 'good' concept (resonance, domain relevance, consistency, fecundity, differentiation, causal utility, and operationalizability). See also Beach and Pedersen's (2016: pp. 101–104) *Causal Case Study Methods* for the criteria of a 'good defined concept' in case-based research.

8   In *Realism and Social Science*, Sayer (2000: p. 19) notes that 'Social systems are always open and usually complex and messy. Unlike some of the natural sciences, we cannot isolate out these components and examine them under controlled conditions. We therefore have to rely on abstraction and careful conceptualization, on attempting to abstract out the various components or influences in our heads, and only when we have done this and considered how they combine and interact can we expect to return to the concrete, many-sided object and make sense of it. Much rests upon the nature of our abstractions, that is, our conceptions of particular one-sided components of the concrete object; if they divide what is in practice indivisible, or if they conflate what are different and separable components, then problems are likely to result'. Referring to concepts in regional studies, Markusen (1999, 2003) uses the notion of 'fuzzy concepts' to describe those concepts that lack clarity and are difficult to operationalize. To her, fuzzy concepts tend to emphasize processes rather than institutions, agents, and behaviour (see also responses in Hudson, 2003; Peck, 2003).

9   While Cresswell (2013) refers to the origin of geographical knowledge and 'theory' in Strabo and Ptolemy, Mayhew's (2011: p. 35) critical survey of Geography's genealogies and the respective ancient texts *Geography* by Strabo (1917–1932) and Ptolemy (2000) argues that both 'originators' of geographical knowledge did not have causal explanation in mind.

10  Since I did not devote a separate section in Chapter 2 to humanistic geography because of the lack of explicitly-named theory in its phenomenological approach to self-knowledge and human experiences (see also Table 2.1), let me quote a brief and recent definition from a leading advocate David Seamon (2015: p. 45; original italics) who characterizes humanistic geography as 'a progressive discovery of the nature of human life, experience, and meaning in relation to geographical phenomena such as space, place, landscape, region, and the natural and human-made environments. Integral to this style of understanding is a sense of wonder at the geographical phenomena of the world and a wish to understand them as they are *in their own right* without having to pay heed to any conceptual, ideological, or practical obligations. This research impulse arises from the wish to know, the satisfaction of knowing, and the intellectual and emotional pleasure taken in finding ways to explore the phenomenon in which one is interested. This manner of understanding incorporates self-knowledge, whereby through studying the *lived* nature of place, space, and environment, we discover more about ourselves. We perhaps become better human beings because of that understanding'.

11  Elaborating on his modest non-representational theory of practices in *Spatial Formations*, Nigel Thrift (1996: p. 30; emphasis added) stresses that he hopes 'to make a clearing for voices that speak from outside the authorised scholarly discourse whilst simultaneously recognising that this ambition is only necessary to an extent, since the scholarly discourse-network is but one of many forms of practice. In other words, I want to point to the *perpetually inadequate* (but not thereby unnecessary) powers of theory'. Such approach has prompted many examples of auto-biographical accounts of the narrating self and experiences of embodied practices in British cultural geography studies, e.g. McCormack (2003) on dance movement therapy in Bristol; Wylie (2005) on walking on the South West Coast Path in North Devon; and more recently Ebbensgaard and Edensor (2021) on single night's walk from Canning Town to Canary Wharf in east London and Simpson's (2021) text on non-representational theory starting with a daily scene from his university office window bordering the city centre of Plymouth. See also Sidaway's (2022) take on walking as an embodied practice from the perspective of psychogeography.

12  See Wright's (2015: p. 392) weak theory approach to understanding belonging as emergent co-becoming.

13  Here, I concur with qualitative sociologists Iddo Tavory and Stefan Timmermans' (2014: p. 128) arguments in *Abductive Analysis* that 'If, after we have thought of other modes of explanation, we still think that there is something about the structure of our explanation that is not captured by other theories, and if our explanation would change the way others see their own work, then our theory is generative… [T]heorizing is not a separate form of research. Theory is part of the research act that emerges as we build and problematize the generalizations produced by others and offer generalizations of our own. Much of qualitative research today either produces relatively descriptive accounts or follows a predetermined theoretical approach'.

14  In his new realist ontology, Gabriel (2015: p. 329) argues that 'if knowledge cannot be unified by specifying any alleged universal and substantial structure holding knowledge as such together, there correspondingly is no position from which to undermine knowledge in one stroke. Epistemological pluralism, therefore, is a bulwark against scepticism, at least to scepticism in its Cartesian form, but also against other forms of scepticism that overgeneralise other epistemic concepts, such as justification'.

15  In his tribute to the late Doreen Massey, Sayer (2018: p. 105) notes that 'Geography deals with complex open systems in which today's activities take place in contexts not of current agents' making, but are nevertheless constrained and enabled by them. In such systems there are at best only temporary and local regularities. Yet one could still explain what happens in them by tracing connections and looking for causal mechanisms. This is effectively what Doreen did in her work on industrial and regional geography'.

16  Fumerton (2018: p. 65) points out that 'Entire books (and lives) have been devoted to the difficult question of how to understand what it is to explain successfully some phenomena. The term "explanation" is itself extraordinarily ambiguous. We talk about philosophical explanations of various phenomena, where we often have in mind something like an analysis, a theory, or an account of some kind of how to understand the phenomena in question. In other quite removed contexts we even talk of excuses as a kind of explanation (e.g. I have a good explanation of why I didn't meet you as promised). But here we will be primarily concerned with causal or scientific (broadly understood) explanations of various phenomena'.

17  To Lipton (2004 [1991]: p. 32; original italics), 'the causal view is still our best bet, because of the backward state of alternate views of explanation [above five accounts], and the overwhelming preponderance of causal explanations among all explanations. Nor does it seem ad hoc to limit our attention to causal explanations. The causal view does not simply pick out a feature that certain explanations happen to have: causal explanations are explanatory *because* they are causal'.

18  These attributes are fiercely debated among different philosophers of scientific realism (e.g. Rinard, 2018: p. 210; Wright, 2018: p. 88).

19  To Schatzki (2019: p. 118), 'Extensive philosophical discussions exist of explanation, especially causal explanation. I agree with those philosophers and social theorists who maintain that all explanations are causal explanations. I recognize that for decades many thinkers have maintained that some explanations, above all, explanations of human activity, are not causal in nature. As I will explicate below, however, even explanations of human activity can be construed as causal on a sufficiently broad sense of "causal." Of course, broad understandings of causality have fallen on hard times in the modern era. Consequent on the emergence of modern science, what was accepted in most intellectual, especially scientific, circles as causality shrunk to efficient causality alone. The efficient cause of an event is what brings that event about. This is an extremely important form of causality. It is, for example, the sort of causality instantiated in interventions in the world and in many material and biological processes'.

20  Elaborating further his realist thought on the importance of explanation vis-à-vis classification, DeLanda argues that we should 'conceive of the activity of the knowing subject as involving not classification but *explanation*. The latter depends on active assessments of significance, that is, on discovering which factors make (or do not make) a difference to the outcome of a process. In addition, when realists conceive of the human subject as *embodied* (as opposed to a disembodied observer), another source of active participation in the production of knowledge is the causal intervention that a body makes possible. Classification may be able to tell us about an object's properties, but not about its capacities if the latter are not currently being exercised. Hence, we need to explore the world, force things to interact with one another so that

their capacities are revealed as they affect and are affected by one another' (DeLanda and Harman, 2017: p. 45; original italics).

21  As argued by Woodward (2003: pp. 4–5; original italics), 'I focus on a much narrower range of explanatory activities – roughly, those that consist of providing *causal* explanations (in a broad sense of "causal," described in more detail below) of why some particular outcome or general pattern of outcomes occurs. A distinguishing feature of such explanations is that they show how what is explained depends on other, distinct factors, where the dependence in question has to do with some relationship that holds as a matter of empirical fact, rather than for logical or conceptual reasons. Thus, for example, explanation in mathematics, if there is such a thing, is outside the scope of my discussion. My reason for proceeding in this way is that I believe that an account that attempts to capture the common elements in everything we may wish to call an explanation is unlikely to be very illuminating and unlikely to tell us much about what is distinctive about causal explanation and the role it plays in inquiry. In the theory of explanation, as in science itself, generality is not always a virtue'.

22  Merton (1968 [1949]: p. 39) further notes that mid-range theory is important because 'It is intermediate to general theories of social systems which are too remote from particular classes of social behavior, organization and change to account for what is observed and to those detailed orderly descriptions of particulars that are not generalized at all. Middle-range theory involves abstractions, of course, but they are close enough to observed data to be incorporated in propositions that permit empirical testing'. More recently and approvingly in *Society and Economy*, sociologist Mark Granovetter (2017: p. 212) focuses on institutional logics as 'the middle range' in his analysis of industry and as his 'perhaps not-so-sly nod to the usage by Robert K. Merton (1957 [1949]) of "theories of the middle range," which was his way of nudging sociology away from grand theory and minor close-range observation to a more fruitful and workable theoretical location'.

23  See also Hedström and Udéhn (2009); Elster (2015); and Kaidesoja (2019a, 2019b). To social theorist Pierre Bourdieu, the task of reflexive sociology is to 'uncover the most profoundly buried structures of the various social worlds which constitute the social universe, as well as the "mechanisms" which tend to ensure their reproduction or their transformation' (Bourdieu and Wacquant, 1992: p. 7).

24  To Ylikoski (2018: p. 406; my emphasis), 'the relevance of the *toolbox vision* is not limited to meta-theory: it also gives new tools to counter the fragmentation of the social sciences. Causal mechanism schemes can be shared among the different subfields, which would allow for a novel type of integration: various subfields employ and develop the same theoretical toolbox and thereby benefit from each other's work. The toolbox vision for sociological theory shows that in the social sciences mechanistic ideas are not confined to discussions about explanation and causation, but they also play an important role in how social scientists think about the nature of social-scientific knowledge'.

25  In Bhaskar's (1975: p. 52) own words in *A Realist Theory of Science*, 'philosophical argument cannot establish which ones actually do; or, to put it the other way around, what the real mechanisms are. That is up to [social] science to discover'. In *Reclaiming Reality*, he further notes that 'Critical realists do not deny the reality of events and discourses; on the contrary, they insist upon them. But they hold that we will only be

able to understand – and so change – the social world if we identify the structures at work that generate those events or discourses' (Bhaskar, 1989: p. 2).

26  This subsection draws upon my earlier work in Yeung (1997, 2019a: pp. 231–233). As noted by philosopher Little (2016: p. 226), 'Realism has been a central and contested part of the philosophy of social science for at least forty years. One reason for its prominence is the fundamental fault line that exists within the philosophy of science between positivism and anti-positivism'. See Harré (1986) for an early discussion of different varieties of realism and Rutzou and Steinmetz (2018) and Danermark et al. (2019) for a more recent take on critical realism in the philosophy of social science.

27  Commenting on Anderson et al.'s (2012a) 'post-relational geography' and assemblage thinking, Allen (2012: p. 191) notes that 'Realism in human geography was in vogue for much of the 1980s and early 1990s, certainly on the European side of the Atlantic, but more or less fell out of favour with the "cultural turn" and the take-up within the discipline of relational ways of understanding the social construction of space, place, identity and countless other phenomena'.

28  Critical realism has retained a strong foothold in heterodox economics and political economy since the 2000s as a coherent critique of mainstream neoclassical economics (e.g. Nielsen, 2002; Lawson, 2003, 2015; O'Boyle and McDonough, 2011; Morgan, 2015). Others have attempted to (re)evaluate critical realism from the perspectives inspired by critical social theories, such as poststructuralism, feminism, and postcolonial theory (e.g. Kaul, 2002; Dean et al., 2005; Gunnarsson et al., 2016; Rutzou, 2017; Rutzou and Steinmetz, 2018; van Ingen et al., 2020). Since the early 2000s, Critical realism has also been well received in sociology (Groff, 2004, 2008; Donati, 2010; Maccarini et al., 2011; Gorski, 2013, 2018; Porpora, 2015; Wan, 2016; Danermark et al., 2019), management studies and organizational science (Tsang and Kwan, 1999; Fleetwood and Ackroyd, 2004; Volkoff and Strong, 2013; Edwards et al., 2014; Tsang, 2014, 2022; Ramoglon and Tsang, 2016, 2017; Kitching, 2018), and the philosophy of social science (Manicas, 2006; Kaidesoja, 2013a; Little, 2016; Rutzou and Steinmetz, 2018; Schatzki, 2019). Meanwhile, the late Roy Bhaskar and his followers have successfully institutionalized critical realism through the establishment of its own journal (*Journal of Critical Realism* since 2002), two Routledge book series on 'Routledge Studies in Critical Realism' (over 33 titles since 2002) and 'Ontological Explorations' (over 50 titles since 2000 related to critical realism), an international association (International Association for Critical Realism since 1997) with its annual conferences, and international research centres (Centre for Critical Realism initially established in 1996 by Roy Bhaskar at the Institute of Education, University of London, with multiple similar groups evolving in different countries in the US, Europe, and Latin America).

29  In this book, I am sticking to Bhaskar's (2016: p. 9) 'basic' (or original first-wave) transcendental version since his 1975 *A Realist Theory of Science* rather than the much more convoluted versions in Roy Bhaskar's further development of dialectical critical realism (his ontology of absence and negation) during the 1990s and the philosophy of metaReality (via two phases of his religious and spiritual 'turn') during the 2000s. As Bhaskar (2016: p. 11) reflects in *Enlightened Common Sense* on the widespread adoption of *different* phases of critical realism, 'it should be borne in mind that, according to critical realism, it is in the last instance the nature of the object that

determines how it should be studied (together with the current state of the research process). Thus it is incumbent on every researcher to determine, in the light of this maxim, which parts of the expanding toolkit of critical realism they wish, in any given instance, to utilise'.

30 See Sayer's (2018: pp. 104–105) reflections on Massey's engagement with critical realism.

31 As argued by Bhaskar (2010: p. 60) in *The Formation of Critical Realism*, the idea of emergence is indispensable to social science because 'we have an ontology, an account of being in which some explanatory structures are emergent from others. If you subscribe to an exclusively materialist ontology, an ontology of material things, in the physical sense only, then you cannot make sense of the emergent powers that are most characteristic of human beings, or of social structures, or very generally of all those social and material states that depend upon, or are in part the outcome of, patterns of human interaction involving such things as reasons'. See also Elder-Vass' (2005, 2010) compositional account of emergence in realist thought and other philosophical discussion of emergence and causation (Clayton and Davies, 2006; Mumford and Anjum, 2011).

32 This social science literature on mechanism thought is very large in analytical sociology (Hedström and Swedberg, 1998a; Hedström, 2005; Gross, 2009, 2018; Hedström and Wittrock, 2009; Demeulenaere, 2011; Ylikoski, 2011, 2012, 2018; Manzo, 2014, 2021; Groff, 2017), political science (Elster, 1989, 2015; Tilly, 2001, 2004; Checkel, 2006; Gerring, 2008, 2010; Falleti and Lynch, 2009; Sil and Katzenstein, 2010; Beach, 2013; Bennett, 2014; Beach and Pedersen, 2018), and the philosophy of science (Illari et al., 2011; Illari and Russo, 2014; Glennan, 2017; Glennan and Illari, 2018a) and social science (Stinchcombe, 1991; Bunge, 1997, 2004; Reiss, 2007, 2015; Weber, 2007; Kaidesoja, 2013b; Runhardt, 2015; Little, 2016; Beach, 2021).

33 In many ways, this discipline-specific reorientation towards mechanism-based explanation in other social sciences has a clear parallel to critical realism in earlier geographic thought during the 1980s and through to the late 1990s. This earlier realist understanding of causal mechanism in human geography (Sayer, 1982a, 1992, 2000, 2010 [1992/1984]; Pratt, 1991, 1995; Yeung, 1997) is consistent with the current conceptions of mechanism in the social science literature. Gorski (2018: p. 27) contextualizes further: 'Long before most sociologists were doing so, early Critical Realists were already characterizing causes as "mechanisms." A mechanism is a structure that reproduces a process (e.g., the exploitation of wage labor or the maintenance of ethnic boundaries). Sometimes, the early Critical Realists also added the word "generative" in order to emphasize the productive powers of causal mechanisms'. See my fuller discussion of this mechanism thought in Chapter 5.

34 In her comparison of critical realism and poststructuralism, sociologist Claire Decoteau (2018: pp. 105–106) also argues that 'Deleuze and Guattari do not address causality explicitly or offer a causal framework, but rather, highlight the radically contingent nature of assemblages and their component parts… In *A Thousand Plateaus*, they also suggest a form of causality that is not only antilinear, but which disrupts simplistic understandings of time and evolution… These theories of contingency, of accidental "swerves," and of relations of exteriority do not provide a strong account of causation that can explain why particular assemblages form or why some endure and others do not'.

35  This subsection draws upon Yeung (2019b: pp. 287–289).

36  See also Peck et al.'s (2018: pp. 9–14) reflections on the intellectual origins and influences of Massey's spatial division of labour.

37  It is necessary to note though that Massey's (1984) original thesis was grounded in then Marxist understanding of capitalist relations of production and did not invoke critical realism. She did cite Andrew Sayer's (1979, 1982b, 1981) earlier work on conceptions of space to argue for why geography matters in such capitalist relations of production. But it is only in the new 'Reflections' chapter in the book's second edition (Massey, 1995: pp. 312, 324) that she engaged briefly with the realism work of Bhaskar (1975) and Sayer (1984).

38  Expressing her distaste for social constructivism in their extreme forms of anti-foundationalism in her *Progress in Human Geography* annual lecture 2000 (see Chapter 2), Massey (2001: p. 10; original italics) bemoans that 'Geographical imaginations (for instance of regions and of regional uneven development) are not simply mirrors; they are *in some sense* constitutive figurations; *in some sense* they "produce" the world in which we live and within which they are themselves constructed. On the other hand, the very fact of the attempt at intervention implies a rejection of that position which would entrap us in a prison house of language to which there is no outside with any force whatsoever. (In other words, I am loathe to turn up on the steps of Downing Street in order to offer another metaphor/story/imagination whose relationship to "the extradiscursive reality" of the North-South divide is either nonexistent or totally unknown)'.

# Chapter Four
## Relational Theory

This chapter offers a critical discussion of relationality and causal powers in different approaches reviewed in Chapter 2 to provide an adequate and yet explicit engagement with these current approaches and debates in Geography (and beyond). Since Doreen Massey et al.'s (1999) edited volume *Human Geography Today*, "relational thinking' has been a highly influential approach to theory and practice in human geography.[1] In this 'relational turn', geographers tend to place their analytical focus on the complex nexuses of relations among subjects, practices, and social entities that effect changes and outcomes in society and space. This relational geography is concerned primarily with the ways in which socio-spatial relations of subjects and identities are intertwined with broader processes of change at various geographical scales. But as argued in my earlier work (Yeung, 2005, 2019b), substantive geographical work adopting this relational thinking and relational turn is often relational only in the *thematic* sense that relations among subjects, networks, and assemblages are an important theme or subject matter in contemporary geographical enquiry. In particular, the causal nature of relationality and power relations – central to developing the kind of mechanism-based explanatory mid-range theory in/for analytical geographies discussed in the previous chapter – remains relatively under-theorized and underspecified (but see important work by Allen, 2003, 2016).

By reconceptualizing relationality, causal powers, and agency and their unfolding in the socio-spatial world(s) in the second section, my *relational theory* aims to offer more analytical purchase for a kind of mechanism-based explanations in mid-range theories than some earlier relational thinking in poststructuralist thoughts (e.g. heterogeneous relations in actor-network theory and processes of

*Theory and Explanation in Geography*, First Edition. Henry Wai-chung Yeung.

becoming or surface relations in non-representational theory) and feminist/post-colonial approaches (e.g. contested relations of difference and representational power). As the second step of my synthetic approach to theory and explanation introduced in Chapter 1's sections on main argument and chapter outlines, this relational theory conceptualizes the dynamic and heterogeneous relationality among actors and practices as causal powers effecting socio-spatial change in context. This conceptual apparatus allows us to go beyond description of these relations and to *explain* why and how relationality and its causal powers make things happen that can better account for events and outcomes taking place in society and space (Woodward, 2003; Glennan, 2017; Yeung, 2019a). As Nigel Thrift (2000: p. 217, 2007: p. 114) recognizes in 'Afterwords', 'Events must take place within networks of power which have been constructed precisely in order to ensure iterability. But what is being claimed is that the event does not end with these bare facts. The capacity to surprise may be latent, but it is always present'. Adopting an anti-essentialist position in their flat ontologies, most poststructuralist approaches in Chapter 2 do not take an explicitly *causal* approach to theorizing such 'networks of power' and 'capacity to surprise' that in turn makes it rather difficult to explain *why* socio-spatial events take place within these networks and in specific ways.

To me, such practically adequate explanation of events and outcomes can be premised on a causal theory of relationality that identifies and traces the emergent properties of actors, practices, and their structures of relations and specifies the multiple pathways or mechanisms through which causal powers work themselves out in what I have termed 'relational geometries' (Yeung, 2005: p. 38). This concept of relational geometries refers to the spatial configurations of more-than-heterogeneous relations among actors, practices, and structures through which power and identities are played out and become efficacious. These relational geometries are neither actors (e.g. individual subjects, social groups, and institutions) nor structures (e.g. class, patriarchy, and the state), but configurations of relations between and among them – connecting actors and structures through horizontal and vertical power relations. Relational geometries are also not networks or assemblages *per se* as conceived in certain poststructuralist approaches because the latter refer mainly to horizontal and, mostly, stabilized ties among actors (e.g. actor-network theory and assemblage theory). Actors in these relational geometries are not static 'things' fixed in time and space. They are dynamic and evolving in such relational ways that their differential practices unleash multiple forms of emergent power in relational geometries (cf. assemblage theory). Building on the concept of different and yet emergent forms of causal powers as *positions* in relational geometries and as *practice* through social action, this relational theory allows us to avoid the two polarized positions in contemporary human geography – over-deterministic capitalist structures in structural Marxism and indeterminant actor-networks and assemblages in poststructuralism (see Chapter 2; Table 2.1). It also taps into the key thinking on power and relationality observed in some ideologically-oriented approaches, such as feminist, queer, and postcolonial geographies, that interrogate and theorize how different binaries in gender relations, sexuality, and colonial relations empower specific and often unjust constructions of social subjectivities and identities.

## Relationality and Relational Thought in Contemporary Human Geography

Before I review critically human geography's recent infatuation with relational thinking in this section, it is useful to trace some of this thought back to the general philosophical discussion of process and relation and to forewarn the potential danger of 'correlationism' in such relational thinking. To begin, one might reasonably argue that relational thinking in general can be traced all the way back to process philosophers Henri Bergson's (1910) *Time and Free Will* and Alfred North Whitehead's (1929) *Process and Reality* in which they argue for the idea of change and temporality as process of becoming or events that constitute a world of interactions and relations (Massey, 2005: ch. 2; Murdoch, 2006: ch. 1; Anderson and Harrison, 2010b). In *Time Matters*, process sociologist Andrew Abbott (2001: p. 24; my emphasis) notes that

> For Whitehead, the world is a world of events. These events can be defined into the stable lineages that we call (social) things. The crucial effect of this [ontological] move is to destroy the micro/macro problem as a difficulty in social theory. For now both individuals and social structures of all kinds are produced instantaneously out of *relationships* defined on the endless flow of events.

This foundational conception of reality as constituted through relations premised on endless flow of events has led some geographers, particularly those of a poststructuralist bent, to declare that 'we will only unlock the power of poststructuralist geography to the extent that we embrace nothing but relations and co-relations, their folding and unfolding' (Doel, 2004: p. 147; see also, Doel, 1999; Roberts, 2014, 2019).[2] Arguing recently for such a kind of correlationism in entangled phenomenologies, Hepach (2021: p. 1281; original italics) insists that 'many phenomena of interest to human geographers (and post-phenomenologists in particular) take place in this space between subject and object; they are, as I argue, inherently *correlational*, that is, they cannot simply be reduced to subjectivity or objectivity, but rather *correlate* subjects and objects in distinctive ways. Erasing the correlational and hence entangled nature of these phenomena would risk obfuscating their very nature'.

To me, process and relation are clearly important in (co)constituting the reality of the socio-spatial world(s) and our being-in-the-world. But the blanket assertion of 'nothing but (co-)relations and (un)folding' and 'no subject/object but only entanglement' in such relational thinking might fall into the danger of 'correlationism' or relationism through which human agency or the reality of objects is expunged from any causal analysis of socio-spatial events and outcomes, and the explanatory goal of causal theories is replaced by the radical empiricism of describing everything as relational everywhere (i.e. internal to the subject as perceived phenomena). This experimental and heuristic approach to describing and analysing unfolding relationality by conceiving everything, including human subjects, as if it were a relationally configured phenomenon presupposes a flat ontology that misses or misconstrues causal powers that really 'make things happen'. To speculative realist Graham Harman (2008: p. 369), 'it makes no sense to think of humans apart from world or world apart from humans, but only of a primal correlation or rapport between the two'.[3] In *After Finitude*, another co-founder of speculative realism Quentin Meillassoux (2008: pp. 5, 53) defines correlationism as a philosophical thought disqualifying the independent existence of subjects and objects and therefore insisting the primacy and constitutive power of relations over any intentional subject or object. He calls for the break-free from this 'correlationalist circle' (see also Sparrow, 2014: pp. 15–16, ch. 3; Gabriel, 2015: pp. 85, 284–287).

Apart from this danger of correlationism, relational thinking may also be rather vague and circular in its familiar platitude that everything is related to everything else. In his sympathetic critique of relational thinking, practice philosopher Theodore Schatzki (2019: pp. 13, 173) argues that this problem of vagueness is often linked to the lack of non-circular definition of relations because almost any such definition brings one back to similar notions such as connection, tie, or link.[4] There is also no reason why relation is given priority over other ontological categories, such as agent, power, substance, structure, event, and process, that collectively constitute the social world(s). Revisiting Massey's relational thought and human geography's recent emphasis on becoming rather than being, Sayer (2018: p. 107) also points to such a danger in the relational view of the world in which everything is always fluid and changing.[5]

Still, I believe relational thinking should not be just about the familiar platitude, but rather about the causal difference (e.g. necessity) a relation can make to a particular event or outcome in society and space. Difference does not emerge on its own; it is likely 'caused' by a certain *(re)working* of a specific combination of events, processes, and sequences – known as causal mechanism(s) in the previous chapter (see more on its conceptual distinction from process in the next chapter). Much relational thinking in the existing theories of social change does not offer a causal explanation of change; it merely describe change and its association with underlying intersections, as in the conception of emergence (cf. Elder-Vass, 2005, 2010; Mumford and Anjum, 2011). This deference to the folding and unfolding of activity-events, which are 'process-like in Bergson's sense' in Schatzki (2019: p. 87) view, is also common in relational thinking and practice-oriented theories in their geographical accounts of socio-spatial change (see further below).

What is generally missing in these relational approaches is a causal explanation (or theory), not just associational or correlational analysis, of socio-spatial change manifested in concrete events and outcomes. In short, what turns processes and events into causal mechanisms that might 'dynamize bundles' of action chains in Schatzki (2019: p. 87) and thereby socio-spatial outcomes? Differences in bundles, in themselves, are not necessarily causal, unless we know what (causal) difference such differences make to action chains. This call for theorizing the causality of relations and relationality necessitates the analytical specification of causal mechanisms that demonstrate *why* a certain relation is crucial to the emergence, happening, and progress of social affairs. Merely pointing out the existence of such a relation and/or a difference is insufficient in a causal theory. Its necessity to a particular event or outcome must be theorized. Consistent with my earlier work on relational thinking (Yeung, 2003, 2005, 2019b), I concur with Schatzki's (2019: p. 175; original italics) reminder of a more ecumenical approach to thinking relationally:

> Instead, however, of hailing relational turns and calling for relational thinking, social theorists should determine which rationally sensible theories and ontologies are most useful for their purposes and work with *whatever* sorts of relations are recognized in these theories and ontologies, thereby letting the relational chips fall where they may... [A]ttempts to analyze everything relationally should be dropped and replaced by a more ecumenical approach that recognizes a plurality of categories of entity – substances, events, structures, and processes – in addition to relations. Calls for relational thinking are dangerous if they are taken to suggest that relations, alone or ultimately, compose social life.[6]

With these broad and brief 'health warnings' in relation to relational thinking, the following two subsections engage critically with relational thought in (1) Marxian and institutionalist geographies; and (2) poststructuralist, feminist, and postcolonial geographies. A brief qualification is necessary here though. Any examination of the nature and emergence of relational thought in human geography can be tricky precisely because in many ways it is hard not to think of geographical problems in relational terms – whether implicitly or explicitly. Again, I can only be brief and selective here, acknowledging the possible unintended consequence of ascribing equivalence to these different approaches (see Chapter 2 introduction). This acknowledgement, however, does not mean that all approaches and theories in human geography, whether structuralist, postmodernist, poststructuralist, feminist, and postcolonial, are relational in nature. Indeed, the *relationality* in any theoretical framework needs to be theorized and demonstrated, as in the cases below.

While acknowledging the existence of an undercurrent of relational thinking in human geography for some time before the 1990s (e.g. Marxism in Table 2.1), I focus more on the geographical work that explicitly addresses how relationality and social relations impinge on and co-constitute the geographies of human activities. In this sense, some of my observations may go against the expectations of some readers who might consider relationality and relational thought as central to/

in many of these critical approaches (e.g. Marxist, feminist, and postcolonial geographies). While I certainly do not deny such expectations, it is important to note that my core concern here is with the kind of *relational theory* in these approaches – how relationality and power work and how they co-constitute to ascribe causal powers to specific mechanisms for explanatory theories. In short, how is relational theory conceived in these approaches and whether causal powers are explicitly theorized in them? Are these various approaches and their associated 'theories' relational in a thematic sense rather than causal in their explanatory apparatuses?

## Relationality in Marxian and Institutional Geographies

I start with the Marxian *social relations of production* framework of the late 1970s and the 1980s and show how it serves as an antecedent of a relational turn in economic geography and urban and regional studies since the 1990s.[7] By the late 1970s, this social relations of production framework had emerged as a radical critique of neo-classical industrial location theory largely because, as Massey (1984: p. 3) notes, 'the changes in industry since the sixties [had] shaken industrial geography and industrial location theory to their foundations'. As noted in Table 2.1, its main tenet was to theorize how uneven development arises from the complex interrelationships between the social divisions of labour underpinned by pre-existing social structures and the spatial organization of capitalist relations of production.[8] Sayer (1985, 1995) thus observes that radical geographers interpreted uneven regional development by emphasizing its structural and productionist causes (e.g. social relations of production as class structures). This analytical focus on capitalist relations and spatial structures was a form of relational thinking in a thematic sense because it examined both the dynamics of social structures and capitalist relations of production and interrogated the complex relational effects of these dynamics on spatial development. As Massey (1984: p. 39) argues in *Spatial Divisions of Labour*,

> Both the broad relations between classes and the very considerable differences within them are fundamental in understanding locational change, both its causes and its wider effects. Both what are called 'interregional relations' and geographical differences in type of employment are in large part the spatial expression of the relations of production and the divisions of labour within society.

The social relations of production approach, nevertheless, often reduced the complexity of concrete processes to the relational effects of abstract capitalist structures such as class and divisions of labour.[9] Its weakest link was not so much the lack of relational thinking, but rather its tendency to overemphasize the structural (over)determination of such concrete relational effects as spatial change and territorial development. This weakness in the social relations of production approach has led Sayer (1995) to note the relative decline of radical political economy in the late 1980s and the 1990s. In the next two chapters, I will revisit in greater detail two newer and more-than-relational-as-thematic frameworks for explaining such spatial change and territorial development that have emerged since the early to the mid-2000s – processual-theorizing of neoliberalization (Chapter 5) and the theory of global production networks (Chapter 6).

In this intellectual context, the development of relational *institutional geographies* since the mid-1990s needs to be situated in a relative decline in the popularity of the social relations of production framework in radical geography and the shift towards mid-range theoretical themes that simultaneously avoid the pitfalls of structural determinism and yet broaden further relational thinking on institutions, networks, agencies, and scales. Interestingly, several theorists of the social relations of production approach have pioneered the broad relational turn since the mid-1990s (e.g. Massey, 1993; Storper, 1997; Massey et al., 1999). Here, I compare and contrast three 'thematic turns' towards the relational-institutional view of local and regional development, embeddedness in networks, and scalar geographies. For heuristic purpose, Table 4.1 summarizes these three relational themes, their conceptual categories and proponents, geographical relevance, and theoretical antecedents. Albeit selective and even contentious, this brief critical survey should be viewed as a necessary step in an 'unfinished project' towards the development of relational theories in human geography (see also Bathelt and Glückler, 2003, 2014; Yeung, 2005, 2021a; Zukauskaite et al., 2017; Fuller, 2022).

One of the mid-range theoretical frameworks in Table 4.1 most closely associated with the relational turn in institutional geographies refers to the analysis of *relational assets* in local and regional development. This body of geographical research moves away from neoclassical models of local and regional development that focus primarily on how economic factors of production and other resource endowments shape the absolute and comparative advantages of specific localities and regions. Instead, the relational assets approach attempts to explain local and regional development as a spatial outcome of the resurgence of regional economies characterized by what Michael Storper (1997: p. 26) terms the 'holy trinity' of technology, organizations, and territories in *The Regional World*.[10] Territorial development is theorized to be significantly linked to relational assets and spatial proximity at the local and regional scales such that 'territorialization is often tied to specific interdependencies in economic life' (Storper, 1997: p. 20). This shift from neoclassical notions of comparative advantage to institutionalist notions of relational assets illustrates how different relational thinking (neoclassical vs. institutionalism) might lead to different conceptual themes and explanatory factors to be explored (comparative advantage vs. relational assets). Instead of exploring transactional factor relations between economic actors developed in clusters and agglomerations, geographers have advocated several interrelated and influential concepts to explain the spatial origins and impact of relational assets (see also concepts in Table 3.1).[11] Collectively, this theoretical emphasis on relational assets offers a variety of such non-economic factors as local rules, reflexive knowledge, and conventions that might explain better the agglomeration of economic activities and the subsequent local and regional development.

**Table 4.1**    Relational frameworks in institutional geographies and their antecedents.

| Relational frameworks | Thematic concepts | Major authors | Spatial manifestations | Antecedents |
|---|---|---|---|---|
| Relational assets in local and regional development | • Institutional thickness<br>• Traded and untraded interdependencies<br>• Agglomeration tendencies<br>• Atmosphere and milieu<br>• Social capital | • Ash Amin<br>• Harald Bathelt<br>• Ron Boschma<br>• Phil Cooke<br>• Anders Malmberg<br>• Ron Martin<br>• Peter Maskell<br>• Kevin Morgan<br>• Allen Scott<br>• Michael Storper<br>• Nigel Thrift | • New industrial spaces<br>• Industrial districts<br>• Clusters<br>• Learning regions<br>• Marshallian nodes in global cities<br>• Regional diversification | • Evolutionary and institutional economics<br>• New economic sociology<br>• Institutional analysis<br>• Organization studies<br>• Urban studies<br>• Political studies of democracy and social movements |
| Relational embeddedness in networks: social actors, firms, and organizations | • Inter-organizational networks<br>• Global production networks<br>• Actor-networks<br>• Hybrid and gender relations | • Ash Amin<br>• Neil Coe<br>• Peter Dicken<br>• Meric Gertler<br>• J.K. Gibson-Graham<br>• Gernot Grabher<br>• Roger Lee<br>• Linda McDowell<br>• Jonathan Murdoch<br>• Nigel Thrift<br>• Sarah Whatmore<br>• Henry Yeung | • Global-local tensions<br>• Differentiated production of organizational space<br>• Path dependency<br>• Hybrid geographies and multiple trajectories | • New economic sociology<br>• Organization and management studies<br>• Institutional analysis<br>• Science and technology studies<br>• Poststructuralism and feminist studies |
| Relational scales | • Geographical scales as relational constructions<br>• Social relations as scalar constructs<br>• Rescaling: globalization and reterritorialization | • Neil Brenner<br>• Kevin Cox<br>• Andrew Herod<br>• Bob Jessop<br>• Sallie Marston<br>• Gordon MacLeod<br>• Jamie Peck<br>• Eric Sheppard<br>• Neil Smith<br>• Erik Swyngedouw<br>• Peter Taylor | • Scalar geographies<br>• Politics of globalization<br>• Urban and regional governance<br>• Social regulation of local labour markets | • Political, economic, and urban geography<br>• Sociology<br>• Institutional analysis<br>• Poststructuralism |

Source: Adapted from Yeung (2005: Table 1, p. 40).

While the relational assets framework has contributed to the relational turn in institutional geographies, its spatial locus of analysis remains largely in local and regional development and its analytical anchor in endogenous (often non-economic) institutional factors. Since the mid-1990s, another strand of relational thinking has emerged that unravels *relational embeddedness* in all kinds of trans-local networks among social and economics actors – individuals, firms, and organizations. In Table 4.1, this broad strand of relational thinking in institutional geographies is highly diverse in terms of theoretical claims, analytical themes, and empirical concerns. Some geographers emphasize *inter-organizational networks* in order to understand industrialization, production, and territorial development. Drawing upon economic historian Karl Polanyi's (1944) notion of differential embeddedness between economy and society in pre-capitalist and capitalist times and its reformulation in 'new economic sociology' since Mark Granovetter's (1985, also 2017) seminal work, Dicken and Thrift (1992: p. 283) argue for studying different organizational forms and processes in geographical industrialization: 'the importance of organization as a cognitive, cultural, social and political (and spatial) framework for doing business has increasingly come to be realized. Indeed, nowadays, organization is often equated with "culture," envisaged as a set of conventions'. In retrospect, the concept of embeddedness represents a telling move away from studying the social relations of production in the Marxian political economy of the 1980s towards a broader conceptualization of the socio-spatial organization of production, prefiguring the extensive discussions that have taken place since the mid-1990s around network paradigms, associational economies, and relational geographies.[12]

Other geographers have taken their philosophical and conceptual cues from critical social theories in poststructuralism and feminism to establish a parallel theme concerned with how *hybridity* and *identities* of actors are relationally constituted via different varieties of actor-networks and social embedding in multiplicities (Table 4.1). The next subsection will delve more on the relational thought in such poststructuralist and feminist/postcolonial geographies. Suffice here to say that this line of relational enquiry argues for the plurality and multiplicity of actors (human and nonhumans) and their relational activities across space and time. Instead of conceptualizing economic units as a singular site of rational, (re)productive, and progressive imperatives, this variant of relational thinking 'decenters' and 'destabilizes' the fundamental categories of organizing socio-economic life. Taking a poststructuralist-feminist approach in *The End of Capitalism*, JK Gibson-Graham (2006 [1996]: pp. 15–16) argues that 'a capitalist site (a firm, industry or economy) or a capitalist practice (exploitation of wage labour, distribution of surplus value) cannot appear as the concrete embodiment of an abstract capitalist essence. It has no invariant "inside" but is constituted by its continually changing and contradictory "outsides"'.[13] Economic actors are seen as embedded in diverse social discourses and practices, and cannot be conceived as rational and mechanistic economic entities. These actors are influenced by a broad array of hybrid relations among humans and nonhumans, and their action is significantly shaped by multiple logics and trajectories whose significance varies in different contexts.

In both strands of relational thought in institutional geographies, however, *geographical scales* seem to be less apparent and held constant in their analytical foci, with the notable exceptions of the global production networks theory and actor-network analysis (see Table 4.1; also more on the former theory in Chapter 6). While implicit elements of relational thinking about spatial scales were evident in radical political economy during the 1980s, it is not until the late 1990s and henceforth that a relational view of geographies of scales has been receiving serious attention.[14] Some of this large body of work attempts to interpret and clarify the role of overlapping scalar geographies and reconfiguring of territorial units in understanding perhaps the most significant contemporary geographical phenomenon – globalization and its underlying industrial-organizational platform known as global production networks (see more in Chapter 6 later).

Most studies of the 'relativization' of scales (Jessop, 1999; Brenner, 2001; Peck, 2002) begin with the view that the socio-political construction of scales is critical to our understanding of globalization tendencies and their territorial outcomes. Certain geographical scales are seen as relationally constructed and historically produced under the aegis of modern capitalism. To Marston (2000: p. 221), geographical scale refers to 'a relational element in a complex mix that also includes space, place and environment – all of which interactively make the geographies we live in and study'. One can think of homes, cities, and regions as socially (re)produced in relation to the advent of different rounds of modernity and capitalism. These geographical scales have mixed fortunes in their political acceptance and social influence during different periods of capitalist regimes of accumulation (Smith, 1984). They are not spatial solutions pre-given at the ontological level such that they can be 'jumped' and 'produced' by globalization tendencies; they are rather contested in a relational manner through social struggles and political means. This relational conception of geographical scales is important to the subsequent understanding of the scalar restructuring effects of globalization (Yeung, 1998b; Amin, 2002, 2004; Peck and Yeung, 2003; Jessop et al., 2008).[15]

Summing up, the above three interrelated strands of thematic approaches have contributed to a relational turn in institutional geographies. While some of them have built on the important relational thought in the earlier Marxian political economy (particularly the social relations of production approach), they have also gone beyond their intellectual predecessors to focus on different socio-spatial phenomena at a variety of spatial scales (e.g. complex relations between economy and culture). In this sense, these relational geographies involve more than old wine in new bottles. An important issue for this chapter, however, is the extent to which this relational turn goes beyond a mere *thematic* turn to rework its conceptual explanations such that we not only place emphasis on relations, but also ascribe causal powers to both relations and relationality in explaining socio-spatial events and changes. This quest for a causal relational theory also involves an epistemological shift from recognizing the de facto differences in relational geographies to theorizing explanations of difference. This kind of relational geography, then, requires causal conceptual apparatuses to explain why and how relationality and power relations matter in 'making things happen' – the main concern of this chapter (and the book in general). In one sense, this concern with causality brings us back to the social relations of production approach in which spatial structures were explained in relation to capitalist structural dynamics unleashed through social relations of production. But before I work towards this relational theory in the second half of this chapter, it is necessary to examine the different kinds of relational thought in several more 'open-ended' and 'ideologically-oriented' approaches already reviewed in Chapter 2.

## Relational Thought in Poststructuralist, Feminist, and Postcolonial Geographies

In the more open-ended poststructuralist approaches (see also Table 2.1), relational thinking premised on the conceptual importance of *relations* and *processes and practices of becoming* tends to prevail among different critical 'theories' of space, actor-networks, and materiality. These different 'theories' reject pre-existing categorization of social entities and prefer processual conceptions of the relational nature of these entities. Instead of focusing on how and why relationality operates and matters, these approaches often settle on theorizing and conceptualizing what relationality is and understanding difference through relations between social entities (Cockayne et al., 2017; Ash, 2020a).[16] While this very diverse and large geographical literature addressed briefly in Chapter 2 is beyond any straightforward summary – perhaps a reflection of their truly 'relational' constructions, I attempt to reflect on three strands of such relational literature in poststructuralist geographies before discussing briefly their articulations in feminist and postcolonial geographies. Table 4.2 provides a reprise of the key concepts and theoretical priorities in:

1. relational space;
2. relationality in actor-network theory;
3. relational-materialism in non-representational theory, assemblage theory, post-phenomenology, and posthumanism; and
4. relational 'turn' in feminist and postcolonial geographies.

(1) relational space

In the first literature strand, a relational conception of space is perhaps one of the most debated issues in human geography.[17] Since her 1991 paper in *Marxism*

*Today*, Massey's various influential works have offered the most coherent conception of *relational space* and *power-geometries*. Massey's (1991, 2004) relational idea of a global sense of place is premised on the notion that however particular and unique, a place is always a meeting place for or a point of intersection with global flows and networks of social relations. As such, power operates through these flows and movements of different people and social groups such that different power-geometries are constructed through their relational interactions and differentiated mobilities in such networks.[18] As argued further in Massey (2004: p. 11), the local is not defenceless against the global precisely because of this local and place-based production of the global (sense of place). The role of local politics and power can have purchase on what she calls 'wider global mechanisms': 'Not merely defending the local against the global, but seeking to alter the very mechanisms of the global itself. A local politics with a wider reach; a local politics on the global'.

In *Post-Structuralist Geography*, Jonathan Murdoch (2006: p. 20) argues that this relational making of space is never neutral, but rather consensual and contested among different social entities that come to dominate or be dominated in these power-geometries. His power-filled conception of relational space draws upon poststructural philosopher Michel Foucault's perspective on the diffuse nature of power (i.e. 'power almost everywhere') and feminist theorists' reworking of this Foucauldian conception of power through the relational process of subject-formation and subjection (e.g. Butler, 1997, 2006 [1990]; Kinkaid and Nelson, 2020; MacLeavy et al., 2021). Concurring with Massey's (1991) relational conception of space, Murdoch (2006: p. 22) argues further that relational space is not necessarily less restricting or confining to people and groups placed within certain power-geometries. Ironically, such 'placing' in different sets of relations can strengthen or weaken the capacity of these individuals or groups in exercising control over these relations.

In *For Space*, Massey (2005: pp. 11–12) takes her relational conception of space to a higher ontological order when she conceptualizes space as a product of interrelations, a sphere of multiplicity, and always in process or becoming. In short, space is and must be open for a future that can be reimagined and changed. Massey (2005: p. 61) thus reckons that 'what has emerged was an argument for space as the dimension of a dynamic simultaneous multiplicity'. This conception of space is really what underlines her conception of 'a relational politics for a relational space'.[19] Questioning the representation of space as a discrete multiplicity or a dimension of quantitative divisibility in continental philosophy and social theories, she argues passionately for a relational space embracing both the process of becoming and the openness of that process of becoming (see Table 4.2). While she acknowledges earlier conception of relations between co-existing elements and terms even in structuralism (see Table 2.1), Massey (2005: p. 39) points to a potential implication that 'not only might we productively conceptualise space in terms of relations but also relations can only be fully recognised by thinking fully

**Table 4.2** Relational thought in poststructuralist geographies and their antecedents.

| Relational thought | Thematic concepts | Major authors in geography | Spatial manifestations | Antecedents |
|---|---|---|---|---|
| Relational space | • Global sense of place<br>• Dynamic simultaneity and multiplicity<br>• Open futures | • Doreen Massey<br>• Marcus Doel<br>• Jonathan Murdoch<br>• Louise Amoore | • Power-geometry<br>• Relational politics and ethics<br>• Process of becoming | • Process philosophy<br>• Feminist theory<br>• Science and technology studies |
| Relationality in actor-networks | • Heterogenous association<br>• Things and actants<br>• Action and practice<br>• Durable social ordering | • Jonathan Murdoch<br>• Nigel Thrift<br>• Sarah Whatmore<br>• Martin Müller | • Acting at a distance<br>• Global-local (un)folding<br>• Hybrid and quasi-object | • Actor-network theory<br>• Science and technology studies<br>• Materialist semiotics |
| Relational-materialism | • Affect<br>• Encounter<br>• More-than-human<br>• Object and (vibrant) matter<br>• Assemblage<br>• Thing-power | • Ben Anderson<br>• James Ash<br>• Paul Harrison<br>• Derek McCormack<br>• Colin McFarlane<br>• Paul Simpson<br>• Nigel Thrift | • Process of becoming<br>• Action and practice<br>• Subject formation<br>• (Un)folding and taking place | • Non-representational theory<br>• Assemblage theory<br>• Post-phenomenology<br>• Posthumanism |
| Relational "turn" | • Feminist new materialism<br>• Agency and subjectivity<br>• Politics of authority and performativity | • Felix Driver<br>• Kim England<br>• Derek Gregory<br>• Jane Jacobs<br>• Eden Kinkaid<br>• Eleonore Kofman<br>• Victoria Lawson<br>• Julie MacLeavy<br>• Sarah Radcliffe<br>• Parvati Raghuram | • Relational politics and ethics<br>• Networks of care<br>• Relations of proximity<br>• Re-imagining the West<br>• Decolonizing practices | • Feminist theory<br>• Queer theory<br>• Postcolonial theory |

spatially. In order for there to be relations there must of necessity be spacing'. To me, this is where her conception of relational space as always open, multiple, unfinished, and becoming becomes quite vague, and her conception of the necessary relation between the relational and the spatial borders on a tautological argument – spacing is not only necessary to relations but it also defines relations (over space). This sort of relational construction of anti-essentialism is also quite common in other poststructuralist approaches to be examined below.

In *World City*, Massey (2007) puts her relational space perspective to a concrete analysis of London's role as a global city and a local place *within* globalization (also in Massey, 2004: pp. 15–17, 2005: pp. 155–159, 166–169, 190–193). More specifically, she has analysed London's success and purpose in relation to local, national, and global processes and its role in the politics and responsibility of the global.[20] Her continual interest in the relational turn is best summarized in the following theoretical exposé: 'Urban space is *relational*, not a mosaic of simply juxtaposed differences. This place [London], as many places, has to be conceptualised, not as a simply diversity, but as a meeting-place, of jostling, potentially conflicting, trajectories. It is set within, and internally constituted through, complex geometries of differential power' (Massey, 2007: p. 89; original italics). In my review of Massey's fascinating book (Yeung, 2008),[21] I note that at times, I feel a little bewildered by her critique of neoliberalism as a major contributor to inequality in London and, for that matter, the United Kingdom as a whole. Massey seems to equate neoliberalism to the wholesale import of the American greed, although I suspect there are surely other complex socio-economic forces at work within the UK, such as pre-existing inequalities so well analysed in her earlier work on spatial divisions of labour (Massey, 1984) and the large influx of – and property ownership by – international capital ranging from Russian oligarchs to Arab sheik monarchs and 'crazy' rich Asians! To me, the American greed is probably the latest *contingent* factor that aggravates further a historical-geographical reality of pre-existing inequality (e.g. Britain's longstanding North-South divide) and foreign ownership. But her targeting of American greed as a particular 'culprit' might appear to be a little mono-causal and narrow in focus for a well-argued book grounded in a relational space approach.

Before we move on to consider relationality in actor-network theory, I offer one recent comparable example of such a relational space approach in human geography – Louise Amoore's (2020a) relational approach to algorithm's 'space of play' in *Cloud Ethics*, i.e. how algorithmic arrangements in the digital era generate ideas of goodness, transgression, and what society ought to be. In what she terms 'cloud ethics', algorithms and machine learning should be understood as 'the political formation of relations to oneself and to others that is taking place, increasingly, in and through algorithms... To consider algorithms as having ethics in formation is to work with the propensities and possibilities that algorithms embody, pushing the potentials of their arrangements beyond the decisive moment of the output' (Amoore, 2020a: p. 7). Empirically, she illustrates this relational approach to the spaces of cloud ethics by examining the diverse interactions between humans and machines embodying algorithms capable of machine learning.

In her fascinating case study of surgical 'da Vinci' robots and interviews with obstetric surgeons, Amoore (2020a: p. 63) shows that these interactions involve different spatially distanciated relations of judgement and decision that are now filtered through and mediated by the algorithms built into the machine learning process of surgical robots. These relational interactions between humans (surgeons and colleagues) and machines in turn accentuate the role of algorithms in what she terms 'double political foreclosure' that condenses multiplicities into a single data output (e.g. optimized surgical procedures suggested by robots) and denies pre-emptively political claims based on the recognizability of data attributes (e.g. untraceability of scattered data elements and distanciated machine learning processes leading to those suggestions). Her relational approach to cloud ethics views (1) algorithms as different arrangements of propositions and thus their outputs are neither true or false: they are contestable subject to ethical and other considerations; (2) algorithms as aperture instruments or technologies of perception that change processes of human perception of things and generate their interest in the data environment (e.g. the problem of 'big data'); and (3) algorithms as giving accounts of themselves, but always partial, contingent, oblique, incomplete, and ungrounded.

In spatial terms, Amoore's (2020a) relational take of ethics that there is no single 'unified I' or actor in algorithms that can be 'tracked down' and held responsible when things go wrong (e.g. surgical damages to organs or 'collateral damage' in precision strike by autonomous weapon systems) appears to be too 'correlationalist' to me. Making such relational arguments is one thing, explaining their causal relations is quite another thing. Where do we draw the line to identify causality, albeit contingently exercised, in this myriad of relational happenings and entities in a world or multiple worlds of algorithms? How do we account for and explain why certain processes of algorithmic applications can go wrong (or right, but perhaps less 'culpable') or sometimes so badly wrong (e.g. her real examples in Amoore, 2020a: pp. 76, 96–97)? Is pointing to the algorithm's reduction of future multiplicities to a single output 'sufficient' for such an explanatory account – the argument seems rather 'mechanical'? Even though she points out the need to render tractable on the horizon of the action triggered by such a single output, the related events and processes should still need to be explained – but by what? The missing agency and causal relation seem to trouble the explanatory power of her relational approach to cloud ethics, even as she recognizes the role of humans in writing prejudicial algorithms by inscribing in them racialized or other biased profiles.[22] Ultimately, are these algorithms 'actor-networks' in their own right?

## (2) relationality in actor-network theory

This brings me to the second literature strand on relational thought in poststructuralist geographies – *relationality in actor-network theory* (Table 4.2). Since I have elaborated quite a bit on the 'theory' itself in Chapter 2, I focus here on its analysis of relationality and its (lack of) possible explanatory potential.[23] In actor-network theory (ANT), relationality and power refer to the strength and the continuous process of heterogeneous associations of actors and entities through which they gain power and act at a distance by enrolling other actors and entities into these actor-networks. As noted in Chapter 2, it is a descriptive sociology of ordering rather than order and how this is done in practice (Murdoch, 1995: p. 748, 2006: pp. 66–69; Thrift, 1996: p. 25). While ANT is not a coherent and unilinear approach to causal analysis, it is safe to state that ANT is a broadly 'materialist semiotic' approach described in Chapter 2; a non-textual relational materialism that focuses on the building of orders, paths of development, and meanings in the pursuit of agendas (Bingham, 1996; Law, 2009; Latour, 2013). Actions or practices, rather than structures, form the focus of its descriptive analysis.

Given ANT's ontology and methodology, Murdoch (1997b: p. 743; my emphasis) defines actor-networks as 'the chains which give rise to natural and social realities, realities which can only be understood as *stabilised sets of relations* which allow the construction of centres and peripheries, insides and outsides, humans and nonhumans, nature and society, and so on'. In short, ANT focuses on the ability of actors to 'act at a distance' by entraining in relational ways both other actors and the necessary material objects, codes, procedural frameworks, and so on to effect the activation of power. Consistent with Massey's (1991) idea of relational space earlier, the adoption of an ANT perspective on the 'global' also implies a rejection of a global-local dualism, with one scale (the global) dominating the other (the local). As noted in some detail by arguably its most famous protagonist Bruno Latour (1999: p. 18; my emphasis),

> by following the movement allowed by ANT, we are never led to study social order, in a displacement that would allow an observer to zoom from the global to the local and back. In the social domain there is no change of scale. It is so to speak *always flat and folded* and this is especially true of the natural sciences that are said to provide the context, the frame, the global environment in which society is supposed to be located. Contexts too flow locally through networks.

In this way, ANT's relational approach is directed at the associations, processes, and performances that give rise to so-called 'purified outcomes' (e.g. nature, society, human, modernity, firm, and so on). Geographical research guided by ANT therefore tends to focus on how (flat) associations and networks are built and maintained across space (Murdoch, 1997a: pp. 334–335). A fundamental part of extended network construction is the ability to create and manage the knowledge, vocabulary, procedures, rules, and technologies through which social activity is conducted. In contrast to a conceptualization of globalization (and the global economy) as a homogeneous and steamroller-like entity (more in my Chapter 6), the new topology in ANT is one of conceiving relationality among nodes that have as many dimensions as they have connections (Latour, 1999: p. 22, 2013: pp. 30–33). National boundaries are insignificant, but the fibrous links shaping social and production systems have no linear, bounded, and fixed character whatsoever: they continually shudder, shatter, mutate and evolve into new constellations of relational connections. The implicit need to deconstruct actors in ANT leads one to resist ascribing causal powers to the notion of unified subjects, firms, nation states or other institutions. Rather, ANT compels the researcher to be interested in the (co)constitution and (re)shaping of social, political, or economic organizations via *tracing* their engagement with an array of actor-networks. This methodological stance reflects its socio-technical constructivist approach to relational thinking.

While the methodological emphasis on relational practices highlighted by actor-network theory is a welcome one, I sense a serious danger of relationism raised by realist philosopher Graham Harman in DeLanda and Harman's (2017: p. 61) *The Rise of Realism*. To me, ANT's concentrated attention on actors *in* networks might descend into a mechanistic approach that atomizes agents and focuses solely on the links or relations between them, without a sense of the unequal social processes that powerfully (co)constitute and (re)shape these relationships. For example, this danger is evident in Murdoch's (1997a: p. 332; my emphasis, also 2006: p. 71) claim that:

> Network analysis is quite simple: it means following networks all the way along their length; there is no need to step outside the networks for all the qualities of spatial construction and configuration of interest will be found *therein*... Actor-network theorists thus reject the view that social life is arranged into levels or tiers some of which determine what goes on in others; everything is kept at 'ground level'.

Keeping things at 'ground level' or the local, however, makes it difficult to retain structural power relations within the global in the same frame. It might well be true that capitalism is too abstract a category to be very useful in understanding spatial specificity in the world today or the finer empirical contexts of embodied socio-spatial life. However, we should surely not discard this level of abstraction *entirely* in favour of the local 'ground level' only. Constraining our analyses of the lifeworld(s) to the 'ground level' and to approach the power relations therein as simply traceable through tangible relations of heterogeneous associations would be a major mistake. As will be explained later in section two, a more practically adequate consideration in a relational theory for understanding the material world and all its complexities should be to acknowledge the points made by actor-network theorists concerning the need to avoid using separate vocabularies for these larger phenomena and entities, and yet at the same time retain causal-explanatory understandings at higher levels of abstraction. In other words, just as we need to incorporate multiple scales and loci of analysis so, too, we should remain sensitive to the insights provided at multiple levels of abstraction.

Furthermore, while ANT explicitly acknowledges the 'powers of association' in actor-networks, it is unclear if causality matters in such powers and causal relations are real and efficacious in empirical outcomes. Contrasting his ANT approach in *Reassembling the Social* with what he calls 'a powerful and convincing account' in which a few global causes generate a mass of effects, Latour (2005: pp. 130–131) prefers a 'weak and powerless account' of the social world. To him, network is a concept and a tool to help description, not a thing out there or something to be described.[24] But as I have already examined in Chapter 2, this seemingly relativist approach to radical empiricism still begs the question if things and quasi-objects in actor-networks are real and possess emergent properties, as in the kind of re-lational-materialism to be discussed next (see also Elder-Vass, 2008, 2010). To Murdoch (2006: p. 67) and Harman (2010: p. 91), the answer is quite affirmative. Examining Latour's (1987, 1993) empirical work on scientific laboratories, they argue that actor-network theory has its 'realist' moments when things and actants are recognized for their real effects on experimental outcomes and scientific find-ings. But the forces of these things and objects are only efficacious or causal when they take shape or engage in heterogeneous associations within actor-networks.[25]

(3) relational-materialism in non-representational theory, assemblage theory, post-phenomenology, and posthumanism

This *relational-materialism* is well featured in the third strand of the more recent literature on relational thought in poststructuralist geographies associated with non-representational theory, assemblage theory, post-phenomenology, and posthumanism (see Chapter 2 and Tables 2.1 and 4.2). Introducing the promise of *non-representational theory* (NRT) in human geography, Anderson and Harrison (2010b: pp. 3, 13) focus on 'non-representational theory's relational-materialism for thinking about the com-position and nature of the social' and note that 'this approach involves three starting points; a commitment to an expanded social including all manner of material bodies, an attention to relations and being-in-relation, and sensitivity to "almost-not quite" entities such as affects'. They also acknowledge NRT's connection with actor-network theory, particularly Latour's (2005) notion of the social as always in the making and subject to reshuffling and new heterogeneous associations of things and quasi-objects. The key difference though is that NRT's conception of materiality takes far many more or even infinite forms of multiplicities and every*thing(s)*.[26] Taking their poststructuralist philosophical cues from Gilles Deleuze's conception of exteriority of relations in assemblages (see my earlier discussion in Chapter 2), Anderson and Har-rison (2010b: pp. 15–16) differentiate their approach from actor-network theory by arguing for an irreducible plurality of relations that must be traced and their durable orderings or assemblages fully unpacked:

> any simple definition of 'relation' is immediately undone by the irreducible plu-rality of relations… The consequence is that it is not enough to simply assert that phenomena are 'relationally constituted' or invoke the form of the network, rather it becomes necessary to think through the specificity and performative efficacy of different relations and different relational configurations.[27]

I certainly agree with their critique of the all-too-common assertion that phenomena are relationally constituted. That kind of relational thinking is only 'thematic' in its descriptive focus. The more significant issue for a relational theory is the specificity and performative efficacy of these relations and relational configurations. This is where I find the NRT approach rather limited in *explaining* the causal powers (i.e. performative efficacy?) of their relational-materialism that does not seem to recognize the existence of anything non-relational or any social entity or property that cannot be defined relationally. This danger of correlationism is raised in realist philosopher Roy Bhaskar's (2016: pp. 55–56) critique of relational-everything (also known as 'relationism' in DeLanda and Harman, 2017: p. 61). While critical realism (see also Chapter 3) adopts a relational conception of the subject matter of social science, e.g. relations of oppression and exploitation and other forms of domination and subjugation and relations of transformation, not everything can be explained relationally and thus his 'scalar' conception of social life.[28] Indeed in another work on assemblage theory, Anderson et al. (2012a: p. 172) have recognized this risk of 'everything is relational':

> For us the risk is that it may become too familiar. Rather than a provocation that forces us to think again, relational thought risks becoming a routine to be mastered and repeated. The danger is that in offering a 'relational' account of the social, it is easy to stop short of a set of subsequent questions. How might we attend to the plurality of relations that might differ in both nature and kind? Are relations internal or external to their terms? Can relations change without the terms also changing? Are actual entities exhausted by their position within relations? How can we understand what we could term 'events' that may break, interrupt or change relations, and may initiate the chance of new relations.

To me, these questions remain more about accounting for different relations in a thematic sense than about explaining their (causal) differences in producing socio-spatial outcomes. The thorny issue of agency is also challenging in these 'seas' of relations – how do things and matters fit into their materialist conception of relations and relationality? Where do causal powers go in enacting and exerting the performative efficacy of these relations and relationality?

These difficult and unresolved issues in non-representational theory's relational-materialism call on other more recent relational thoughts in *assemblage theory*, *post-phenomenology*, and *posthumanism* that collectively bring materiality and 'thing-power' into their conceptualization and analysis of what political theorist Jane Bennett (2004, 2010) calls 'the force of things' or 'vibrant matter' (see Table 4.2). These vital things and matters can range from trash, waste, and the elements to human bodies (skins, sweat, and so on), and their relational co-presence enables thing-power to rise to the surface that cannot simply be reduced to the semiotics and contexts of their appearance. In some recent geographical studies of matters and materiality (e.g. McCormack, 2017, 2018; Ash and Simpson, 2019; Adams-Hutcheson and Smith, 2020; Ash, 2020a; Engelmann and McCormack, 2021), different socio-spatial manifestations of affect, emotion, and encounters with matters and the elements have been accounted for through such descriptive analyses of the contingent co-presence of objects and things in relation to their affective effects on subjects and their subjectivities. Engelmann and Mc-Cormack (2021: p. 1433) argue further that the circumstantial relations between the four elemental orientations of matter, molecule, milieu, and media shape but not determine the composition and conditions of their 'elemental worlds' that are entangled with bodies and forms of life.

While this vitalist view offers a more thematic focus on things and matters in relational thought in poststructuralist geographies, some nagging questions remain outstanding – what is *not* thing-power and what use is there if everything, including human powers, can be conceived as thing-power? Bennett's (2004, 2010) conception of materiality in things and even bodies might also be tautological because it necessitates thing-power – things are material and since materiality has intrinsic vitality, things are vital and therefore 'powerful'! To me, this begs at least three further sets of questions for empirical disciplines such as human geography:

1.  In what sense a matter is vital and what is its vitality and in relation to what (matter and/or subject)? Do we count these relations between matters as matter as well? In short, is relationality itself a (vibrant) matter?
2.  How do we know the nature and magnitude of vitality? Is it merely an empirical question? Does vitality matter more than matter itself? To whom, really, does vitality matter?[29]
3.  Even granted matter's thing-power, how does causality play out in this ontology of every 'thing' as vital?

Let me take a leaf out of Jane Bennett's (2010: ch. 7) section on the 'small agency' of worms in *Vibrant Matter* – 'leaf' in both metaphorical and materialist senses! What is a leaf's affective vitality in relation to the subject (humans) and other objects (e.g. worms eating leaves)? Are there differences in both the quality (nature) and magnitude of the leaf's vitality in these cases? How do we know? Do we merely leave it to empirical disciplines to figure it out? Can we theorize the different conditions and, in the spirit of my earlier argument for explanatory theories, different causal mechanisms through which this heterogeneous nature and degree of vitality takes place? As outlined in my three key considerations of/for theory in Chapter 1, what are its implications for our immanent critiques of knowledge production (i.e. politics of theorizing) and our normative strive towards positive social change (i.e. practical adequacy)? Can the politics of such thing-power be even debated in parliamentary democracies or only in Bennett's own political utopia?[30] In short, theorizing thing-power seems necessary but not sufficient in fulfilling these considerations, unless the differential nature and degree of thing-power can be ascertained. This analytical task might well go beyond relational thinking (of 'everything' and as 'always') in flat ontologies and necessitate actual and explanatory theories in empirical disciplines such as human geography.[31]

In Abrahamsson et al.'s (2015) critique of vitalist thought, they examine the materiality of another matter, omega-3 fatty acids, by 'borrowing' the case from Jane Bennett's (2010: ch. 3) *Vibrant Matter* and interrogating closely the methods of several scientific studies of omega-3 effects on humans quoted in Bennett. While they agree with her on the importance of matter, they have doubts about matter's agency or the idea of thing-power. To them, Bennett's case for omega-3's agential power is paradoxically drawn from causal studies in normal science, and yet her strategy of drawing more members, such as fatty acid's particularities in ocean fishes and their environmental concerns, into the role of 'actors' is unwise and sidesteps the causality study of such matter. They prefer the removal of this agency-versus-causality divide to explore what they term other 'modes of doing' or 'matter in relation', such as affording, responding, caring, tinkering, and eating.[32]

But as argued in Chapter 1 and by Tolia-Kelly (2013), Joronen and Häkli (2017), and Doucette (2020), even this more relational approach to matter and vitalism might still incur the risk of doing descriptive 'surface geography' and suffer from an onto-theological 'lock-in'. Joronen and Häkli (2017: p. 569; original italics) thus lament that:

> Few scholars, including us, deny the urgency of complex environmental problems and the need to critically question modes of thinking that have led to their escalation globally. Nonetheless, when the notion of non-human agency forms a steady onto-theological stance, it risks projecting a totalizing account of the political. *Everything* non-human is thought of as having political *potential* because everything can have an effect on something.[33]

Most recently in his text *Non-Representational Theory*, Paul Simpson (2021: p. 119) cautions that these related questions on matter and relationality are significant and remain unresolved. He urges us to think much more carefully about the difference between agency and causality. Overall then, post-phenomenology and posthumanism seem to sidestep what theory and explanation are about (subjects, objects, their relations, or what?) and how they should be conducted in an epistemological sense. The relational thought in these approaches is primarily concerned with the ontological explication of the nature of subjects, objects, matters, the elements, relations, and materiality. In this chapter's second main section, my relational theory aims to take into account both the causal powers of relationality (matter and its constitutive relations) and the autonomous existence of such objects and non-objects (e.g. structures) outside human experiences and practices.

(4) relational 'turn' in feminist and postcolonial geographies

In the fourth strand of literature on feminist and postcolonial geographies, relational thought represents a significant 'turn' when feminist and postcolonial geographers critically and persistently theorize relationality in various binaries associated with subjectivity, identity, and subject formation (see Table 4.2). Having examined feminist and postcolonial approaches in Chapter 2, I shall be brief here by way of a selective illustration of geographical work incorporating such relational thought in feminist theory and postcolonial theory.

In *feminist geography*, Kinkaid and Nelson (2020) refer to such a relational turn by turning to the more recent work of feminist theorist Judith Butler (2015a, 2015b). In Chapters 1 and 2, I have already discussed Butler's (2015a) work on the practice of a performative theory of assembly in which she theorizes the body as a living set of relations rather than an autonomous entity. In this ontological claim, the body can live and act in the social worlds only in relation to its dependency on different infrastructural structures and environmental conditions (Butler, 2015a: p. 130). In this 'ethics of cohabitation', she argues for the relational interdependency of our bodies 'up against' the distant suffering of other bodies and thus the interconnections of there and here in the public assembly of our bodies. In *Senses of the Subject*, Butler (2015b) turns towards a post-phenomenological account of subjectivity and emphasizes the fundamental relationality and dependency of such subjects – the idea that the 'I' and 'we' are always necessarily produced through our relations with others and 'I'/'we' are never fully 'myself' or 'ourselves' in an autonomous way.

To Kinkaid and Nelson (2020: p. 96), such a relational turn in feminist theory provides rich resources for geographers to engage with parallel theoretical shifts, such as feminist new materialisms, actor-network theory, non-representational theory, and queer theory. These new relational thoughts in feminist geography seem to be concerned mostly with rethinking the problems of representation, materiality, and agency. While some feminist geographers have taken this relational approach to rework the reference of performativity as a network of relations, others have focused on processes of (un)becoming in the constellation of identities and subject formations (see Kofman and Raghuram, 2015, 2020; Datta et al., 2020; MacLeavy et al., 2021).

For example, England et al. (2020: p. 336) focus on a relational ontology of care that view people as embodied and interdependent beings and examine the provision of healthcare among women immigrants, healthcare workers, and asylum seekers within the UK.[34] Their study finds that the different experiences of the same healthcare system by these diverse people demonstrate the need for a relational understanding of the taken-for-granted categories such as health, care, and 'immigrant woman'. Taking a plural and embodied feminist approach, Brigstocke et al. (2021) further conceptualize authority and its relation with power in order to examine the 'crisis' of authority in its different forms, from algorithmic and experiential (affective) to expert and participatory authorities. Their relational approach helps establish authority as distinct from power and yet imbued and reproduced in everyday life and experiences. Similarly, MacLeavy et al. (2021) deploy feminist relational concepts of resistance, resilience, and reworking, first evoked in Cindy Katz's (2004) *Growing Up Global*, in new processual ways to gesture at the emerging, performative, and generative moments of undetermined futurity and subjects-in-formation.

In *postcolonial geographies*, the relational turn has also been influential since the geographical works of Derek Gregory (1994, 2004), Jane Jacobs (1996), and Felix Driver (2001). The issue of unequal power relations coordinated through practices of textual inscription and circulation has led some geographers to engage with the process of 'decolonising the mind' by challenging the self-image of the West as a self-determining and self-contained entity (Barnett, 2015: p. 177). These new decolonizing practices range from challenging the politics of authority and knowledge production to the (re)enactment of particular effects of texts and other aesthetic forms within the broader networks of social relations in society and space. In fact, one might argue that Edward Said's (2003 [1978]) Orientalism can be conceived relationally as a 'discursive formation' in Foucault's (2002 [1969]: p. 41) sense that lay the foundation for the exercise of colonial powers. But then to say that this discursive formation suffuses our everyday life and taken-as-given thought can be vague and limited for explanatory purpose. Surely we need to specify and unpack much more explicitly these very authoritative representations and their *actual workings* on the ground as causal mechanisms if we were to deploy them as explanations of coloniality and effects in manufacturing consent and (re)producing hegemony. Deconstructing Orientalist representations is one thing; connecting the relational politics of these representations and empirical outcomes in both macro- and micro-spaces is quite another thing and represents, perhaps, a much more daunting challenge (see also Hallaq's, 2018 critique and my further discussion in Chapter 6).

Taken together and as noted in Tables 4.1 and 4.2, the above diverse strands of literature on relational thinking in human geography have collectively contributed to a broadly relational turn that affords conceptual primacy to institutional embeddedness, networks, rescaling of space, processes of becoming, multiplicities, heterogeneous associations, vibrant matters and things, and relational politics and ethics. These new concepts of relationality became the dominant *themes* in many geographical approaches and empirical enquiries during much of the 2000s and the 2010s. As noted at the chapter's beginning, the relational thinking in some of these approaches runs into the danger of correlationism and/or relationism because of their missing conception of causal powers in relationality and agency that make things happen in society and space. A relational theory needs to overcome this tendency towards correlationism in relational thinking and to inscribe causal powers into its explanatory frame.

## Making Things Happen: Towards a Relational Theory

In this section, I aim to rework three important conceptual tools of/for a relational theory in analytical geographies – relationality, causal powers, and actors – in order to identify their underlying causal properties.[35] As introduced in Chapter 1, this is an important second step in my synthetic approach to theory and explanation because some extreme variants of the relational turn in human geography, such as some of the above more open-ended approaches, have been accused of anti-essentialism and weak in explanatory power. Sayer (1995: p. 23) has aptly pointed out this problem for theory and explanation: 'The danger of anti-essentialism is that it switches straight from determinism and reductionism to voluntarism. Extreme versions of anti-essentialism which suppose that anything can happen in any situation therefore render explanation impossible, for there is nothing that theory can say about what determines what' (see also Chapter 3).

The generic and perhaps metaphorical concepts of relations and networks – as conceived in the various open-ended approaches – are in themselves descriptive categories or metaphors and often devoid of explanatory capacity. This is mainly because their material and substantive influences need to be mediated through social action and human agency. After all, relations and networks do not act in their own right and produce concrete socio-spatial outcomes without actor-specific agency. These action and practices are embodied in and performed by actors, however co-constituted they are through these relations and networks. As a description of complex webs of actors and structures, these concepts are thus less effective in theorizing how concrete socio-spatial outcomes are produced through them (see also Schatzki, 2002, 2019; Hannah, 2019). As sociologist Laurent Thévenot (2001: p. 408; my emphasis) notes, '[t]he notion of network is very compelling because of its power to embrace in its *description* a potential list of entities which is much broader than the one offered by models of action and practice. But this notion tends to overlook the heterogeneity of links for the benefit of a unified picture of interconnected entities'.

I argue that one key missing link in the earlier relational frameworks and relational thought summarized in Tables 4.1 and 4.2 is the conceptualization of *causal powers* practiced by social actors through relationality in these networks and relations. We must not only unpack *what* the nature of such powers might be in relational terms, but more importantly also demonstrate *how* the more-than-heterogeneous configurations of power relations or what I term 'relational geometries' can generate certain emergent effects and spatial tendencies that account for concrete events and change in society and space. Put in different empirical contexts, some of these emergent effects in the inherent relationality of different configurations of power relations may become more important than others and thus may have more capacity to produce concrete socio-spatial outcomes. In this sense, relationality exercised through causal powers in relational geometries is 'more-than-heterogeneous' in nature because of the different degrees of capacity and differentiation in exercising power relations. This differentiated importance and capacity of relationality in generating empirical outcomes is premised on the specificity of causal mechanisms in such explanatory theories, as introduced in the previous chapter. While the next chapter will elaborate further on such mechanisms, this section begins with relationality before theorizing its differentiated causal powers in relational geometries.

## *Rethinking Relational Thought: Relationality and Power*

To clarify the nature of relationality, we first have to revisit relational thinking. As defined by Massey et al. (1999: p. 12), relational thinking represents 'an attempt to reimagine the either/or constructions of binary thinking (where the only relations are negative ones of exclusion) and to recognize the important elements of interconnection which go into the construction of any identity'. Some critical clarifications of this quotation are necessary. First, relationality presupposes binaries such that relations between these opposing binaries can be 'reimagined'. Figure 4.1 shows how relationality works through the conceptual connections between/among actors and structures, global-local scales, the social and the spatial, and gendered identities. It is through these matrix-like interconnections and tensions that each end of the binary achieves its meaning. It is thus impossible to think of the global without presupposing its relation to the local and other spatial scales (see Massey, 2005).

Second, it follows that not all binary relations are necessarily 'exclusive'. Such exclusiveness in binary thinking needs to be demonstrated in relation to the implied 'inclusiveness' of relational thinking, not merely asserted. In other words, some binaries can be useful insofar as they stimulate relational thinking. As noted

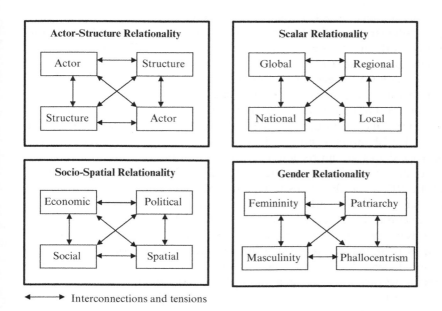

◄────► Interconnections and tensions

**Figure 4.1**   The nature of relationality in human geography.

Source: Adapted and developed from Yeung (2005: Figure 1, p. 43). Reproduced with permission.

earlier in realist philosophers Meillassoux's (2008: p. 5) critique of correlationism and Harman's distaste for relationism (DeLanda and Harman, 2017: p. 61), it is not necessarily productive to insist that we can never grasp a subject just because it is not always-already related to an object. The assumed primacy of the relation over the related terms, such as the global and the local or an actor and a structure, can also be premature and risky in terms of an onto-theological 'lock-in' (Joronen and Häkli, 2017: p. 569).

To me, relationality refers to an inherent quality embedded in an iterative process of drawing or building interconnections between two or more discrete categories and phenomena that may not necessarily be binaries. Thinking about relationality necessitates an analytical movement away from abstract phenomena (e.g. the subject or the network) to examine the interconnections between discrete phenomena and to transcend their dichotomization. As argued by organizational theorists Hilary Bradbury and Benyamin Lichtenstein (2000: p. 551), 'Taking a relational orientation suggests that the real work of the human organization occurs within the space of interaction between its members. Thus the theorist must account for the relationships among, rather than the individual properties of, organizational members'. Clearly, such an emphasis on relationality has strong parallels in earlier studies in the physical sciences (e.g. quantum physics) and social sciences (e.g. systems analysis and social theory). A relational conception of actors and structures also presupposes an understanding of sociologist Anthony Giddens' (1984) classic conception of structuration in which the discursive consciousness and reflexivity of human agency can arguably shape the structures that both enable and constrain their activities (see Elder-Vass, 2010).

What might then be useful in this theory of relationality for relational approaches in human geography? I believe it has something to do with the *inherent tension* in relationality that in turn gives rise to the analytical significance of different forms of emergent power. The contingent realization of these different forms of emergent power is an empirical matter because it depends on specific historical-geographical contexts (see also Chapters 5 and 6). The process of connecting different discrete categories necessitates an appreciation of the tension between these categories. For example, in arguing for an analytical shift from the social relations of production of the 1970s and the 1980s to relations between actors and their embedded networks in the 1990s and beyond, we often invoke an analytical tension in theorizing the connections between these categories. This tension in relationality, nevertheless, is not necessarily a bad thing for theory development. To understand this tension in relationality, we need to bring different forms of *emergent power* back into our theorization – a missing epistemological process in much of the thematic relational turn in human geography that too frequently tends to privilege particular categories, such as the local, the multiplicity, the network, the actant, the thing, matter, the performative, the affective, and so on.

I now give a few short examples of such unintended privileging of power's diverse categories in critical approaches that range from actor-network theory and non-representational theory to feminist theory (see Table 4.2). In *actor-network theory*, power is regularly thought of as power-through-networks and/or 'network as solidified actor'. Taking a topological view of power and networks, Murdoch (2006: p. 78) notes that:

> Actor-network theory builds on Foucaultian [*sic*] theory by showing how power is conducted within network formations. Power, in this view, lies in the heterogeneous materials assembled in networks in accordance with the need to make actions (scientific or otherwise) durable through space and time. Networks draw materials together into new configurations. Each network traces its own trajectory and this trajectory reflects a convergence of factors, including the combination of entities used in network construction, the relations established between these entities, and the ordering impulses of the network builder. If all these elements work in concert then the network becomes a solidified actor – an 'actor-network'.

This conception of power seems rather slippery and diffuse, as Murdoch (2006: p. 78) recognizes as deliberately 'oxymoronic' – citing ANT theorist John Law (1999: p. 3). But such a hybrid 'mixing' of actants (heterogeneous materials), relations (their interactions in networks), and durable structures (networks) in 'making things happen' makes it rather hard to tell *who* exactly is indeed 'the network builder' – is it an actant, a relation, or even the network itself? Who should 'the need to make actions (scientific or otherwise) durable' be attributed to? Murdoch (2006) seems to claim it is the network that does this and traces that. But isn't the network itself an *effect* of relations and interactions among its (co)constitutive actants, some of whom are more (or less) powerful than others? I believe a robust theory of relationality and power must necessarily specify these inter-actant power relations and trace the sources of power and 'ordering impulses' that make things happen and 'all these elements work in concert'. In short, actors cannot be networks that are durable and, possibly, complex configurations of relations among these actors. Actors must be defined in relation to their agency, i.e. identifiable sources and efficacy of intention, choice, and power. Network relations matter, but only insofar as their (co)constitutive actors can be specified and the pathways of transmitting and effecting power among these actors, i.e. causal mechanisms, can be identified.

In *non-representational theory* and its leading work on affect, power relations are acknowledged in terms of their working through affective life. As Ben Anderson (2014: p. 8) proclaims in *Encountering Affect*,

> The urgency of the 'affective turn' follows from a simple claim: forms of power work through affective life. Whether or not this is a transformation unique to 'late capitalist culture' is beside the point. Understanding how power functions in the early twenty-first century requires that we trace how power operates through affect and how affective life is imbued with relations of power, without reducing affective life to power's effect.

In Anderson (2016), he takes this affective approach to power further by examining empirically what he terms 'neoliberal affects' that are defined as affective atmospheres and structures of feelings (in terms of qualities and senses) in conditioning the rise of neoliberalism in the United States and the UK during the 1980s. To him, these affects provide 'the *real conditions of emergence* for particular neoliberalisms and the continual *(re)conditioning* of emerged but still in formation neoliberalisms' (Anderson, 2016: p. 735; original italics). Nevertheless, the functioning of these real and 'powerful' affects has not been theorized as necessary relations to neoliberalism and their actual workings as discursive formation have also not been demonstrated empirically (despite his two examples of the Mont Pelerin Society and Milton Friedman's workshop in Chicago[36]). The concept of neoliberal affect becomes more an 'intuition', a 'generic descriptor', an 'umbrella category', and a 'vocabulary' in Anderson (2016: pp. 735–736), rather than a causal explanation or even a (affective) theory of the emergence of neoliberal reason and neoliberalism (cf. Peck, 2010; Peck and Theodore, 2015; see also my discussion of the process/mechanism conflation of neoliberalism in the next chapter).

Many other geographical studies of affect tend to follow this poststructuralist view of power as affective in the process of becoming that might be useful in accounting for the (un)folding of relationality. But as introduced in this chapter's beginning, this processual view of power still begs the key question of *why*, in Thrift's (2000: p. 217, 2007: p. 114) view, events must take place within networks of power? What forces or causal mechanisms 'compel' such events to do so? Answering these causal questions requires unpacking such networks of power and their propensity towards iterability or reproducibility. But who drive these processes and how do they (actors) go about doing so (mechanisms)? Much work on affect seems to focus on individual thought, experiences, and feelings in different/situated unfolding events and encounters, such as rhythms, habits, emotions, doing, feelings, sitting, moving, and so on (see also Simonsen and Koefoed, 2020; Simpson, 2021).

In *feminist thought*, power is often conceived as performative through the performance of bodily enactments and the embodiment of gender norms. Moving from her 1990 theory of gender performativity to a consideration of precarious lives, Butler's (2015a) performative theory of assembly discussed in Chapter 2 offers a performative form of power in the struggles for democracy due to the problem of demarcation and delimitation of the people it represents – who are/define 'the people'? Even though they are often transitory, public assemblies and demonstrations matter as (concerted) bodily enactments of such performative power in excess of discursive demands. Her performative theory thus conceptualizes bodily enactments in the political, such as public assemblies, as 'powerful' struggles against precarity and dispensability associated with the demand for self-responsibility, as in neoliberalism's twin processes of the 'precaritization' and 're-sponsibilization' of individuals. Similar to Butler's (2015a) theory built on political theorist Hannah Arendt's work on the space of appearance and the politics of bodies, Simonsen and Koefoed (2020: pp. 112–114) also draw upon Arendt and her 'politics of relationality' to examine the politics of action in urban encounters.

To sum up, what might be lacking in some strands of such relational thought (e.g. actor-network theory and non-representational theory) is an analytical focus on the tension and power relations between – not within – different categories (see also Figure 4.1). Focusing on the inherent tension in relationality and its manifestation through differential power relations (e.g. in some feminist and postcolonial geographies) also allows us to incorporate actor-specific *practices* into our analysis of socio-spatial events and change. This theory of relationality thus compels us to analyse the tension in the differential (dis)embedding of actors and things in diverse networks and to explain socio-spatial outcomes in relation to how these actors negotiate and act on this tension *differently*. Any explanatory analysis of the differential capacity of actors in this negotiation process needs to take into account different forms of causal powers (e.g. 'thing-power' and relations of domination and control) and their manifestation through actor-specific practices in society and space.

### Causal Powers and Relationality in Relational Geometries

What then are causal powers in this relational theory? If relationality is constituted through interactions, interconnections, and tensions, there is clearly a great deal of heterogeneity and unevenness in these relational processes. This heterogeneity and unevenness does not refer to the diverse socio-spatial events and processes themselves – as well documented in the voluminous literature examined in this chapter's first section (and in Chapter 2). Instead, I refer to the inherent heterogeneity and unevenness in the (co)constitution and (re)configuration of relational geometries that in turn produce concrete outcomes. There are therefore different emergent forms of causal powers embedded in these diverse configurations of relational geometries. In realist sociologist Dave Elder-Vass' (2010: ch. 2) *The Causal Powers of Social Structures*, this relational approach to emergence stipulates that emergent properties or causal powers originate from the particular relations holding different parts in a particular kind of whole.

The works on causal powers by realist geographers John Allen (2003, 2016), Andrew Sayer (2004, 2015), and others in the social sciences have been most useful here.[37] As made abundantly clear by Sayer (2015: p. 109),

> By 'cause' we mean simply that which produces (or perhaps blocks) change. A cause is not… a consistent regularity between one event and another, such that one is inclined to say: 'if A, then B'. Rather, a cause is a mechanism that produces change. All objects – including people, institutions and discourses – have particular 'causal powers'; that is, things they are capable of doing, such as a person's power to breathe or speak. They also have particular 'causal susceptibilities', such as an individual's susceptibility to certain changes.

In *Lost Geographies of Power*, John Allen (2003) analyses the relations between spatiality and power at a general level and developed a relational notion of the spatial assemblages of power in which spatiality is imbued with power *and* power is intertwined with spatiality (cf. Lefebvre, 1991 [1974]; Massey, 2005). In *Topologies of Power*, Allen (2016: p. 39) argues further that relations between people and groups are viewed as spatially distanciated and thus their interactions are necessarily intertwined with material connections and social practices that help bridge this distanciation. In short, their power relations involve the (co-)presence of other subjects and objects in different relational configurations that can be 'stretched' and 'worked through' in socio-spatial life. This relational view of power has also been emphasized in the earlier 'institutional turn' in human geography (Jessop, 2001; Amin, 2001a; Bathelt and Glückler, 2014). To understand how power is unleashed through more-than-heterogeneous relational geometries, we need to unpack its causal nature and concrete forms. But the concept 'power' is a particularly tricky one to define. On power, political theorist Steven Lukes (1986: p. 17) concludes that 'there are various answers, all deeply familiar, which respond to our interests in both the outcomes and the location of power. Perhaps this explains why, in our ordinary unreflective judgements and comparisons of power, we normally know what we mean and have little difficulty in understanding one another, yet every attempt at a single general answer to the question has failed and seems likely to fail'.

Still, Sayer (2004: pp. 260–261) has identified some inherent linguistic difficulties in Allen's (2003) experiment with thinking of power differently:

1.  tendency to conflate power/cause with effects;
2.  tendency of committing what realist philosopher Roy Bhaskar (1975, 2008 [1993]) terms epistemic or ontic fallacy when power is seen as 'co-extensive with its field of enquiry' – power is both reality (ontology) and knowledge (epistemology); and
3.  tendency of circularity in definition when power is constituted by relationships that compose it.

To him, 'These kinds of description [of power] are familiar in post-structuralist literature... On closer examination, however, such formulations are actually deeply puzzling in terms of their implied metaphysics. At worst, the more we ponder phrases such as "power is inseparable from its effects," the more they begin to look like "x is just what x is"' (Sayer, 2004: p. 261)!

We are thus seemingly stuck in a rather paradoxical situation that has indeed plagued much of relational thinking in human geography – defining power or providing a singular general answer to its nature and outcome is likely to fail or to go circular/tautological, and yet relational theory cannot be causal and explanatory without a better grip on the nature and operation of power. To remedy this paradox, Sayer (2004) offers an alternative conception of power that does not necessarily need to eschew the 'bad habit' of thinking and speaking of power as centred and as capacity, in comparison to Allen's (2003) conceptions of power as networked, as dependent on mobilization, or indeed as immanent. In fact, Sayer (2004) argues that the former (power as centred) is actually *necessary* for understanding how the latter conception of power as diffuse and immanent works.

He proposes the crucial idea of 'double contingency' (Sayer, 2004: p. 262) in understanding the realization of power when (1) the activation of emergent power by A is contingent on *its relation* to other objects (B, C, and so on) and (2) the causal effects of this activation of power by A is also contingent on *the powers* of these objects that may disrupt, facilitate, or enhance A's realization of power. This double contingency in the realization of power leads to several key observations on causal powers in Sayer (2004: pp. 262–264, 2015: p. 109). Causation is unlikely to be linear and the exercise of power will not likely form regularities over space due to the mediating effects of different objects in relation to A (i.e. contingency 1). We can better understand emergent power as potential or disposition/susceptibility (before double contingency in action) and actual power as exercised or practiced through changes brought about by any object (including the body) and representation in textual or material forms (e.g. reason and discourse).[38]

Taking further cues from Allen's (2003: p. 2) conception of power as 'a relational effect of social interaction' and his later topological frame of power as 'the same, but different' through relational processes in space and time (Allen, 2016: p. 3), I define power as the relational properties of the capacity to influence *and* the exercise of this capacity through actor-specific practices. As these properties can be reproduced and transformed through different registers and relational networks, they are, as expressions of power, indeed same, but different. Power is thus defined in neither simply a static positional term nor a processual practice manner because it is encapsulated in *both* ongoing (dis)position and practice.

Defined as such, power is both a relational construct of position(ality)/disposition and an emergent property manifested through practice. Power is a *relational* attribute because its effects are experienced through the process of its mobilization and practice. For example, we think of an actor as powerful or having power when we know of prior outcomes arising from the networks of relations in which this actor is embedded. This actor can be deemed to possess a *capacity/disposition* to act within those networks of relations. Its power is dependent on the fact that this capacity is exercised eventually and successfully. Power is therefore not an inherently possessed quality nor an actor-specific property, as often assumed in social network analysis.[39] In the latter literature, an actor's power in a network is a function of its positionality within the network (e.g. centrality) or of 'the strength of association between actors in the composition of the network' (Bridge, 1997: p. 619). But the structure of a network tells us little about the qualitative nature of the relations among actors that are far more important than structures *per se.*

Instead, I see power as the emergent properties of *social practices* among actors who have the capacity and resources to influence. Social actors are critical in the mediation of power as relational effects, although they do not possess power per se. While capacity might be conceived as inscribed in more-than-heterogeneous relations in a structural sense in some critical approaches (e.g. feminist and postcolonial geographies), its causality can only be effectual through actor-specific practices and therefore cannot be determined a priori. The relational properties of power are multi-directional because some actors derive their capacity to influence from privileged structural positions, whereas others experience power through relational practice and contestation. My relational conception of causal powers as emergent properties exercised through relationality in networks and relational practices of social actors is consistent with Bhaskar's (2010: p. 60) critical realist view of emergent powers as providing the causal link or causation between explanatory structures and human reasoning and practices. But it is not the same as the idea of immanent power in Allen (2003) and Foucauldian conceptions of 'power everywhere' because, as Sayer (2004: p. 266; original italics) argues, 'Critical realism thus also allows a *relational* concept of power, without ignoring or obscuring what it is *about* the *relata* and the relations which produce such power, as tends to happen where "immanence" is invoked'.

Taking a similar realist approach, philosopher of social science Daniel Little (2016: pp. 137–142, 200–205) puts the idea of emergence into his notion of causal powers and causation in how things work. To him, causal powers and causal mechanisms can be mutually compatible since they answer different questions within the causal nexus: power questions on 'what does something do' and mechanism questions on 'how does something work' (see also my Chapter 3 on causal mechanisms and relational thinking in mid-range theories). This *necessary* connection between causal powers and causal mechanisms goes a long way to resolving one key challenge in explanatory social science – the request for the specification of causal mechanisms at work is often answered with vague notions that some components of a mechanism have certain powers to affect other entities. But this answer in itself offers no particular explanation of *what* these causal powers are and *how* they actually work through causal mechanisms to produce socio-spatial changes and effects.

Consistent with political philosopher Ruth Groff's (2017, 2019) non-determinist conception of causal powers, my relational theory of power can be useful to explaining why the causal effects of the same power geometry may not be applicable to *all* actors within these networks and relations. The practice of differential power relations among actors of different endowment and capacity can actually jeopardize the structural tendencies of such power geometries. The dominant positionality of some actors in such networks can only explain concrete socio-spatial outcomes in partial terms. A more robust explanation in this relational theory requires an examination of the practices of such power relations among different actors in relation to their respective structural positionalities and their mutual interconnections. It also entails a better specification of the causal mechanisms or links through which such powers in social relations can be mediated and realized to make things happen. In this sense, Schatzki's (2019) view on the relevance of power in explaining contemporary social life is quite useful. While appreciating Allen's (2016) topological position on spatially stretched power relations as 'extremely fruitful', Schatzki (2019: pp. 190–191) argues that we need to unravel the causal efficacy of the existence or nonexistence of these mediating connections and chains of practices.

My relational theory also conceptualizes power as an *emergent quality* such that the sum of more-than-heterogeneous relations is much greater than that of individual parts. In Figure 4.1, this emergent effect of causal powers is illustrated by the summation of various interconnections and tensions within each box. This emergent power from diverse sets of relations represents a particular kind of causal effects because the presence of their constitutive parts (e.g. actors or structures) precedes any concrete effects or outcomes in society and space. Revisiting my earlier subsection on institutional geographies, the emergent power of relational assets and institutional thickness is clearly greater than the sum of individual assets or institutions in a particular region. The sheer presence of local assets (e.g. human and technological competencies) or local institutions (e.g. pro-development coalitions) does not necessarily constitute an emergent effect propelling superior regional performance. This is because the efficacy of such an emergent effect is contingent on the practice of a variety of regional actors, such as workers, firms, unions, and agencies entering into all sorts of more-than-heterogeneous relations – a relational practice that *activates* and *actualizes* this emergent effect. In other words, the emergent nature of power is experienced through action and practice by such actors. Mediated and realized through actor-specific practice, the emergent power embedded in these relations provides a major force to drive association and interconnections and to produce concrete socio-spatial outcomes.

The above abstract theorization of power perhaps explains why the existing relational frameworks and relational thought in Tables 4.1 and 4.2 tend to ignore or downplay the role of causal powers in relational constructs. Instead, most of these frameworks and approaches focus on relational *categories* as analytical themes (e.g. institutional thickness, network embeddedness, process of becoming, subject formation, identity politics, and so on). The causal nature of relationality and power is often implicit, rendering most of these thematic approaches incomplete as a relational theory in human geography. In the context of economic geography, Faulconbridge (2012) takes seriously Allen's (2003) conception of power's modalities and spatial manifestations and reconciles them with Sayer's (2004: p. 262) 'double contingency' in understanding economic change brought about by global firms and their local suppliers and customers. As summarized in Table 4.3, his relational reworking of the economic geographies of power starts with the initial contingencies in the exercise of power before its switching of modalities of exercise contingent on changing power relations due to unpredictable second- or third-order repercussions over time. As argued further by Faulconbridge (2012: p. 740),

**Table 4.3**    Modalities and techniques of power and their spatiality and economic effects.

| Modalities of power | Techniques of power | Spatiality and economic effects |
| --- | --- | --- |
| *Authority* – power to make demands and define legitimate behaviour | Construction of recognition and legitimacy of demands | Rapid, sustained, and comprehensive change to behaviour, with little contestation (e.g. a supplier quickly changes delivery routines to align completely with those promoted by customer firms that they believe represent best practice). |
| *Coercion* – power to compel a particular form of conduct by others despite alternatives | Production of logics limiting the possibility of alternative perspectives | Change after debates over legitimacy but often superficial, resented, and reversible without coercion (e.g. a firm agrees to adopt new standards of waste management after threat of sanction, but does not properly monitor its implementation leading to fewer environmental benefits than anticipated). |
| *Domination* – power to ensure demands begrudgingly accepted and fulfilled by others | Effective dismissal of alternatives by responding to the reactions of contending parties | Change and demands met but feelings of exploitation and/or resentment by contending parties (e.g. a dominant firm lowers its order price to a supplier who profits little and has to cut wages against workers' wishes; local unions prevent a global firm changing working practices by using regulation as a barrier). |
| *Manipulation* – power to conceal intent of requests and ultimately compel voluntary compliance by others who think they will benefit | Covert shaping of thinking and reactions of individuals and other parties | Fragile and risky compliance secured (e.g. significant initial benefits for a host region due to state-led deception of a foreign investor into believing it is receiving preferential treatment through incentives in return for know-how; withdrawal of cooperation by the investor later upon discovery of other firms receiving the same incentives). |
| *Seduction* and *enticement* – power to attract or induce others to support and comply with requests | Strengthening the case for and creating desire by contending parties to choose freely | More time needed for change in behaviour and reliance on the effective construction of seductive narratives or relationships (e.g. many rounds of consultations, case studies, meetings, and votes among national regulators to reach consensus and adopt the principles of international bankruptcy law). |
| *Displaced* and *veiled register* – power to make others do and think without a direct sense of authority or coercion | 'Quieter' forms of power to be leveraged topologically through relational proximity | Diffuse and decentralized change in behaviour (e.g. data analytics firms editing and adjusting their missives in real time to resonate with their intended audience, to leverage a direct presence in their everyday life, and to engage in political and economic influences). |

Sources: Simplified and reworked from Faulconbridge (2012: Table 1, pp. 738–739) based on Allen (2003); updated with Allen (2016, 2020).

'Studying the contingent influences on the exercising of resources and the resultant production of one modality of power or another is thus vital to explore power's spatiotemporal specificities'.

To give more spatiotemporal specificities to causal powers, I develop the concept of *relational geometries* to specify this double contingency in the exercise of power relations. In my relational theory, I conceptualize two particular forms of power relations in which the causality of relational geometries can be unleashed – relational complementarity and relational specificity – further theorizing work might specify more forms and modalities of such power relations. By complementarity, I refer to a form of power relations where the constituents of relational geometries benefit from each other's co-presence and engagement. These constituents can be actors (e.g. human subjects, firms, and institutions), structures (e.g. capitalism, markets, and geopolitical dominance), or both. Greater complementarity in the power relations among these constituents likely enhances its emergent power to produce socio-spatial change and outcomes. This is because the complementary 'fit' between actor strategies and structural imperatives reduces conflicts and resistance, and therefore leads to higher likelihood of realizing the intended outcomes in society and space.

Let me put these abstract ideas in more concrete terms by way of a 'real world' example of local unions in times of global change (see also examples of neoliberalization in Chapter 5 and global production networks in Chapter 6). Such complementary power relations can be observed in many different socio-spatial contexts, such as the cooperative practices of such local actors as labour unions in growing regions. Despite their unequal power relations, local actors with different endowment and capacity may enter into cooperative relations with trans-local actors, such as national governments and international organizations, in order to tap into each other's complementary 'assets' such as political access and communicative networks. Through this complementary process of relational interaction, a new set of relational assets can be produced in such ways that bind some local actors to a particular set of relational geometry. These local actors thus enjoy relational complementarity – a relational advantage defined by and practiced through their cooperative relations. Their mutual benefits (e.g. better rights for union members) and spatial tendencies (e.g. stronger connections between local and national unions) are not necessarily explained by the sheer fact that they are embedded in relational networks – a thematic descriptive approach often taken in the relational literature summarized in Tables 4.1 and 4.2.

Rather, these concrete benefits and tendencies for local unions and their members are explained by the processes through which their complementarity is relationally constructed and the ways in which they realize this complementarity. The former processes may involve discursive constructions of cooperation within each labour union to legitimize its politics of cooperation. The latter may entail the practice of complementary power relations such that the local union may encourage its members to be less combative towards local entities and domestic firms in order to 'fit' into the more open-ended approach taken by union actors at the national and international scales. The fact that different local unions are embedded in the same network does not explain the socio-spatial outcomes of their respective fight for worker rights. Such a causal explanation needs to be located in the ways through which relational complementarity among unions and actors at different geographical scales is constructed and realized through the practice of power and its relational effects.

*Relational specificity* refers to a particular form of power relations in which dedicated commitment is enforced among constituents in dyadic and more-than-heterogeneous relations. It is determined by the extent to which (co)constituents in relational geometries are dependent on and 'locked-in' to their ongoing power relations for access to resources, information, and identity formation. This dependency is specific to particular relational geometries (e.g. union networks or social groups) and therefore requires dedicated commitment from these constituents to make their relational geometry 'work'. The capacity of a relational geometry to produce concrete outcomes among its constituents is proportional to the degree of this relational specificity. In more concrete terms, the performance of some local unions may be highly dependent on specific kinds of relations with local states and international investors (see also Table 4.3). Some networks are more exclusive and dedicated than others and thus their relational specificities vary quite significantly that in turn explain why substantial variations in socio-spatial events and outcomes remain visible in the social world(s). Understanding the origins of such variations in different relational geometries allows us not only to explain better the differential effects of causal powers in society and space, but more importantly to challenge these unjust and unequal outcomes and to achieve our normative goals as critical social science.

Before developing further the explanatory mechanisms of this relational theory in the next chapter, I conclude briefly by making the case that the relational turn in human geography during the past three decades has indeed broken some significantly new grounds in our (re)thinking of space, networks, embeddedness, rescaling, materiality, and subjectivity. But this turn remains incomplete in our explanation of what really make things happen in society and space. Most of the relational frameworks and approaches examined in this chapter are oriented towards developing new descriptive *themes* and *vocabularies* for understanding the relational co-constitution of socio-spatial life, events, and outcomes. Going beyond this thematic focus in the relational turn, I have reworked into a relational theory some under-theorized conceptual tools, particularly the notion of relational geometries and the nature of relationality and causal powers in such relational geometries.

To 'operationalize' our relational thinking and give it more explanatory uptake, we must bring power back into our relational theories and yet move from the descriptive vocabularies of power to developing a relational notion of what Allen (1999, 2003) terms the spatial assemblages of power. This relational conception of causal powers explains why we need to reorient our analytical focus away from individual subjects or broader structures as if they were causal and explanatory in their own right. Instead, we must unpack relational geometries imbued with causal powers capable of effecting socio-spatial events and change. In this epistemological sense, my approach towards a relational theory goes beyond the kind of relational conceptions that focus merely on understanding and accounts of intentions and strategies of actors and their relational ensembles in society and space.

How then do we apply this relational theory without being accused of creating greater fuzziness of concepts and fragmentation in critical human geography? After all, the kind of relational theory developed here might appear to be imprecise and fuzzy because it does not clearly specify – beyond forms of emergent power and relational geometries – operationalizable variables for further empirical testing. Striving a balance between the kind of onto-theological lock-in of correlationist thinking in relational thought and the Humean positivist conceptions of empirical regularities as causal covering laws, my reworking of a relational theory is intentionally reflexive and, therefore, opens up some spaces for further conceptual refinement and spirited debates. This reworking of causal powers represents a conscious strategy to establish causality between relational geometries and concrete (socio-spatial) outcomes.

The success of this epistemological effort, nevertheless, depends critically on how we get out of the atomistic/individualist conceptions of human experiences/activities and spatial changes that are so ingrained in some existing geographical imaginations. Thinking about these socio-spatial experiences, activities, and changes in relational terms is only a first step towards unveiling the explanatory capacity of analytical geographies expounded in the previous chapter. Ascribing causal powers to relational geometries represents quite another leap towards a kind of explanatory geography that can be inherently reflexive and contextual without over-privileging or over-socializing any categories of relational thought. To explain this 'making things happen', we need to go further in our relational journey to conceptualize how causal powers are actually mediated and transmitted through specific *mechanisms* that must be clearly distinguished from general processes of becoming and change. The next chapter will take on this third step in my synthetic approach to theory and explanation in/for Geography.

# Notes

1   For key references on relational thinking across different subfields in human geography since the early 2000s, see Bathelt and Glückler (2003, 2014); Massey (2005); Yeung (2005, 2019a); Murdoch (2006); Jessop et al. (2008); Anderson and Harrison (2010b); Anderson et al. (2012a); Müller and Schurr (2016); MacFarlane (2017); Hart (2018); Glückler and Panitz (2021); and Woods et al. (2021). Relational thinking has also been revived in relational sociology (Emirbayer, 1997; Donati, 2010; Donati and Archer,

2015), processual sociology (Abbott, 2001, 2016), anthropology (Holbraad and Pedersen, 2017), and management studies (Dyer and Singh, 1998; Gulati, 2007; Kano, 2018; Deng et al., 2020).

2   Arguing that sociology should be about social relations and social process, Abbott (2001: p. 124; original italics) elaborates further that 'at the heart of sociology are those phenomena that are fully enmeshed both in social time and social space, what I have elsewhere called interactional fields. It is because we study interactional fields that we are a discipline of social *relations*, concerned with the social *process*' (see also Abbott, 2016: pp. ix–x).

3   In *Towards Speculative Realism*, Harman (2010: p. 157) argues further that 'relationality [has become] a major philosophical problem. It no longer seems evident how one thing is able to interact with another, since each thing in the universe seems to withdraw into a private bubble [of relations], with no possible link between one and the next'. In his dialogue with Manuel DeLanda with reference to realist philosopher Roy Bhaskar's work on reclaiming reality, Harman uses the term 'relationism' to critique this conception that everything real is simply whatever affects something else and ultimately it is nothing more than its effects, as in Bruno Latour's actor-network theory: 'This is relationism, not realism. It cannot account for currently unexpressed realities that may not be affecting anything right now and might never affect anything at all. Ultimately, this is the problem with actor-network theory in the social sciences: it cannot handle *counterfactual* cases, and can't really do justice to the sorts of things you (and Bhaskar) say about experiment' (DeLanda and Harman, 2017: p. 61; original italics).

4   As noted by Schatzki (2019: p. 173) in *Social Change in a Material World*, 'Contemporary social theory is replete with calls for, invocations of, and homages to relations and relational turns. I can only partly endorse this chorus: although relations help compose the practice plenum and, thereby, social life, they are not qua relations crucial to the happening and progress of social affairs. The entire topic of relations and social life is vexed by the vagueness of the notion of a relation. This vagueness is reflected in the familiar platitude that everything is related to everything else'.

5   To Sayer (2018: p. 107), 'there's a danger here, albeit one avoided by Doreen [Massey], of flipping from an overly structured view of the world to one in which it is represented as wholly unstructured and uniformly fluid, or no more than a mess. (Exaggeration is the besetting sin of avant-garde social theory.)'!

6   Taking a similar practice approach to develop his rudimentary theory of directed practice in *Direction and Socio-Spatial Theory*, Matthew Hannah (2019: p. 6) recently makes a strong case for recognizing such entities as embodied human practices in intentional relations so that 'however relational, ontogenetically and phylogenetically derivative, differentially positioned or performative we are, human beings are not simply featureless knots or bundles of external determinations or fleeting stabilizations. Nor are we merely some kind of deceptively stable-looking but actually effervescent foam thrown up by performative events. We inherit generically human biological features, acquire and develop specific embodied properties – some likewise universal to the species – that we need to understand in order to understand social reality. These [human] properties shape intentional relations with the world in fundamental ways regardless of our positionality. A relational perspective that pays no attention whatsoever to the generic characteristics of the relata (in this case, embodied human subject and external world) is incomplete. It is from this perspective that the importance of the inherent directedness of embodied human practice can be most easily perceived'.

7  This subsection draws upon my earlier work in Yeung (2005: pp. 39–42).

8  See pioneering studies of Marxian political economy in Harvey (1973, 1982, 1985); Massey (1973, 1979, 1984); Walker and Storper (1981); Smith (1984); and Storper and Walker (1989). For debates on social relations and spatial structures, see Gregory and Urry (1985). For useful recent reviews, see Cox (2014, 2021), Henderson and Sheppard (2015), and Peck et al. (2023).

9  As noted by Henderson and Sheppard (2015: p. 66; original italics), 'Marx argued that the social relations deemed "necessary" for the material basis of human life were outcomes of antagonistic group relations, struggles over ideas, and often the exertion of brute force by a ruling class. Social relations are not *naturally* necessary but are historically wrought through struggles over material and political interests'.

10  See also reviews of this large body of literature on clusters and regional economies in Bathelt et al. (2004); Storper (2013); Harris (2021); and Wu (2022); and my recent reworking of these thematic approaches in Yeung (2021a).

11  Examples of such relational assets in regional economies are 'institutional thickness' (Amin and Thrift, 1994; Zukauskaite et al., 2017), 'untraded interdependencies' (Storper, 1997), 'learning regions' (Morgan, 1997; cf. Hudson, 1999); 'associational economies' (Cooke and Morgan, 1998), and 'local buzz' (Bathelt et al., 2004; cf. Wu, 2022).

12  For key geographical studies of networks and embeddedness, see Cooke and Morgan (1993, 1998); Yeung (1994, 2018); Dicken et al. (2001); Coe et al. (2004); Hess (2004); Coe and Yeung (2019); and Glückler and Panitz (2021). This emphasis on networks and their associated power relations has also facilitated the rediscovery of the firm in economic geography (Yeung, 2018; Clark et al., 2018: Part IV), in part because it establishes an alternative analytical path between the methodological individualism of narrowly firm-centric approaches (e.g. industrial location models) and the strong sense of structural determinism that is evident in macro-process studies of geographical industrialization and uneven development (e.g. the social relations of production framework; see also Peck, 2003; Peck et al., 2023).

13  See geographical examples in Thrift and Olds (1996); Whatmore (1997); Olds and Yeung (1999); Nagar et al. (2002); Ettlinger (2003); Gibson-Graham (2006, 2008); Larner (2009); and Weller and O'Neill (2014).

14  See such long-standing geographical debates on scales over the past three decades in Swyngedouw (1997); Brenner (2001, 2019); Cox (1998); Marston (2000); Sheppard (2002); Marston et al. (2005); Moore (2008); Herod (2010); MacKinnon (2011); and Linder (2022).

15  Drawing on the embodied experiences of people during the COVID-19 pandemic, Linder (2022: p. 81) recently argues for a humanistic sense of scale approach to understanding the widespread 'scalar stress' associated with the forced and contested upending of previous scalar arrangements during and after the pandemic. To him, the scalar restructuring effects of the pandemic are 'not simply produced and experienced through the machinations of political economy and discourse but through affective, emotional, and tactile engagements with particular sites. As people lose touch with these sites, they sense the dissolution of particular scales as well as the reinvigoration and transformation of others'.

16  Examining the flat ontologies in these open-ended approaches on actor-networks, affect and practice, and assemblages, Ash (2020a: p. 348) notes that 'Such perspectives are united in that they tend to reject the categorisation of entities into ontological

hierarchies, units, sets or groups that would distinguish things as fundamentally different from one another... Flat ontologies are thus considered an antidote to such violent forms of distinction, because they point to the interconnected, relational nature of entities that cannot be distinguished from one another through some preexisting category. While these positions are united in their focus on relationality, how they differentiate between entities differs depending on how they theorise and conceptualise what relationality is'.

17   For some of the more prominent writings on different conceptions of space in human geography, see Tuan (1977); Sack (1980); Massey (2005); Harvey (1996); Thrift (1996); and Malpas (2018).

18   To Massey (1991: pp. 25–26), 'different social groups and individuals are placed in very distinct ways in relation to these flows and interconnections. This point concerns not merely the issue of who moves and who doesn't, although that is an important element of it; it is also about power in relation to the flows and the movement. Different social groups have distinct relationships to this anyway differentiated mobility: some people are more in charge of it than others; some initiate flows and movement, others don't; some are more on the receiving end of it than others; some are effectively imprisoned by it'. See a recent reprise of Massey's relational space conception in Peck et al. (2018: pp. 21–26).

19   This thought on space and the world as an open multiplicity is also echoed in Latour's (2013: pp. 48–49) work on a new way of enquiry into modes of existence, Thrift's (2021: pp. 4–5) recent work on urban animals and more-than-human species, and the emergent conception of more-than-human becomings and belongings in indigenous geographies (Wright, 2015; Bawaka Country et al., 2016).

20   In her earlier paper, Massey (2004: p. 17) takes on a more political position *for* London(ers): "Londoners' are located in radically contrasting and unequal positions in relation to today's globalisation. The political argument should be about how those small and highly differentiated bits of all of us which position us as "Londoners" give rise to responsibility towards the wider relations on which we depend. And that "London" voice is a powerful one. In the past it has been a subversive voice, and it could be so again'.

21   My book review caught the attention of the late Doreen Massey! In her email to me on 7 August 2008 reproduced in full here, she gave me her seal of approval: 'Dear Henry, I have just caught up with your review of *World City* on the EGRG website and wanted to say how happy I was to read it. Not only is it very positive (for which many thanks) but also – and even more importantly – it really gets at what I was trying to say. It made me really happy to read it. I hope all goes well with you. Best wishes, Doreen'. I cannot be more grateful for benefiting from reviewing her book and this generous appreciation note. Here, I particularly want to thank Doreen's incredible scholarship and generosity that should remain forever a great(est) source of inspiration for us all.

22   Acknowledging Safiya Noble's (2018) important work on data discrimination and racist/sexist algorithms driving search engines such as Google, Amoore (2020a: p. 69) argues that 'the regimes of recognition I have described actively exceed profiles written into the rules by a human'. To be fair though, she does recognize such possible critiques of her relational approach: 'At this point, one might reasonably ask how

giving such an account of the contingent politics of machine learning algorithms is of any possible critical use. How might a cloud ethics work with the incompleteness, the undecidability, and the contingency of the algorithm's space of play?' (Amoore, 2020a: pp. 80–81). Her answers to these critical questions seem to raise further 'unanswerable questions', such as reawakening the multiplicity present within algorithms, such as the processes and arrangements of weights, values, bias, and thresholds in neural nets that are not part of our 'statutory political domain' (after Michel Foucault). See also feminist literary critic Katherine Hayles' (2017: ch. 5) *Unthought* for a thoughtful discussion of such cognitive assemblages of technical agency and human subjectivity as automatic traffic surveillance and control systems, personal digital assistants, sociometers, and unmanned aerial vehicles (UAVs) or drones.

23   This critical discussion of relationality in actor-network theory draws upon my earlier collaborative work utilizing this relational approach (Olds and Yeung, 1999: pp. 538–540; Dicken et al., 2001: pp. 101–105). See Bosco (2015) for a concise review of actor-network theory in relational geographies.

24   In *Reassembling the Social*, Latour (2005: p. 131) argues that 'ANT will take as a weak and powerless account that simply repeats and tries to transport an already composed social force without reopening what it is made of and without finding the extra vehicles necessary to extend it further. Masses of social agents might have been invoked in the text, but since the principle of their assembly remains unknown and the cost of their expansion has not been paid, it's as if nothing was happening. No matter what their figuration is, they don't do very much'.

25   Taking on ANT's narrowly defined conception of agency (i.e. things are efficacious through relationality), postcolonial critic Wael Hallaq (2018: p. 199) uses the term 'Latour's Stone', not without a pun, to critique Latour's ascription of things to their *presence*, not agency, in actor-networks. To Hallaq, such consideration of the (relational) presence of things as Latour's Stone 'precludes a human structure of intent, a necessary condition for agency. Intent presupposes a rational action of choice, for when choice does not ontologically exist, there cannot be intent'. In the context of colonialism, he argues that agency matters because it refers to intentional choices made by colonialists embedded in dominant discursive formations and epistemic sovereignty, such as Orientalism (cf. Said, 2003 [1978]).

26   Anderson and Harrison (2010b: p. 14; original italics) offer a glimpse into these infinite forms of *everything* material: 'Consider, for example, the sheer multiplicity of materialities that are mixed together in non-representational [theory] inspired empirical work; beliefs, atmospheres, sensations, ideas, toys, music, ghosts, dance therapies, footpaths, pained bodies, trance music, reindeer, plants, boredom, fat, anxieties, vampires, cars, enchantment, nanotechnologies, water voles, GM Foods, landscapes, drugs, money, racialised bodies, political demonstrations… Non-representational theory is unusual, then, in being *thoroughly* materialist. It does not limit *a priori* what kind of beings make up the social. Rather everything takes-part and in taking-part, takes-place: everything happens, everything acts. Everything, including images, words and texts'.

27   See also comparisons in DeLanda (2006, 2016); Müller and Schurr (2016); Bridge (2021); and Woods et al. (2021).

28   As noted by Roy Bhaskar (2016: p. 56; original italics) in *Enlightened Common Sense*, 'the relational conception is itself perhaps unduly restrictive, in so far as it would seem

to prohibit the study of entities and properties in the social world that cannot be defined relationally. So I have subsequently further elaborated this in terms of a conception of social science as operating at different *levels of scale*. This ranges from the sub-individual scale at the psychological level upwards to individual (e.g. biography), micro- (e.g. specific encounter), meso- (e.g. work functional roles), macro- (e.g. whole economy), mega- (e.g. whole formations such as Islamic fundamentalism), and planetary levels (e.g. world systems theory and geohistory).

29  Similarly, Ash and Simpson (2016: p. 57) raise some important and difficult questions on the theory of subject formation in post-phenomenology: 'This sort of rethinking of the subject also asks the question: "where does this leave 'us'"?… what implications do the multitude of vibrant materials that we might engage with have for understanding such intersubjectivity? Ultimately, how do we account for what remains of the inter-subjective when any such subject entering into a relation has already been decentred amid the givenness of the world and so cannot form the foundation or origin of that relation to be built upon?'

30  In *The Ascent of Affect*, historian of thought Ruth Leys (2017: p. 349; my emphasis) argues that such quandaries in Bennett's vital materialist thought are indeed insurmountable since her affect theory 'explains how things can be included in a parliament of things by imagining that they don't have to speak or represent themselves at all, because they necessarily transmit materially the vital affects that are immanent in them. And if conceiving politics in this way makes it hard to imagine what *parliamentary debates* would look like, this would appear to be precisely her point: for Bennett, debate over ideology is irrelevant. Her fantasy is rather of a language of nature that isn't itself a representation because it consists of material vibrations or neural currents by which the affects are inevitably passed on, though not exactly understood. In her *political utopia*, we are invited to imagine a pluralism of vital, affective energies impinging on each other and producing new, if unpredictable, lives and effects'.

31  See critiques of vitalist thought in Abrahamsson et al. (2015: pp. 5–6); Joronen and Häkli (2017: pp. 569–570); and Simpson (2021: p. 119). More recently, Roberts and Dewsbury (2021) call for a 're-vitalization' of vitalism grounded in Deleuze's 'non-organic vitalism'. But their excessive focus on vitalism as a philosophical aspiration for thought has undermined its causal efficacy in empirical explanation. In *Unthought*, Katherine Hayles (2017: p. 67) warns us such a danger of Deleuzian emphasis on affects, forces, intensities, and assemblages at the expense of subject consciousness and cognition. To her, 'the enthusiasm for all concepts Deleuzian threatens to ensnare some of the more extreme instances of new materialism in a self-enclosed discourse that, although it makes sense in its own terms, fails to connect convincingly with other knowledge practices and veers toward the ideological, in which practices are endorsed for their agreement with the Deleuzian view rather than because they adequately represent acts, practices, and events in the real world'.

32  To Abrahamsson et al. (2015: p. 13), 'rather than getting enthusiastic about the liveliness of "matter itself," it might be more relevant to face the complexities, frictions, intractabilities, and conundrums of "matter in relation." For it is in their relations that matters become political, whether those politics are loudly contested or silently endured. It is here that the question arises of which relations to foster and in which direction to go'.

33   Critiquing human geography's surge towards a notion of new materialisms and orien-
     tations as a 'surface geography', Tolia-Kelly (2013: p. 153; original italics) similarly
     argues that 'Occasionally, the promise of the imagination within the research process
     to refigure the worldly materializes, whereas in other accounts there is simply only a
     shallow engagement presented. This is where the *political* engagement with the con-
     cept of material is absent; this is what I term a *surface geography*. In these research
     projects, there is use of the concept of "materiality," but without any reflection, cri-
     tique, engagement or evaluation; leaving a *surface* recording, a description, a mapping
     or illustration of materialities within a site or those which are observed'. Taking a
     Gramscian approach, Doucette (2020: p. 320) further critiques the hyper- or objective
     determination of political will in this vitalist approach to materialism.
34   To England et al. (2020: p. 336), 'At the core of feminist care ethics is a relational
     ontology of connection that positions people as embodied, interdependent beings. We
     are all vulnerable and dependent on others at numerous points throughout our lives,
     and we are each enmeshed in networks of care relations'. See also McDowell (2004)
     and Lawson (2007) on feminist care ethics and Dufty-Jones and Gibson's (2022)
     feminist-inspired arguments for an ethic of care in the pedagogy of research writing.
35   Some parts in this section are based on Yeung (2005: pp. 42–49).
36   Anderson (2016: pp. 742–744) does examine briefly two examples of the meetings of the
     Mont Pelerin Society (founded by Friedrich von Hayek in 1947) and the Milton Fried-
     man's workshop in the Chicago School of Economics to illustrate 'neoliberal atmo-
     spheres' during the birth and momentum of neoliberalisms and use his 'reading against
     the grain to draw out traces of affect' of works by Stuart Hall and others on UK's Thatch-
     erism to illustrate 'structures of feelings' in everyday life (Anderson, 2016: pp. 746–749).
     But the cause-and-effect relationship between affect and neoliberalism seems rather
     confusing to me when he argues that 'Atmospheres are complex conditions that simulta-
     neously imbue and undo distinctions between occasions, organizations, styles of thinking,
     and objects. Perhaps the atmospheres of occasions/organizations have an *emergent causal-
     ity* that can be retrospectively traced in the tone of policies, ideas, and so on. However,
     atmospheres are not simply reproduced or expressed without differences. And they do
     not simply pre-exist the formation of organizations or neoliberal objects/reason. Undoing
     distinctions between cause and effect, atmospheres emanate from and fold back into
     dynamic constellations of people, things and ideas' (Anderson, 2016: p. 744; my empha-
     sis). I wonder how can something with an emergent causality (i.e. atmospheres) 'emanate
     from and fold back' into the very effects (i.e. neoliberal reason as 'dynamic constella-
     tions')? Are they not both sets of affective outcomes of causal mechanisms *outside* them
     altogether? Similarly, he notes that 'These examples remind us that structures of feeling
     *are* the resonances that create a dispersed but shared "affective present" felt across diverse
     phenomena (an "affective present" that is multiple and will be differentially related to
     and lived)' (Anderson, 2016: p. 747; original italics). But how can 'resonances' be causal
     since it is already so 'dispersed' and 'differentiated'? These quasi-causal arguments of
     affective atmospheres seem rather vague and discursive – ironically a point well recog-
     nized by Anderson (2016: p. 749) later on: 'Perhaps vague, possibly amorphous, such
     affects do not add up to a single dominant mood. My aim has been to avoid reproducing
     a totalizing account of the affective present by holding onto the multiplicity and ambiva-
     lences of affective life'. Still, I believe claiming such multiplicity is one thing, but making

it work as a practically adequate causal explanation needs careful specification and un-packing of causal mechanisms. Otherwise, it is not much different from the very totaliz-ing account that Anderson (2016) and other affect theorists so eagerly want to avoid (see also a book-length critique of affect work in Leys, 2017).

37 See also Groff (2008, 2017, 2019); Clegg and Haugaard (2009); Elder-Vass (2010); Mumford and Anjum (2011); Groff and Greco (2013); and Little (2016). Political philosopher Ruth Groff (2019: p. 182), for example, argues that 'Causation is about the display of the powers of powerful things – activity that may or may not occur, and which, if it does, may or may not issue in any given outcome'. As such, she advocates a non-determinist approach to causal powers. Similarly in *Getting Causes from Powers*, philosophers Stephen Mumford and Rani Anjum (2011: p. 1) argue for a theory of causal dispositionalism in which causal powers are derived from properties of things and events: 'It is properties that do the causal work, and they do so because they are powerful. Nevertheless, objects, facts and events can all be involved in causation, on our view. But they are involved because of the powerful properties that they contain'. They note further that 'A theory of causation has been developed, the basic tenet of which is that a cause is something that disposes towards its effect. All causation, on this view, is powers at work. An effect is caused when a disposition or dispositions exercise' (p. 143).

38 On bodies, Sayer (2004: p. 264) notes that 'The activation of causal mechanisms and their consequent effects always depends on the other objects with which they are in contact. Since bodies have their own powers and susceptibilities (socially acquired, not merely innate), this is consistent with the idea of power$_2$ operating through bodies and not merely externally'. On reasoning and discourses as possible causal mecha-nisms, see Fairclough et al. (2003) on realism and semiosis and Bhaskar (2010: p. 60) and Elder-Vass (2010: ch. 5, 2012: ch. 8).

39 See some examples of these power-as-property views in Burt (1992); Kilduff and Tsai (2003); and Knoke and Yang (2020).

# Chapter Five
# Mechanism and Process in Causal Explanation

This book has so far made an epistemological case for the importance of mechanism-based explanatory theory in Geography grounded in a realist understanding of causal mechanisms and a relational thinking in developing mid-range theories. Addressing various relational thoughts in institutional, poststructuralist, feminist, and postcolonial geographies, the previous chapter has developed a relational theory to account for causal powers and relationality in the more-than-heterogeneous formations of relational geometries that 'make' things and events happen in society and space. This relational theory is useful insofar as it helps explain *why* events and things take place through the exercise of causal powers by social agents via their relational practices. But the specification of *how* these causal powers and relational practices interact through particular mechanisms has not yet been adequately conceptualized. As I have recently argued in Yeung (2019a, 2019b), this analytical procedure is both necessary and critical because there is a tendency in much critical human geography to conflate process with mechanism. The previous chapter's first section on relationality has already examined how process-like thinking tends to permeate in much of Geography's relational thought. In this processual thought addressing events, becoming, and practices, process is viewed in causal terms, as if it were a 'force' in its own right to account for eventual outcomes. Causal powers and their exercise through relational practices are often either missing or underspecified in this processual/relational thinking.

Revisiting my three key considerations of, and for, theory and explanation in Chapter 1, I argue here that the kind of analytical geographies grounded in mechanism-based explanatory theories, as discussed in Chapter 3, should make a

*Theory and Explanation in Geography*, First Edition. Henry Wai-chung Yeung.

much more explicit distinction between mechanism and process. This procedure can enhance substantially the explanatory power of mid-range theories deploying causal mechanisms. In turn, this analytical approach to causal theorizing can better (1) address *normative concerns* through immanent critiques of the limits to theories in open-ended 'surface geographies'; (2) consider the operation of these mechanisms in different *socio-spatial contexts* and therefore the contingency and situatedness of our knowledge production; and (3) offer *practical adequacy* in making real-world interventions for positive social change. As the third step in my synthetic approach to theory and explanation in Geography, this chapter develops a theory of mechanism that engages with the rapidly growing 'mechanism thought' in analytical sociology, political science, and the philosophy of social science during the past two decades (literature first introduced in Chapter 3 endnote 32). Writing in *Comparative Political Studies* a decade ago, political scientist John Gerring (2010: p. 1500) calls it 'social science's current infatuation with causal mechanisms' (see also Hedström and Ylikoski, 2010; Gross, 2018 in sociology; Groff, 2017 in philosophy; and Yeung, 2019a in human geography).

This chapter's theorizing of mechanism and process in causal explanation is conducted in three sections. First, I draw on the distinction between necessary and contingent relations in realist thinking (Yeung, 1997, 2019a; Sayer, 2000, 2010 [1992/1984]) to theorize *process* as a contingent change in a general recurrent series of actions/events and *mechanism* as a particular and necessary relation or process of working out causal powers to produce concrete outcomes in specific socio-spatial contexts. A causal mechanism is therefore a particular kind of process, but it is distinct from process as a contingent and general series of actions and events. The particularity in specifying a causal mechanism is premised on the socio-spatial context of its operation. This discussion of context engages with contingency and practice in contemporary human geography. Overall, specifying concrete mechanism(s) is an indispensable analytical procedure to work out how processes unfold and relate causally to geographic outcomes in particular contexts, i.e. making things happen (Chapter 4). It entails careful empirical and substantive theoretical analysis to move towards more coherent and integrated causal explanations.

The second section engages with the kind of processual or process-based thinking common in critical human geography (e.g. Marxist, poststructuralist, post-phenomenological, and posthumanist work) and explains why a conceptual rethinking of the process-mechanism distinction is necessary. Paradoxically though, this important discussion is largely missing in the philosophical and epistemological work of leading critical realists (e.g. Roy Bhaskar and Andrew Sayer). Revisiting the diverse body of geographical literature examined in Chapters 2 and 4, I argue that the process/mechanism conflation is significant in different theories of socio-spatial change and encounters (e.g. actor-network theory, non-representational theory, assemblage theory, and so on). I link this process-mechanism discussion back to the processual thinking in Marxist geography (e.g. Harvey, 1982, 1996 on social relations of production and dialectics) and poststructuralist geographies (e.g. Thrift, 1996, 2007; Murdoch, 2006; Anderson and Harrison, 2010a; Simpson, 2021).

The third section builds on my conceptual clarification of the process-mechanism distinction to argue for the importance of causal mechanisms in explanatory theory and theorizing in human geography. By way of a more developed example, I illustrate the analytical importance of this distinction in relation to contemporary geographical studies of neoliberalization. Taken together, this theory of mechanism offers a more focused discussion of causal explanations and reconciles processual thinking, often found in open-ended relational thought (discussed in the previous chapter), with mechanism-based explanatory theories for future geographical research.

## Theorizing Mechanism in Causal Explanation

As noted towards the end of Chapter 3, there is now a very substantial body of literature on mechanism as a conceptual and methodological apparatus for developing causal explanations in the diverse fields of analytical sociology, political science, and the philosophy of science and social science.[1] As philosophers of science Stuart Glennan and Phyllis Illari (2018b: p. 1) argue at the beginning of their recent handbook on mechanisms, 'Mechanical philosophy is of ancient origin. For philosophers and scientists in many epochs, thinking about mechanisms has proven to be a fruitful way to understand nature. Although mechanical philosophy receded for much of the twentieth century, it is again resurgent'.[2] What then is mechanism in this large and diverse literature? There are two distinct traditions in understanding mechanism. Table 5.1 summarizes alternative conceptions of mechanism offered by philosophers and social scientists. In general, the philosophy of science literature tends to focus on *mechanical* systems or structures and often refers to the *functions* of a mechanism (e.g. Machamer et al., 2000; Pearl, 2009 [2000]; Craver and Darden, 2013; Garson, 2013, 2018; Glennan, 2017). It is often this kind of 'scientific' mechanism-based thinking and language that gives rise to the common perception and even dismissive reading of mechanism as too 'machine-like', i.e. mechanical, technical, or even macho-mechanical-technical.[3]

In the social sciences, the focus is much more on *causal* processes and *events* leading to the identification and specification of (causal) mechanisms. By emphasizing causal powers and dynamic processual unfoldings in the social world, this more open-ended conception of (social) mechanisms should give critical human geographers a reasonable sense of relief or even immunity from allergic reaction to the above scientific-mechanical view of mechanisms (i.e. don't be afraid and read on!). This causal-processual view of mechanism is also consistent with the idea of generative mechanism in scientific realism (e.g. Harré, 1972; Salmon, 1984, 1998). Political scientist John Gerring (2008: pp. 163, 178) thus argues

**Table 5.1**    Definitions of mechanism in the philosophy of science, philosophy of social science, and social science disciplines.

| Authors | Definitions |
|---|---|
| *Philosophy of science* | |
| Machamer et al. (2000); Craver and Darden (2013) | Mechanisms are *entities* and *activities* organized such that they produce regular changes and underlying relations from start to finish. |
| Glennan I (2002) | A mechanism for a behaviour is a *complex system* that produces that behaviour by the interaction of several parts, where the interactions between parts can be characterized by direct, invariant, change-relating generalizations. |
| Woodward (2002, 2003) | A model of a mechanism describes an organized or structured *set of parts or components*. The overall output of the mechanism will vary under manipulation of the input to each component and changes in the components themselves. |
| Bechtel and Abrahamsen (2005) | A mechanism is a *structure* performing a function by virtue of its component parts and component operations and their organization. |
| Pearl (2009 [2000]) | Mechanisms are stable and deterministic *functional* relationships between variables, some of which are unobservable, and organized in the form of an acyclic *structure*. |
| Garson (2013, 2018) | Mechanisms are identified by the *functions* they serve, where 'function' is understood as having a connotation of teleology, purposiveness, or design. |
| Glennan II (2017); Glennan and Illari (2018b) | A (minimal) mechanism for a phenomenon consists of *entities* (or parts) whose *activities* and *interactions* are organized so as to be responsible for the phenomenon. |
| *Philosophy of social science* | |
| Bhaskar (1975, 1986); Collier (1994) | A mechanism is a *triggerable causal power* that coexists with a host of other mechanisms, processes, and factors that inhibit that triggering or otherwise interfere with the causal relationship. |
| Little I (1991) | A causal mechanism is a *series of events* governed by law-like regularities that lead from the explanans to the explanandum. |
| Stinchcombe (1991) | Mechanisms serve as lower-order social processes that constitute a higher-order theory. |
| Bunge (1997, 2004) | A mechanism is a *process* in a concrete system that is capable of bringing about or preventing some change in the system. |
| Little II (2011, 2016) | A mechanism is a *particular configuration* of conditions that always leads from one set of conditions to an outcome. Mechanisms bring about specific effects. |
| Bengtsson and Hertting (2014) | Mechanisms are regular *patterns* of specific kinds of actions and interactions, patterns that are causally productive, meaning that they bring about certain outcomes. |
| *Social sciences* | |
| Elster I (1989) | A mechanism explains by opening up the black box and showing the cogs and wheels of the internal machinery. A mechanism provides a continuous and contiguous *chain of causal or intentional links* between the explanans and the explanandum. |

**Table 5.1**    (Continued)

| Authors | Definitions |
| --- | --- |
| Elster II (1999, 2015) | Mechanisms are frequently occurring and easily recognizable *causal patterns* that are triggered under generally unknown conditions or with indeterminate consequences. |
| Reskin (2003) | Mechanisms are observable processes that do not require the positing of motives and convert inputs (independent variables) into outputs (dependent variables). |
| Hedström (2005) | A mechanism is a concept used to describe a *constellation of entities and activities* that are organized such that they regularly bring about a particular type of outcome. |
| Gross (2009) | Mechanisms are *chains or aggregations* of problem situations and the effects that ensue as a result of the habits actors use to resolve them. |
| Yeung (2019a) | A mechanism is a particular and necessary *relation* that connects a specific *cause* with its eventual *outcome* in broadly similar *contexts*. A cause can be an action or a practice by an actor, institution, object or their combinations. |

Sources: Based on Hedström (2005: Figure 2.2, p. 25); Gross (2009: pp. 360 – 362); Hedström and Ylikoski (2010: Table 1, p. 51); Bengtsson and Hertting (2014: pp. 710 – 714); Little (2016: p. 191); and Glennan and Illari (2018b, 2018c).

that his minimal (core) definition of mechanism as 'process' is consistent with all contemporary usages and practices within the social sciences. In what sociologist Philip Gorski (2015: p. 28) calls a 'connector' approach to defining mechanism, cause and effect are typically defined in positivist terms of temporal linearity (cause preceding effect), and causal mechanisms are the chains or links that connect them. To political scientists Michael Zürn and Jeffrey Checkel (2005: p. 1049), these chains or causal mechanisms are 'intermediate processes' that 'connect things; they link specified initial conditions and a specific outcome'.[4]

Indeed, this social science conception of mechanism does not deviate much from sociologists Peter Hedström and Richard Swedberg's (1996: p. 288, 1998b) influential definition of social mechanisms as theoretical or analytical constructs connecting observed relationships between explanans and explanandum (phenomenon to be explained). Their own explanatory approach is to address 'a further and deeper problem: how, i.e. through what process, was the relationship actually brought about?' This process-based conception of mechanism, however, is not the only established definition of social mechanisms. In Table 5.1, different understandings of mechanism tend to revolve around defining mechanisms variously as processes, structures, systems, chains, links, patterns, constellations, events, entities, activities, interactions, parts or components, and so on (see a recent critique in Groff, 2017). Two key 'components' seem to emerge from these definitions (see also Kaier, 2018): (1) *material objects*: entities or parts that are stable bearers of properties or causal powers; and (2) *actualized activities*: interactions or operations that are more than just emergent potential or capacities and produce real changes in society and space.

Despite these diverse definitions of mechanisms, philosopher of social science Petri Ylikoski (2018: p. 405) argues that social scientists should not worry too much insofar as we are thinking in terms of mechanism-based explanations. And yet even this vast literature on mechanism exhibits a tendency towards *conflating* mechanism with process. To Ylikoski (2018), this is a more serious problem because in such processual thought, mechanism is often conceived as a 'black box' under the illusion of achieving a certain depth of understanding. This dangerous ambiguity in process-mechanism conflation leads me to rethink the two conceptual tools in light of Chapter 3's discussion of the development of mechanism-based explanatory theory in critical human geography. Unpacking the 'black box' of mechanism, not as an effect but as a practically adequate causal explanation, is imperative in Geography and the social sciences.

This conceptual section offers a theory of mechanism that differentiates it from process in novel ways that can inform geographical research and afford greater precision in causal explanations. My epistemological approach is not meant to produce a single universal definition of mechanism. Instead, I argue that (re)conceptualizing mechanism allows for a better and more robust form of theorizing. As noted by Hedström and Swedberg (1996: p. 299; original italics) in one of the earliest works on social mechanisms, 'it is not so much the definition *per se* that is important, as the type and style of theorizing it encourages'. By 'theorizing', I follow Sayer's (1992: p. 81) advice that it involves a process of 'normative explication' through which 'problematic concepts' are explicated and concise definitions are given to 'important but vaguely understood terms through re-working their relations with other terms in the network'.

To me, 'process' and 'mechanism' are such problematic concepts and vaguely understood terms in the network of causal explanations that require reworking/theorizing in order to link better their sense-relations in critical human geography. My theory of mechanism is developed in two steps: (1) a clearer (re)conceptualization of what mechanism and process are – the former a necessary relation with the outcome and a more specific kind of the latter; and (2) the introduction of actors and their action into the specification of mechanisms for producing concrete outcomes in the socio-spatial world(s). Because of this critical role of actor-specific intentions and actions, social mechanisms are often different from those operating in the physical/natural world (e.g. in biology and physics; see also Table 5.1). These human intentions and actions also make social mechanisms much more conjunctural and much less mechanical-technical than nature-based mechanisms.

## Reconceptualizing Mechanism, Process, and Context

While causal explanation is important in social science and the identification of mechanism is a necessary step, we cannot realistically claim processual concepts, such as time-space compression (Harvey, 1989), neoliberalization (Harvey, 2005), actor-network (Latour, 2005, 2013), mobility (Cresswell, 2006), affect (Anderson, 2014), strategic coupling (Yeung, 2016), and bodily regime (Pile, 2021), as *causal mechanisms* unless we can clearly differentiate mechanism from process. In fact, I argue that *both* mechanism and process are integral to any causal explanation and thus this conceptual issue matters far beyond their semantic distinctions. To resolve this important issue, I go back to Sayer's (1992: pp. 89–92) useful distinction between necessary/internal and contingent/external relations of connection in critical realist thought (see also Chapter 3 on realism). This relational necessity is material or natural and does not refer to logical or discursive necessity.[5] The connection between two objects, such as people, institutions, and practices, is necessary and internal if one cannot exist without the other (e.g. slave-master or landlord-tenant relations cited by Sayer). Otherwise, such connection is contingent and external in nature (e.g. British governments and North Sea oil). This realist conception of necessary relations differs from the kind of assemblage theory/thinking in human geography in which necessary relations are deemed socially constructed and contingently framed through specific historical processes (see Chapters 2 and 3 on assemblage theory). To me, causation in assemblage thinking remains vague and indeterminant due to its social ontological commitment to unravelling processes of assembling a wide range of heterogeneous social entities to form wholes or assemblages.[6]

Applying the above realist conception of necessary relations to the process-mechanism distinction, I define *mechanism* at the simplest level as a *particular* and *necessary* relation that connects a specific cause and the working of its causal powers with an eventual outcome in broadly similar contexts. As theorized in the previous chapter on causal powers, a cause can be an action or a practice by an actor, institution, object, or their combinations. Without activating this mechanism through powers embedded in a causal condition (i.e. emergent properties in relational geometries), the concrete outcome or phenomenon will not happen. In short, this mechanism is both necessary and specific to a particular socio-spatial outcome; their cause-and-effect relation is not contingent on something else external to such relation (see also Table 5.1). In *Method in Social Science*, Andrew Sayer (1992: p. 105) thus argues that '[t]he particular ways-of-acting or mechanisms exist necessarily in virtue of their object's nature. The nature or constitution of an object and its causal powers are internally or necessarily related'. This realist conception of mechanism as necessary and internal relation differs from the focus on the 'exteriority of relations' and non-linear causality in poststructuralist assemblage thinking (DeLanda, 2006, 2016; Anderson et al., 2012a; see also my review in Chapter 2).

On the other hand, *process* refers to a contingent and recurrent series of changing configurations and relations among its constitutive elements or entities over time and space that *can* relate to intended and unintended outcomes. These entities can be individual actors (e.g. bodies, emotions, minds, and things) or broader collectives (e.g. social groups, firms, networks, states, and institutions).

This contingent change in relations is neither internal nor necessary to specific outcomes though. The term 'process', such as neoliberalization, embodiment, or intersectionality is often used to describe a sequential change in recurrent configurations and relations among its constituents. But as will be discussed in the next two sections, it is often not used to connect causally this change with its eventual outcomes, intended or otherwise. These contingent and recurrent attributes thus mean that process is open-ended in nature. A process *of* change itself requires unpacking (i.e. description) and explanation that may draw upon other causal mechanisms in conjunctural and yet consequential ways to form causal explanation. Its outcomes cannot be specified a priori because this specification requires a causal analysis of change in the form of a necessary mechanism or multiple mechanisms. My claim does not imply that processes such as neoliberalization, embodiment, or intersectionality cannot be causal mechanisms – they can, provided that their causal necessity to the phenomenon at stake is carefully specified.

In addition, an action or an object cannot be a process and a mechanism at the same time because the latter is specified from the former and is internal or necessary to a concrete outcome. Often, the causal working of a mechanism entails a process-like sequence of change (cause) and outcome (effect). In this sense, a mechanism can be derived from a process (the working of causal powers), but it is a *particular* kind of process because of its necessary role in connecting change and outcome. This particularity in any mechanism is derived from the necessary relation(s) between its causality and the phenomenon in question. Meanwhile, a process cannot be derived from a mechanism since a process needs not be a necessary and an internal connection between cause and effect – it may simply represent *contingent* change in the recurrent configurations of entities and this change itself needs explanation. Despite some common (mis)understanding of space as contingency in human geography, my distinction here does not accept such assumption a priori. The processual ways in which space matters – often termed 'spatial relations' – can sometimes be specified as necessary in relation to particular phenomenon. Such spatial relations can indeed be causal mechanisms, rather than merely contingent or contextual factors.

Mechanism also operates at lower levels of abstraction than process, with which it has a many-to-one (or many-to-many) relationship; it illuminates the explanatory pathway through which particular relation operates in specific context(s). The constitutive elements of a mechanism are real entities or actions/objects with emergent powers and potentialities discussed in Chapter 4. A mechanism therefore cannot be a pure idea or an abstract object, as in logic, mathematics, and general linguistics (Bunge, 1997: p. 418). This particularity in mechanism helps us distinguish clearly process (of change) from mechanism (for purpose-specific, directional, and causal outcomes) in social science analysis. In this sense, philosopher Mario Bunge (1997: p. 416) is right to assert that '[e]very mechanism is a process, but the converse is false'. Some processes may never be specified into particular mechanisms for causal explanations; not every process is and can be a mechanism.[7]

Figure 5.1 illustrates my theory of mechanism (and process) in causal explanation. Operating at the more *general* level (external/contingent) and a higher level of abstraction, process represents change in recurrent series of relations that brings about new series of relations and constitutive elements. To account for outcomes at the *concrete* and 'lower' level (e.g. mid-range theories discussed in Chapter 3), we need to specify the causal necessity of an action/object or a process *for* a particular purpose of connecting change or recurrent events at the general level with its specific outcomes at the concrete level (middle boxes in grey). This specification of particularity can transform an abstract process into a concrete mechanism and demonstrates how a causal change works out to produce its specific outcomes, i.e. making things or events happen. However, it should not be read as mechanism being 'caused' by process. The 'downward' arrows from 'process' to 'mechanism' refer to the analytical procedure of specification, not causal powers flowing from one to another.

This conceptual move from a general process of change itself to a concrete/ necessary mechanism or several mechanisms for a socio-spatial outcome requires careful specification of the outcomes to be explained and the working of the causal powers through this mechanism(s). Missing out this crucial step of specification will render process to remain as a descriptive tool at the general/contingent level (upper section in Figure 5.1). As examined in Chapters 2 and 4, many critical 'theories' and relational thoughts in human geography have adopted such

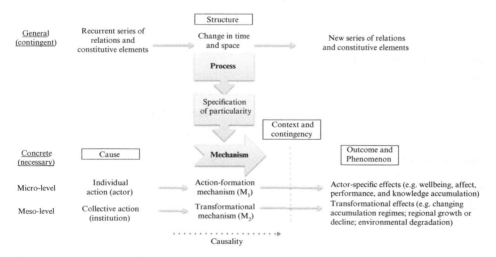

**Figure 5.1**  A theory of mechanism and process in causal explanation.

a processual approach, but have not specified causal mechanisms in their descriptive accounts of socio-spatial change and events.

In the spirit of building mid-range theories discussed in Chapter 3, this formulation of mechanism and process allows for meso-level concepts (in different processes) to be situated in multi-scalar analyses involving multiple actors and institutions at the general level. And yet the concomitant requirement of specification of particularity in the production of causal explanations tends to reduce the temptation of simply identifying a large list of factors and interactions in these process-like concepts, such as neoliberalization and embodiment. This epistemological exercise likely limits the number of causal mechanisms in each explanatory mid-range theory to just a few, as evident in the examples in Table 5.2.[8] As such,

**Table 5.2**    Examples of social mechanisms and mid-range concepts.

| | |
|---|---|
| **Contention** | **Social communications** |
| Escalation | Interpersonal network |
| Brokerage | Broadcast |
| Paramilitary organizations | Rumour |
| Competition for power | Transport networks |
| Boundary activation | **Economic activity** |
| **Collective action** | Market |
| Prisoners' dilemma | Auction |
| Free rider behaviour | Ministry direction |
| Convention | Contract |
| Norms | Democratic decision making |
| Selective benefits | Producers' control |
| Selective coercion | **Government** |
| **Organizational enforcement** | Agenda setting |
| Audit and accounting | Log rolling |
| Supervision | Regulatory organizations |
| Employee training | **State repression** |
| Morale building | Secret police |
| Leadership | Informers |
| **Norms and values** | Spectacular use of force |
| Altruistic enforcement | Propaganda |
| Person-to-person transmission | Deception |
| Imitation | **System** |
| Subliminal transmission | Flash trading |
| Erosion | Interlocking mobilization |
| Charisma | Overlapping systems of jurisdiction |

Source: Little (2016: Table 6.1, p. 193).

any causal explanation needs to specify one or more mechanism(s) necessary to the concrete phenomenon under investigation. This phenomenon can be an outcome or a process that forms the beginning of our causal investigation.

A political-economic phenomenon such as over-determination, neoliberalization, or strategic coupling is a process. So is the social-cultural process of affective performativity, gendered embodiment, or bodily encounter. But if the necessary relations between a process and concrete outcomes can be specified through theoretical and substantive work, such as neoliberalization specified with geographical uneven development later in this chapter, a process *of* change can be reconceptualized to become a mechanism *for* these outcomes. As a cover concept (e.g. neoliberalization or bodily encounter), a process in itself is insufficient in specifying these changes triggered by the interactions of elements or entities within a necessary causal mechanism. This specification of concrete outcomes and their causal connections to changing entities affords greater analytical precision and explanatory power to mechanisms than processual descriptions of change that are neither internal nor necessary to these concrete outcomes (and thus their reading as vague, confusing, and indeterminant). As argued by philosopher Renate Mayntz (2004: p. 239; original italics), 'to use a terminological label merely to *allude* to a process that remains unspecified has no more explanatory value than the simple statement of a correlation' (see also Beach and Pedersen, 2016: pp. 71–91).

This theorization of mechanism in causal explanation brings to the fore the importance of *context* because particularity in causal mechanisms is often dependent on the existence of the 'right' context in which causal powers operate efficaciously and produce expected outcome(s). This context-dependent nature of a mechanism's particularity is also important in avoiding the sort of transcendental finality in the Cartesian explanation of open systems (i.e. social worlds), a key consideration of/for theory and explanation in Geography discussed in Chapter 1. Mechanism-based mid-range theories and explanations must always be well grounded in different socio-spatial contexts.

More specifically, context is integral, not external, to the subjects/objects under investigation, and therefore serves as the relevant broader setting for a causal mechanism to operate and produce its expected outcome. In Chapter 4, I have already examined Sayer's (2004: p. 262) crucial idea of 'double contingency' in understanding the realization of causal powers in context. Illustrated further in Figure 5.1, context serves to enable the causal powers of mechanism to act upon and produce empirical outcomes in society and space. In short, context is not outside this operation of causal powers at the concrete level – from cause via mechanism to outcome.[9] Context shapes the conjunctures in which different causal mechanisms work to generate specific phenomena and events. It enables a less 'machine-like' and a more dynamic and open-ended view of mechanisms in the social world(s). My approach is similar to the arguments in support of context in human geography (Sunley, 1996; Frangenheim et al., 2020; Gong and Hassink, 2020; cf. Barnett, 1999), analytical sociology (Gross, 2018), political science (Falleti and Lunch, 2009), and the philosophy of social science (Pozzoni and Kaidesoja, 2021).

A useful causal explanation is constituted by the specification of mechanisms and their interaction with operating contexts. Political scientists Tulia Falleti and Julia Lynch (2009: p. 1144) thus contend that 'credible causal social scientific explanation can occur if and only if researchers are attentive to the interaction between causal mechanisms and the context in which they operate'. In *Realism and Social Science*, Sayer (2000: p. 15) notes that 'the same mechanism can produce different outcomes according to context, or more precisely, according to its spatio-temporal relations with other objects, having their own causal powers and liabilities, which may trigger, block or modify its action'. As political-economic and social-cultural action takes place contingently within the socio-spatial world(s), there is no reason why this action can be ontologically separated from the same world as a separate category for description and analysis. In other words, context sets the contingent conditions in which socio-spatial action can be realized and analysed (Yeung, 2003: p. 445, 2019a: p. 235; Beach and Pedersen, 2016: pp. 89–90).

My theory of mechanism and causal explanation, nevertheless, does not endorse the universal applicability and efficacy of the same mechanisms in *all* empirical contexts (that would be far too macho-mechanical for my taste!). Unlike the planetary claims of deterministic structures in structuralist theories (Chapter 2) and relational thought in some critical theories (Chapter 4), mechanisms are neither universal nor deterministic because they do not always produce the same expected outcomes in different socio-spatial contexts. This contextual contingency, however, does not mean that mechanism is only one-off because it is particular for, and specific to, a phenomenon or an event. In the social world, a phenomenon or an event may recur over time and space such that the same mechanism might be evoked in its causal explanatory account. My conception of causal mechanisms in mid-range theories is not about their generality or recurrence per se, but about their necessary epistemological role in explaining why and how things and events happen in specific contexts (i.e. no straightforward generalizations or law-like 'regular'/invariant mechanisms). Most socio-spatial phenomena have multiple mechanisms operating in conjunction, in sequence, or in parallel – a methodological condition known as 'equifinality' (see Beach and Pedersen, 2016: p. 90; Goertz, 2017: pp. 52–55). To me, the causal chains linking these mechanisms and their enabling contexts must be brought to the analytical forefront in any practically adequate mechanism-based explanation. This methodological step goes beyond merely recognizing the conjunctural workings of such mechanisms to theorizing and specifying their differential causality in relation to the phenomenon or outcome in question.

In contrast to grand theories or more totalizing explanations outlined briefly in Chapter 2, mid-range theories can be helpful in uncovering causal mechanisms without the epistemological commitment to theorizing the underlying universal structures of social life and relations. Instead, such mechanism-based theorizing in context allows for more pluralistic explanations precisely because we can have many different mid-range theories and multiple causal mechanisms *for* explaining complex geographical realities and outcomes in different socio-spatial contexts.[10] Over time, more explanatory mechanisms can be developed such that broader theories of the more generalizable kind might be developed on the basis of these mid-range theories and their concomitant causal mechanisms – a 'concatenation' strategy for causal theory development.

Methodologically, context is not necessary in the specification of mechanism from process (though it is integral to the *operation* of a mechanism). The abstraction method separating the necessary from the contingent requires us to remove the contextual material in order to reach the causal properties of an underlying mechanism and to make inference in similar contexts. As argued by Sayer (1992: p. 86), this realist method 'must "abstract" from particular conditions, excluding those which have no significant effect in order to focus on those which do. Even where we are interested in wholes we must select and abstract their constituents'. Through what Pike et al. (2016: p. 132) describe as the 'deep contextualization' method tracing historical contingencies and institutional genealogies, geographers can uncover a fuller set of actors and their internal and external relations that are involved in co-producing specific socio-spatial change and trajectories.

## *Causal Theory and Actors*

As alluded in Chapter 3, a causal theory describes why and how certain variable relationships conceptualized in one or more mechanisms operate to produce the expected outcomes from the initial conditions – it is fundamentally explanatory in nature. While these conditions and outcomes are empirically observable, their causal mechanisms are not necessarily amenable to direct observation. Developing causal theory therefore requires an analytical procedure to render these mechanisms visible and intelligible to our empirical analysis. In critical realism (e.g. Sayer, 1982a, 1992; Pratt, 1991, 1995; Little, 2016), this methodological procedure of abstraction refers to the analytical specification of causal mechanisms in relation to the existing processes of socio-spatial change. To Cox (2013b: p. 50), human geographers have taken for granted this crucial realist method to an extraordinary degree without attributing it to critical realism. This explains my contention in Chapter 3 that certain elements of realist methodology are well and alive in human geography today, despite fewer current renditions of its philosophical underpinnings.

In Roy Bhaskar's (1986: p. 11, note 26, 1989: p. 19) realist philosophy for social science expounded in his *Scientific Realism and Human Emancipation* and *Reclaiming Reality*, this procedure is embedded in the broader realist conception of *retroduction* in which an argument 'moves from a description of some phenomenon to a description of something which produces it or is a condition for it'. Retroduction necessitates an iterative and reflexive methodology involving analytical movements from understanding the empirical phenomenon to its underlying necessary and contingent conditions and the abstraction and specification of causal mechanisms (see Pratt, 1995; Yeung, 1997, 2003; Elder-Vass, 2010; Gorski, 2018). In the social mechanisms literature, Hedström and Swedberg (1996: p. 290, 1998b: pp. 15, 25) argue that 'It is through abstractions and analytical accentuation, however, that general mechanisms are made visible'. Instead of focusing just on 'providing theoretical accounts of what happens as it actually happens', they believe firmly in the value of analytical abstractions (Hedström and Swedberg, 1998b: p. 14). Others social scientists and philosophers of social science call this highly popular method 'process tracing' or the use of within-case evidence for making inferences and reconstructing causal explanations (Beach and Pedersen, 2013, 2019; Weller and Barnes, 2014; Bennett and Checkel, 2015; Tsang, 2022).

Revisiting Figure 5.1, the specification and transformation of a process of change into a causal mechanism for explaining an outcome requires abstraction and specification of its necessity to these outcomes. In this conception, *action* is one of the core principles in my theory of mechanism. This conception relates specifically to the social world(s) in which actors are the conscious agent whose action and choice – intentional or otherwise – can produce concrete outcomes. In Chapter 4, I have already discussed the importance of actors and their agency in unleashing the causal powers and relationality in relational geometries and practice philosopher Schatzki's (2019: p. 87) 'dynamize bundles' of action chains in effecting social change in a material world. In short, human agency should go beyond what postcolonial critic Wael Hallaq (2018: p. 199) terms 'Latour's Stone', i.e. the physical presence of things.[11] As argued forcefully by Hedström and Swedberg (1998b: p. 24), 'it is actors and not variables who do the acting. A mechanism-based explanation is not built upon mere associations between variables but always refers directly to causes and consequences of individual action oriented to the behavior of others' (see also Elster, 2015: Part III; Beach and Pedersen, 2016: pp. 79–80). Similarly arguing for an action theory of causation in human geography, Cox (2013a: p. 12) notes that socio-spatial '[c]hange occurs because people act. They act on and with other things or conditions, but these too should be seen in their relation to human agents: as products of a human action that also transforms them and gives them new properties' (see also Hannah, 2019: pp. 6–7).

Since mechanism is a particular and necessary relation between causal powers and an outcome, I argue that this particularity in the socio-spatial world is premised on the specificity of effective actions at the individual and collective levels and their outcomes. Differentiated at the micro-level and the meso-level in Figure 5.1, this specification requires the articulation of action or initiatives taken by actors, such as people, politicians, firms, workers, and states, with their collective outcomes (e.g.

social-cultural change and/or political-economic transformation). After all, mechanism in the social world will not be efficacious unless actors do what they intend to do. This intentionality is where individual beliefs and bodily strategies matter. It is human action that gives the *modus operandi* of mechanism for effecting particular change in society and space. But this intentionality of actors does not mean that mechanism itself has intention(s) or is a social construction. As explained in Chapter 4's relational theory, mechanism is the particular relational link or set through which purposeful action and its causal powers can be transmitted to, and connected with, its intended or unintended outcomes. When these actors do take initiatives that can be specified through empirical analysis, a process – as a contingent and general set of changing events and relations – can be redefined as a (particular) mechanism in the causal explanation of such an outcome. Without this specification of particularity in action and outcome, we cannot determine a posteriori if a set of events is necessarily a mechanism.[12]

In geographical analysis, this particularity can produce different types of mechanisms connecting social and/or institutional action with their individual and collective outcomes. At the micro-level in Figure 5.1, individual action by actors can produce concrete outcomes through what sociologists commonly call 'action-formation mechanisms' ($M_1$). Grounded in James Coleman's (1986, 1990) well-known schema of sociological explanation, Hedström and Swedberg (1996, 1998b) suggest that specifying a mechanism requires articulating the purposive action of actors in a specific social situation, through which a variable produces necessary change in another variable (see also Beach and Pedersen, 2016: pp. 85–89). This micro-level mechanism is known as a situation mechanism or an individual action-formation mechanism, such as cognitive dissonance or self-fulfilling prophecy. But when actors interact with each other and individual actions are transformed into a collective outcome, a micro- to meso-level transition is deemed to have taken place, and the resultant mechanism is known as a transformational mechanism ($M_2$), such as the tragedy of the commons or accumulation by dispossession. At this more meso-level, collective action beyond individual actors can bring about transformational effects in society and space.

By way of examples familiar in my fields of specialization, a good number of these actor-level and institutional-level mechanisms can be identified in the existing geographical research into uneven development in economic and political geography and urban and regional studies (see also Chapter 4 on institutional geographies and Table 4.1). At the actor-level, we can think of adaptive learning and emulation as particular mechanisms ($M_1$) for 'fast policy transfer' among regulatory authorities (Peck and Tickell, 2002; Peck and Theodore, 2015) or for knowledge spillovers among regional actors (Boschma and Frenken, 2006; Boschma et al., 2017). Martin (2010) and Martin and Sunley (2015) also describe different micro-level mechanisms for institutional change: layering, conversion, and recombination, whereas I have proposed in Yeung (2016) several actor-specific mechanisms of strategic coupling for promoting national industrial transformation: strategic partnership, industrial market specialization, and lead firm formation (see also my further reflections in Chapter 6 of this book). The operation of these mechanisms entails both specific action on the part of these actors and authorities and necessary changes in the configurations of their relations with other entities in order to produce the eventual outcomes of changing local/national governance or innovative activities or new path formation in regional/national development.

At the more meso-level, transformational mechanisms $(M_2)$ can take the form of particular collective action through privatization, commercialization, commodification, (re)regulation, financialization, and political constructions of markets that transform existing socio-spatial relations into neoliberal patterns of institutional shifts and regulatory restructuring. A similar mechanism-based approach can be pursued to identify the transformational mechanisms at work that explain the path dependence or self-organization – a process – of uneven regional evolution. These mechanisms may be product diversification or 'branching' at the collective level (Frenken and Boschma, 2007; Boschma et al., 2017) or convergence and increasing returns to capability development at the institutional level (Martin and Sunley, 2006, 2015). As will be illustrated further in Chapter 6, inter-organizational networks are also important meso-level mechanisms for regional and national growth (Huggins and Thompson, 2014; Hamilton-Hart and Yeung, 2021; Yeung, 2021a) and global economic development (Yeung, 2016, 2022). In all of these instances, significant political-economic processes and uneven regional evolution can often be explained by individual action-formation mechanisms $(M_1)$ or transformational mechanisms $(M_2)$ that connect causal powers with their particular empirical outcomes in context.

## Processual Thought in Geography

But how do processes (and mechanisms) unfold in diverse geographical accounts of social relations, encounters, practices, and phenomena in their variegated socio-spatial contexts? Before I demonstrate the relevance of mechanism-based theorizing in rethinking neoliberalization and explaining its socio-spatial outcomes in the final section, it is useful here to examine briefly the dominant kind of processual thought in some critical geographical approaches to socio-spatial changes and encounters that exhibits a general tendency towards conflating process with mechanism. Some of these literature strands have also been examined in the previous chapter's section on relationality and relational thought in contemporary human geography (i.e. Marxist geography, poststructuralist geographies, including actor-network theory, non-representational theory, and assemblage theory).

To begin with *Marxist geography*, one might argue that its epistemological emphasis on dialectics as method offers one of the most directly processual thought. Such dialectical thinking conceives processes (and relations) as having ontological autonomy in creating and sustaining entities and things in capitalism. These processes in the conflictual social relations of production in turn account for real world events and socio-spatial outcomes. On this processual thought in Marxist geography, it is useful to quote at length David Harvey's (1996: p. 49; my emphasis) first principle of dialectics among his 11 propositions in *Justice, Nature and the Geography of Difference*:

> Dialectical thinking emphasizes the understanding of processes, flows, fluxes, and relations over the analysis of elements, things, structures and organized systems... There is a deep ontological principle involved here, for dialecticians in effect hold that elements, things, structures and systems do not exist outside of or prior to the processes, flows, and relations that create, sustain or undermine them. For example, in our contemporary world, flows of capital (goods, and money) and of people give rise to, sustain, or undermine places such as factories, neighborhoods, and cities understood as things. Epistemologically, the process of enquiry usually inverts this emphasis: we get to understand processes by looking either at the attributes of what appear to us in the first instance to be self-evident things or at relations between them... On this basis we may infer something about the processes that have generated a change in state but the idea that the entities are unchanging in themselves quickly leads us to a causal and mechanistic thinking. Dialectical reasoning holds, however, that this epistemological condition should get reversed when it comes to formulating abstractions, concepts, and theories about the world. This transforms the self-evident world of things with which positivism and empiricism typically deals into a much more confusing world of relations and flows that are manifest as things.

Here, Harvey's (1996) processual view is that nothing exist outside of or even prior to processes and thus dialectical theorizing must not take entities and things as self-evident, but rather as *products* of 'a much more confusing world' of processes and relations. In this processual thought, however, it is not clear where processes themselves come from and how their causal powers can be unleashed to produce things, events, and outcomes. All we know is that entities and things do not exist unless they are continually (re)produced through processes and relations (see a critique in Hart, 2018: pp. 379–380). While Harvey seems adamant about mechanistic thinking because of its allegedly static conception of things or their relations as self-evident and reified, his dialectical reasoning offers no clear analytical pathway on how processes and relations must necessarily create, sustain, or undermine these events and outcomes in *particular* ways. In short, this Marxist processual view has no place for causal mechanisms in its explanatory theorizing. If any, it tends to conflate process with mechanism when it comes to empirical explanations (see the case of Harvey's possible conflation of neoliberalization in the next section).

This ontological privileging of processes and relations is also evident in much of the work in *poststructuralist geographies* (see my discussion in Chapters 2 and 4; also MacFarlane, 2017). In *Post-Structuralist Geography*, Jonathan Murdoch (2006: ch. 2) examines Michel Foucault's (1975) work on discipline and punishment in prisons through enclosed spatiality and the Panopticon as spatial mechanisms of monitoring and surveillance. But in the same sentence, he seems to conflate these spatial mechanisms with what he terms 'processes of observation and normalization':

> It is therefore the suppression of potential dangers that drives the development of Panoptic monitoring and surveillance. Moreover, Foucault argues these *mechanisms* are increasingly adopted beyond the prison gate in a host of institutional settings – schools, factories and hospitals – where *the same* processes of observation and normalization are valued. Foucault claims that these new Panoptic spaces come to comprise a 'carceral archipelago', organized in line with the ubiquitous strategies of hierarchical observation and normalizing judgement. It seems, then, that the prison has spread, heralding the emergence of what might be called a 'disciplinary society' (Murdoch, 2006: p. 40; my emphasis).

And yet he concurs later on with Allen's (2003) work on power and the need to specify the precise mechanisms of how governmental power works in these processes of disciplining and normalizing otherwise spatially dispersed and seemingly autonomous and independent subjects (Murdoch, 2006: p. 52). In his concluding chapter on poststructuralist ecologies, Murdoch (2006: pp. 197–198) argues for a poststructuralist geography as 'a way of shifting spatial imaginaries so that new forms of geographical practice come into being'. This seems to me all good and fine. But he goes on to discuss some 'steering mechanisms' that seem to be conflated with processes of spatial (de)formations. It is not clear what mechanism and process mean in his call for 'steering the spatial', admitted paradoxically by him as 'perhaps not a slogan likely to inspire great enthusiasm'!

In his three empirical cases of processes of division and transgression in English countryside, processes of planning practice in the UK, and processes of industrialization, standardization, and differentiation in food networks, Murdoch (2006: chs. 5–7) attempts to 'translate' the processes of heterogeneous associations in *actor-network theory* into his empirical accounts of spatial formations (cf. Thrift, 1996; Whatmore, 2002). In this enactment of processual thinking in Latourian actor-network theory (e.g. the distinction of networks as result or 'set-ups' from networks as process of heterogeneous associations in Latour, 2013: pp. 31–33), it remains unclear what material processes of socio-spatial change are at work. Even less clear are the primary (causal) mechanisms for explaining the (dis)ordering of nature and society in these spatial formations. In this kind of processual analysis, there is a tendency of taking all spatial relations as network relations. This seems to be a danger of the tyranny of networks if the causality of network processes is not well specified into spatial mechanisms of some sorts. If everything is about/ inside heterogeneous networks, how is this claim different from the totalizing theory of capital(ism) in Marxist thought already noted in Chapter 2?

In *non-representation theory*, my earlier discussion in Chapters 2 and 4 has already shown that processes and practices are its key themes for radical empirical accounts.

But can these processes and practices become causal explanations of performative outcomes, such as bodies, emotions, embodiment, and so on? To Anderson and Harrison (2010b: p. 2; original italics), 'non-representational theory has a *practical* and *processual* basis for its accounts of the social, the subject and the world, one focused on "backgrounds," bodies and their performances'. In this processual view, the analytical attention is placed on what they call 'emergent processes of ontogenesis' through which bodies are actualized and individuated through diverse sets of practical relations. In particular, affect is theorized as such an emergent process of repopulating the social. As argued by Wright (2015: p. 392) and Simpson (2021: p. 8), this kind of processual accounts and 'weak theory' provides an open-ended experimentalism with the world that is attuned to the processes, performances, and practices of a wide range of human and more-than-human agents.

In my view, this epistemological commitment to an open-ended processual account does make it much harder to offer mechanism-based causal explanations that might constitute mid-range theories examined in Chapter 3. For example, can the process of 'subjectification', a key concept in non-representation theory, be a causal explanation of performative outcomes? If so, why and how? Is subjectification too broad and general since, as noted by Simpson (2021: p. 8; also Thrift, 2007: p. 7), 'Subjectification proceeds from an ever-shifting composition of human and non-human things – various objects, people, technologies, texts, ideas, discourses, rules, norms, and so on – perpetually encounter and shape one another'? Here, practice philosopher Schatzki (2019: p. 179) might have gone too far by arguing that social reality is just too complex and contingent to make it possible for a particular event to occur under any specifiable conditions for a given process. Surely few critical social scientists are naïve enough to believe in such 'iron clad' invariant connections between cause and effect in different socio-spatial phenomena. As argued in the previous section, context and contingency matter much in mechanism-based explanations, as they always do in such processual and practice-oriented theories of the social world(s). In my specification of mechanism as particular process specific to the phenomenon to be explained, context and contingency are not bracketed (out) but should rather be fully unpacked to illustrate how a particular mechanism brings cause to work on its effect in specific context(s).

Taking a different poststructuralist route to this kind of processual thought, McCormack (2012) offers an affirmative critique of abstraction as a necessary element in understanding the experiential and material complexity of lived worlds.[13] To him, abstraction in geographical thinking refers to both process and noun. As a process of selective reduction, abstraction represents

> generalization and simplification through which the complexity of the world is reduced at the expense of the experience of those who live in the concrete reality of this world... It is taken to involve isolating or identifying the most *essential* processes driving or shaping phenomenon, temporarily bracketing these from extraneous

influences and background empirical noise. As such, it provides a way of synthesizing the results of individual observation and description (McCormack, 2012: pp.
715, 717; my emphasis).

As a noun, abstraction refers to a form of representation through which this
process of simplification is stabilized and its results circulate. Examples are contemporary forms of organizational consistency and technologies for ordering the
world, e.g. economic projections, traffic management systems, software and code,
and graphics and diagrammes. He cites critical urban theorist Henri Lefebvre's
(1991 [1974]) work in *The Production of Space* to illustrate Lefebvre's strong critique of abstract space in social and scientific thought and public policy (e.g.
urban and environmental planning). Pursuing a revisionist view on the relevance of abstraction as an open question, he argues for lively, dynamic, or 'warm
abstractions' that 'affirm the importance of being open to the multiple ways in
which abstraction participates both in the worlds we inhabit and in our efforts to
make sense of them' (McCormack, 2012: p. 716).

To me, the conundrum in this processual view of abstraction as both a process of isolating 'essential processes' and a noun for representational forms is
that the sort of reductionist, homogenizing, and technocratic-instrumentalist
abstraction in Lefebvre's (1991 [1974]) critique is not the same as abstraction as
a method. As noted earlier in the first section, this abstraction method is useful
in identifying causal mechanisms that are not the same thing as McCormack's
(2012: p. 717) 'essential processes'. Indeed, abstraction as a method is necessary
to go beyond the banality of everyday lived experiences and practices to uncover
the underlying power relations and causal mechanisms – some of these mechanisms need not even be underlying and can be as just as banal and mundane,
e.g. self-fulfilling prophecy as a causal mechanism of social outcomes (see also
examples in Table 5.2).

In McCormack's (2012) writing and examples, he often switches between
these different forms of abstractions – abstraction in epistemology (as method)
and abstraction in reality (as noun/object or 'participant'; p. 727). The former
can be termed 'theoretical abstraction' (i.e. ways of thinking) and the latter as
'concrete abstraction' (i.e. from thought to practice and participant in social
worlds). Here, I think the critiques levelled against either form are not necessary
the same and thus this rather uncritical 'switching' (or conflation) is unhelpful
in illustrating the nature of abstraction in geographical thinking and writing. The
Lefebvrian kind of critique against the alienating effect of software and code as
abstraction surely is not the same thing as the epistemological critique against
abstraction as a way of theorizing beyond the direct human experiences. At stake
here is more than just a matter of the *level* of abstraction (i.e. how 'abstract'),
but as, if not more, important is the *nature* of abstraction – as epistemology to
'reclaim reality' (as argued in this chapter) or as forms, technologies, or even
objects (as in McCormack, 2012).

Let me give one more specific example of possible process/mechanism conflation in the context of work on bodies and affects in *psychoanalytic geographies* (Kingsbury and Pile, 2014a; Pile, 2021). In their studies of psychoanalysis founder Sigmund Freud's work on his patients, Kingsbury and Pile (2014b) examine Freud's 'idea of a repressed unconscious and the psychic mechanisms of repression' (Pile, 2021: p. 91). Despite this emphasis on psychic mechanisms of repression, they go on to outline a processual conception of repression as an ongoing worldly process.[14] In his psychoanalysis of the repressed experiences of Freud's patient Dora, Pile (2021: p. 101) brings to the fore many different processes of the unconscious, such as the contiguity of ideas, reversal into opposites, repression, over-determination, trains of thought, chains of association, timelessness, contradictoriness, and preservation. To him, repression 'is generative of Dora's symptoms'. As a process of the unconscious, repression seems to be a generative mechanism *for* Dora's symptoms since it is specific and particular to her conditions. But repression, as a general process of psychic (un)consciousness, may not necessarily be a generative mechanism for another body suffering from even similar symptoms, such as confusion, anxiety, and trauma over emerging sexuality. This begs the question of how we can understand 'bodies' as actors, 'bodily regimes' as structured relations, and 'repression' as a process until it becomes particular to specific bodies or bodily regimes, i.e. repression as a psychic mechanism.

In *assemblage theory*, I have already examined in Chapters 2 and 3 Manuel DeLanda's (2006: p. 32) arguments in *A New Philosophy of Society* for focusing on causal mechanisms as a solution to the recalcitrant micro-/macro-problem in social theory. To him, these complex mechanisms behind the synthesis of emergent properties refer to the inner workings of concrete assemblages that are constituted by relations of exteriority. But in his rush to champion mechanism and causality in assemblage theory against totalities in a mechanical world of linear causality, he has somewhat glossed over the crucial distinction between process and mechanism. While he draws on the Deleuzian notion of processes of territorialization and coding (in Deleuze and Guattari, 1987 [1980]), DeLanda (2006: pp. 19–20; original italics) claims that:

> to speak of processes of territorialization and coding which may be instantiated by a variety of mechanisms implies that we have an adequate notion of what a mechanism is. In the case of inorganic and organic assemblages these mechanisms are largely causal, but they do not necessarily involve *linear causality*, so the first task will be to expand the notion of causality to include nonlinear mechanisms. Social assemblages, on the other hand, contain mechanisms which, in addition to causal interactions, involve *reasons and motives*. So the second task will be to show what role these subjective components play in the explanation of the working of social assemblages... Hence if assemblages are to replace totalities the complex mechanisms behind the synthesis of emergent properties must be properly elucidated.

As I have noted critically in Chapter 2, DeLanda (2006) does not work through this important task of elucidating nonlinear causal mechanisms in his empirical analysis, leaving only 'forces' and 'processes' to carry the full weight of his causal analysis of these complex mechanisms. For example, classifying different 'factors' or 'forms' into 'territorializing' (centripetal) or 'deterritorializing' (centrifugal) processes – a rather cumbersome Deleuzian binary terminology anyway (in addition to his much-evoked 'machine' metaphor) – is not going to give a mechanism-based causal analysis nor a proper analysis of processes of differentiation.[15] This is because of its binary or bifurcative orientation towards a descriptive typology of what different assemblages might look like, rather than a full-fledged causal analysis of their emergence and transformation focusing on cause and effect within specific historical and geographical contexts. Much of DeLanda's (2006: chs. 3–5) descriptive analysis focuses on processes of differentiation (primarily through Deleuzian territorialization and deterritorialization) that are seemingly disguised or mis-specified as causal mechanisms. To sum up my critique, processual description cannot substitute for detailed and precise specification of mechanism – causal (linear or non-linear) or otherwise.[16]

Focusing on the similarities or conjunctions between actor-network theory and assemblage thinking in human geography, Müller and Schurr (2016) have identified three processes for cross-fertilizations between these two strands of poststructuralist processual views:

1. the stabilization of relations across distance (actor-network theory's [ANT] forte that can be useful for assemblage thinking);
2. the need to deal with change and unforeseen events (fluidity central to assemblage thinking, but picked up later by actor-network theorists); and
3. the central role of desire and affect in binding elements into the network.

In their further elaboration on these conjunctions and cross-fertilizations, Müller and Schurr (2016) inadvertently seem to conflate process with mechanism. In their empirical case on assisted reproduction as an actor-network, Müller and Schurr (2016: pp. 221–222) not only describe 'the whole process' of governing the network, but also its 'mechanisms of stabilisation' through reliance on various intermediaries across transnational space and the failure of the various 'mechanisms of control'. To them,

> What an ANT-inspired description adds over and above an assemblage approach in this analysis of how stability is achieved is a more nuanced understanding of the *mechanisms* that make the elements of the network cohere but at the same time produce unexpected multiplicities. The enrolment of elements with the help of intermediaries, the restricted gaze of the oligopticon when intermediaries convert to mediators, are concepts that allow not just a fine-grained description of the labour involved in governing at a distance, but it offers an analytical vocabulary for the processes of stabilisation (Müller and Schurr, 2016: p. 222; my emphasis).

As evident in the above quotation, it is unclear how such 'network-coherence mechanisms' are conceptually different from 'processes of stabilization'? Müller and Schurr (2016) seem to refer to the same stabilization process/mechanism, at least metaphorically. This problem of process/mechanism conflation is perhaps grounded in the lack of causal explanatory orientation in actor-network theory (see my discussion of Latour, 1988, 1996 in Chapter 2). When they discuss mechanisms of desire/wish as affect in assemblage thinking, Müller and Schurr (2016) further conflate these mechanisms with processes of assembling.[17] To give more substance to this conflation problem and to exemplify its significant implications for geographical analysis, the following section critically examines a relatively large body of literature on *neoliberalization* and demonstrates how this kind of process/mechanism conflation can occur and why resolving it matters much in the development of explanatory theory/theorizing in Geography. As noted in Chapter 1, my choice of illustrative materials from my own subfield in economic geography and urban and regional studies is simply pragmatic because familiarity allows me to reflect better on the conflation problem and the intellectual origins and geographical situatedness of this literature strand. Geographers from other subfields, such as those discussed briefly in this section on processual thought, will no doubt pick up this process/mechanism conflation issue in their specific domains of geographical knowledge and reflect on their own journey towards explanatory theory.

# From Process to Mechanism: Explanatory Theory/Theorizing in Geography

As one of human geography's key contributions to the social sciences, contemporary geographical analysis of uneven development has focused primarily on uncovering diverse processes of spatial formations in late capitalism.[18] Eschewing the deterministic grand theories of the earlier era in the 1970s and the 1980s, geographers are concerned with understanding the dynamics of capitalist production through variegated social and institutional practices and uneven spatial processes in context (Sheppard, 2011, 2016; Peck, 2016, 2023; Clark et al., 2018; Leyshon, 2021; Werner, 2021). When economic-geographical processes are theorized through mid-range concepts in recent decades, such as neoliberalization, path dependence, strategic coupling, and financialization,[19] they are often used as heuristic devices for explaining socio-spatial changes and institutional practices leading to uneven development (see also my earlier discussion of institutional geographies in Chapter 4). But what is the explanatory efficacy of these *process*-based concepts, and is it fundamentally the same as *mechanism* – another key conceptual building block for coherent causal explanation in mid-range theories examined in Chapter 3? How can a clearer conceptual distinction between mechanism and process strengthen causal explanation in such geographical analysis?

Further to the earlier two sections and in the spirit of constructive dialogues, this section engages directly with recent geographical work on *neoliberalization* and the causal analysis of uneven development. I argue for theorizing and explaining uneven development in a more robust manner on the basis of causal explanations grounded in mechanism-based thinking, rather than stopping at the kind of processual analysis as often is the case in many strands of critical human geography, including those discussed in the earlier section. In this more focused and precise way, I believe geographical research can achieve more effective analytical purchase and engage better with the wider social science community. However, the mushrooming of meso-scale or mid-range conceptions of geographical phenomena during the past two decades sometimes exhibits a lack of analytical rigour and therefore potentially weakened explanatory power. More recent work in the geographical analysis of uneven development has deployed the terms 'process' and/or 'mechanism' to describe influential mid-range concepts, such as neoliberalization and path dependence.

Similar to some critical approaches examined in the previous section, followers in these large genres of literature tend to use process and mechanism interchangeably, as if these two concepts refer to the *same* causal connection in specific empirical events or geographical episodes. Sometimes influenced by and couched in critical social theories, this common linguistic and/or conceptual slippage can erode the explanatory power of mid-range concepts and theories because of the differential analytical specificity embedded in the two terms. Their possible conceptual conflation thus requires rethinking and further clarification in order for geographers to develop more coherent causal explanations based on these mid-range concepts.

In particular and as theorized in Chapter 4, the concept of causal powers exercised through generative mechanisms in critical realist thinking has thrown into sharp relief the fundamental relationality of cause and effect in socio-spatial dynamics (Hudson, 2003; Yeung, 2005; Sheppard, 2008; Varró, 2015). Contributing towards such a renewed effort in theorizing causal mechanism, I argue that explanation in current geographical analysis cannot be adequately performed by the thick description of socio-spatial processes, no matter how nuanced and contextualized they are as often found in a large swath of geographical literature purportedly 'explaining' the process of neoliberalization itself and related affective atmospheres (e.g. Anderson, 2016; see also discussion in Chapter 4) and lived/embodied experiences (e.g. Dowler et al., 2014; Phipps, 2014).[20] To increase the explanatory efficacy of mid-range concepts describing these processes, more careful analytical specification is required to identify the causal mechanisms *for* the empirical phenomena under investigation.

## *Why Neoliberalization?*

Cognizant of the highly diverse geographical literature on uneven development, I have chosen neoliberalization and the political-economic production of capitalist uneven development to illustrate the conceptual conflation of mechanism and process and to showcase how my distinction of the two concepts might help improve its explanatory efficacy.[21] Indeed, process and mechanism are often used interchangeably in this literature that leads to its explanations being more gestural than carefully constructed and exemplified. As Jamie Peck (2013: pp. 152–153; original italics) concludes in his critical realist moment, 'Citing the process of neoliberalization must not be a substitute for explanation; it should be an *occasion* for explanation, involving the specification of particular causal mechanisms, modes of intervention, hybrid formations, social forms and foibles, counter-mobilizations, and so forth'. My choice here reflects the concept's rapid emergence since the late 1990s and its significant impact in human geography and adjacent social science fields. My intention is not to evaluate or even summarize the vast geographical literature on neoliberalism, as distinct from its processual conception in 'neoliberalization', in substantive and empirical terms – an almost impossible task in itself. Readers interested in neoliberalism should read some of the cited work here for how the concept is very much alive and working in practice (see also focused critiques in Ferguson, 2010; Weller and O'Neill, 2014; Venugopal, 2015; Birch and Siemiatycki, 2016; Green and Lavery, 2018). My purpose below is more in the spirit of offering an immanent critique – to raise critical questions on the process/mechanism conflation within its conceptualization and contradictory empirical deployment (e.g. in explaining China's uneven development).

My argument for incorporating both process and mechanism in coherent geographical explanations is consistent with, and complements, human geography's current infatuation with variegation/conjunctural/assemblage thinking. As examined in Chapter 4 and the earlier section in this chapter, this kind of processual thinking tends to focus perhaps too much on contextualizing socio-spatial changes and thereby often underspecifies the causal 'work-out' of key processes and/or relationality. The final subsection will put my conception of mechanism and process 'back' into the discussions of neoliberalization. Referring to a working example of neoliberalism 'with Chinese characteristics' – a phenomenon popularized by David Harvey (2005: pp. 120–151) in his well-known book *A Brief History of Neoliberalism*, my critical evaluation illustrates the problematic tendency towards the process/mechanism conflation in the literature and elucidates how a more precise distinction can alleviate some of the shortcomings and improve the existing causal explanations.

As argued throughout this chapter, an analytical focus on processes at the general level is inadequate without specifying precisely how these processes can become mechanisms *for* particular socio-spatial events and outcomes under peculiar conditions or contexts. Just like how social relations of production – as a key relational process in the Marxian political economy of capitalism in Chapter 4 – 'need' mechanisms such as exploitation, commodification, and dispossession to produce conjunctural over-determination and diverse concrete outcomes, neoliberalization – as process of neoliberalism – cannot be the precise mechanism for a particular form of uneven geographical development. The lack of internal/necessary relations between neoliberal tendencies and these changes can render neoliberalization a 'chaotic' concept discussed in Chapter 3. And this is more troubling than the idea of neoliberalization as a 'rascal concept' (Brenner et al., 2010: p. 184; Peck, 2013: p. 133, 2023: ch. 4), a 'deeply problematic and incoherent term' (Venugopal, 2015: p. 165), or even a form of 'theoretical determinism' (Pow, 2015: p. 464). As critiqued by Ann Markusen (1999: p. 871) almost two decades ago, this kind of 'process-preoccupied writing' can easily lead to 'fuzzy' concepts because 'The analysis is reduced to characterizing the process, with no clear attribution of power, responsibility or range of possible response on the part of actors'. I believe we need better and more concrete specification of causal mechanisms that can make a concept and/ or a process 'work', i.e. creating the possibility of, and responsibility for, socio-spatial change.[22]

In more specific terms, whereas a general process such as neoliberalization or path dependence (or even labour process) can exist independently of particular geographical outcomes (e.g. local unemployment or the rise of high tech clusters), there is no such thing as a 'general' or a 'universal' mechanism without its purpose and outcome(s) clearly identified and theorized; a mechanism is always a necessary mechanism *for* something – connecting cause and effect as identified in a robust explanatory theory. This is why the process-mechanism distinction matters much in the efficacy of causal explanations. Indeed, the key problem or 'fuzziness' is that these 'general processes', not well-specified mechanisms, are often presented *as* causal explanations of geographical outcomes. The conflation is about using process as an explanation in itself. For an explanation to be causal and complete, concrete mechanism(s) must be specified in relation to contingent general process(es). The critical issue is not just that outcomes are glossed as processes, but rather processes are glossed as mechanisms that are necessary and particular in context (see also Figure 5.1).

The next section first begins with some of the canonical works on neoliberalization, starting with Peck and Tickell (2002), as part of the 'process tracing' of the emergence of this influential body of literature. This mid-range concept was originally developed in the context of a post-Fordist regime of accumulation in the United States and Britain – a clear indication of its Anglo-American situatedness in origin, standpoint, and application. As other researchers adopt this processual concept, often uncritically, in their supposedly 'causal' analyses of different empirical contexts and geographical outcomes over time, neoliberalization – as a process of neoliberalism – gets conflated with causal mechanisms for specific forms of uneven development *everywhere*. Certainly not intended by such pioneer geographers as Jamie Peck and Adam Tickell (2002), this conflation by followers reflects the key problem of under-theorization of process-mechanism in the existing geographical studies of neoliberalism.

## Neoliberalization: What's in a Process and What Can Go Wrong?

In their highly influential paper on neoliberalizing space, Peck and Tickell (2002: p. 380) explicitly call for a 'process-based analysis' of *neoliberalization* that has subsequently stimulated much debate in the geographical analysis of urban and regional governance, socio-spatial lifeworld(s), and uneven development. To them, 'neoliberalization should be understood as a *process*, not an end-state. By the same token, it is also contradictory, it tends to provoke counter-tendencies, and it exists in historically and geographically *contingent* forms' (p. 383; my emphasis). Conceptualized as a process of neoliberalism, neoliberalization refers to a dominant political-economic project of regulatory restructuring emanating from North America and, later, Western Europe that has its creative and destructive moments; it is 'driven by a family of open-ended social processes and associated with polymorphic forms and outcomes' (Peck et al., 2010: p. 101). Responding to the caricatured critique of neoliberalization as monolithic unity by scholars in the varieties of capitalism approach (see Hall and Soskice, 2001; Hancké, 2009), Peck and Theodore (2007: p. 757; my emphasis) argue further that 'process-based conceptions – sensitive to conjuncture, contingency, and contradiction – are less vulnerable to such blunt critiques, since they are explicitly concerned with the manner in which (partially realized) *causal* processes generate uneven and divergent outcomes'. Many subsequent geographical studies have focused on the 'rolling out', 'rolling back', and 'rolling with' phases in these 'causal processes' and their variegated temporal-spatial outcomes (see Craig and Porter, 2006; England and Ward, 2007; Park et al., 2012; Springer et al., 2016; Peck, 2023).

While this process-based conception of neoliberalization as both an 'out there' and an 'in here' phenomenon can be useful for understanding neoliberalism's planetary diffusion as a political-ideological project, I argue that the concrete mechanisms constitutive of this process have not been adequately theorized and specified in subsequent geographical studies, leaving the causal claims about neoliberalization somewhat underspecified and fuzzy. In short, we know quite a great deal about the unfolding and 'rolling' of neoliberalization as a set of geographically variegated processes, but we are less certain of its actual operationalization through specific causal mechanisms that can connect hegemonic regulatory transformation in neoliberalism (cause) with its intended and unintended socio-spatial change on the ground (geographical outcome). As argued by Barnett (2005: p. 9) sometime ago, this process-based conception of neoliberalization 'lacks any clear sense of how consent is actually secured, or any convincing account of how hegemonic projects are anchored at the level of everyday life, other than implying that this works by "getting at" people in some way or other'. To him, theorists of neoliberalism have set up 'a simplistic image of the world divided between the forces of hegemony and the spirits of subversion' (p. 10) – the concept is unable to account for the causal relationship between top-down initiatives (e.g.

political-economic change) and bottom-up developments (e.g. individual action-formation $M_1$ in Figure 5.1).[23]

Lacking clear referents such as the political origins of modern liberalism, many geographical studies of neoliberalism and neoliberalization are far too general in their process-based analysis and much more circumscribed in their causal explanation of *how* and *why* the critical intersections between this general process of political change and everyday socio-economic life are governed. And yet neoliberalism has often been invoked a priori as *the* theoretical explanation for diverse outcomes, such as dystopic narratives in urban studies (Pow, 2015). This has led to what anthropologist James Ferguson (2010: pp. 166, 171) calls 'empty analysis' yielding 'an unsurprising conclusion' in much progressive scholarship: 'neoliberalism is bad for poor and working people, therefore we must oppose it'; it serves 'as a kind of abstract causal force that comes in from outside (much as "the world system" was reckoned to do at an earlier theoretical moment) to decimate local livelihoods'.[24] The normative outcome of these studies tends to be about denouncing neoliberalism rather than thinking through what can be done about it, as in my positive social transformation consideration of/for theory and explanation discussed in Chapter 1 (see also Weller and O'Neill, 2014; Venugopal, 2015).

I illustrate this analytical conundrum with specific reference to David Harvey's (2005) extremely influential book *A Brief History of Neoliberalism*.[25] Without really specifying how neoliberalism moves from being a particular theory/doctrine of political-economic practices – 'incorporated into the common-sense way many of us interpret, live in, and understand the world' – to becoming a multifaceted set of causal mechanisms, he argues that this '*process of neoliberalization* has, however, entailed much "creative destruction," not only of prior institutional frameworks and powers (even challenging traditional forms of state sovereignty) but also of divisions of labour, social relations, welfare provisions, technological mixes, ways of life and thought, reproductive activities, attachments to the land and habits of the heart' (Harvey, 2005: p. 3; my emphasis, also, 2006b). The causality of neoliberalization as process is fairly obvious in Harvey's analysis. To him, any state – capitalist or socialist, which takes on the pathway of market-oriented liberalization (e.g. China in 1978, India in the 1980s, and Sweden in the early 1990s), is deemed a neoliberal state and the 'creative destruction' in their partial moves towards neoliberalization is responsible for subsequent geographical uneven development (see case studies of India in Ahmed, 2010 and Finland/Sweden in Ornston, 2018). And yet, Harvey (2005: p. 9; my emphasis) laments that such 'uneven geographical development of neoliberalism on the world stage has evidently been a *very complex process* entailing multiple determinations and not a little chaos and confusion'.

It is indeed chaotic and confusing if this 'very complex process' or, dare I say, Marxian conjunctural over-determination of uneven geographical development were conceived as synonymous with the process of neoliberalization itself! If so, what are its explanatory (co-)determinants and forces of 'creative destruction', i.e. (conjunctural) causal mechanisms? How can the process of neoliberalization serve as the *explanans* of spatial outcomes (the *explanandum*), such as uneven development? Pointing to the difficulty of constructing the moving map of neoliberalization, Harvey (2005: p. 87; my emphasis) argues further that 'The general progress of neoliberalization has therefore been increasingly impelled through *mechanisms* of uneven geographical developments'. In this even more conflated account of multiple causation and mechanisms, the causal relationship seems completely reversed such that uneven developments (the *explanandum*) become the causal mechanisms 'impelling' the process/progress of neoliberalization (the *explanans*)! While this possibly reciprocal or dialectical form of causality (outcome feeds back on cause) may appear 'normal' to a processual Marxist theorist like Harvey (see my critique of his first principle of dialectics in the earlier section), its unintended conflation of process and mechanism can lead to a significant degree of analytical chaos and misattribution of causality because neoliberalization is constructed in one broad stroke as a cause, a process, and an outcome.

To retain the explanatory power, if any, of neoliberalization and to prevent it from becoming a catch-all phrase to account for 'everything that has happened since the 1990s' (see my Chapter 6 on another such term/concept 'globalization'), it is necessary to translate this abstract political-economic thought and ideas of neoliberalism at the conceptual level into a concrete set of institutional practices in the empirical domain that interact with pre-existing social-spatial conditions (context) to produce uneven developmental outcomes (see also Birch and Siemiatycki, 2016; Peck, 2023). Extending the arguments in my theorization of mechanism in the first section, this analytical translation requires careful specification of internal and necessary relations that turns the general process of neoliberalization into concrete mechanisms on the ground that can 'get at' people and (re)shape their everyday life. Otherwise, neoliberalization-based explanations will suffer from the same fate as 'class reductionism' in earlier radical political economy (see Sayer, 1995) because not all (uneven) geographical outcomes can be reduced to neoliberalization.

Notwithstanding some uncritical applications of the abstract and processual conception of neoliberalization, I argue that greater conceptual clarity between mechanism and process can partially resolve this analytical problem. To Ferguson (2010: p. 172), 'Such insistence on specificity and precision would undoubtedly improve the analytical clarity of many of our discussions'. One key missing link in reconciling this analytical divergence between neoliberalization as a macro-hegemonic process and its relationship – contingent or necessary – with micro-individual collective action is the lack of a clearly articulated theory of the concrete mechanisms through which neoliberalization is actually put to work in shaping everyday life. Much of the literature focuses on the hegemonic ideas, macro-practices, and assemblages of neoliberalization rather than the specific 'mechanics' – what Ferguson (2010: p. 173) calls 'governmental mechanisms' and Povinelli

(2011: p. 132) terms 'modes of exhaustion and endurance' – for socio-spatial changes on the ground. As well noted by one of its pioneers Jamie Peck (2010: p. 14) in *Constructions of Neoliberal Reason,* the concept is often used 'as a no-more-than approximate proxy for a specific analysis of mechanisms or relations of social power, domination, exploitation, or alienation. The forms and registers of the phenomenon can seem almost without limit'.[26]

In principle, a causal explanation may comprise multiple mechanisms that connect initial conditions or changes with empirical outcomes. While the same process may lead to many possible outcomes because of their contingent relation, this causal path is specified in a few necessary mechanisms that operate within particular contexts. A mechanism-based explanation is indispensable in a mid-range theory that draws upon meso-level concepts and analyses to intermediate between pure description/story-telling in radical empiricism and universal laws in Humean positivism and Marxian grand theories. Some of these mechanisms can indeed be 'components' of broader mechanisms at the higher level of abstraction. As argued by sociologist Arthur Stinchcombe (1991: p. 367), a mechanism usually 'gives knowledge about a component process (generally one with units of analysis at a "lower level") of another theory (ordinarily a theory with units at a different "higher" level)'. These context-specific mechanisms interact with one another and constitute what sociologists Diego Gambetta (1998: p. 104) calls 'concatenations of mechanisms' or Doug McAdam et al. (2001: p. 8) term 'component mechanisms' of the overall process (see also Hedström, 2005: pp. 56–60; Kaidesoja, 2019b). To Sayer (2000: p. 14; original italics), 'many mechanisms are *ordinary,* often being identified in ordinary language by transitive verbs'.

Putting this conceptual distinction back into neoliberalization studies, we can broadly identify neoliberalization as a contingent political-economic *process* of evolving hegemonic projects instituted in different places and contexts. This recurrent process *of* change in itself needs to be theorized, historicized, and substantiated, as evident in the existing literature on the history and (re) constructions of neoliberalism (see Harvey, 2005; Peck, 2010, 2013; Anderson, 2016). But the actualization of this political-economic process on the ground necessitates the careful specification of the relevant actor- and institutional-level mechanisms illustrated in Figure 5.1. This theoretically grounded specification procedure can potentially transform the process of neoliberalization into a series of necessary mechanisms for producing concrete socio-spatial outcomes. These mechanisms must demonstrate how causal powers work in specific instances and/or contexts to create intended and unintended consequences. If well specified (i.e. not to be conflated with process), these mechanisms can be the substantive answer to Peck's (2010: p. 276; original italics) call for 'grounded assessments, not blanket pronouncements' that show '*How* social formations and relations are neoliberalized, and with what path-forming consequences, really makes a difference'.

## *Explaining Neoliberalism 'with Chinese Characteristics': How might the Process-Mechanism Distinction Work?*

Revisiting Harvey (2005: pp. 120–151), I briefly examine the empirical case of China since he has devoted an entire chapter to its contemporary transformations and pointed to the apparent parallels of neoliberalism in China's post-1978 economic reform, such as the move towards 'free' trade, the privatization of former state-owned enterprises, the 'growth-first' phenomenon, and the rise of the market economy. Calling this a form of 'neoliberalism "with Chinese characteristics"', he has identified competition and privatization, a democracy of consumption, the massive proletarianization of workforce, and urban speculation, as the key *logics* in this process of 'economic neoliberalization'. In particular, he argues that 'In so far as neoliberalism requires a large, easily exploited, and relatively powerless labour force, then China certainly qualifies as a neoliberal economy, albeit "with Chinese characteristics"' (Harvey, 2005: p. 144). Still, his 'empirical' analysis remains mostly descriptive of the broad historical transformations in China under socialist market reform. It is unclear how such transformations are necessarily *caused* by neoliberalization as we know it. Attributing China's uneven geographical development – itself a very complex process comprising multiple different dimensions (e.g. the uneven emergence of wealthy coastal regions, the domination of mega cities, the exploitation of a large army of surplus labour from rural areas in inner provinces, and so on) – to such neoliberalization process reflects a possible conflation of process and mechanism.

As a process of change characterized by market-based capitalist logics, certain elements of neoliberalization might well have occurred in contemporary China. Even though Harvey (2005: p. 81) finds it 'interesting to note how neoliberalization in authoritarian states such as China and Singapore seems to be converging with the increasing authoritarianism evident in neoliberal states such as the US and Britain', I argue that the concrete working of this convergence process on the ground in China differs substantially from its political origins in the US and Western Europe. This is because the resemblance of China's economic opening-up with the 'syndromes' of neoliberalization may well be impelled by other counterfactual historical forces, such as the Chinese political regime's legitimization imperatives and survival strategies. However neoliberal look-alike or family resemblances of its economic reforms and uneven outcomes, China's economic transformations are likely to be driven mostly by internal political forces premised on the reproduction of the Chinese Communist Party's monopoly power and the complicated and yet evolving political dynamics of central-local state relations.[27] Wu (2008: p. 1095) thus argues that 'the market was initially introduced as a survival strategy for the state' to break the impasse of capital accumulation under state socialism and its efficacy 'relies very much on the state's ability to maintain social order'. Even though neoliberalization is clearly a political project often constituted by disparate actors and forces, a point well recognized by Harvey (2005: p. 19) and others, his book has not examined in any detail the crucial role of *party politics* in China's alleged 'neoliberal turn'.

More specifically in sinology and social science, the Communist Party state in China has been well theorized as *the* causal mechanism of economic transformation through its adoption of marketization and neoliberalizing practices (Lim, 2019; Tan, 2021). Exercising its control over ideology, polity, economy, and society through coercive and even violent means, the Party state confronted its own crisis of legitimacy since the late 1980s through further economic reform and marketization during the 1990s. This politics of reinventing the market and remaking the economy with Chinese characteristics, such as the consolidation of state-owned enterprises alongside the proliferation of entrepreneurial township and village enterprises and private firms, was well illustrated in many social science studies as orchestrated by the Party state for its own regime reproduction, political stability, and modernist nation-building (Naughton and Tsai, 2015; Fuller, 2016; Huang, 2022). As such, it was the Party state that activated and turned the (contingent) process of neoliberalization in China – identified by Harvey (2005) and others – into a specific and necessary set of social relations for the (re)production of geographical uneven development.

In short, the devil is really in the details, and this is where the specification of mechanisms and their concrete contexts of operating efficacy matters much. This careful analytical specification can respond effectively to Peck et al.'s (2010: p. 96) important question on contemporary China as a key frontier in, or even a bold exception to, neoliberalization and serve as 'a kind of radical Rorschach test, separating those prone to divine neoliberalizing tendencies (however contingently expressed) from those inclined to focus on the kinds of exceptions that ostensibly disprove the (neoliberal) rule'. In practice and well demonstrated in the wider literature on China, marketization is fundamentally shaped by China's unique political-economic structures and socio-spatial contexts, such as the political domination of its one-party central state (Liu, 2019; Huang, 2022), the highly corporatist nature of the local state (Huang, 2008; Breznitz and Murphree, 2011; Ang, 2016; Lim, 2019), the extensive role of inter-personal networks in everyday life (Yang, 1994; Nee and Opper, 2012), the land-based logic of development (Lin, 2009; Hsing, 2010; Zhou et al., 2019), and the continual domination of state-owned enterprises (Naughton and Tsai, 2015; Fuller, 2016; Norris, 2016).

These specificities in China's contemporary political economy or 'socialism with Chinese characteristics' mean that the apparently same process of neoliberalization can work out very differently through particular mechanisms that in turn (re)produce uneven geographical development. This is where the process-mechanism distinction becomes most critical in our causal explanation of China's contemporary uneven development. It may render neoliberalization, as a process-based concept, less useful than mechanism-based explanations in causal accounts. In China and under the domination of its Party state, the redistribution of urban land and the pervasiveness of local corporatism and social networks are some of the concrete and necessary mechanisms for explaining diverse socio-economic outcomes on the ground (e.g. the incessant drive for mega projects in large cities and the plight of rural-urban migrant workers). This urban-biased development also reflects the continual vested interest of large state-owned enterprises that have substantial *de facto* control of urban assets (e.g. land) and easy access to the state-led financial system (e.g. loans). In the absence of specifying these concrete mechanisms at work, the socio-spatial outcomes of China's uneven geographical development cannot be easily reduced to, and let alone explained by, the all-encompassing capitalocentric logics of neoliberalization (see recent work on Greater Bay Area development in southern China in Peck, 2021; Meulbroek et al., 2023). As argued by Pow (2015) and Zhou et al. (2019), the preoccupation of these logics of neoliberalization with capital and class interests has failed to appreciate the distinctive nature of entanglement of capital, state, and society in urban China, underspecifying the driving role and the competing rationalities of China's authoritarian state and the rapid reconfiguration of urban society and social aspirations among its people.

What might then be some plausible examples of such necessary mechanisms connecting causal forces with concrete socio-spatial outcomes? Short of an in-depth empirical analysis (see above cited works), let me be a little speculative here. To be fair, most causal explanations are elliptical to some degree and tend to gloss over multiple component mechanisms. Still, a good number of actor-level ($M_1$) and institutional-level ($M_2$) mechanisms can be 'abstracted' and identified from the existing studies of neoliberalization – these two types of mechanisms are not necessarily sequential to each other, but they can be combined conjuncturally or treated separately in an actual empirical study. At the actor-level (see Figure 5.1), we can think of adaptive learning and emulation as action-formation mechanisms ($M_1$) for 'fast policy transfer' among regulatory authorities (Peck and Tickell, 2002; Peck and Theodore, 2015). Instead of defining the process of neoliberalization as policy diffusion in itself, it is conceptually more useful to think of such diffusion as but just *one* mechanism of the general process. In turn, this mechanism of policy diffusion can be constituted by the concatenation of component mechanisms, such as adaptive learning and inter-agency emulation (e.g. best practices, consultancy, and benchmarking) in China.

Once the problem of aggregation is resolved through this distinction between process as the general/contingent and mechanism(s) as the particular/necessary, geographical analysis of uneven development can gain better explanatory traction by linking the causal powers of neoliberalization as a broader process of capitalist change with the dynamics of socio-spatial life on the ground. For example, specifying such actor-level mechanisms as regulatory and planning mechanisms and rent-seeking mechanisms in the context of changing urban policy regimes in China can add much value to linking neoliberalization tendencies with concrete outcomes in its urban governance and rural transformations, e.g. the emergence of rural industrialization, the rapid rural-urban migration, and social (in)justice and the right to the city.

Action-formation mechanism can also connect the ground-up accommodation and negotiation by actors, however contingently, with top-down forces of neoliberalization. In China, populist tendencies such as the massive shift towards consumerism and materialistic experience and the politics of (in)difference to wealth and inequality are constitutive of this mechanism of action-formation. This kind of bottom-up socio-cultural change produced through particular actor-level mechanisms may make top-down neoliberal 'fixes' (e.g. national policy shifts and market opening) look like highly coherent and effective in their operationalization when it may in fact be these very actor-level mechanisms that *do* the actual work on the ground. This analytical focus on the actor-level mechanisms of neoliberalization can bridge the macro-spatial orientation of the existing geographical studies and the key concern of some critics with the governmentality of everyday socio-economic life. It also brings actors and their intentionality into the causal explanations of socio-spatial outcomes associated with neoliberalization.

At the more meso-level (see Figure 5.1), transformational mechanisms $(M_2)$ can take the form of particular collective action, such as privatization, state redistribution, and political constructions of markets. In Harvey's (2005: pp. 159–161, 2006b: pp. 153–155) analysis of neoliberalism, some of these are conceived as features of 'accumulation by dispossession' – the main mechanism through which the outcomes of neoliberalization can be achieved, such as redistribution of wealth and income. A mechanism-based explanatory theory, however, must specify each of these as a particular mechanism for specific outcome(s) of neoliberalization. In this operationalization, transformational mechanisms serve as the analytical tool to give explanatory substance to such a general process as neoliberalization. A causal explanation of these outcomes in China therefore necessitates a (re)combination of all these differentiated component mechanisms, and this explanation cannot be reduced to the process of neoliberalization alone. In all of these instances, neoliberalization as a political-economic process can be (re)made necessary through the specification of its individual action-formation mechanisms $(M_1)$ and/or transformational mechanisms $(M_2)$ for connecting causal powers with their particular empirical outcomes.

Taken together in this chapter, I have argued that robust mid-range theory in critical human geography needs causal explanations underpinned by a conceptually precise and valid distinction between process and mechanism. Adopting a non-deterministic and mechanism-based approach to causal explanation and theory development, this epistemological approach can serve as a possible zone of engagement with other reflexive and critical approaches in human geography examined in Chapters 2 and 4. Geographical theory can be explanatory in nature, but its explanatory power depends on the identification and specification of generative mechanisms connecting causal powers with socio-spatial events and outcomes. While performing a necessary role in causal explanation, however, mechanism can be conflated with process even in canonical works by some of the most influential geographers discussed in this chapter – the conceptual problem goes well beyond linguistic slippages. This conflation in turn reduces the analytical efficacy of geographical theory and its potential contribution to theory development in the wider social sciences – an important theme I will return to in the final concluding Chapter 7.

In particular, I have explained the critical importance of distinguishing conceptually mechanism from process in order to develop more realistic mid-range concepts and causal explanations that can account for individual action and emergent powers connecting initial causes and their concrete outcomes and, yet, offer analytical clarity and explanatory precision in this procedure. As the third step in my synthetic approach based on certain elements of realist thought and relational theory already discussed respectively in Chapters 3 and 4, this chapter has demonstrated that the conception of mechanism as a particular and necessary relation for producing outcomes in context is a robust and pragmatic one. In this conceptualization, a mechanism is central to causal explanation because a general and contingent process of change, while integral to this explanation, may not be causal 'enough' to explain concrete empirical outcomes.

By explicitly developing a mechanism-based approach to account for socio-spatial events and outcomes, geographers can avoid what Hedström and Ylikoski (2010: p. 54) call 'lazy mechanism-based storytelling' or what Gerring (2010: p. 1504) and Kalter and Kronberg (2014: p. 100) term 'mechanism talk' (i.e. a mechanistic application of mechanisms – even in some poststructuralist thought pointed out in this book). My immanent critique shows that identifying and specifying these mechanisms in relation to the general processes of socio-spatial change, such as neoliberalization in this chapter, can go a long way to advancing such geographical knowledge of uneven development. It can also contribute to the renewed purpose of explaining the 'big pictures' of uneven global development as a core intellectual project in economic geography (James et al., 2018; Martin, 2018; Peck, 2023) and other subdisciplines in human geography that are concerned with the critical understandings of major contemporary political and societal debates. The robust specification of mechanisms will also enable geographical theory to be more compatible and comparable with those mechanism-based analyses in other social science disciplines. It allows for a more reciprocal form of 'engaged pluralism' emergent in human geography and the wider social sciences. As will be illustrated in the next chapter, one such causal mid-range theory on global production networks – the underlying platform of globalization and global capitalism – has indeed emanated from my own field of economic geography and urban and regional studies and engaged successfully with the wider social sciences.

## Notes

1   This section draws upon my earlier work in Yeung (2019a: pp. 230–238). See this large literature in key books by Hedström and Swedberg (1998a); Hedström (2005); Demeulenaere (2011); Kincaid (2012); Manzo (2014, 2021); Elster (2015); Little (2016); Glennan (2017); and Glennan and Illari (2018a).

2   Philosopher of science Sophie Roux (2018: pp. 30, 34) traces the origin of mechanical philosophy to the 1660s after certain founding members of the Royal Society in England, such as Robert Boyle, Henry Power, and Robert Hooke, coined the term 'mechanism' as a neologism and began to use 'mechanical philosophy' to denote a particular kind of philosophy of science as a reaction against Aristotelian natural philosophy. To me, this mechanical philosophy says much more about mechanism in an epistemological sense without its necessary and corresponding philosophy on ontology – what would the world (being, nature, and society) be like in order for mechanism to be recognizable and efficacious in causal terms. Indeed, much of the philosophy of science literature on mechanism remains rather 'mechanistic' in the sense that it is primarily concerned with the scientific practices of discovering, representing, and/or modelling mechanisms in causal explanations in order to avoid the pitfalls of the Humean search for universal causal laws of nature.

3   Let me point out an irony here. It might be useful to remind readers that the term 'abstract machine' is evoked rampantly throughout Gilles Deleuze and Félix Guattari's (1987 [1980]) *A Thousand Plateaus* – a key poststructuralist referent in open-ended approaches in critical human geography. 'Machine' and its derivatives have appeared almost 1,000 times in the influential text.

4   This intermediary process view of causation and mechanism is commonly found in political science and sociology (e.g. Mahoney, 2001: p. 581, 2008: p. 413; Gerring, 2005: pp. 166, 179; Gross, 2009: p. 363) and the philosophy of social science (e.g. Bunge, 1997: p. 414, 2004: p. 191; Mayntz, 2004: pp. 241, 253; Reiss, 2007: p. 166) and science (e.g. Illari and Russo, 2014: pp. 121–126).

5   See Sayer (1992: pp. 164–169) for his strongest defence of natural necessity in relation to logical necessity in causal explanation (e.g. mathematics). See also a similar view against logical necessity by two speculative realists in DeLanda and Harman (2017).

6   See also applications of assemblage theory/thinking across diverse fields in human geography since the late 2000s in McFarlane (2009); Allen and Cochrane (2010); Anderson and McFarlane (2011); Edensor (2011); Anderson et al. (2012a); Dittmer (2014); Ouma (2015); Müller and Schurr (2016); Kinkaid (2019, 2020); Bridge (2021); and Woods et al. (2021).

7   Many philosophers of mechanism support this particularity view of mechanism *for* explaining natural or social phenomena. To Petri Ylikoski (2012: p. 22; original italics), 'a mechanism is always a *mechanism for something*; it is identified by the kind of effect or phenomenon it produces'. Declaring the new mechanical philosophy for science, philosopher Stuart Glennan (2017: p. 2) points out that 'one of the most important general things we can say about mechanisms is that they are particulars – each one different from the next'. In their handbook of mechanisms, Glennan and Illari (2018c: p. 92) also argue that 'It is a truism among new mechanists that mechanisms are individuated by their phenomena or behavior. All mechanisms are mechanisms for. This usage is common in scientific and technological contexts'. Similarly, Garson (2018: p. 104) notes that 'A mechanism is always a mechanism for a phenomenon. The phenomenon that a mechanism serves is not somehow incidental to that mechanism, but constitutive of it: mechanisms are identified, and individuated, by the phenomena they produce'. What is missing in this 'mechanism-for' view though is the workings of causal powers as conceived in Chapter 4 and this chapter.

8   Critiquing the danger of anti-essentialism for its denial of causal explanation, Sayer (1995: p. 23; my emphasis) argues that 'To explain a complex *process* no less than a simple one, we have to say what *mechanisms* (causes including reason) co-produced it and in virtue of what structures those mechanisms exist. There is no point in an anti-essentialist even mentioning all the possible factors in a concrete situation if they were not responsible for determining what happened'. As such, causal explanation is not about listing all the possible factors in a process-like concept.

9   In this sense, I concur with Nigel Thrift's (1996: p. 3) 'performative' view of context and contingency in *Spatial Formations*: 'By "context" I most decidedly do not mean an impassive backdrop to situated human activity. Rather, I take context to be a necessary constitutive element of interaction, something active, differentially extensive and able to problematise and work on the bounds of subjectivity'.

10  This realist argument for mechanism-based mid-range theories responds to earlier critiques of realism for missing out the necessary capitalist structures of social relations (e.g. Harvey, 1987; Cox, 2013a). As noted by Cox (2014: pp. 177–178), 'In critical realism, the identification of the structures proceeds through the separation of the necessary from the contingent. A consequence of that in terms of ideas of social process is pluralizing – so many independent social structures like capital, the division of labor, gender, and so forth – putting critical realism in an uncomfortable relation with the categorial approaches discussed previously'. See also Chapter 3's discussion of critical realism and its conception of contingency.

11  See also my quote on agency from Hallaq (2018: p. 199) in Chapter 4 endnote 25.

12  Following sociologist James Coleman (1986, 1990), Ylikoski (2018: p. 403) argues for the importance of mechanism-based explanations in linking micro-level individual actions with macro-level social outcomes: 'Social scientists know a great deal about how individuals' desires, beliefs, and opportunities, for example, are influenced by the social contexts in which they are embedded (situational mechanisms), and about how these desires, beliefs, and opportunities influence actions (action-transformation mechanisms), but when it comes to the link between individual actions and social outcomes, they are often forced to resort to hand-waving' (see also Ylikoski, 2012).

13  In *How We Became Posthuman*, feminist literary critic Katherine Hayles (1999: p. 12) cautions against the disembodying nature of abstraction during theorizing or what she sees as the 'Platonic backhand' at work: 'The Platonic backhand works by inferring from the world's noisy multiplicity a simplified abstraction. So far so good: this is what theorizing should do. The problem comes when the move circles around to constitute the abstraction as the originary form from which the world's multiplicity derives. Then complexity appears as a "fuzzing up" of an essential reality rather than as a manifestation of the world's holistic nature'. See also discussion of embodiment in posthumanism and post-phenomenology in Simonsen (2013); Ash and Simpson (2016); Ash (2020b); Simonsen and Koefoed (2020); and Hepach (2021).

14  As noted by Pile (2021: p. 92; my emphasis) in *Bodies, Affects, Politics*, 'This [processual view] aligns, then, with a reworked understanding of the assignment of bodies to proper places and the distribution of the senses, in which more than one bodily regime is in play. Where repression is a set of processes, rather than a set of locked away contents; the assignment of bodies to proper places requires ongoing work to achieve; and the sense get continually worked over to achieve and ensure consistency'.

15 This bifurcating approach to concepts in Deleuzian thought is well recognized by Roberts and Dewsbury (2021: p. 1525): 'With Deleuze, there are no two ways about it: neither hybridization nor middle ground, only bastardization perhaps; no more-than nor less-than, only bifurcation like representation or non-representation'.

16 See also Woods et al.'s (2021: pp. 290–293) recent attempt to 'apply' the same 'mechanics' of Deleuzian territorialization/deterritorialization and coding/decoding to their study of rural towns in Ireland, Wales, Canada, and Australia in relation to global economic restructuring and international migration.

17 As noted by Müller and Schurr (2016: pp. 224–225; my emphasis), 'Where ANT has recognised the necessity of the virtual in general terms, desire/wish in assemblage thinking works through its *mechanisms* and effects… The stability of the global assisted reproduction assemblage is tied up with the ability of relations between (non-)human bodies located in different sites to produce desire/wish. Desire/wish does not emerge as a result of the assemblage, but emerges with and in the *process* of assembling. This makes desire/wish and assemblage co-constitutive'.

18 This section draws upon my earlier work in Yeung (2019a: pp. 238–247).

19 Key references on these concepts in geographical political economy are: neoliberalization (Peck and Tickell, 2002; Castree, 2008a, 2008b; Peck, 2010; Green and Lavery, 2018), path dependence (Boschma, 2004; Boschma and Frenken, 2006; Martin and Sunley, 2006, 2015; Harris, 2021), strategic coupling (Coe et al., 2004; Yeung, 2005, 2016, 2021a; MacKinnon, 2012), and financialization (Pike and Pollard, 2010; Christophers, 2015; Ioannou and Wójcik, 2019).

20 In feminist geographies, for example, a number of empirical studies have been conducted on gender-based violence arising out of neoliberalization (e.g. Dowler et al., 2014; Phipps, 2014; Phipps and Young, 2015; Pain et al., 2020). But similar to much of the geographical political economy literature on uneven development to be examined in this section, the theorizing and specification of how this process (neoliberalization) is turned into a causal mechanism *for* explaining gender-based violence remains mostly lacking.

21 Space constraint does not allow me to take up fully the other three influential mid-range concepts familiar to me: 'path dependence' in evolutionary economic geography, 'strategic coupling' in global production networks research, and 'financialization' in financial and urban geography. The process-mechanism problematic in these three strands of geographical analysis tends to be more a matter of mixing up of terms and conceptual slippage.

22 In their responses to Markusen (1999), Peck (2003) and Hudson (2003) concur that processes need to be worked out better in relation to their theoretical necessity and analytical plausibility. To Peck (2003: p. 731) – a self-confessed 'process fetishist', this entails concrete research 'to investigate the working out of causal processes or tendencies in different settings, to trace the effects of contingent interactions, and to corroborate and triangulate findings in relation to extant (and emergent) theoretical positions'.

23 Arguing from the perspective of non-representational theory, Anderson (2016: p. 737) critiques that 'Whilst this research is timely and important, neoliberalism acts as the starting point of analysis, is given a causal role, and becomes the dominant framing context. Neoliberalism is made into a "big Leviathan" that determines affective life… Indeed, most approaches to neoliberalism make some kind of implicit claim about affect and how neoliberalism reorders contemporary affective life'. In a reversal of this causal logic of neoliberalism as the causation for affective life, he points to how affects,

through atmospheres and structures of feelings, condition the emergence and organizing of neoliberalism. But as discussed in my Chapter 4 endnote 36, his own approach remains ambivalent on process and causal mechanism. Anderson (2016: p. 749) thus concludes that 'neoliberalisms happen as/in the midst of dynamic structures of feeling that are more than neoliberal, and become part of the processes whereby the unfinished logic of neoliberalism is differentially actualized. This means that claims about "neoliberal affects" are always claims about a particular geo-historical conjuncture, the constitution and limits of which are empirical questions'. While these 'dynamic structures' may seem causal in terms of their capacities (to affect), their process tracing (i.e. *how* they become causal mechanisms) remains unclear and ambiguous, rendering their explanatory power rather weak. Anderson (2016: p. 750) has conveniently left all these crucial 'how' questions to future research!

24 See also critical theorist and anthropologist Elizabeth Povinelli's (2011: p. 128) *Economies of Abandonment* for her rendition of the sharing of 'certain exhausting conditions of neoliberalism and late literalism' and 'the different modalities of this sharing' in various social projects among diverse groups of indigenous and marginalized people in Australia and the US.

25 The choice of Harvey's (2005) book can be controversial to some readers who may perceive the book more as a popular and broad-stroke account of neoliberalism and its consequences, rather than a carefully designed research monograph aiming to specify the kind of causal mechanisms theorized in my book. However, I believe Harvey's book sits somewhere between a popular 'airport book' and a research monograph: it has some broad claims that can be quite journalistic (and indeed journalist reports have been cited), but it also has thought-provoking theoretical exposition, quite some facts, and a fairly comprehensive reference to key academic works in its nine pages of references (pp. 226–234). Given the book's status as *possibly* the most influential and certainly already the most cited work on neoliberalism inside and outside human geography (also Harvey's second most cited work after his 1989 *Condition of Postmodernity*), a brief analysis of Harvey's conception of process and mechanism can inform future researchers and students alike when they embark on a causal analysis of neoliberalization and its uneven geographical outcomes – both themes are explicitly linked in Harvey's book. Nevertheless, space constraint means that my attempt is neither a full-fledged critique nor a 'straw-person' argument; it is rather an *illustration* of why and how careful specifications of mechanism and process can be important for the geographical analysis of uneven development.

26 To cite a few good examples though, Ferguson's (2010) study of South Africa presents a carefully constructed case of how major policy transfers and initiatives can be, all at once, 'pro-poor', redistributive, and neoliberal. Larner's (2009) process tracing of Mike Moore's neoliberalization of the World Trade Organization agenda offers a bottom-up approach to such policy transfer mechanisms. Peck and Theodore's (2015) *Fast Policy* also contains very detailed analysis of the global mobility of conditional cash transfers and participatory budgeting.

27 See work by geographers, e.g. Wu (2008, 2010, 2018); Peck and Zhang (2013); Lim (2014, 2019); Zhang and Peck (2016); and social scientists, e.g. Shirk (1993); Yang (2004); Ang (2016); and Tan (2021).

# Chapter Six
# Theorizing Globalization: Explanatory Theory, Situated Knowledges, and 'Theorizing Back'

Having developed my three-step synthetic approach to mechanism-based mid-range theory and explanation in Geography in Chapters 3–5, I now seek to 'stress test', in a metaphorical sense noted in Chapter 1, the practical adequacy and normative stance of this synthetic approach. As elaborated more fully in Chapter 1, these two key considerations of, and for, theory and explanation are necessary for positive social change because our theories must be both causal and reflexive in order to account for complex and yet interconnected relations of more-than-human struggles, inequalities, and socio-spatial outcomes. My stress-testing comprises two parts that demonstrate the politics of causal theory development in this chapter and the appeal and relevance of such kind of geographical theory for the broader social sciences and public communities in the next and concluding chapter.

Here, I have chosen to focus on one key contemporary geographical phenomenon – *globalization* and its underlying political-economic organizational platform known as *global production networks*. This pragmatic choice of theorizing globalization as inherently geographical processes and grounding it in the mid-range causal theory of global production networks reflects my own positionality as an economic geographer based in East Asia and my familiarity with, and involvement in, such scholarly debates in human geography and the wider social sciences – I encourage readers to reflect critically on their own theory development journeys in different approaches and subfields in human geography that were examined in Chapter 2 (see examples in Massey, 2005; Thrift, 2007; Peck, 2010, 2023; Cox, 2021).[1]

*Theory and Explanation in Geography*, First Edition. Henry Wai-chung Yeung.
© 2024 John Wiley & Sons Ltd. Published 2024 by John Wiley & Sons Ltd.

For about three decades since the beginning of my PhD in October 1992, I have been fascinated with how globalization has been widely conceived as *the* causal force powerfully integrating diverse localities and regions into what some prominent hyper-globalists term 'borderless world' (Ohmae, 1990, 1995), 'the end of geography' (O'Brien, 1992), and 'flat world' (Friedman, 1999, 2005). I have engaged with critical scholarship in human geography and the wider social sciences to contest such misplaced discourses that distort and caricature the intricate and multiplicitous relationships among capital, state, and space (Yeung, 1998b, 2009a; see also Graham, 1998; Leamer, 2007; O'Dowd, 2010). But reflexively challenging and deconstructing such globalization discourses is one thing, rebuilding and reconstructing a situated theory of globalization and its multifarious processes is quite another, and indeed much more challenging, matter altogether![2]

Situated in my own East Asian context – often on the *receiving end* of globalizing 'Western' theories (see my early reflections in Yeung, 2001) and concrete processes of globalization (e.g. capital, elite, and technology flows from the Global North), I have been intimately involved in major international efforts to develop novel and yet less grand and more modest theories of globalization. In economic geography, one such body of mid-range causal theory work refers to the theory of *global production networks* that has now become a fairly influential theory for explaining economic globalization and its concrete socio-spatial outcomes in human geography and the wider social sciences (Dicken et al., 2001; Henderson et al., 2002; Coe et al., 2004; Coe and Yeung, 2015). My situatedness in East Asia not only allows me to participate in the international collaborative development of this theory and to test its empirical specificities in East Asia (Yeung, 2009b, 2016, 2022), but also enables my longstanding epistemological effort since Yeung (2001) in 'theorizing back' at dominant Western theories in different subfields in the social sciences, such as economic geography (Yeung and Lin, 2003; Yeung, 2007), regional studies (Yeung, 2009b, 2015, 2021a), and international political economy and East Asian studies (Yeung, 2014, 2016; Hamilton-Hart and Yeung, 2021).

This chapter has three sections. The first two sections elaborate on the above conceptual efforts in theorizing globalization as geographical processes and developing a causal theory of global production networks that illustrate the kind of causal explanations and mechanism-based mid-range theory proposed in Chapters 3–5. In particular, I *re*-present the entire process of theorizing in relation to the critical definition of the geographical phenomenon under investigation (i.e. globalization), the original development of conceptual framing (e.g. global production networks) and core concepts (e.g. strategic coupling), and the further refinement and consolidation of these conceptual framing and core concepts into a causal theory capable of practically explaining economic development and industrial transformation in an interconnected world of diverse localities and regions.

The third and longer section reflects critically on the normative stance of this theory building practice. Indeed, such conceptions of situated knowledges have been much explored in feminist and postcolonial geographies.[3] As Tariq Jazeel (2019: p. 32; original italics) notes in *Postcolonialism*, 'even critical human geography betrays a certain Anglophonic and EuroAmerican squint, and likewise I stress that even postcolonial theory (as well as postcolonial geography) is not immune to this. It perennially runs the risk of being reified as a body of *theory*, codified as a skill set to acquire from books like this one in ways that can easily become anathema to the very post-colonial ethical disposition to always look for the more excluded'. In 'development' geography, the work by David Slater and others has shown the imperialistic nature of earlier theories of 'development' in which the Global South was *always* postulated as un(der)developed in the image and norms of the Global North. Taking a strongly postcolonial stance, Slater (1999: p. 67) calls for 'reverse discourses' in order for non-Western work to 'theorize back' at the West through 'counterposed imaginations and visions emanating from different sites of experience and subjectivity'.[4]

Similarly in postcolonial studies, cultural anthropologist Arjun Appadurai (1999: p. 237; my emphasis) argues for a conversation about, and an imagination of, research 'to which scholars from other societies and traditions of inquiry could bring their own ideas about what counts as new knowledge and about what communities of judgment and accountability they might judge to be central in the pursuit of such knowledge'. More bluntly, he contends that 'the more marginal regions of the world are not simply producers of data for the *theory mills* of the North'![5] To me, this theorizing back at Northern 'theory mills' is necessary to transcend what postcolonial literary critic Homi Bhabha (2004 [1994]: pp. 29–30) identifies in *The Location of Culture* as 'the relations of exploitation and domination in the discursive division between the First and Third World, the North and the South'.[6]

Despite this widely acknowledged importance of recognizing one's situatedness and positionality in geographical knowledge production, the development of reverse discourses in order to theorize back at situated knowledges emanating from Western Europe and North America remains a daunting epistemological challenge. As another postcolonial literary critic Gayatri Chakravorty Spivak (1988: p. 271; my emphasis) reflects a long time ago at the beginning of her highly influential chapter *Can the Subaltern Speak?*, 'calling the place of the investigator into question remains a meaningless piety in many recent critiques of the sovereign subject. Thus, although I will attempt to foreground the precariousness of my position throughout, I know such gestures can *never* suffice'.

In this final section, I argue that the recognition of situated knowledges is necessary but perhaps insufficient in theorizing back at and advancing social science understanding of complex socio-spatial worlds in the post-pandemic era. Extending my reflections on the collaborative development of the theory of global production networks in the first two sections, I explain how its key concept 'strategic coupling' is grounded in the transformative material realities of East Asia (Yeung, 2009b, 2016, 2022) and has been conceived and deployed to theorize back at dominant conceptions of endogenous regional development in Western theories and to 'speak back' to mainstream Anglo-American human geography. As I push further this situated discourse of 'global economic geographies', I believe there are necessary reflexive steps for making the theory of global production networks work better, as evident in explaining the recent 'trouble' with global production networks, deglobalization, and decoupling during and after the COVID-19 pandemic and escalating geopolitical tensions in the 2020s and beyond (see also Yeung, 2023).

## Globalization as Geographical Processes

'Geography is still important. Globalization has not diminished the economic significance of location' – John Kay, then one of Britain's leading economists, proudly declared over two decades ago in the headline of his fortnightly column in the world's famous pinkish newspaper, *The Financial Times* (10 January 2001: p. 14; see also http://www.johnkay.com).[7] The fact that business gurus and media analysts like John Kay, Kenichi Ohmae (1990, 1995), Richard O'Brien (1992), and Thomas Friedman (1999, 2005) write about globalization is nothing new. Indeed, prominent geographers such as Taylor et al. (2001), Cox (2004), Dicken (2004), Massey (2005), and Taylor (2007) have long associated the dreaming up of 'globalization' as *the* lexicon in the new millennium with such hyper-globalists (as well as CEOs, global financiers, business schools, and international organizations). What is particularly interesting in Kay's FT column, however, is his unreserved defence for the importance of place and location even at the peak of globalization. Coming from outside Geography as an academic discipline, his views on globalization ironically provide significant legitimacy for theorizing globalization as inherently geographical processes. In their laudable efforts relating Geography to globalization in the new millennium, Peter Taylor, Michael Watts, and Ron Johnston (2001: p. 1; my emphasis) note that 'Whatever your own opinion may be, any intellectual engagement with social change in the twenty first century has to address this concept [globalization] seriously, and assess its capacity to *explain* the world we currently inhabit'. What these prominent geographers did not say much about is that this assessment of the capacity of globalization as a concept and a set of political, economic, and socio-cultural tendencies to explain the ever-more complex geographical world can be very challenging.

Globalization, by its very nature, demands serious attention from geographers. Over the last few decades, the processes that have led to dramatic increases in the intensity and extensiveness of international economic interdependence and integration are inherently and unavoidably spatial in character (Dicken, 1986, 2015; Yeung, 1998b; Sheppard, 2002, 2016). The multifarious actors involved in these economic processes are also culturally situated in diverse societies and regions.

Geographers have thus coined the metaphor 'mapping globalization' to highlight what we see as a pressing need for globalization studies to analyse the phenomenon from theoretically and empirically rigorous geographical perspectives. As argued passionately by Ash Amin (2001b: p. 6276), 'the distinctive contribution of this discipline [Geography] within the congested study of globalisation, has lied in the study of the spatiality – social, economic, cultural and political – of what is increasingly being seen as a single and inter-dependent world'.

Certainly, the first step towards undertaking effective mappings of globalization is to be explicit about how the phenomenon is being conceptualized and delineated. In one of the earliest geographical contributions to globalization debates, Peter Dicken et al. (1997: p. 158) argue that 'definitions are not mere semantic peccadilloes; they remain crucial not least because they caution against the kind of caricaturing of globalization which has become all too common'. The tendency in the popular media and certain political and academic circles to label simply any kind of 'international' relation as indicative of globalization quite simply destroys its usefulness as an analytical category. In other words, we have to be clear about what we mean by globalization and how it relates to, and contrasts with, other forms and processes of international activity (e.g. migration and cultural diffusion known as McDonaldization). This is of course not a new argument – albeit it is still not made forcefully enough – and there is now a wealth of critical literature that can help in formulating effective and usable definitions of globalizing processes.

Cognizant of the enormous amount of critical social science literature on the multi-faceted nature of globalization (see Appadurai, 1996, 2013; Sassen, 1996; Mittelman, 2000; Stiglitz, 2006, 2017; Sparke, 2013; Dicken, 2015; Sheppard, 2016), I argue that globalization is an inherently geographical phenomenon, and therefore its alleged causality and uneven socio-spatial outcomes might be better understood and accurately assessed from a geographical perspective (Yeung, 1998b, 2009a). Globalization processes are conceived as spatial tendencies contingent on, and accounted for by, certain stringent and necessary requirements, some of which are geographical while others are political, economic, social-cultural, and/or technological. Contrary to the efforts of what sociologists Mike Featherstone and Scott Lash (1995) called 'the spatialization of social theory', this geographical perspective attempts to destabilize the hegemonic mobilization of globalization as the universal explanation of empirical outcomes. Our analytical concern should not just be about explaining how globalization, and more recently deglobalization since then American president Donald Trump's trade war with China starting in 2018, reshapes our lives – a key observation made by most social/(de)globalization theorists of grand narratives.

Rather, geographers should be interested in the geographical preconditions that enable globalization to take place in tandem with the reshaping of socio-spatial life – a geographical theory *of* globalization. This geographical perspective views the spatiality of globalization as an outcome of social constructions of space that are mediated through historically specific political-economic, socio-cultural, and technological processes. As a description of spatial tendencies, globalization does not have an independent existence outside these processes, and thus cannot be mobilized to explain empirical outcomes in their absence (see Sheppard, 2002, 2016; Yeung, 2019a). As Spivak (2012: p. 105) argues in *An Aesthetic Education in the Era of Globalization*, the 'double bind' of globalization is such that 'in postmodern electronic capitalism, globalizing capital, finance capital, is also virtual. You cannot be against globalization; you can only work collectively and persistently to turn it into strategy-driven rather than crisis-driven globalization'.

It is now generally agreed among human geographers that globalization should be viewed as both a set of material processes of transformation and resistance *and* a set of contested ideologies and discourses that operate across a variety of spatial scales. Globalization is certainly not akin to a mega-trend 'out there' to be grappled objectively by social scientists. We cannot understand globalization as concrete processes of socio-economic and political restructuring on a global scale without underscoring its ideological foundations on the basis of which these processes operate (e.g. neoliberalism, as discussed in Chapter 5). To presage next section's causal theory of global production networks, I focus more specifically on *economic* globalization, defined as the rapid proliferation of cross-border production, trade, and investment activities spearheaded by global corporations and international financial institutions that facilitate the emergence of an increasingly integrated and interdependent global economy. There are three specificities to this conception of economic globalization. First, it includes only material processes of economic transactions and linkages across borders, and excludes other globalization imperatives that may have significant economic consequences (e.g. migrations, civil society networks, and diffusion of 'global' cultures).

Second, the conception encapsulates an actor-oriented approach to understanding globalization by focusing specifically on the transformative role of global corporations, financial institutions, and other powerful organizations. This specificity avoids the often-flawed structural view of globalization as some sort of mega trends. It allows us to bring back the Prince of Denmark (actors) in the discussion of *Hamlet* (globalization), even though such actors as the state might no longer be quite so autonomous in an era of globalization besieged by all sorts of challenges from the above and from below (e.g. environmental movements, human right considerations, geopolitical contests, and so on). To theorize globalization, we must identify both the 'captors' and 'captives' of globalization.

Third, it refers explicitly to the global scale as critical in defining *globalization*. Whatever its constituents, contestations, and consequences at different geographical scales, globalization is necessarily an integrating set of tendencies that operate on the global scale and intensify connections and flows across a larger number of territories and regions. This stricter conception of globalization avoids the dangerous tendency to use 'globalization' loosely as a catchall phrase for describing all kinds of contemporary processes of socio-spatial change (see also the same kind of epistemic abuse of 'neoliberalization' in Chapter 5). Despite its causal links with the contemporary capitalist imperative, globalization is certainly not just about the latest phase of uneven geographical development, de/reterritorialization, or crisis-induced capitalist restructuring (cf. Smith, 2004; Harvey, 2006c, 2014; Sheppard, 2016; Peck, 2023).

Although Peter Dicken's (1986, 2015) *Global Shift*, unquestionably the most influential geographical text on globalization, was published as early as 1986, geographers had not been very evident in the globalization debate until the early 1990s when 'the end of geography' thesis became increasingly popularized in the media, policy circles and even academic worlds (and thus prompting John Kay's comment in *The Financial Times* at the beginning of this section). The critique of this strong convergence thesis of globalization has reverberated seriously in the social sciences and notably in human geography. Globalization has seemingly led to significant material transformations in the global economy, most appropriately termed 'global shift'. These global transformations entail the rapid proliferation of cross-border trade and investments by global corporations and financial institutions, the ruthless penetration of global cultures epitomised by McDonald's, Hollywood movies, the Internet and subsequently social media and digital platforms, and the reluctant power shift from nation states to global and private governance.

These global transformations, nevertheless, are not geographically even and without their resistance at different spatial scales and in different territories and regions. The global reach of corporate activities has failed to transform the world economy into a singular global factory or a unified market. In fact, what appears to be more convincing is the phenomenon of regionalization through which city-regions have emerged as the major motor of the global economy (Scott, 1988, 2012; Storper, 1997, 2013). Global production activity seems to be taking place in high-tech regions in the Global North and low-cost assembly sites in the Global South, as epitomized in the iconic case of Apple's iPhone (Yeung, 2022). And yet global finance remains highly rooted in existing global finance centres such as the City of London, New York, and Tokyo (Sassen, 1991; Hall, 2018), and new international financial centres such as Hong Kong, Singapore, and Shanghai (Haberly and Wójcik, 2022). Geographers have therefore argued for an examination of specific regions and territorial ensembles to appreciate the inherently geographical nature of globalization processes and place-based institutional limits to globalization.

Globalization is also as much a set of material processes as a set of contested ideologies and discourses. The ways through which globalization is represented can have equally significant impact on material processes and contested politics (Amin, 2002, 2004; Sparke, 2013). As well critiqued by Doreen Massey (2005: p. 77) in *For Space*, most uncritical imaginations and discourses of globalization represent 'a move straight through from a billiard-ball world of essentialised places [as in modernism] to a claustrophobic holism in which everything everywhere is already connected to everywhere else [as in postmodernism]. And once again it leaves no opening for an active politics'. She argues that globalization should not be conceived as an inevitable/ineluctable process or a law of nature, but rather as a political project seeking to turn the world's geography into the world's (single) history and to render coexisting spatial heterogeneity as a single temporal series. In *Nomadic Theory*, feminist philosopher Rosi Braidotti (2011: p. 173) also points out that this constitutive difference in emergent subjectivities is critical in political projects for social change: 'The historical era of globalization is the meeting ground on which sameness and otherness or center and periphery confront each other and redefine their interrelation. The changing roles of the former "others" of modernity, namely, women, natives, and natural or earth others, has turned them into powerful sites of social and discursive transformation'.

While we cannot equate globalization with neoliberalism *per se* (see Chapter 5), it is true that neoliberal politics and practices have greatly facilitated the advent of globalization up to the mid-2010s and, since then, its reversal via deglobalization/ decoupling spearheaded by techno-nationalist politics in the post-Trump era of US-China geopolitical contestation. Just think of how liberalization and market-based economic policies have enabled certain giant corporations to emerge and dominate in the global economy. In other words, globalization cannot proceed smoothly without its corporate supporters and institutional and political champions that are also culturally situated in specific business and social systems (e.g. American vs. German vs. Japanese systems). As expected, business gurus, media pundits, and policymakers (and even academics) are often the strongest supporters of globalization. In championing for globalization and making it appear as a natural force, these people have 'naturalized' globalization processes and portrayed them as 'necessary', 'inevitable', 'beyond our control', and 'there is no alternative (TINA)'. Powerless citizens have to choose either wholesale embracing of globalization or economic decline and social exclusion (see critiques in Stiglitz, 2002, 2017).

What geographers have plainly shown in their recent work is that this either/or ideological choice of globalization should be seriously questioned. In fact, localities can reassert their power in the global economy through certain discursive practices and/or constructing alternative globalizations (e.g. Gibson-Graham, 2006, 2008; Gibson-Graham et al., 2013). These practices include the building up of social capital, the experimentation with non-market forms of socio-economic exchanges, the reorganization of local work practices, and so on. To challenge the ideological supremacy of neoliberalism and the much broader processes of globalization, some localities and communities have actively demystified globalization as a necessary and inevitable phenomenon. Geographers' greatest contribution to the globalization debate is the recognition of how spatial scales matter in our understanding of the complex operations of globalization processes. Globalization is sometimes highly localized, whereas in other times it is a region that witnesses most of the effects of globalization. Viewed in this geographical perspective, globalization is *not* necessarily an essentialized global force that homogenizes national and local differences. It has as many local and regional dimensions as being a global force (Smith, 2004; Massey, 2005; Sparke, 2013).[8]

What then are the implications of this geographical perspective on globalization for the development of new *theory* and *explanation* of global change and transformation? As a start, what is clear in the above conceptual interventions is the explanation of globalization tendencies in relation to their various socio-spatial formations, not the other way around as so often done in what might be termed 'globalization theory' where globalization is pretended as the causal force to explain those very formations. Spatiality does play a critical role in any explanation of globalization tendencies, although this role is *not* exclusive to Geography, or other social science disciplines. As noted by sociologist Saskia Sassen (2007: p. 4) in *Deciphering the Global*, 'Two disciplines more than any others have contributed significantly to the study of the global as it gets constituted subnationally. They are geography and anthropology, specifically, particular branches of each. Economic and political geography have done so especially through a critical development of scale and scaling. This work recognizes the historicity of scales and thus resists the reification and naturalization of the national scale as present in most of social science' (see also my discussion of scales in Chapter 4 on institutional geographies).

Another important implication is related to an agency-focused approach to theorizing globalization that places more significance on actor transformation and resistance. Much of the literature on globalization takes on an abstract macro and structural view of the global economy. What is missing in this globalization agenda is the attention to social actors who are not only constructing globalization in their various capacities, but also experiencing significant transformations in their everyday social life. By focusing on these actors in globalization processes, we can make a much better connection between the apparently non-human processes of globalization and their manifestations in all sorts of more-than-human activities, practices, and struggles. This approach also allows us to theorize the contested socio-spatial production of scales and globalization discourses. In short, we have to pay attention to globalization as a *living* and *lived* experience, which entails both transformations of social practices and resistance from social actors.[9] The empirically grounded orientation of human geography as an intellectual discipline allows us to bridge the still largely unfilled gap between overwhelmingly stylized abstractions in globalization studies and the contradictory experiences of most people who are living with globalization as an everyday fact.

Last but not least, we need to move beyond the simplistic notion of globalization as merely a set of end-state or 'placeless' phenomena. There is clearly room for 'bottom-up' studies of globalization that take a less grand and a much more agency-oriented approach. We certainly need to understand and critique the strategies of global corporations and international organizations. But equally important is the pressing need – both intellectual and practical – to theorize how globalization is connected with, and contested at, various scales by social actors, such as cocoa farmers in West Africa, automobile component suppliers in Germany and Detroit, and 'factory daughters' throughout East and South Asia, whether at the level of the embodied racial/gender identity, the individual household decision, the workplace, or the international mobilization of labour unions. We also need to think creatively about new kinds of spaces created and/or destroyed by globalization tendencies, from new areas of 'graduated sovereignty' such as special economic zones (Ong, 2006) to the emergence of translocalities within major cities that are well connected to global networks (Beaverstock et al., 2000; Coe et al., 2010). We need globally coordinated research that is well executed locally. Globalization research requires the construction of international networks that parallel, overlie, and crisscross the very global networks we are concerned to investigate. Only through such cross-national/regional efforts can we improve our chances of coming to terms with globalization as a complex set of *geographical* processes and phenomena that have impinged upon everyday lives in most, if not all, parts of the world.

## A Causal Theory of Global Production Networks: Explaining Globalization and Its Socio-Spatial Outcomes

Following the above critical reflections on globalization as geographical processes, I now elaborate on how a 'bottom-up' theory of globalization has been developed in economic geography, a major subfield in Geography, that conceptualizes key actors and their translocal relationships in globalizing *production* processes connecting multiple localities across different spatial scales.[10] Most importantly, this mid-range theory of global production networks, as the underlying political-economic organizational platform of globalization, can offer causal explanations of the diverse 'syndromes' and contested socio-spatial outcomes of globalization tendencies. Since the late 2000s, theoretical advancement and empirical studies of global production networks – also known as global value chains – have emerged as an influential research foci in human geography and the wider the social sciences.[11] Grounded in this conceptual literature, the theory explains why and how actor-specific organizational and geographical configurations of production networks can connect disparate 'dots' and 'hot spots' – places, sub-national regions, and national and macro-regional economies – in different worlds of innovation and production. To readers not familiar with the theoretical literature on global production networks, this brief section serves as a concise and non-technical introduction to the theory's key concepts and explanatory variables. Other readers interested in how this theory helps address substantive empirical issues, such as economic restructuring, urban and regional change, environmental governance, social upgrading and inequalities, labour processes and outcomes, technological innovation, and so on, should consult the various empirical studies cited in my endnotes that build on this theory and its underlying key concepts.

In my international collaborative work developing this causal theory of global production networks (known as 'GPN 2.0 theory')[12], we conceptualize production networks as the key industrial-organizational platform bringing together the strategic activities and developmental trajectories of firms and non-firm actors in different places and sub-national regions across the world economy. Explaining the nature and emergence of these interconnected worlds of innovation and production requires both a political economy understanding of changing national-institutional and industry contexts and an elucidation of why and how this industrial-organizational platform has come about. This network-based theory of the interconnected worlds of globalization not only provides an analytical window for examining global production networks as the core backbone of today's world economy. It also eschews the excessive geographical focus on endogeneity and national-territorial dynamics in much of the dominant literature on local and regional development in human geography and the social sciences (see the next section).

As illustrated in Figure 6.1, GPN 2.0 theory explains why and how three *competitive dynamics* – optimizing cost-capability ratios, sustaining market development, and working with financial discipline – interact with firms and non-firm actors under different *risk conditions* (a fourth independent variable) to produce four different *firm-specific strategies* for organizing global production networks: intra-firm coordination, inter-firm control, inter-firm partnership, and extra-firm bargaining. Each of these firm-level strategies is dependent on and thereby explained by a unique combination of causal dynamics and firm-specific characteristics. Together, these causal dynamics and firm-specific strategies constitute the causal mechanisms of global production networks. In reality, a lead firm may adopt multiple strategies at any time and its network effects on industrial transformation may be differentiated in relation to peculiar national-institutional and industry contexts, as evident in my empirical work on East Asia (Yeung, 2016, 2022).

For analytical purpose though, we can generalize at a higher level of abstraction to specify the conditions (or causal dynamics) under which a lead firm pursues a specific strategy for a particular product line and/or production network activity. This in turn enables a useful comparison of different lead firms in terms of their most dominant network configurations and firm-specific strategies. Causal dynamics are the independent variables driving firm-specific strategies, which then lead to differential organizational innovations and geographical configurations of production networks and thereafter value capture trajectories and uneven development outcomes – as shown in Figure 6.1. But as cautioned in Chapter 5 on mechanism and process, context matters much in mechanism-based causal explanations in social science. In GPN 2.0 theory, these causal dynamics are themselves geographically variegated within and across differ-

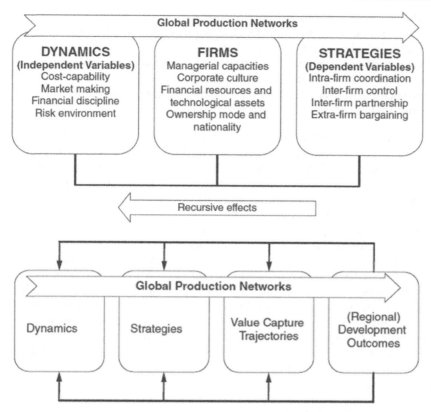

**Figure 6.1**   GPN 2.0 theory and the causal mechanisms of uneven development.

ent regional/national economies and industrial/product segments – a historical consequence of industrial restructuring and co-evolutionary transformations within specific geographical and institutional contexts. Their causal outcomes on firm-level strategies and network configurations are likely to be geographically specific and yet uneven.[13]

In short, GPN 2.0 theory explains globalization and its geographical processes and uneven socio-spatial outcomes in relation to four conceptual steps:

1.   the necessary role of production networks in connecting multiple worlds of innovation and production through different *geographical configurations* (the 'where' question);

2.  competitive dynamics and risk environment as *causal drivers* shaping lead firms and their network members in specific historical and geographical contexts (the 'why' of production networks);
3.  their *firm-specific strategies* and organizational innovations in production networks (the 'how' issue); and
4.  uneven socio-spatial *development outcomes* in an interdependent world of global production networks (the 'so what' issue).

In line with my arguments for developing modest mechanism-based theory in Chapter 3, this GPN 2.0 theory is pitched as a mid-range theory because it does not explain the more fundamental, and perhaps planetary, capitalist dynamics that constitute those causal mechanisms in Figure 6.1. It also does not theorize the ontological nature and constitution of networks, as in various critical social theories examined in Chapter 2, nor the discursive human or more-than-human subjectivities in these networks, as commonly found in feminist and posthuman approaches. As a causal theory, GPN 2.0 theory focuses epistemologically on context-specific network mechanisms to explain why and how uneven socio-spatial outcomes occur in different localities and regions in the interconnected worlds of innovation and production. In doing so, GPN 2.0 theory exemplifies the kind of relational thought expressed in Chapter 4 that utilizes causal powers in relational geometries (i.e. firm-specific heterogeneous power relations in production networks) to explain why and how things happen (i.e. uneven socio-spatial development outcomes). Unlike some relational theories and processual thought discussed in Chapters 4 and 5, this causal theory does not eschew the autonomous role of actors (i.e. firms and non-firm institutions such as the state and private governance organizations). Indeed, these actors are the fundamental building blocks of GPN 2.0 theory.

In this mechanism-based explanatory theory, *strategic coupling* is arguably the most widely known concept deployed to explain the complex geographical configurations of production networks that connect diverse worlds of innovation and production and through which uneven socio-spatial outcomes are produced. As I have theorized at length in Yeung (2009b, 2015, 2021a), strategic coupling with global production networks refers to the intentional convergence and articulation of actors in both local/national economies and global production networks for mutual gains and benefits.[14] Unlike earlier theories of globalization, it should not be viewed as a static concept resulting in an end-state articulation of local economies and national worlds into global production networks. The strategic nature of these interconnections, mediated through different actors such as firms and non-firm institutions, necessitates continual and evolving interactions among these actors at different spatial scales.

This key geographical concept of strategic coupling allows us to connect and bridge two critical and yet relatively independent sets of competitive dynamics – territorial dynamics at the local or national scale and network dynamics at the global scale. As conceptualized in Coe and Yeung (2015: pp. 67–74), *territorial dynamics* refer to the pre-existing political and social institutions and economically productive assets that give rise to the unique character and composition of the multi-national worlds of innovation and production, such as Silicon Valley in California and Taipei/Hsinchu in Taiwan. My earlier empirical work on East Asia also shows that these territorial dynamics are strongly embedded in the political economy of evolving national and institutional contexts (Yeung, 2016, 2022). In this sense, global production networks are not just about transnational interrelationships among actors at the global scale; there are critical territorial 'forces' at work in specific localities and regions that bind and couple with these multiscalar relationships.

Meanwhile, *network dynamics* are much less governed by pre-existing institutions at the local or even the national level. Instead, they are constituted primarily by a wider range of economic actors, such as global lead firms, strategic partners, specialized suppliers, industrial users, industry groups, final customers, workers, non-governmental organizations, and so on. Some of these are large transnational corporations, whereas others are national or domestic actors. While embedded in specific national worlds of production, lead firms are mostly driven by the competitive network dynamics of seeking cost efficiency, market access and development, financial and capital gain, and risk mitigation through the innovative (re)configuring of their production networks (see Figure 6.1). These network logics are therefore firm- and industry-specific, and do not necessarily align with those political and institutional logics in their home origins and/or host localities, i.e. specific local or national economies. In short, global production network dynamics are qualitatively different from localized territorial dynamics.

A good recent example of these two sets of multi-scalar competitive dynamics shaping strategic (de)coupling with global production networks is the United States sanctions and export controls on key American technologies destined for China's information and communications industry since 2019 under then Trump Administration (exacerbated further under the Biden Administration), and the reluctant compliance of many American high-tech firms with such techno-nationalist imperatives couched invariably in geopolitical and national security terms (i.e. non-economic/market considerations). The former refers to the *territorial* dynamics of techno-nationalism within the US, the practical understanding of which requires a separate set of (geo)politically-oriented explanatory theories well beyond the modest conceptual confines of GPN 2.0 theory. The latter concerns the disruptive *network* dynamics within the global ICT industry, such as heightened regulatory risk in Figure 6.1 for American firms. This changing network dynamic in turn can lead to the widespread geographical reconfiguration of production networks in various industry segments, notably in semiconductors. As a mid-range causal theory of industrial organization, GPN 2.0 theory can adequately explain this complex strategic (de/re)coupling and spatial reorganization, from reshoring and friend-shoring to China Plus One (see Yeung, 2022 for empirical details).

Strategic coupling with global production networks therefore refers to a mutually dependent and constitutive process involving shared interests and cooperation between two or more groups of network actors who otherwise might not act in tandem for a common strategic objective. It is a dynamic process through which local actors in sub-regional or national economies coordinate, mediate, and arbitrage strategic interests with 'global' actors – their counterparts in various global production networks. Connecting diverse worlds of global production, these translocal processes involve both material flows in transactional terms (e.g. equity investment and movement of production inputs, intermediate or final goods) and non-material flows (e.g. technologies and knowhow, software and information technology services, market information and intelligence, and organizational practices) among firms within specific geographical configurations of global production networks.

Geographically and as illustrated in Figure 6.2, the integration of these intra-, inter-, and extra-firm relationships takes place across the world at different spatial

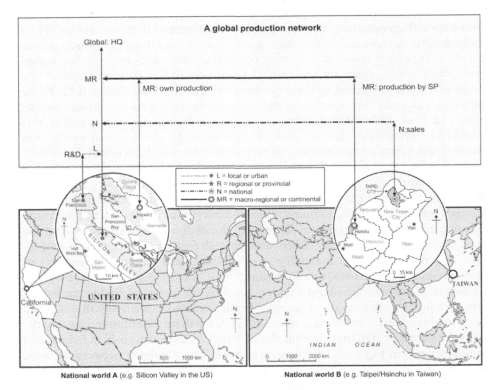

**Figure 6.2**    Global production networks: integrating national worlds of production.

scales, from the local and the sub-regional to the national, the macro-regional, and the global scale. The organization and flow of value activity can be conceived in multiple spatial scales from the local to the global. Each of these organizational relationships, however, must be embedded within a national territorial formation, aggregating from localities, such as Santa Clara (California) and Hsinchu/Taipei (Taiwan), to sub-regional ensembles and from these regions to their respective national economy, i.e. the United States or Taiwan (see more in Yeung, 2021a, 2022). This geographical conception of production networks 'taking place' incorporates both complex organizational relationships of network actors and their territorial embedding. The two are mirror images of each other because irrespective of their functional scales (e.g. global or macro-regional), firms in global production networks must eventually 'touch down' or locate in specific territorial ensembles within national economies – be they local or sub-regional. Once this touching down takes place, value activity tends to spread across different localities and sub-regions within national economies. Such processes can include contested local labour market dynamics, geographical spillover in technological innovation, the spatial diffusion of management and work practices, and the geographical integration of production activity.

Though rather complex, this intersection of industrial-organizational relationships and territorial embeddedness is precisely the reality of today's global production networks through which different 'worlds' of innovation and production can be 'stitched together' to form a global mosaic of *interconnected worlds*. In this GPN 2.0 theory, the territoriality of production networks should not be construed exclusively at just one spatial scale (e.g. national or country-level). The common global value chain analysis focusing only on the global scale for assessing value capture and industrial upgrading may not inform us sufficiently about how the reconfiguration and changing governance of value activity can impact differentially on localities and sub-national regions with diverse resource endowments, institutional settings, and growth trajectories. Equally, a regionally oriented geographical analysis specific to the local scale may be limited because it tends to take for grant extra-local/national processes and competitive dynamics that operate at the wider spatial scales (see more on this endogenous regional view in the next section).

Summing up, the GPN 2.0 theory of interconnected worlds focuses on the geographical configurations, causal dynamics, and firm-specific strategies of global production networks that crisscross and integrate different territories and macro-regions in today's global economy. The key competitive drivers of global production networks, such as optimizing cost-capability ratios, sustaining market access and development, working with financial discipline, and managing risks, are theorized as the causal dynamics of empirical outcomes in society and space. In theoretical terms, these causal dynamics are independent variables that explain the different strategies adopted by lead firms and their partners in global production networks. Conceptualizing these firm-specific strategies is an indispensable part of the theory because they translate the causal powers in competitive dynamics and risk environment into differential geographical configurations of value activities that in turn produce diverse co-evolutionary outcomes throughout the world.

While this theorization of causal dynamics can provide robust explanations to address the question of *why* global production networks are formed, the conceptual exposition on firm-level strategies should offer compelling answers to the question of *how* these networks work and operate in the different industries and local/national institutional contexts. In line with my arguments for relational theory in Chapter 4 and mechanism-based explanations in Chapters 3 and 5, these causal dynamics in GPN 2.0 theory provide the structural properties of network causality and emergence, whereas firm-specific strategies serve as the corresponding and actor-centric mechanisms for organizing these networks. Taken together in Figure 6.1, these causal drivers and firm-specific strategies co-constitute the causal mechanisms of global production networks that integrate diverse worlds of production in different localities and regions and account for uneven socio-spatial outcomes (see empirical studies cited in endnotes).

## Beyond Situated Knowledges: 'Theorizing Back' and Making Theory Work

While the above 'case study' of my theory development journey might sound rather abstract and post-hoc in rationalization, I now turn to the 'for what' and 'so what' questions of normative theorizing in this final section. In particular, I reflect critically on my own positionality as an economic geographer from East Asia who undertook doctoral training in British geography during the early 1990s and has since engaged in international research collaboration with geographers in both the Global North and within East Asia. This reflexive process allows me not only to interrogate my own situated knowledge, but also to explain what kind of reverse discourses outside dominant Western theories and intellectual contexts might be pragmatically developed. In this theorizing back at Western theories, I think it is imperative that our situated theory and concept(s) must be practically adequate in causal explanations. In short, the explanatory efficacy of causal theory is necessary in any reverse discourse that not only 'can speak' and 'can narrate' in a critical epistemological sense, but also 'can gaze/talk *back*', 'can speak *back*', and 'can diffract *back*' in pragmatic terms and thereby gain traction in global knowledge production beyond Western theories, as so well argued in postcolonial and feminist studies.[15]

Building on this line of argument for proactive 'speaking back' without subscribing to some postcolonial critics' Marxist positionality (e.g. Spivak, 1999; Chakrabarty, 2008 [2000]), I question the practical adequacy of merely reporting on the non-represented or more excluded subject (as in situated knowledges) and theorizing as a transparent relay of practice (as in some dominant 'open-ended' approaches in human geography examined in Chapter 2). After discussing why this recognition of the situatedness of our knowledges might not be enough for theorizing back, I proceed to illustrate how the concept 'strategic coupling' in GPN 2.0 theory has emerged in my own process of theorizing back at Anglo-American geography and how making theory work entails a continual commitment to grounding our critical theories and explanations in appropriate socio-spatial contexts. As examined in my three key considerations of/for theory and explanation in Chapter 1, this epistemological commitment to what Louise Amoore (2020a: p. 145) calls the 'doubtfulness of partial perspectives' in *Cloud Ethics* can help us avoid the kind of apolitical radical empiricism in some open-ended approaches to weak theories of subjectivities and the sort of mechanistic insensitivity in structuralist thought oriented towards championing grand theories of capitalism.

## *Are Situated Knowledges Good Enough?*

Let me begin this reflexive process by asking why we should be bothered with our positionality as a situated knowledge worker and the normative concerns of our theories and explanations. My own reflexive moment of decentering Eurocentrism in knowledge production came quite a long time ago – some three decades back! When I started my PhD with renowned economic geographer Peter Dicken in Manchester in late 1992, I asked him pointedly 'Why is it that we in Asia must always use theories from "the West" [then meant England!], "apply" them to our case studies back home, and explain any abnormality using those Western theories as the benchmark'? In his usual witty way, Peter said 'Indeed, why should that be? Come up with your theory or else I won't pass your PhD'![16] To a fairly innocent graduate student coming freshly from my first degree in Geography obtained in postcolonial Singapore, travelling via then British colony Hong Kong where I received my secondary education in Geography, this provocative wake-up call must be *the* singular most important moment in my entire academic life. It has forever sustained my interest and ambition in decentering Anglo-American knowledge production through new theory work, albeit admittedly a particular kind of explanatory theory as argued throughout this book.[17] This in turn necessitates us not granting Western theories any conceptual carte blanche.

Almost a decade later when the journal *Environment and Planning A* announced my appointment as an Editor starting from 1 January 2001, it noted that the appointment 'demonstrates our commitment to periodic renewal of editorial talent, and our intention is to keep in touch with our expanding readership in Asia' (Yeung, 2001: p. 1). In my editorial accompanying this announcement then, I took the unexpected opportunity to argue for redressing the geographical bias in social science knowledge production that had deeply troubled, and still troubles, me. I argued that this geographical bias arises from two main inequalities – extremely limited knowledge about certain geographical regions (i.e. the Global

South, such as Africa, Asia, and South America) and the dominance of social science knowledge production and dissemination by authors from core countries/regions (i.e. the Global North). Failing to anticipate the enormous significance of postcolonial thought in critical human geography today, I even went so far to claim boldly that:

> Although this two-faceted inequality might perhaps have been fine during the 'good old days' of empires and dynasties, when the Foucauldian notion that knowledge equals power prevailed (compare Said, 2003 [1978]), I believe that its perpetuation poses a serious obstacle to the development of a truly progressive social science in the postcolonial globalising era (Yeung, 2001: p. 2).

Perhaps foreseeing my future endeavour in theorizing back through new theory development, I ended the editorial by calling for 'a more productive and progressive engagement with this world by social science scholars from outside the Anglo-American world. This is a necessary step for social sciences to be a truly global enterprise that not only advances our understanding of the world we live in, but also helps us change it as we go along and cope with global forces increasingly beyond our own control' (Yeung, 2001: p. 8). I believed that this engagement by authors from outside the Anglo-American world of knowledge production must go beyond the lingering issue of vernacular languages, despite the dominant power of English and its suspicious 'linguistic privilege' in global knowledge production.[18] In what might then appear to be a rather idealistic call, I contended that 'These authors must also attempt to speak to their counterparts from the "North" by relating their research work and findings to ongoing debates in the "mainstream," even though this may show major contradictions and lead to conflicts with existing "paradigms." In fact, this challenge from the "outside" in both empirical and theoretical terms may prevent the [Anglo-American] social sciences from gravitating towards a dogmatic worldview in which only one voice dominates' (Yeung, 2001: p. 7). In short, decentering and theorizing back at dominant Western theories and voices would be imperative in a renewed social science that is truly progressive, global, and devoid of one-voice domination.

This opening reflection on my evolving positionality in human geography illuminates my deep epistemological conviction that is consistent with Derek Gregory's (1994) questioning of critical (Western) theory as symbolic capital. In *Geographical Imaginations*, Gregory (1994: p. 181; original italics) notes that 'It is, I think, significant that the contemporary circulation of ideas within the international academy is dominated by a flow of "theory" *from* the West and a return cargo of empirical materials *to* the West'. These Western theories are not universal knowledges precisely because of their situatedness in the historical and geographical specificities of their own origins and, dare I say, provincialized production networks. These intellectual 'goods' must be treated with caution when we import them into non-Western contexts (e.g. Africa and East Asia). As Gregory (1994: p. 182; original italics) argues further,

> My own view, at present, is that one ought not to reach to the 'European' in European high theory (or the 'Western' in Western Marxism) as the marks of Cain. But since they *are* signs of privilege, since they are the traces of both knowledge *and* power, they need to be examined: neither accepted without comment or dismissed out of hand. For those theoretical ideas are invested with their origins, scored by their tracks, and so their genealogies need to be interrogated, their politico-intellectual baggage declared and their closures prised open. None of this implies embargoes, to continue the metaphor, but it may well require import duties. For traveling theories are not innocent gifts.

As will be discussed in the next two subsections, I argue that theorizing back requires us not only to impose Gregory's 'import duties' that will still sustain this unidirectional flow of even more expensive 'goods' (Western theories) after such duties are added to the cost of imports and 'paid' in full by impoverished consumers in the Global South. More importantly, theorizing back compels us to engage in exports of new theories/theoretical insights from the Global South to the Global North and to challenge critically those Western theories. Of course, this theorizing back or 'speaking back' might entail a new round of trade barriers and import duties imposed by the North and the West!

This intellectual conundrum is precisely what has seemingly happened to the field of critical urban studies of the Global South. Despite the very productive challenges to Eurocentrism in urban theory exemplified by Jennifer Robinson's (2006, 2016) work on 'ordinary cities' and comparative urbanism and Ananya Roy's (2009, 2020) call for 'new geographies of theory', the long shadow of Eurocentric theories remains casting over the field of critical urban studies. As lamented recently by Roy (2020: p. 19), after over two decades of such decentering of dominant/Western urban theory, 'Arguably, a Southern turn is underway in urban studies, with growing attention to the production of knowledge grounded in research and scholarship concerned with geographies that are the (post)colonial other of the North Atlantic. But I am not convinced that such a turn entails the re-worlding of our fields of inquiry and disciplines, be it geography or urban studies'.

To Roy, this unsatisfactory outcome of decentering reflects a process known as 'citationary alibis', including the notion of 'engaged pluralism' or what she terms 'respectability politics' (cf. Barnes and Sheppard, 2010; Hassink et al., 2014; Van Meeteren et al., 2016a; Rosenman et al., 2020). Through this process of inclusion and integration, the critics of Eurocentric theories are included, cited, and respected, but the reality of hegemonic and universal theory embedded in Eurocentrism persists.[19] To break this self-reinforcing cycle of Eurocentric knowledge production, Roy advocates not only the repeated rewriting of Western theories, but also more importantly a radical break with the gestures of inclusion and integration in such citationary alibis and respectability politics (cf. Peck, 2015; Scott and Storper, 2015; Van Meeteren et al., 2016b; Cox and Evenhuis, 2020). To me, this radical break may entail what subaltern scholar Dipesh Chakrabarty (2008 [2000]: pp. 45–46) calls the 'politics of despair' in provincializing Eurocentrism in social science knowledge production.

To a large extent, I share Roy's frustration that the recognition and assimilation of difference and situated knowledges in Appadurai's (1999: p. 237) 'theory mills of the North' are clearly insufficient in decentering Euro-North American knowledge production. I see the same intellectual conundrum in my own sub-field – *economic geography*. As critically examined in depth in my earlier work with urban geographer George Lin who works on China (Yeung and Lin, 2003), economic geography has for a very long period of time taken for granted that theories emerging from geographical studies of Silicon Valley, Los Angeles, or the City of London would be naturalized unequivocally as what might be termed 'mainstream economic geography' or the influential core of Anglo-American human geography.[20] This heavy concentration of economic geography theories in relation to their dominant sites of production and dissemination has certainly shaped the directions of research in economic geography in many other countries and/or regions, albeit each at a different pace of diffusion and adoption. Studies of economic geography of other localities have not only tended to follow the theoretical impulses and templates that have been institutionalized and legitimized by this mainstream economic geography, but also have earned the strange title as some kind of 'regional geography' (and thus my wicked question to Peter Dicken in late 1992!).

In this vein, geographical research on industrial locations in China and export processing zones in Malaysia is often labelled as 'Asian geography'; studies of the informal sector in African economies, as 'African geography'; and investigations of gender relations in Latin American labour markets, as 'Latin American geography'. As vividly described by geographer Rob Potter (2001: p. 423; original italics), this epistemological bias in economic geography (and human geography at large) can be both daunting and self-reinforcing:

> Those who work outside the Euro-North American orbit are excluded, or at best marginalized, from the specialisms which see themselves making up the *core* of the discipline of *Geography*. Quite simply, they are regarded as 'ists' of the Latin American, Caribbean, African or Asian variety. If they endeavour to be comprehensive in their consideration of other regions of the globe, then they may qualify as the ultimate 'ists': as full-blown 'developmentalists'!

To me, the persistence of this bifurcation in epistemology and methodology has led to the phenomenon of 'the tragedy of the commons' in economic geography – theories derived from specific historical geographies become universalized among

the Euro-North American group of economic geographers, and descriptive specificities of regional geographies have little generality to offer to geographical studies
in other countries and/or regions. And yet in Yeung and Lin (2003: p. 110), we
questioned this recognition of the situatedness of dominant theories in economic
geography and asked two perhaps rather 'inconvenient' questions:

> First, why are economic geography theories, from the quantitative revolution and
> Marxism to flexible specialization and the recent 'cultural turn,' so dominant as
> if they were universal theories capable of explaining diverse economic geographic
> processes? Yet, why are they so little used in the economic geographic studies of
> other regions? Second, why have theoretical insights that have emerged from area
> studies and regional geography failed so far to capture the imaginations of main-
> stream economic geographers?

Despite the long history in postcolonial thought (Said, 2003 [1978]; Jazeel,
2016) and feminist critiques (Harding, 1986, 1991; Haraway, 1988, 1991; Rose,
1993, 1997; England, 1994) inside and outside Geography recognizing the situatedness of our knowledges, we clearly need more than the deconstruction and
critiques of Eurocentric texts and dominant Western theories. In short, I believe
deconstructing Orientalism (à la Edward Said) and provincializing Europe (à
la Dipesh Chakrabarty) are likely insufficient in their own right – a key point
also well argued recently in Wael Hallaq's (2018) *Restating Orientalism*. Going
beyond such situated knowledges, we need new knowledges, both theoretical and
empirical, from the more marginal or excluded regions of the world that not
only can speak on behalf of the region(s), but also can be connected with – and
exported back to – the Global North.[21] This epistemological process of making
connections and theorizing back through reverse discourses must go beyond the
kind of 'authoritarian thinking' examined in Jazeel (2019: p. 208). Focusing on
postcolonial theory and critical geography, he warns us the danger of authoritarian forms of theorization such that theory exists as something in which to
specialize (see my discussion of Geography's theory exceptionalism in Chapter 1
introduction) and we lose our sense of the geographical contexts and specificities
of theory – Western or otherwise. To Jazeel (2019: pp. 209–210),

> in moments of theoretical (over) specialization without recourse to the grounded con-
> texts in and through which one might want to both locate and use an intellectual
> methodology, the retreat from place is a very real prospect. In such instances there
> is the risk that truth claims are generated without tangible connections to grounded
> political or spatial contexts, despite the fact that, as I have stated above, all theorization
> is always-already grounded. My argument here is… to stress that to avoid authoritar-
> ian thinking we should retreat from simple bifurcations of the 'theoretical' and the
> 'empirical'; from truth claims made in the absence of particular fields, contexts and
> place-specific political or cultural questions. The discipline [Geography] cannot be
> split into those who theorize and those who do empirics, and the authoritarian agenda

is only enhanced by work whose contribution aims towards the 'purely theoretical'. In essence, and simply, this is an argument for the 'so what?' of intellectual work.

As discussed thus far in this book, this 'so what' question for theoretical and/ or intellectual work is immensely important because it not only questions the authoritarian agenda of 'pure' theorists (as discussed in Chapter 2), but also seeks a more productive engagement with the practical reality of theory as an adequate explanatory tool for social transformation. This practical adequacy and normative nature of theory brings me back to the notion of *theorizing back* as originally evoked in the work of geographer David Slater (1992, 2002). Calling for the recognition of 'other domains of democratic theory', Slater (2002: p. 256) asks an important question on the origin and representation of theory. Going beyond Gregory (1994: p. 181) and others, Slater (2002: p. 270) draws insights from his analysis of democratic politics in Latin American (Peru and Bolivia) to argue for a kind of reversal of the limitations of Western universalism that does not necessarily seek an alternative non-Western perspective, but rather disrupts and unsettles the claims of Western theory: 'Moving beyond the universalism of much Western political theory on democratic change does not have to mean that there is an alternative non-Western perspective which functions as a polar opposite. Rather, by disrupting and unsettling the customary sorts of questions and issues that are posed by Western-based theory, it may be possible to amplify, diversify, and globalize our frames of analysis'.

This call gels well with his earlier idea of theorizing back in Slater (1993, 1999, 2004) that favours reverse discourses as counterposed geographical imaginations from diverse experiences and multiple trajectories.[22] In the next two subsections, I will (re)turn to my own experience in such theorizing back at economic geography and adjacent social science in urban and regional studies through what I have termed *global economic geographies* that 'must be built on comparative understandings of economic geographic processes emerging from and interconnecting different regions of the global economy' (Yeung and Lin, 2003: p. 111; emphasis omitted). This kind of global economic geographies must go beyond the mere recognition of situated knowledges and local differences, as advocated recently in Hassink et al.'s (2019a: p. 163) call for an 'international economic geography' wherein each region/locality of the world does its own kind of (economic) geography in its own language(s) and local conceptual vocabulary. As argued rightly by Trevor Barnes (2019: p. 173), this 'one big happy global family of difference; a big-tent contented "international economic geography"' is inherently problematic precisely because of the danger of it becoming a parochial version of the fragmented old-time regional geography. Instead of championing this vision for multiple and self-contained national/local knowledges, I believe we can achieve much more through the *comparative understandings* of economic-geographical processes and outcomes across the world. Theorizing back is an indispensable mechanism *for* this decentering of dominant Anglo-American thought in human geography.

## Theorizing Back: Strategic Coupling and Global Economic Geographies

So how did I theorize back, really? In my editorial for the journal *Economic Geography* (Yeung, 2007: p. 341), I argued that "theorizing back' at Anglo-American economic geography can be understood as either making original theory that emanates from research on sites outside Anglo-American countries or remaking key economic-geographic concepts in light of new insights from East Asia'. In this subsection, I illustrate theorizing back in relation to the role of 'strategic coupling' as a key concept in the original theory of global production networks re-presented earlier in section two.[23] In fact, both the theory of global production networks and the key concept strategic coupling have emanated from empirical research on East Asia, even though their initial theoretical development was based on international collaboration with the so-called 'Manchester school' in British geography (Bathelt, 2006: p. 225; Clark et al., 2018: p. 10; Barnes, 2019: p. 175). As discussed at length in my *Regional Studies* Annual Lecture 2020 (Yeung, 2021a), strategic coupling enables me to theorize back at the key concepts and theories associated with the highly prominent new regionalism literature since the 1990s (e.g. flexible specialization, institutional thickness, untraded interdependencies, regional innovation systems, and learning regions) and its recent incarnation in evolutionary economic geography (e.g. related diversification and regional resilience) during the 2010s. As examined in my monograph *Strategic Coupling* (Yeung, 2016), equally significant is the epistemological role of strategic coupling as an important conceptual corrective to the pre-existing and dominant theories of the developmental state in East Asian capitalisms – a very substantial social science literature since the early 1980s (Johnson, 1982; Amsden, 1989; Haggard, 1990, 2018; Wade, 1990; Evans, 1995) that has well predated human geography's current infatuation (or even hegemonic obsession?) with state capitalisms (e.g. Alami and Dixon, 2020, 2023; Whiteside et al., 2023).

Indeed, one of the most visible differences in capitalist trajectories between advanced industrialized economies and East Asian economies is related to the extent of *endogeneity* – defined as the degree to which the causal mechanisms responsible for economic change in regions and nations can be adequately theorized as emanating from *within* those places. In North America and Western Europe, the post-Fordist transformations theorized in the earlier new regionalism literature (Scott, 1988, 1998; Amin and Thrift, 1994; Storper, 1997; Cooke and Morgan, 1998) and, more recently, evolutionary economic geography (Boschma, 2004, 2017, 2022; Martin, 2010, 2012; Martin and Sunley, 2015; Boschma et al., 2017) are clearly situated in a context of global economic change thoroughly traced and illustrated for over three decades in Peter Dicken's (1986, 2015) *Global Shift*. Nevertheless, the key concepts and their variants in new regionalism and evolutionary economic geography are primarily endogenous in their explanatory framing; they are defined and explained mostly in relation to dynamic processes *within* these capitalist economies in the Global North (see Bathelt and Glückler, 2014; Zukauskaite et al., 2017; Hassink et al., 2019b; Frangenheim et al., 2020; Harris, 2021; Peck et al., 2023).

For example, triggered by the crisis of accumulation within Atlantic Fordism in the 1980s, these two literature strands argue that the rise of new industrial spaces and the drive for knowledge-based economies since the 1990s have led to the institutionalization of innovation systems and, in their spatial forms, creative clusters and industrial districts in specific city-regions in North America and Western Europe. The post-Fordist growth of interfirm networks also gives rise to flexible production systems and learning regions, even though these network dynamics are endogenously driven by changing industrial organization. In East Asia, however, such endogenously specified concepts as flexible specialization, untraded interdependencies, learning regions, and related diversification are much less useful in accounting for the dynamic growth and transformation of diverse East Asian economies since the 1990s. Rather, these East Asian capitalisms are more appropriately characterized by significant *exogeneity* in their historically compressed and geographically variegated developmental trajectories (see Yeung, 2016, 2022; Hamilton and Kao, 2018; Nem Singh and Ovadia, 2019; Whittaker et al., 2020; Kalleberg et al., 2021; Tan, 2021).

This exogeneity is expressed in East Asian capitalisms' earlier preoccupation with export-oriented industrialization, as well as their more recent concern with grounding translocal knowledge flows and production networks. Instead of looking mostly inward towards their domestic economies for new growth dynamics, key actors and institutions in East Asian economies are continuously searching for new ways of articulating their local and national economies with the global economy. In this sense of grounded reality, the strategic coupling of East Asian economies with the 'flows' and 'networks' that are global and translocal in scope serve as a better or more *situated concept* for understanding changing East Asian capitalisms since the 1990s. Unlike Atlantic Fordist or even post-Fordist modes of developmental trajectories (and David Harvey's neoliberalism 'with Chinese characteristics' critiqued in Chapter 5), these exogenous flows of goods and services and networks of capital, people, and knowledge/technologies are fundamental to the causal dynamics of East Asian capitalisms (see also Saxenian, 2006; Hamilton and Kao, 2018; Hamilton-Hart and Yeung, 2021). These flows and networks also help avoid the analytical problem of place-based 'Asian exceptionalism' (i.e. Asia is different because it is Asia) – commonly found in area studies and international relations – as they highlight the exogenous connections shaping East Asian growth dynamics. They enable the careful examination of the differentiated ways in which East Asian economies play a more significant role in shaping future global economic geographies.

To date, this idea of global-local coupling of non-territorialized flows and networks with territorialized institutions and structures has clearly emerged as one key research frontier that can yield significant and enduring theoretical breakthroughs. While it comes as no surprise to geographers familiar with East Asian developmental dynamics, it does pose a significant conceptual challenge to pre-existing theories of uneven development in North America and Western Europe. With hindsight, the dramatic economic-geographical transformations in North America and Western Europe also did *not* occur without significant exogenous influences and articulations – their neglect in dominant theories reflects more the intellectual myopism of Euro-North American theorizing of uneven development. These post-Fordist transformations were not self-contained, but rather co-evolved with changing international divisions of labour incorporating what political economist Alice Amsden (2001, 2007) calls 'The Rest' (Yeung, 2019c).[24] Global-scale flows (e.g. manufactured exports from Japan and, later, East Asian newly industrialized economies) and networks (e.g. global shifts in corporate organization, vertical disintegration, and international outsourcing) were just as important as endogenous processes in restructuring and transforming the industrial core of the Global North. Western theories of the turbulent transition from Fordism to post-Fordist production systems and regional development trajectories should indeed have examined and incorporated such transformative developments *elsewhere* in 'The Rest'! Failure in doing so represents the epistemological ignorance of Western theories that are blindsided by their own imperialist tendencies. In this sense, I concur with Spivak's (1988: p. 291, 1999: p. 279; my emphasis) postcolonial critique of French poststructuralist intellectuals, such as Michel Foucault and Gilles Deleuze, for ignoring both the epistemic violence of imperialism and the international division of labour such that 'to buy a self-contained version of the West is to ignore its *production* by the imperialist project'.[25]

Overall and as discussed in Chapter 4 on institutional geographies, there is a tendency in mainstream economic geography towards overemphasizing the endogenous evolution of localized and territorialized dynamics, such as agglomeration economies, learning and innovative capacities, institutional building, and distinctive socio-cultural practices, as universal explanations of urban and regional transformations. These endogenous approaches to spatial dynamics and uneven development are perhaps more appropriate in the study of advanced industrialized economies, where most regions and territories have established substantial territorialized assets in the forms of immense social capital, pro-growth institutions, absorptive capacities, and so on (e.g. the ongoing smart specialization programme of place-based development within the European Union since 2011). When applied uncritically to the East Asian and other macro-regional contexts, however, these endogenous views tend to exceed their contextual specificity (i.e. situatedness) and become too myopic in analytical foci.

This significant theoretical lacuna has prompted the development of a new geographical theory of economic development in an interconnected world. Since the early 2000s, global production networks research has fundamentally addressed the global-local tensions identified in Peter Dicken's (1994) Roepke Lecture in

Economic Geography. This research in economic geography has undergone two phases of significant theory development, transiting from the earlier broad and general GPN *framework* (Dicken et al., 2001; Henderson et al., 2002; Coe et al., 2004) to the more recent and explanatory GPN 2.0 *theory* (Coe and Yeung, 2015; Yeung and Coe, 2015). During this fairly long period of collaborative theory development, the concept strategic coupling, first developed in Coe et al. (2004) and substantially further refined in my work on East Asia (Yeung, 2009b, 2015, 2016), has become one of economic geography's competitive 'exports' to the social sciences at large.

In retrospect, the discovery of strategic coupling based on empirical work in East Asia (e.g. the case of BMW in Thailand in Coe et al., 2004) and its further conceptual development was serendipitous in nature, when we were frustrated with then the rather inward-looking debate about endogenous learning and new regionalism in Anglophone economic geography and urban and regional studies (see Yeung, 2021a). We wanted to 'globalize' a geographical approach to regional transformation and thus the concept was developed, first as part of GPN 1.0 framework, to describe how East Asian regions can be strategically 'coupled' with translocal actors and global production networks (e.g. BMW from Germany). But theorizing back was not in the original intent and remit of GPN 1.0 that was primarily concerned with developing a general analytical framework for explaining uneven development outcomes. As noted in the earlier subsection, this epistemological process towards theorizing back was started before my GPN 1.0 work, since in fact as early as my PhD in the first half of the 1990s and my subsequent interest in decentering Anglo-American knowledge production through new theory work.

Consolidated further in my editorial work published in *Environment and Planning A* (2001) and *Economic Geography* (2003, 2007), I have incorporated theorizing back as a core epistemological pillar of my theory work on global production networks and my empirical research on East Asian development. All these efforts have culminated in my monograph *Strategic Coupling* (Yeung, 2016) that demonstrates much further the concept's empirical efficacy in explaining the industrial transformation of East Asian economies in the new global economy. My aim was to challenge and theorize back at the predominant and inward-looking narrative that this transformation in East Asia had been driven primarily by the so-called 'developmental state' in Japan, South Korea, and Taiwan (Johnson, 1982; Amsden, 1989; Haggard, 1990, 2018; Wade, 1990; Evans, 1995; cf. Yeung, 2014; Hamilton-Hart and Yeung, 2021).

As illustrated conceptually in Figure 6.3, through strategic coupling with global production networks, domestic actors and institutions in East Asian economies have since the late 1980s become disembedded from dwindling developmental state control and policy influences and reembedded in such translocal production networks that offer unparallel access to new capital, technology, and markets in the changing global economy. Further theorized as sociologist Diego Gambetta's

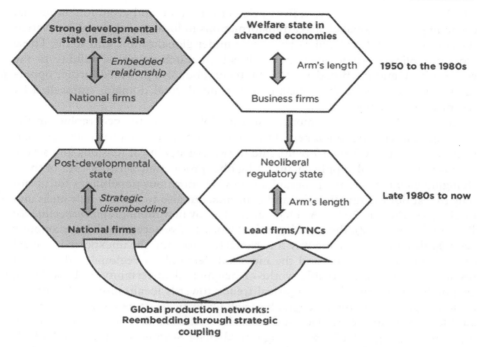

**Figure 6.3**   Theorizing back: embedded autonomy, developmental state, and global production networks.
Source: Yeung (2016: Figure 3.1, p. 57). Reproduced by permission of Cornell University Press.

(1998) concatenations of component mechanisms, such as strategic partnership, industrial market specialization, and (re)positionings as global lead firms, strategic coupling has been developed as a new causal mechanism for explaining industrial transformation in the new global economy.

This theorizing back at Western theories, via the concept strategic coupling and the broader GPN 2.0 theory (co-developed with Neil Coe in Singapore), seems to have gained some traction by now. Throughout the 2010s and thereafter, the concept has been hotly debated within the cross-disciplinary fields of economic geography (e.g. MacKinnon, 2012; Horner, 2014; Lim, 2018; Hendrikse et al., 2020; Fu and Lim, 2022), regional studies (e.g. Henry et al., 2021; Wu, 2022), international political economy (e.g. Neilson et al., 2014; Behuria, 2020), international business studies (e.g. Kano et al., 2020), and development studies (e.g. Henderson and Hooper, 2021). Many empirical studies across the social sciences and in area studies have found the concept relevant to their diverse empirical specificities and explanations of local, regional, and national developmental trajectories in the changing world economy. In particular, most of these studies have deployed the concept to explain investment and technological linkages between local and foreign firms, cluster formation and evolution, industrial upgrading and regional change, transformations in local and regional innovation systems, urban and regional restructuring under globalization, and so on. These cross-disciplinary studies have not only added much empirical validity to the concept itself and the broader GPN 2.0 theory, but also provided further opportunities for us to take the concept to new intellectual domains unravelled by recent unprecedented events.

In the always-changing empirical world, global economic geographies in the 2020s are undergoing fundamental transformations due to several complex challenges, from the COVID-19 pandemic to rising geopolitical tensions and severe disruptions to global supply chains and global production networks. All of these changing global economic geographies provide enormous possibilities for us not only to test our existing theories and concepts, but also to identify new ideas and thinking (see Yeung, 2023). As I have argued in my new monograph *Interconnected Worlds* (Yeung, 2022), the interdependent worlds of yesteryear's global economic geographies might be giving way to, or intertwined with, the unexpected reversal of economic globalization and the incessant demand for regional and national resilience in a post-pandemic world of heightened uncertainty and escalating geopolitical tensions. These empirical trends towards localization and regionalization in global economic geographies will likely kickstart new rounds of strategic (de/re)couplings worldwide such that the restless landscape of contemporary capitalism, as argued a long time ago in Michael Storper and Richard Walker's (1989) *The Capitalist Imperative*, will again be reshaped and reorganized. This time though, I believe East Asia may well take the lead to re-*Orient* the global economy in its image – much like what economic historian Andre Gunder Frank (1998) has argued in *ReORIENT* about the importance of moving back to an Asian-centred global economy in our historiography. But developing practically adequate theories of this new round of global economic change and reorientation must entail a careful reworking of our existing situated knowledges and gestures of theorizing back in order to make theory work better. This brings me to the recent immanent critiques of, and critical reflections on, GPN 2.0 theory and the real world(s) of global production networks.

## *Making Theory Work: The Trouble with Global Production Networks*

Lately, global production networks are in trouble! In the midst of the COVID-19 pandemic in 2020 through to 2023 (and exacerbated by Russia's invasion of Ukraine in February 2022), most countries and people experienced unexpected and yet severe disruptions in global supply chains, from shortages in critical medical supplies to semiconductor chips and even automobiles and toys. Given these unprecedented challenges, one would expect the theory of global production networks to be particularly relevant for explaining the causal industrial-organizational dynamics underpinning these global supply chain disruptions and their consequences for everyday livelihood and uneven development outcomes.[26] In such uncertain times, there are seemingly enormous practical reasons for, and normative expectations on, making GPN 2.0 theory work (better).

This expected practical efficacy of GPN 2.0 theory in explaining the ongoing restructuring of the global economy, however, has been questioned in recent debates that have intensified since the late 2010s. Some sympathetic critics of GPN 2.0 theory have pointed out its perceived relative lack of engagement with the state, finance, labour, the environment, and so on (see review in Coe and Yeung, 2019). Others have lamented its 'hegemonic' positionality as the 'GPN paradigm' in economic geography (Phelps et al., 2018). Most recently, Bryson and Vanchan (2020: pp. 531–532) even allege that 'In 2010, [Michael] Taylor argued that clusters had become a mesmerising mantra in economic geography. By 2020, the new mesmerising mantra has become the GPN approach'. And yet, they argue that GPN 2.0 theory is unable to analyse the new kinds of value and risk revealed by the COVID-19 pandemic, such as non-price-based value (e.g. the secured availability of locally produced critical medical supplies) and extra-network risks (from microbes to national security and climate change).

In all fairness, some of these are legitimate epistemological and normative concerns that might justify their intellectual trouble with GPN 2.0 theory. Using the moniker 'GPN trouble' for these recent and mostly immanent critiques, I focus on two main issues here. First, I believe part of this GPN trouble has much to do with some critics' unrealistic expectation of GPN 2.0 theory's epistemological reach. As a mid-range theory of industrial organization and economic development, GPN 2.0 theory in itself simply cannot cover all relevant dimensions of socio-economic change (see also my arguments in Chapter 3). It is imperative to be mindful of what GPN 2.0 theory really entails and how it should be 'operationalized' in two stages. Second, I take issue with some recent GPN-like or GPN-lite work that incorporates the state, labour, and so on. I find some of this work troubling because they do not convincingly answer the key normative question of 'in what sense a GPN problem?' – the primary litmus test of making theory work.

Taking on useful immanent critiques, the GPN 2.0 theory developed in Coe and Yeung (2015) has become relatively 'narrower' in the sense that it is envisioned as a mid-range theory of industrial organization and economic development in an interconnected world economy. Focusing on the 'network box' and its underlying causal dynamics in different global industries (see Figures 6.1 and 6.2), GPN 2.0 theory explains what constitutes a global production network, why various actors work with each other in such a relational network, how they organize it differently under variegated strategic circumstances, and what all these patterns and processes mean for the diverse trajectories of value capture and uneven geographical development. In short, it entails a necessary two-stage explanatory approach to geographical political economy – first, explaining the nature and logic of cross-border production networks in specific industries or sectors and, second, explaining their unequal consequences for localities and regions that are 'plugged' into or strategically coupled with these networks. Some of these consequences can indeed be rather devastating for local and regional actors that may lead to their unplugging or decoupling from such networks. In fact, GPN 2.0 theory does not assume a priori that cross-border production networks are necessarily good for local development nor always expansionary and resilient. The key to understanding the geographical impact of these networks is to unpack and explain their recursive logics in dynamic evolutionary terms over time (see Figure 6.1). GPN analysis should therefore necessitate at least some focus on what firms and their network partners do *before* one can meaningfully dissect the consequences of these unique industrial-organizational dynamics for uneven development outcomes (Yeung, 2018, 2021a).

More specifically and for it to be useful as a mid-range theory in the geographical analysis of uneven development, this two-stage conceptual approach compels us to ask the most fundamental question: in what sense a GPN problem? Any explanatory approach taking on GPN 2.0 theory and answering such a crucial question requires not only the assumption of implicit links between network dynamics and uneven development outcomes, as is often done in many existing GPN-like/lite studies. More importantly, the litmus test also asks for the empirically grounded explanation of *explicit* causal links between industrial-organizational change at the level of global production networks and the variegated socio-spatial outcomes in labour, technology, capital formation, and social change in different localities and regions. And yet, there is a common tendency in the critical literature to attribute different manifestations of socio-spatial inequalities in global capitalism to the 'black box' of global supply chains or global production networks and, by implication, the failure of GPN 2.0 theory to account for such causal links (e.g. Bair and Werner, 2011; McGrath, 2018).

Cognizant of the current infatuation in some poststructuralist approaches with such discursive thinking in analysing uneven geographical development (see Chapters 2 and 4), I argue that this thinking tends to focus too much on the discursive *context* of socio-spatial changes and underspecifies the *causal mechanisms* through which network dynamics are directly implicated in producing such changes. But even granted the need for a more discursive approach to making GPN 2.0 theory work, there still begs the crucial question of in what sense are these geographical variegated socio-economic inequalities and consequences really problems directly related to, and caused by, something specific in/to global production networks? Are there historically and/or geographically specific political structures and social relations, as the 'constituent outsides' of these firm-based production networks, that are complicit or even directly implicated in producing such 'dark sides' to the strategic coupling of localities and regions with global production networks? What might these outcomes be if such production networks and their key actors are entirely domestically or locally based, i.e. the counterfactuality question to causal thinking explained in Chapter 3? Would development outcomes be more equal and/or any different? If so, in what sense is it a GPN problem?

This seemingly tough two-stage explanatory work in GPN analysis can be rather elusive because of its heavy demand for detailed empirical knowledge of global production networks in different industries and sectors impinging on, and/or originating from, these localities and regions in an interconnected world economy. I have experienced this first-hand during the past several years doing intensive empirical work on the global electronics industry (Yeung, 2022; see also Yeung, 2016)! Still, I believe this detailed knowledge of network dynamics is crucial to making GPN 2.0 theory work, irrespective of one's research focus on production networks at the industry level or uneven development outcomes in specific territories and localities. Indeed, I would go further to argue that a GPN-lite study focusing solely on development outcomes on the ground, such as rural livelihood, worker subjectivities, and gender or racial relations, needs not be couched as a geographical study of global production networks or in terms of GPN 2.0 theory. The absence of network dynamics does not automatically constitute an analytical problem insofar as such grounded studies eschew explanatory claims of *causal links* between uneven socio-spatial outcomes on the ground and competitive dynamics in global production networks. Ultimately though, this detailed empirical knowledge of broader network dynamics can be useful to the formulation of relevant political initiatives (state and policy) and social interventions (reproduction and livelihood) to address the real-world trouble with global production networks in most cases, e.g. during and after the COVID-19 pandemic and geopolitical wars in the 2020s.

In terms of the politics of theorizing discussed in my key considerations in Chapter 1, some critics of GPN 2.0 theory – vis-à-vis their claims on its (mis) treatment of value/risk, the state, and labour – seem paradoxical by giving the mid-range theory too much explanatory (over)reach and coverage only to render it as 'unproductive', 'impoverished', 'mesmerising', and 'losing touch'. These critics are also unable to answer fully the substantive difference such causal network dynamics make to their analytical outcomes. By way of illustration, let me focus on just one element – *the state* (see Yeung, 2021b on labour). The state has recently been in vogue in human geography, partly due to the rise of so-called 'state capitalisms' in Western democracies since the 2008/2009 global financial crisis and the urgent demand for strong and capable state leadership in steering economy and society during and after the COVID-19 pandemic. As noted in Figure 6.3 and for decades since the 1960s, such an institutionalized form of state capitalism has been around and put into practice in certain Asian and Latin American countries, with drastically different developmental outcomes (e.g. Japan, South Korea, Taiwan, India, the Philippines, and Brazil; see Haggard, 1990, 2018; Wade, 1990; Evans, 1995; Kohli, 2004; Yeung, 2016). Not surprisingly, some critics of GPN 2.0 theory have lamented its (mostly) 'missing' analysis of the state. While many scholars of global production networks have already recognized the state's differentiated roles in variegated articulations of, and strategic coupling with, global production networks (Yeung, 2014; Smith, 2015; Horner, 2017; Lim, 2018; Hess, 2021; Werner, 2021; Fu and Lim, 2022), this GPN trouble needs further unpacking and clarification.

To begin, the state is a constitutive part, but not necessarily the central driver, of global production networks – global lead firms are, in conjunction with their strategic partners, key suppliers, and major customers in different national jurisdictions. As well illustrated in the development state literature on East Asia, the state can undoubtedly influence these lead firms through specific policy interventions such as strategic industrial policy and/or trade restrictions, but the state does not directly 'do' production networks, except in a small number of cases of sovereign wealth funds (e.g. Singapore), state-owned enterprises (e.g. Saudi Aramco), and private firms with alleged state links (e.g. China's Huawei). Bringing the state into a full-blown analysis of global production networks thus requires us to be attentive to both the state as a political institution for collective action and national security *and* the state as an economic actor in its own right. In line with my arguments on causal explanations in Chapter 5, it compels us to specify much more explicitly the causal mechanisms through which the state is complicit in disrupting or reshaping the competitive logics of global production networks and its ramifications for network dynamics and socio-spatial outcomes (e.g. my earlier discussion of US sanctions on China in section two).

Summing up this entire chapter, the trouble with global production networks in both the real world and our epistemic community might have perhaps come at the right time. Decades of unfettered economic globalization discussed in section one has led to a far more interdependent world economy characterized by extensive cross-border production networks. And yet the recent COVID-19 pandemic and geopolitical contestations have exposed the inherent vulnerability and weak resilience in these 'global' production networks. The post-pandemic world economy will likely undergo another global shift towards less globalized production – through the massive restructuring of global production networks in search for more diversified production bases, supply stability, and network resilience. Still, this remaking of the global economy throughout the 2020s will not occur in a vacuum devoid of state manoeuvres, geopolitical tensions, social conflicts, and environmental challenges.

Somewhat paradoxically, making GPN 2.0 theory work better and making good real-world sense of transformative restructuring processes are both necessary to make global production networks more stable and less risky in the future world economy. These key considerations of, and for, theory and explanation demand greater analytical resilience in GPN 2.0 theory and the broader GPN approach discussed in this chapter. The next iteration of GPN theory must incorporate not only new network dynamics arising from ongoing technological shifts and digital disruptions in the production domain, but also potentially very different geographies of subjectivities, work, and livelihood in the social arena of the post-pandemic 2020s. Most importantly, it must demonstrate explicitly how and why these network dynamics causally matter in their interaction with the changing geographies of everyday socio-economic life well understood in feminist and postcolonial geographies. As a mid-range theory of industrial organization and economic development, GPN 2.0 theory and its future (re)conceptualizations must continue to offer robust explanatory insights into a fairer and more just world for people and society. In this sense, there might be a theory-led solution to the GPN trouble and geographers can make substantial contributions to a new kind of social science and public engagement. The next and concluding chapter will elaborate on this productive role of mid-range geographical theories and explanations *for* the wider social sciences and public/policy communities.

## Notes

1   My confidence in presenting this theory work on globalization and global production networks here also stems from its scholarly recognition by the respective research awards for 'pioneering publications in the field of globalisation' from the Royal Geographical Society (with IBG) and 'lifetime contribution to the field of regional studies' from the Regional Studies Association in the United Kingdom, and scholarship honours for 'fundamental insights into the geographic nature of global production networks and the relationship between states and firms' from the American Association of Geographers in the United States. In short, my two-decade long epistemological attempt of 'theorizing back' at Anglo-American geography and urban and regional studies seems to have gained some tractions in those research communities. For obvious reasons related to my own intellectual shortcomings, I find it much harder to present in a similar vein full 'case studies' of theory development work in Marxist, poststructuralist, feminist, and postcolonial geographies (see an excellent recent example in Tariq Jazeel's 2019 *Postcolonialism*). Seeking readers' forbearance, I confess that there is inadvertently a sense of self-indulgence and autobiographical reflection in this chapter's narrative approach.

2   In her *Southern Theory*, postcolonial sociologist Raewyn Connell (2007: ch. 3) offers a trenchant critique of the 'the Northernness of globalisation theory', particularly those theories in her home discipline of sociology. But her work remains limited when it comes to (re)constructing a situated theory of globalization – what she advocates admirably as 'Southern theory', i.e. theories emanating from outside the metropoles of Euro-American knowledge production. In her reflection on social science, she notes further that 'The permanent revolution of corrigibility, in fact, provides one of the best arguments against metropolitan domination. If social science in the periphery is dependent on theory in the metropole, that theory is protected from its rightful vulnerability – since metropolitan theorists rarely pay attention to the research from the periphery, while social scientists in the periphery rarely feel authorised to rewrite the ideas of the metropolitan expert' (Connell, 2007: pp. 224–225). My theory development project, detailed in this chapter, has indeed aimed at reversing such unequal relationships in global knowledge production.

3   In her most influential 1988 work on situated knowledges in response to Sandra Harding's (1986) *The Science Question in Feminism* (reproduced in *Simians, Cyborgs, and Women*), Marxist feminist Donna Haraway (1991: p. 111; original italics) argues that 'Situated knowledges are always *marked* knowledges; they are re-markings, reorientatings, of the great maps that globalized the heterogenous body of the world in the history of masculinist capitalism and colonialism'.

4   There is now a very large postcolonial literature on this critique of situated knowledges, such as the highly influential work of Edward Said, Homi Bhabha and, Gayatri Chakravorty Spivak in postcolonial cultural/literary studies, Dipesh Chakrabarty in subaltern studies, and Raewyn Connell in sociology. See Jacobs (1996); Slater (2004); Sharp (2009); Jazeel (2019); and Jazeel and Legg (2019) for geographers' engagement with this postcolonial literature. My evocation of the term 'the West' is also meant to be tentative and contingent on our current epistemic practices, rather than as an ontological fixity. As well noted in Said's (2003 [1978]: p. x) preface to *Orientalism* shortly before his untimely passing in September 2003, 'neither the term Orient nor the concept of the West has any ontological stability; each is made up of human effort, partly affirmation, partly identification of the Other. That these supreme fictions lend themselves easily to manipulation and the organization of collective passion has never been more evident than in our time [the post-9/11 "war on terror"]'. See also feminist science studies scholar Sandra Harding's (2008: pp. 235–236, 245–247) reflections on her choice of the 'North/South' distinction in *Sciences From Below*.

5   In her 2017 postscript to the 10th Anniversary Expanded Edition of *Terrorist Assemblages*, feminist queer scholar Jasbir Puar (2017 [2007]: p. 226; my emphasis) makes a similar argument on the American-centrism of queer theory: 'there was scant attention to the relationship of queer theory to empire, and to queer theory as embedded in an imperial knowledge production project. Further, queer theoretical production and archives from global south locations were often lauded as the particular evidence of elsewhere, as the *raw data* of the "local." Often denoted as sexuality studies (when in other contexts it would simply be embraced as queer theory) these archives were read as challenging and modifying the "global" instead of counting as queer theory proper (a queer theory both transcendent and yet particular to the United States)'. And yet in her 2017 book *The Right to Maim*, she made no claim of any epistemological correctives for such EuroAmerican-centric theorization (of biopolitics): 'My goal, however, is not to affirm an instrumentalist use of such a blueprint or to mobilize Palestine in order to foreground a corrective to Eurocentric theorizations of biopolitics. The ultimate purpose of this analysis is to labor in the service of a Free Palestine' (Puar, 2017: p. 154; see also quote in my Chapter 2 endnote 48).

6   But I do not entirely subscribe to Bhabha's epistemological commitment to theory as rhetoric and textuality. As he notes further, 'the historical moment of political action must be thought of as part of the history of the form of its writing. This is not to state the obvious, that there is no knowledge – political or otherwise – outside representation. It is to suggest that the dynamics of writing and textuality require us to rethink the logics of causality and determinacy through which we recognize the "political" as a form of calculation and strategic action dedicated to social transformation' (Bhabha, 2004 [1994]: pp. 33–34). His approach might work better in cultural studies and literary critiques of colonial texts and history, but it has serious limits for rethinking the logics of causality in contemporary capitalist uneven development and social transformation.

7  This section draws upon my earlier work in Yeung (2009a: pp. 581–586).

8  In his 2004 new preface to *The Location of Culture*, postcolonial literary theorist Homi Bhabha (2004 [1994]: p. xv) takes a similar view of the persistent inequality and immiseration at the local and regional level produced by unequal and uneven development under globalization. To him, 'Globalization, I want to suggest, must always begin at home. A just measure of global progress requires that we first evaluate how globalizing nations deal with "the difference within" – the problems of diversity and redistribution at the local level, and the rights and representations of minorities in the regional domain'. See also Tomaney's (2013) explication of how the local or parochialism matters in challenging the universalist claims of cosmopolitanism.

9  See Pratt and Rosner (2012a) and Datta et al. (2020) for some good examples of feminist work on contesting cultures and identities in an era of neoliberal globalization. As well noted by Pratt and Rosner (2012b: p. 11), 'The intimate forces our attention on a materialized understanding of the body when we theorize on a global scale. Is it possible to theorize global processes while remaining attentive to the pleasures and travails of individual embodiment? How might we find ways to hold on to emotion, attachment, the personal, and the body when we move into a more expansive engagement with the world? How, in other words, can we find the intimate in the global?'.

10  This section draws upon my earlier work in Yeung (2018, 2022: ch. 3).

11  For some examples of such conceptual advancements in the social sciences, see Dicken et al. (2001); Henderson et al. (2002); Coe et al. (2004, 2008); Yeung (2009b, 2018, 2021a); Coe and Yeung (2015, 2019); and Yeung and Coe (2015) on global production networks, and Gereffi (2018); Gereffi et al. (2005); Ponte et al. (2019); Agarwal et al. (2022); and Boschma (2022) on global value chains. See Coe and Yeung (2019) and Kano et al. (2020) for recent critical reviews of this very substantial literature on global production networks and global value chains.

12  This GPN 2.0 theory was fully developed in my conceptual monograph with Neil Coe *Global Production Networks* (Coe and Yeung, 2015). It emerged from our earlier theoretical work that had set up GPN 1.0 as an analytical framework in the early 2000s (Dicken et al., 2001; Henderson et al., 2002; Coe et al., 2004). While most book-length monographs on global value chains have strong empirical components (e.g. Neilson and Pritchard, 2009; Posthuma and Nathan, 2011; Pickles and Smith, 2016; Sun and Grimes, 2017; Barrientos, 2019; Xing, 2021; Ruwanpura, 2022), they do not have theory development as the central goal. See also Coe's (2021) advanced introduction to the global production networks approach and my recent critical reflections on its empirical application (Yeung, 2021b).

13  Many empirical studies have 'projected' these industrial-organizational dynamics of global production networks onto broader development issues, such as labour, industrial upgrading, environment, and the state/politics (e.g. Smith, 2015; Liu, 2017; Horner, 2020; Teixeira, 2022). See Coe and Yeung (2015, 2019) for more on such uneven development outcomes. As I have argued in Yeung (2021b) and this chapter's final subsection, the focus on the 'network box' and its underlying causal dynamics represents only the necessary *first* step in a two-stage approach to empirical analysis utilizing GPN 2.0 theory; it is also highly relevant for development scholars interested in the unequal and contentious consequences of the differential organization of global production networks for people and society in different localities, regions, and nations.

14  See conceptual development in Coe et al. (2004) and Yeung (2009b, 2015, 2016). My 2016 monograph *Strategic Coupling* provides the first book-length analysis of how strategic coupling with global production networks can serve as a causal mechanism for explaining industrial transformation in national and regional economies; it also offers an important conceptual corrective to the dominant literature on the developmental state in driving national economic growth and change. Many journal papers and book chapters have now deployed this key geographical concept to explain the variegated spatial outcomes of economic globalization. In the third section of this chapter, I will elaborate further on the epistemological importance of this concept in my attempt at 'theorizing back' at Western theories of local and regional development.

15  The idea of 'can speak'/'can narrate' comes from postcolonial critics Gayatri Spivak (1988, 1999) and Edward Said (2003 [1978]) and Homi Bhabha's (2004 [1994]: p. xx) 'right to narrate', whereas the need to 'gaze back'/'talk back', to 'speak back', and to 'diffract back' originates from the clarion calls respectively by feminist critics of science and philosophy Sandra Harding (1991: p. 163, 2008: p. 8), Sara Ahmed (1998: p. 16, 2017: p. 134), and Karen Barad (2007: p. 36). Spivak (1988, reproduced in 1999: pp. 248–308) starts her chapter *Can the Subaltern Speak?* with a trenchant critique of French intellectuals and, in particular, the friendly exchange between two poststructuralist philosophers Michel Foucault and Gilles Deleuze on power, desire, and subjectivity (Foucault, 1977). Taking a staunchly Marxist position, Spivak (1988: p. 279, 1999: pp. 264–265, 357; my emphasis) argues that their poststructuralist approach to culture has reduced Marx to a benevolent but dated figure in order to serve their interest in launching a new theory of cultural interpretation that is devoid of ideology and class formation and yet rather uncritical of the historical role of the intellectual: 'In the Foucault-Deleuze conversation, the issue seems to be that there is no representation, no signifier (Is it to be presumed that the signifier has already been dispatched? There is, then, no sign-structure operating experience, and thus might one lay semiotics to rest?); theory is a relay of practice (thus laying problems of theoretical practice to rest) and the oppressed can know and *speak for* themselves. This reintroduces the constitutive subject on at least two levels: the Subject of desire and power as an irreducible methodological presupposition; and the self-proximate, if not self-identical, subject of the oppressed. Further, the intellectuals, who are neither of these S/subjects, become transparent in the relay race, for they *merely report* on the nonrepresented subject and analyze (without analyzing) the workings of (the unnamed Subject irreducibly presupposed by) power and desire'. To Spivak (1988: p. 280, 1999: p. 265), such interested individualistic refusals of the institutional privileges of power bestowed on the subject must be taken very seriously. Indeed in *A Critique of Postcolonial Reason,* Spivak (1999: pp. 246–311) reproduces her famous 1988 chapter and revisits her earlier (misconstrued) concluding claim that 'The subaltern cannot speak' (Spivak, 1988: p. 308). She now reflects that her earlier declaration was driven by her immediate passion from the despair of Bhuvaneswari Bhaduri, the subaltern woman in her case, and we should indeed recognize the *possibility* for the subaltern to speak (e.g. she was able to read the case of Bhuvaneswari who therefore has spoken in some way)! As Spivak (1999: pp. 308–309) notes further, 'I was so unnerved by this failure of communication that, in the first version of this text, I wrote, in the accents of passionate lament: the subaltern cannot speak! It was an inadvisable remark'. In his 1995

Afterword to *Orientalism*, Said (2003 [1978]: p. 335; original italics) also takes a more positive stance on subaltern speaking by pointing out that 'if you feel you have been denied the chance to speak your piece, you will try extremely hard to get that chance. For indeed, the subaltern *can* speak, as the history of liberation movements in the twentieth century eloquently attests'. But as argued by postcolonial critic and Islamic law scholar Wael Hallaq (2018: p. 4) in *Restating Orientalism*, speaking out against Orientalist representations of the East is one thing (as eloquently done in Said's critiques of Orientalism), questioning the foundational categories and conception of nature, state, capitalism, secularism, anthropocentrism, and so on in the modernity project is quite another in the critique of modern knowledge. In short, 'scapegoating Orientalism' is inadequate in the face of structural impediments in the larger epistemological context of knowledge production: 'In the process of scapegoating Orientalism, Said and the very discursive field his work has created have left untouched the structural anchors of the sciences, social sciences, and humanities, as well as their political manifestations in the larger modern project' (Hallaq, 2018: p. 6).

16   As the saying goes, the rest is history. For example, I could have ended up doing nonrepresentational theory with Nigel Thrift in Bristol! See my personal anecdote in Chapter 2 endnote 13.

17   Coincidentally at about the same time in 1992, subaltern scholar Dipesh Chakrabarty wrote a long essay entitled 'Postcoloniality and the artifice of history' published in *Representations* precisely about this everyday paradox in Third World knowledge production. Reproduced in his *Provincializing Europe* (2008 [2000]: ch. 1), it notes that 'For generations now, philosophers and thinkers who shape the nature of social science have produced theories that embrace the entirety of humanity. As we well know, these statements have been produced in relative, and sometimes absolute, ignorance of the majority of humankind – that is, those living in non-Western cultures. This in itself is not paradoxical, for the more self-conscious of European philosophers have always sought theoretically to justify this stance. The everyday paradox of third-world social science is that *we* find these theories, in spite of their inherent ignorance of "us," eminently useful in understanding our societies. What allowed the modern European sages to develop such clairvoyance with regard to societies of which they were empirically ignorant? Why cannot we, once again, return the gaze?' (Chakrabarty, 2008 [2000]: p. 29; original italics). In his preface to the 2007 edition, he argues further for this need to question the silent and everyday presence of European thought in the Global South because 'The global relevance of European thought, then, was something I took for granted. Nor did I question the need for universalistic thinking' (Chakrabarty, 2008 [2000]: p. xiii). In racial and black studies, Alexander Weheliye (2014) similarly questions Eurocentrism in the 'bare life and biopolitics discourse' of Giorgio Agamben and Michel Foucault. In *Habeas Viscus*, he argues that 'Foucault's and Agamben's ideas are frequently invoked without scrutinizing the historical, philosophical, or political foundations upon which they are constructed, which bespeaks a broader tendency in which theoretical formulations by white European thinkers are granted a *conceptual carte blanche*, while those uttered from the purview of minority discourse that speak to the same questions are almost exclusively relegated to the jurisdiction of ethnographic locality' (Weheliye, 2014: p. 6; my emphasis).

18   Some subsequent publications in human geography have argued that the dominant role of English language in scholarly publications in the social sciences offers too

much of a linguistic privilege and prevents progressive engagement by non-native English speakers with the dominant theories and voices in Anglophone social science (e.g. García-Ramon, 2003; Rodríguez-Pose, 2004; Hassink, 2007; Hassink et al., 2019a; Müller, 2021; cf. Haraway, 1991: ch. 7 on her reverse experience as an anglophone writing on *Geschlecht* [sex/gender *system*] for a Marxist dictionary in German). Despite my discussion of this linguistic privilege in Yeung (2001: p. 7) and as a non-native speaker learning my ABC only at 11 years old after arriving at colonial Hong Kong in 1979 (from my birthplace Guangzhou in China), I think the epistemological issue goes far beyond language barriers to include striking a judicious balance between theory and data, the strict requirements for originality in research and arguments, and, most significantly, the 'style' of theorizing and scholarly engagement (i.e. how critical should and could one be?). If it were primarily a question of linguistic privilege, the fix might well be relatively easy – getting more non-native speakers to be bilingual or multi-lingual! The reality is that non-native English speakers from *both* the Global North and the Global South often thrive intellectually as faculty members and researchers in Anglophone academic institutions and, by comparison, much less so in their home country institutions (see Edward Said's (2003 [1978]: p. x) reflection in the 2003 preface to *Orientalism* on the critical importance of his home institution, Columbia University in New York city, as almost a utopia for his work; also Spivak, 2012). Moreover, the sheer weight of social science publications in English, exacerbated by some extremely esoteric writings and obfuscating styles (e.g. some poststructuralist work in French and postcolonial work in English, as discussed in Chapter 2 and its endnote 57), has not only perpetuated this linguistic privilege, but even put native English speakers to a linguistic *dis*advantage – both French and English in this case! I therefore concur with Van Meeteren's (2019: p. 186) observation that 'If there existed a silver bullet to resolve these conundrums, we would not have been pressing the issue so fruitlessly over 20 years. Nevertheless, it is irresponsible to therefore just let it slide, especially at the moment when the discipline is growing globally at breakneck pace'.

19  As argued by Roy (2020: p. 20), 'in urban studies, citationary structures have moved in order to incorporate and address the critique of Eurocentrism but epistemologies and methodologies have barely changed. The critics of Eurocentrism have become citationary alibis, included and cited but ultimately incorporated into the liberal progress[ive] narrative of critical geography. Difference is thus managed and assimilated as is precisely the case with the bureaucracies of diversity, equity, and inclusion that many decades of academic organizing and struggle have yielded at the global universities of the North Atlantic'.

20  In Yeung and Lin (2003), we examine a very large body of literature in economic geography since location theory and quantitative revolution. For brevity in this chapter, I do not cite them. Interested readers can go back to our paper in *Economic Geography* and my other writings (e.g. Yeung, 2007, 2012, 2021b). See also recent debates on moving beyond Anglo-American economic geography in Hassink et al. (2019a).

21  In this sense, my argument aligns with Harding's (1986, 1991) and Haraway's (1988, 1991) advocacy for epistemological connections in their feminist writings on situated knowledges and embodied objectivity: 'We don't want a theory of innocent powers to represent the world, where language and bodies both fall into the bliss of organic sym-

biosis. We also don't want to theorize the world, much less act within it, in terms of Global Systems, but we do need an earth-wide network of *connections*, including the ability partially to translate knowledges among very different – and power-differentiated – communities. We need the power of modern critical theories of how meanings and bodies get made, not in order to deny meaning and bodies, but in order to live in meanings and bodies that have a chance for a future' (Haraway, 1991: p. 187; my emphasis).

22   This call is particularly well echoed in critical development geography and postcolonial geographies, such as Corbridge (1993); Radcliffe (2015, 2017); Craggs and Neate (2017, 2020); Jazeel and Legg (2019); Faria and Mollett (2020); and Narayanan (2021).

23   Some parts of this subsection draw upon my earlier work in Yeung (2012: pp. 117–118, 123).

24   The debate in development studies of this new international division of labour has a long history since development scholars Folker Fröbel et al.'s (1980) pioneering work *The New International Division of Labour* that focused on the international relocation of German-owned textile and garment production over the 1960–1975 period, both within Europe and beyond to North Africa and Asia. See a recent collection in Charnock and Starosta (2016).

25   See also feminist Sandra Harding's (1991: ch. 9, p. 234) *Whose Science? Whose Knowledge? Thinking from Women's Lives* for a causal account of the historical *over*-development of science and technology in Europe and its *de*-development in the Third World. In his call for provincializing European historical thought, Chakrabarty (2008 [2000]: p. 45) makes the same point when he disagrees fundamentally with Richard Rorty's position against Jurgen Habermas' conviction '"that the story of modern philosophy is an important part of the story of the democratic societies' attempts at self-reassurance." Rorty's statement follows the practice of many Europeanists who speak of the histories of these "democratic societies" as if these were self-contained histories complete in themselves, as if the self-fashioning of the West was something that occurred only within its self-assigned geographical boundaries'. Similarly, Hallaq's (2018: endnote 39, p. 277) critique of European coloniality derivative and constitutive of modernity and capitalism argues for the uniqueness of the capitalist structures arising in Western Europe, 'a differential that possessed exclusively European roots but one that undeniably harnessed the global world as its laboratory'.

26   This subsection draws upon my earlier work in Yeung (2021b). See also Yeung (2023).

# Chapter Seven
# What Kind of Geography for What Kind of Social Science?

This book began with David Harvey's (1969: p. 486) plea in *Explanation in Geography* that 'By our theories you shall know us' – Geography should be known for its theories in the wider social sciences. But his epistemological claim begs the crucial 'what kind' question: what kind of Geography, what kind of theories, and what kind of social science that matter most to us? In this book, I have made an explicit attempt to specify a kind of analytical geographies that aims for developing explanatory theories of socio-spatial phenomena and their outcomes. Engaging with and yet eschewing the deterministic grand theories of everything and the discursive styles of open-ended theorizing of socio-spatial life, I have argued for the epistemological importance of mid-range theories grounded in mechanism-based causal explanations. These causal theories are mid-range in nature because their explanatory power within certain substantive domains of real-world research is premised on the specification of the causal mechanisms necessary for particular empirical events or outcomes in these domains and the contingent historical-geographical contexts in which such causal mechanisms become efficacious. In short, mid-range theories in analytical geographies require *both* causal explanations and specific contexts of operationalization to work; their explanatory capacity goes beyond individual cases and embodied subject experiences, and yet they are not about planetary laws and over(ly)-deterministic generalizations. Theory needs to be explanatory, and contextualized explanation should be grounded in theory. Geography should embrace more mid-range explanatory theories in all of its persuasions, from critical human geography to physical geography, GIS, and remote sensing.

*Theory and Explanation in Geography*, First Edition. Henry Wai-chung Yeung.

To substantiate this conception of the kind of Geography and its theory and explanation, I started the book with two important caveats such that my gesture for non-deterministic mid-range theory and mechanism-based explanation does not champion a particular theory of the socio-spatial world, nor a philosophy in/ for Geography and/or even a new ontological-epistemological 'turn'. Instead, my gesture for theory and explanation in Geography was premised on three key considerations in terms of normative concerns in our politics of theorizing, the importance of socio-spatial contexts in geographical accounts, and the necessary yardstick of practical adequacy for positive social change. Focusing on critical human geography and its multitude of approaches and concepts since the 1990s, I examined in Chapter 2 the nature and meanings of *theory* in Marxism, post-structuralism, post-phenomenology/posthumanism, feminism, and postcolonialism. At the inevitable risk of caricaturing and 'thin-reading' the enormous range and diversity of 'theories' in these approaches, I noted that many critical theories are ontological in their discursive orientation and often become theoretical critiques of other theories, leading to what social theorist Pierre Bourdieu (1988: p. 774) terms 'theoretical theory'. Other social scientists and philosophers of social science, such as Richard Swedberg (2014: p. 15) in *The Art of Social Theory* and Theodore Schatzki (2019: p. 24) in *Social Change in a Material World*, have also cautioned that such theoretical theories or abstract theories found in different ontological or philosophical debates are practically inadequate in accounting for social change in a material world. Taken together, I argued that we need to recognize the inherent dangers of excessive ontological lock-in or abstract theorization in certain philosophical quarters that underpin critical human geography today.

Developing my synthetic approach towards theory and explanation in Geography, the book's next three Chapters 3–5 examined at great length (1) the nature of mid-range theories and mechanism-based explanations; (2) the role of causal powers practiced by social actors through relationality or relational geometries in making things happen in a kind of relational theory; and (3) the analytically significant difference between mechanism in causal explanation and process in processual thought for such kind of relational-explanatory theory development. My epistemological position thus views theory not as an abstract device for open-ended discursive critiques and/or ontological meandering, but more importantly as a causal explanation of life-changing struggles, persistent inequalities, and uneven outcomes in society and space. In this position, an abstract or 'theoretical' critique is not necessarily a theory, nor must a theory be only critical in its core tenet(s). Rather, a theory must be explanatory and its explanandum must be clearly specified. Explanatory theory therefore entails a different kind of normative position in critical human geography that views causal explanations as a necessary step towards academic research relevant for and contributing to positive social transformation. Our socio-spatial interventions can be better developed if we have a clearer sense of why and how carefully theorized causal mechanisms interact with contingent contexts to produce specific socio-spatial events and outcomes.

As I argued in Chapters 2 and 3, describing, contextualizing, situating, thinking about, and empathizing with embodied practices, subject experiences, and identity formation in socio-spatial phenomena can only go so far in normative terms. Without the explanatory clarity of causal mechanisms at work, these descriptive procedures and processual approaches are ultimately insufficient in helping us understand, change, and transform uneven and unjust socio-spatial realities. In sum, my arguments in these chapters for robust mid-range theory and causal explanation in analytical geographies necessitate a conceptually precise and valid distinction between process and mechanism. This non-deterministic and mechanism-based approach to causal explanation and theory development can serve as a productive zone of engagement with other reflexive and critical approaches in human geography and the wider social sciences. Geographical theory can be explanatory in nature, but its explanatory power depends on the identification and specification of generative mechanisms connecting causal powers with specific events and outcomes in society and space. These generative mechanisms refer to the 'how' of social-spatial outcomes – the recursive ways in which causal powers and agency (the 'why') make things happen in socio-spatial events and phenomena. Such mechanisms for navigating the *terra firma* of geographical reality are certainly not the kind of machine-like macho-mechanical-technical systems in Humean scientific explanation that almost always trigger allergic reactions from critical and reflexive readers and approaches in human geography. This epistemological approach has good potential in making important contributions to theory development in the wider social sciences.

Taking a reflexive stance on my own positionality and situated knowledges, the previous Chapter 6 on theorizing globalization offered a 'stress test' of the practical adequacy and normative stance of my synthetic approach towards theory and explanation in Geography. In particular, I showcased how a mid-range theory of global production networks (GPN 2.0) not only can explain the contested socio-spatial outcomes of economic globalization in the contemporary empirical contexts of interconnected worlds, but also enables me to 'theorize back' at the dominant Western theories of geographical industrialization and regional development. In this final and forward-looking chapter, I take further this notion of theorizing back to argue for a kind of analytical geographies, i.e. Geography premised on mid-range theories and explanations, that can engage with and advance important social science concerns and priorities in the post-pandemic world. Taking seriously Kevin Cox's (2014: p. 201) complaint in *Making Human Geography* that 'the other social sciences have, and with some important qualifications, given human geography short shrift', I believe analytical geographies can enable geographers to theorize back at the other social sciences through a more reciprocal form of engaged pluralism and subvert our subservient role as providers of geographic data for their theory mills. In the mid-2020s and beyond, this intellectual task is particularly urgent in a post-pandemic world of immense uncertainty and widespread disruptions, massive human suffering and dislocation, and unprecedented environmental challenges associated with (de)globalization, climate change, geopolitical shifts and wars, economic restructuring, socio-spatial inequalities, digitalization, healthcare and work-life changes, and so on.

Over a decade ago in 2010, Nigel Thrift reflected on his own intellectual journey(s) in a panel on space and spatiality at the New York meeting of the American Association of Geographers: 'I was able to make that journey in the company of other much more inspired contemporaries who taught me an awful lot, even when I disagreed with them, and many of them are here today. At the same time, of course, while all this intellectual rambling was going on, the world was *changing*' (Merriman et al., 2012: pp. 9–10; my emphasis). Indeed, whatever our ontologies and epistemologies might be, the world around us was changing and has changed much faster since then, including the latest pandemic and the Russian invasion of Ukraine during the 2020–2023 period.

So how and what should geographers be doing, in theory and in practice, that goes far beyond what Thrift characterizes as 'intellectual rambling' and what Natalie Oswin (2020: p. 10) criticizes as our content in merely maintaining our status quo?[1] Perhaps we have been 'rethinking' too much (myself guilty as charged[2]) and we must now translate our (re)thinking into actual practice. We need to figure out better these politics of change by (1) theorizing and explaining them better; (2) building alliances with other like-minded scholars across the social sciences in advancing these explanations; and (3) fashioning out real-world changes through education and active involvement in policy and practice. In short, we must go beyond intellectual rambling and academic esotericism to develop analytical geographies for real-world engagement and policy and practice. This call for practical theories and meaningful explanations echoes the recent arguments in organizational theorists Mats Alvesson et al.'s (2017) *Return to Meaning: A Social Science with Something to Say* in which:

> we unashamedly use the word 'problem' to denote the extensive failure of social science to address the burning issues of our time, the anxiety and frustration engendered by the proliferation of esoteric and meaningless texts, and the resulting instrumental and cynical attitudes about academic work both inside and outside universities… Most seriously, however, the problem results in an enduring disconnection between the generation and dissemination of knowledge in social science and the pressing needs of a society facing major challenges… Research in social science is *potentially* meaningful to wider society if it addresses the political, economic, or existential realities that face it and affect the lives of the public. Whether or not this potential is realized depends on whether the study is available for public scrutiny, which, in turn, requires for it to be communicated in a widely comprehensible way (Alvesson et al., 2017: pp. 5, 18; original italics).

Taking a postcolonial approach, feminist sociologist Raewyn Connell (2007) also argues eloquently in her *Southern Theory* for a kind of 'dirty theory' grounded in land (a new meaning for 'grounded theory') and theoretical generalizations that are context-sensitive:

> I want to suggest a new meaning for the term 'grounded theory': linking theory to the ground on which the theorist's boots are planted. To think in this way is to reject the deeply entrenched habit of mind... by which theory in the social sciences is admired exactly in the degree to which it escapes specific settings and speaks in abstract universals (Connell, 2007: p. 206).

My arguments in this book for mid-range explanatory theory that identifies causal mechanisms and their practical operation grounded in specific socio-spatial contexts are in line with Connell's (2007) grounded theory. In contrast with those open-ended and ideologically-oriented approaches in which the local is the only site of knowledge or the only legitimate site of politics, such as postmodernism, feminism, and post-structuralism discussed in Chapter 2, Connell (2007) still favours a *particular* kind of generalization through (Southern) theory. Commenting on such discursive approaches favouring the local site of knowledge and politics, she argues that:

> This line of thought is damaging if it leads to a rejection of generalisation – the life-blood of social science as a cultural formation. Generalisation is involved in com-munication, in the testing of claims, in scientific imagination and the search for new data, in the application and use of knowledge, in the capacity of knowledge to grow. To reject generalisation in social science would immobilise us. But that does not mean that we are committed to generalise in abstract universals... The power of social science generalisations is multiplied if they can be linked to the characteristics of the context *within* which they apply... Our interest as researchers is to maximise the wealth of materials that are drawn into the analysis and explanation. It is also our interest to multiply, rather than slim down, the theoretical ideas that we have to work with (Connell, 2007: p. 207; original italics).

In the following two sections, I elaborate further on how such engagement with social science theory development and public policy relevance can be engendered through a kind of analytical geographies premised on developing mid-range the-ories and mechanism-based explanations. At times, the forward-looking nature of this relatively short concluding discussion can be quite polemical and speculative, and I genuinely hope my provocation can stimulate renewed thinking in future geographical work on theory and explanation in Geography.

## Towards Analytical Geographies: Mid-Range Geographical Theories for Social Science

Throughout this book, I have implicitly taken social science as the epistemological-institutional context in which many different approaches in critical human geography have evolved. And yet in this social science with methodological pluralism, I have argued that the search for mid-range geographical theories and mechanism-based explanations in analytical geographies can help us avoid the danger of falling into the two extremes of strong naturalism (positivism) and relativist constructivism (anti-naturalism) in our explanatory accounts of socio-spatial phenomena. In his critical evaluation of varieties of social explanation, social science philosopher Daniel Little (1991) concludes that neither the strong naturalism of 'physics envy' nor the strong anti-naturalism of relativist accounts can provide a credible basis for social science.[3] Rather, a pluralist method grounded in weak versions of naturalism or anti-naturalism might work better (see also Little, 2018). In his *New Directions in the Philosophy of Social Science*, Little (2016) takes this pluralist approach further and argues for meso-level causation in an actor-centred sociology that is consistent with this book's call for mid-range theory and explanation in Geography (see also my discussion in Chapter 3 and Figure 3.1).

Let me discuss further these extremes of strong naturalism and relativist constructivism. In *For Space*, Doreen Massey (2005: ch. 2) has examined the philosophical underpinnings of positivism and the epistemological origin of physics envy in the sciences. To her, physics envy has led 'both to an imagined hierarchy among the sciences (with physics at one end and, say, cultural studies and humanities at the other) and to a phenomenon of physics envy among a range of scientific practices which aim to ape, but find they cannot, the protocols of physics' (Massey, 2005: p. 34). This was physics based on Newtonian-mechanics or 'mechanical' or 'mechanistic' explanations (see my discussion in Chapter 3). To Massey, this view of science, starting as early as in Henri Bergson's (1910) *Time and Free Will*, is outdated and so should the idea of physics envy in social science.[4] Into the post-pandemic 2020s, it would be rather strange to appeal to physics when making an argument for why and how we study society and space. Instead of physics envy, we should aim to contribute to theoretical debates beyond Geography and, at the very least, across the social sciences, while bearing in mind Massey's (2005: p. 73) caution that we should be explicitly aware of the terms of the conversation.

But what about a different kind of envy – critical human geography without 'philosophy envy' or what Nigel Thrift (2021: p. xi) terms 'phiction' in *Killer Cities*?[5] After all, most of us are 'doctors' of philosophy (PhDs) or 'Dr Soon'! This book has demonstrated quite explicitly that the strong anti-naturalism of relativist approaches in critical human geography might have gone too far the other way round. Instead of physics envy, human geography today might be more appropriately deemed *philosophy envy*. As I have pointed out in Chapter 1 and revisited in various chapters on these approaches, geographers' appeal to philosophy, particularly continental philosophy, has led to the general tendencies of such geographical work to be overtly theoretical, textual, and re-presentational. Instead of philosophy serving as an underlabourer or, in feminist philosopher Rosi Braidotti's (2011: p. 6) view, a technician for knowledge production and projects of human emancipation by clearing away what philosophers John Locke (1975 [1690]) and Roy Bhaskar (2016: p. 2) term 'philosophical rubbish' as obstacles to progress in social science, it has become a kind of dogmatic thought dictating the substantive content of critical human geography. The discursive tactics of geographers appealing to favoured ontological registers to justify their theoretical claims often amount to picking out for quotation one's favourite, or most compatible, philosopher(s). Instead of the 'harder' scientist in Massey's (2005: p. 72) warning about physics envy, it is the 'esoteric' philosopher, often continental or more specifically French in origin, who dictates the terms of abstract 'theoretical' engagement in such critical human geography work.

As argued throughout this book, this philosophy envy should not be read, and thought about, as some kind of transcendental philosophical truth or deference about ontology and epistemology. In this sense, I share Eric Sheppard's disdain for 'my ontology versus yours' (quoted in Merriman et al., 2012: p. 8) and Mikko Joronen and Jouni Häkli's (2017: p. 568) concern with excessive 'onto-theological lock-in' in critical human geography. I am certainly not against geographers bringing in and engaging with philosophers' work, as evident in my own arguments in this book augmented with quotes from philosophers and my own foray into both critical and speculative variants of realist philosophy. Rather, I believe we should treat philosophy and ontology as simply a sceptical thought on the nature of being and reality that helps clear the philosophical rubbish for our substantive theorizing and explanatory work to proceed. Even though we often borrow conceptual vocabularies from philosophers to constitute our theoretical statements, we must also be aware of the terms of the philosophical conversation in which these vocabularies are situated. In short, substantive geographical theories of contemporary socio-spatial phenomena cannot be solely premised on and/or justified by philosophical concepts and vocabularies. Our discursive rules and/or causal explanations derived from such philosophical thought – French variety or otherwise – must be interrogated and reworked further into something more appropriate for understanding the complex and uncertain geographical reality in the post-pandemic 21$^{st}$ century. After all, while many philosophical thoughts might appear to be transcendental in their ontological and metaphysical claims, we must take note too that their very origins as social texts took place in specific historical and geographical contexts during the 19$^{th}$ and 20$^{th}$ centuries or much earlier (see Chapter 6's brief critique of Eurocentrism in dominant philosophical thought such as Marxism and poststructuralism).

In the kind of analytical geographies *without* physics and philosophy envy, I believe we can make useful contributions to the wider social sciences by developing mid-range geographical theories and explanations. Arguing for making space for human geography in the social sciences, Cox (2014: p. 200) points further to 'the thesis that human geography has been parasitic on the other human sciences; that human geography, in fact geography altogether, has no theory of its own but must rely on other fields... The latter claim is particularly interesting since it demeans the recentering forces in the field, what it specifically has to offer as a set of abstract concepts'. To me, it is unclear what these 'recentering forces' might be and how 'abstract concepts' could perform their role in enabling geographical knowledge to be useful to social science. In pragmatic terms, I think mid-range geographical theory might be more 'transferrable' across different social science disciplines due to its concern with the specific dimension or domain of socio-spatial phenomena and its less abstract approach to theory and explanation (see earlier Chapters 3–5). This kind of transferrable causal explanations can serve as a productive zone for human geographers to engage with the wider social scientific debates on the formation and causation of diverse events, processes, and outcomes in society and space. To philosophers of social science Timothy Rutzou and Dave Elder-Vass (2019), such 'transposability' of causal explanations can help reconcile the ontological focus on formation stories in poststructur-alist assemblage theory and the critical realist concern with causation stories.[6] In Figure 7.1, such productive zones of theoretical engagement across different disciplines (1–3) can take place over time such that transferrable geographical

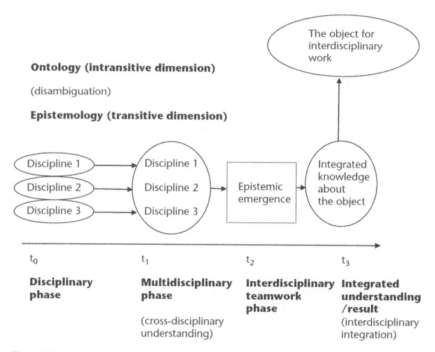

**Figure 7.1**    Interdisciplinary knowledge production in social science.

Source: Danermark et al. (2019: Figure 7.1, p. 182). Copyright ©2019 From *Explaining Society: Critical Realism in the Social Sciences* by Mats Ekstrom and Jan ch. Karlsson. Reproduced by permission of Taylor and Francis Group, LLC, a division of Informa plc.

theories and explanations can be well placed in specific epistemic emergence that in turn provides the foundation for integrated knowledge and interdisciplinary work in social science.

This call for developing transferrable mid-range geographical theories necessitates at least two renewed efforts on the part of geographical work. First, it compels geographers to go beyond our traditional reliance on common concepts in human geography, such as space, place, scale, location, landscape, settlement, territory, network, and so on. As demonstrated conceptually in Chapter 6's causal theory of global production networks, such kind of mid-range geographical theory entails the development of new substantive concepts (e.g. strategic coupling) and causal mechanisms (e.g. competitive dynamics and strategies) that provide practically adequate explanations of empirical events and outcomes in geographical reality (e.g. industrial transformation in specific East Asian national and regional contexts). Merely elaborating on human geography's common concepts in such theory development journey cannot take us far enough to lead broader social science debates, such as the emergence of global production networks and global value chains as the key object for interdisciplinary work since the 2010s.

Second, it necessitates the reorientation of our theorizing work beyond human geography's midwifery/husbandry role in social science. For too long, human geographers have been preoccupied with the 'geographical deconstruction' of other social sciences – adding space into or spatializing other social science theories. But this epistemological approach has led other social sciences to dictate the terms of the conversation. As well recognized by Cox (2014: p. 208; original italics),

> social theories are only as good as the degree to which and the way in which they recognize the disturbing effects of space – of geographic differentiation, scalar relations, territoriality, the stretching of ecological relations over space. But by the same token, spatialization can only be as good as the (social) theory being spatialized. Even where there *is* a spatialization, it may be in question because of the underlying theory and assumptions about the world.

To me, surely we want to contribute to such (social) theories at their formation and conceptualization phase, not only after they have been (re)made with the underlying assumptions about the (a)spatial world. Mid-range theories in human geography might well serve as such critical building blocks in new social science theories – geography should not matter only as an afterthought or 'add-on variable', but our mid-range theories in Geography should be central and integral to the building of broader social science theories during their epistemic emergence and formative phase (see Figure 7.1; also the example of the geographical theory of global production networks in Chapter 6). If such kind of geographical theorizing efforts can eventually take off and strategically shape specific social science theory development in the 2020s and beyond, we would be able to measure our success as a theory 'exporter' by the extent to which other social scientists read and learn from our two broad and intra-disciplinary journals in human geography – *Progress in Human Geography* and *Dialogues in Human Geography* – respectively as 'progress from human geography' (papers by geographers *for* social science) and 'dialogues with human geography' (papers by social scientists to engage *with* geographers). This brings me to the final and puzzling issue of academic esotericism in geographical writings that may not be conducive for developing transferrable mid-range geographical theories for social science.

## Beyond 'Academic Esotericism': Analytical Geographies for Public Engagement and Policy

In *Ideology, Science and Human Geography* published some 45 years ago in the midst of 'quantitative revolution' and the emergence of humanistic and Marxist geography, Derek Gregory (1978: p. 165; original italics) reminds us Geography's normative impulses by concluding that 'It is simply not enough to construct metatheoretical frameworks, important though they are; critical theory has to provide an understanding of the structure of *specific* theoretical systems and of *specific* social mediations. In so far as it is possible to isolate one discipline's contribution to what is effectively a programme of ideology-critique, we can clarify the role of geography'. While my book has thus far demonstrated the relevance of both open-ended and ideologically-oriented approaches in such a programme of ideology-critique since Gregory's important work, it remains unclear their role and contributions in relation to understanding and transforming the structure of specific social mediations.

To a significant extent, this lack of clarity in critical human geography's role in specific social mediations, understood as public engagement and policy interventions, is related to the degree of what might be termed 'academic escapism' in dominant ontological/philosophical debates in recent decades. In this form of knowledge production, geographers have taken the route of debating highly abstract and 'theoretical' notions of being, subjectivity, process- and event-formation, practices, and so on, as if such 'critical' theorizing *alone* would suffice in addressing normative issues confronting diverse societies and geographical realities in today's uneven, unjust, and yet highly interconnected worlds. In spite of Geography's theory exceptionalism discussed in Chapter 1 – no separate ghettoized subfield known as 'Geographical Theory', this escape or retreat into esoteric academic debates might be intellectually satisfying (and career-enhancing) to some theorists, but it may be rather limited in transforming specific social mediations.[7] In this sense, incestuous critiques, 'theoretical' theorizing, and nonfigurative ontologizing in Geography can become a form of academic escapism that yields far too little explanatory insights into real-world practices and interventions of common interest to other social sciences. When judged from the stark reality of pressing real-world problems in the post-pandemic era, it may come across as an elitist academic indulgence whose critical edge is driven more by what postcolonial critic and Islamic law scholar Wael Hallaq (2018: p. 275) calls 'the hem and haw of a bourgeois ethic' in *Restating Orientalism*.[8] Offering her sympathetic critique of the (over)use of opaque terminology and dense argumentation in the existing social studies of finance by humanists, feminist literary critic Katherine Hayles (2017: pp. 176–177) has gone even further – perhaps far too much in the eyes of my readers – in her *Unthought* to argue for a rapprochement with economists and finance professors in such critical studies of finance capital's cognitive assemblages!

> To be taken seriously in this endeavor, humanists will need to learn the vocabulary, mechanisms, and histories of finance capital... The work of building bridges between finance capital and the rich critical and philosophical traditions of the humanities requires that humanists learn to write and speak in ways legible to the finance community, for only so can there be a successful transmission of ideas across these fields. The price to gain admission to discussions with economists, business school professors, traders, politicians, and other influential actors is steep, but the potential contributions humanists can make more than justify the investment. If there is no way out of the global financial system, then the way forward may require going more deeply into it.

Regardless of one's critical stance and ontological-epistemological position, there are seemingly inherent limits to intellectual critiques in critical theories. In *Vibrant Matter* – itself a fairly abstract philosophical work discussed in Chapters 2 and 4, political theorist Jane Bennett (2010) claims to take a more pragmatist turn by pointing out the limits to the political efficacy of what she calls 'demystification' – possibly the most popular practice of critical theory through which the 'hermeneutics of suspicion calls for theorists to be on high alert for signs of the secret truth (a human will to power) below the false appearance of nonhuman agency' (Bennett, 2010: p. xiv). To demystify this false conception of 'demystification', she quotes critical theorist Michel Foucault for his involvement in proposing reforms in the specific domain of penal law on sexuality and child rape for the French government in his time. As acknowledged with a twist by Foucault (1988 [1977]: p. 209) himself, 'But, in the end, I've become rather irritated by an attitude, which for a long time was mine, too, and which I no longer subscribe to, which consists in saying: our problem is to denounce and criticize; let them get on with their legislation and reforms. That doesn't seem to me like the right attitude' (quoted in Bennett, 2010: p. xv). Introducing a collection of interviews with Foucault between 1977 and 1984, comparative literary theorist Lawrence Kritzman (1988) points specifically to Foucault's concern with breaking away from the totalizing ambition of the universal intellectual. Instead, he argues that Foucault prefers the 'specific intellectual' who 'is cognizant of the discursive operations of the institution that he or she analyzes without aspiring to guru status. The role of

theory [to Foucault] is therefore not to formulate a global analysis of the ideolog-
ically coded, but rather to analyze the *specificity* of the mechanisms of power and
to build, little by little, "strategic knowledge" (Kritzman, 1988: xiv; my emphasis). To Bennett (2010), such a productive critical theory must go beyond demystification (i.e. critiques) and offer positive formulations of alternatives that will
eventually become the objects of later critiques and reforms.

My book's interest in mid-range theory and mechanism-based explanation seems
to align quite well with Kritzman's (1988) understanding of theory, the analytical
specificity of power mechanisms, and 'strategic knowledge' in Foucault's work and
Bennett's (2010) pragmatic concern with theory's role in formulating alternatives
and new objects for reforms. Still, the proof of the pudding is in the eating – explanatory theory as the pudding and practical adequacy in normative interventions as
the eating! How might we formulate real-world alternatives on the basis of our critical enquiry and theory development and yet ensure such alternative formulations
can be understood by, and useful to, the engaged public and policy practitioners?
After all, social justice cannot be achieved by our discursive critiques and narratives
alone – no matter how cogent and powerful they might be; it requires the concomitant action and practice of the very subjects (or victims) of injustice and those acting on behalf of them in the hope of making the world a better and more just place.[9]

However critical we might be of our own politics and practice of theorizing
in human geography, I believe we can make significant contributions to public
engagement and policy agendas. In this regard, mid-range theories and explanations in analytical geographies can make a difference because they are deliberately developed to address domain-specific real-world issues in their historical
and geographical contexts. Such kind of Geography might help alleviate some
geographers' concern with the policy (ire)relevance of geographical research.
While acknowledging 'this is by no means true of the discipline as a whole', Tim
Unwin (2011: p. 279; my emphasis) notes that 'This failure of geographers to be
recognised as having important contributions to make to public policy may well
be because much geographical research is indeed irrelevant to the contemporary
agendas being discussed in global policy arenas – and *deliberately so*'. I have noted
earlier that this deliberate attempt to avoid policy relevance might be a form of
academic escapism. But we need to be mindful too that the opposite – deliberate
avoidance of theory and critique – can be equally damaging and problematic for
various reasons, such as the lack of acknowledgement of reflexivity, positionality,
and situated knowledges (see my discussion in Chapter 6).

To improve our reaching out to the engaged public and policy communities, we
need to take a more *pragmatic* approach to our knowledge production. In critical
human geography, there is a long tradition of participatory action research (see
Popke, 2003; Harney et al., 2016; Shannon et al., 2021). Some visible and impactful examples stand out, such as Gibson-Graham's (2006, 2008) action research in
diverse/local economies (mostly in the Global South), and mrs kinpaisby's (2008)
participatory geographies in the study of the communiversity. Writing under the

penname of 'mrs kinpaisby', Sarah Kindon, Rachel Pain, and Mike Kesby argue that the communiversity is about mobilizing research practices and resources to serve the needs of non-academic communities by allowing them to produce knowledge and take action around the critical issues that matter to them (see also Kindon et al., 2007). On the other hand, Gibson-Graham (2011) calls for thinking holistically about interdependencies that can forge sustainable ethical communities through geographical engagements focusing on well-being and happiness rather than economic growth and targets. To Tolia-Kelly (2013) who critiques human geography's surge towards 'new' materialisms and material geographies (see discussion in Chapters 1 and 2), Gibson-Graham's project goes beyond such 'surface geographies' to embrace action and affirmative change:

> At the heart of their account their aim is to *actively connect*, methodologically, philosophically, pragmatically, rather than *see* and iterate material connections. A different mode of humanity is embraced here... towards an interdependent, human-centred process of becoming and belonging. The materiality of living, creating and politics is emergent, non-hierarchical and posthuman. The important aspect of materialism for these authors is a possibility for political change and reimagining of a complex of living that is situated in resolving human and non-human violence, alienation, resource-poverty and environmental desertification of the seas and land (Tolia-Kelly, 2013: p. 155; original italics).

Paradoxically, this pragmatic concern with action and affirmative change seems to be missing in Gibson-Graham's more recent work on beyond the Anthropocene.[10] Based on her 2016 Neil Smith Lecture delivered at St. Andrews University and published in *Antipode*, Gibson-Graham (2020) offers a retrospective 'reading against the grain' of the regional geography works of Joe Spencer and Oskar Spate conducted in the 1950s and the 1960s for insights into missing community economic practices in tropical Asia then:

> I wanted to find out how did a knowledge commons become an absence? I 'met' two thoughtful scholars and keen observers of the complexity of the worlds they inhabited. Reading their texts for economic difference I found an *ambivalence* towards the inevitability of a modern (capitalist) development trajectory and useful observations about resilience practices (Gibson-Graham, 2020: p. 30; my emphasis).

Taking further cues from my theorizing back in Chapter 6, I question whether this reading against the grain might be too ambivalent for 21$^{st}$ century social science. I wonder what is the reading for and how are these observations from dated texts by two 'thoughtful' white men/geographers insightful for developing new theory and explanation for the lecture/paper's primary topic – the Anthropocene? How does this reading for difference contribute to her keen feminist interest in mapping community economies and ecologies in order for us to perform other more equitable worlds and navigate global climate change in the Anthropocene?

Some useful answers to these questions can be found in recent pragmatic work on confronting the Anthropocene. In her book *Staying with the Trouble*, feminist theorist Donna Haraway (2016) takes a more pragmatic approach to the question of the Anthropocene by arguing that we should learn to be truly present and becoming-with by 'staying with the trouble' of what she calls the Chthulucene (in lieu of the Anthropocene) – the idea of living and dying together on a damaged earth by making kin with each other (not necessarily as family but as persons). Still, she raises the burning question of 'What is decolonial feminist reproductive freedom in a dangerously troubled multispecies world?'. To her, the Anthropocene 'cannot be explained away by blaming Capitalism or any other word starting with a capital letter. The need is stark to think together anew across differences of historical position and of kinds of knowledge and expertise' (Haraway, 2016: pp. 6–7). But she remains hopeful for the pragmatic possibility of such living with the trouble. As noted further by Haraway (2016: p. 55), 'unlike either the Anthropocene or the Capitalocene, the Chthulucene is made up of ongoing multispecies stories and practices of becoming-with in times that remain at stake, in precarious times, in which the world is not finished and the sky has not fallen – yet. We are at stake to each other'.[11] In this unfinished and yet troubled multispecies world challenged profoundly by what Kathryn Yusoff (2018) calls 'a billion Black Anthropocenes'[12], there is indeed still much at stake for us all (see also my example of the 'GPN trouble' in Chapter 6)! As argued affirmatively by feminist philosopher Rosi Braidotti (2011: p. 297; original italics) in *Nomadic Theory*, '"We" are in *this* together' and let us move beyond the dominant melancholic lament in critical theory, for love of our multispecies world.[13]

Taken together, pragmatic research and theorizing in critical human geography cannot be just about empty slogans or critical reading (against the grain) of historical and/or philosophical texts. More importantly, we need to (re)imagine the future by staying with the trouble to come and developing different and yet new kinds of knowledge and expertise for such future (un)inhabitable world(s). We need to be hopeful with better theories and explanations! After all, this future is itself evolving and performative such that we, as academics and theorists, are merely a group of performers in the endless production of (new) knowledges to which this book has hopefully contributed. As well reflected by process sociologist Andrew Abbott (2001: p. 33; my emphasis) in *Time Matters*, 'We are not discoverers, but performers. We have our time, perhaps, in the public eye. But other performers and other performances will come. For us, it is enough to have mounted the work as often as we could and to have recognized that in fact there is no original score, only *endless* succession of productions'.

Filled with the optimistic spirit of this endless ebb of knowledge flows and yet cautioned by our existential crisis in the Chthulucene, let me 'end' this book on theory and explanation in Geography by paraphrasing David Harvey's (1969) ending slogan that he wished geographers pinning up on their study walls for the 1970s. For the 2020s and beyond, I wish you will put this apparently dull motto on your desktop/screen savers and digital wallpapers and make it fun and sexy through your future theory work and real-world practice:

'By our explanatory mid-range theories you shall know and learn from us'!

# Notes

1   Some critical geographers are clearly frustrated by this intellectual rambling and Geography's lack of engagement with real-world differences by changing them. As argued passionately by Oswin (2020: p. 10; original italics), 'We have the research. We *know* that access to space everywhere on earth is societally unequal. We *know* that through all kinds of policies, practices and discourses, a global minority is stripping a global majority of land, home, shelter, privacy, public space, education, opportunity, capital, nutrients, air, water, bodily autonomy, freedom of movement, security, infrastructure, health, comfort, kin, speech, resources, territory, national belonging, time, possibility, dignity, life. And we *know* that race, ethnicity, class, ability, citizenship status, sexuality, gender identity and species clearly influence all experiences and that those who are produced and read as "normal" take up a disproportionate amount of everything. These are the realities of our social, political, economic and environmental conjuncture. They always have been, and the situation in the world worsens every day. So why, when we so desperately need to think and act against-the-grain, is our discipline generally content to maintain its status quo?'.

2   I am a guilty party too (Yeung, 2005, 2019a), though my culpability might be relatively lower than some reviewed in chapters 2, 4, and 5.

3   See also Sandra Harding's (1991: ch. 4) feminist critique of physics envy and relativism in her *Whose Science? Whose Knowledge?* and Karen Barad's (2007: chs. 3–4) *Meeting the Universe Halfway* for a 'diffractive' methodological approach to bringing Niels Bohr's quantum physics to bear on various critical social theories reviewed in my chapter 2.

4   Massey (2005: p. 72) notes that 'Given the kind of imagination of space that I am proposing I could easily appeal to witnesses in some branch of the natural sciences in corroboration of my argument. But I could also – being honest – find a bunch of natural scientists who propose quite a contrary point of view. And, within the natural sciences, I am not competent to judge. Perhaps, therefore, we ought not to resort to tactics that in reality amount to picking out for quotation one's favourite, or most compatible, "harder" scientist'. Claiming that she is not against engaged conversation between fields, she argues further that 'it is to urge caution and, most importantly, an explicit awareness of the terms of the conversation' (p.73).

5   See chapter 1 endnote 22 for what Thrift means by 'phiction'.

6   Rutzou and Elder-Vass (2019: p. 421) conclude that 'more fundamentally, causal explanation in general rests on the transposability of explanation between cases in which similar causes operate, and this transposability depends on the presence in those cases of objects with similar powers arising from similarities in their composition and structure. Accordingly, formation stories are necessarily interwoven with causation stories'.

7   As noted in Häkli's (2020: p. 372; original italics) commentary on Ash's (2020a) flat ontology of machine guns (see also discussion in chapter 2), 'Yet, if we wish the ontological turn to function as more than a novelty machine, to yield more-than-academic outcomes and be consequential beyond the neoliberal university, we need convincing ways to link this work back to social practices in real societies. To this end, it would be useful to every now and then perform a reality check by asking, for instance, can I theorize something *better* with an alternative ontology'?

8   See full quote from Hallaq (2018) in chapter 2 endnote 54. Let me offer one brief example on the mundane and everyday life from non-representational theory work in human geography – many other examples from the different approaches reviewed in chapter 2 can also be used but space constraint applies here. Quoting critical theorist Michel Foucault's (1988 [1980]: p. 326) interview response published in *Le Monde* about the masked philosopher and his 'dream about a kind of criticism that would not try to judge, but to bring an oeuvre, a book, a sentence, an idea to life', Anderson and Harrison (2010b: p. 2; my emphasis) introduce their collection of chapters on non-representational theories as 'a sense of affirmation and experimentation… [in] the ethos of Foucault's dream and, moreover, its invitation to do and think otherwise'. They note further that 'If one single thing can be said to characterise nonrepresentational work in Human Geography over the past 15 years it is the attempt to invent new ways of addressing *fundamental* social scientific issues and, at the same time, displacing many of these issues into new areas and problems'. I wonder what social science issues are indeed 'fundamental' in such non-representational accounts? Given its non-representational epistemology, it does seem rather paradoxical for non-representational theorists to emphasize something as 'one single thing' and as 'fundamental' as social science issues that are not well defined, perhaps because these very issues are perpetually 'displaced' into new problems before they can ever/even be represented (see also critique in Cresswell, 2013: pp. 234–235 and reflections in Simpson, 2021: p. 221)!

9   In *Southern Theory*, Raewyn Connell (2007: p. 214) warns against endlessly descriptive efforts in such theory development (e.g. in some postcolonial and feminist work): 'We cannot arrive at a new formation of knowledge by heaping description on description, however subtle and comprehensive they might be… What matters, then, is not just the subject-matter of experience but also its vector or intentionality, its relation to the structures around which a politics of change may form'.

10  A quick note of clarification on the Anthropocene is necessary here (thanks to one reviewer for prompting me). Chapter 2's subsection on post-phenomenology and post-humanism does address some recent geographical work on the Anthropocene, but this book does not focus on any specific research themes that commensurate with the Anthropocene. So while it is true that the Anthropocene is 'only' mentioned here in the last section of the final chapter, I do not intend at all to render this more-than-human existential issue of climate change emergency peripheral or insignificant among many geographical concerns named in this book. Quite the contrary, the very fact that I want to end the book with this enormously important issue is precisely to accentuate its significance in two ways. First, it helps us reconnect the two 'halves' of Geography – human and physical geography – and speak to the wider field of sustainability and environmental sciences. Second, ending the book with the Anthropocene compels us to do an even better job in future geographical research into the Anthropocene that is

grounded in solid theory and explanation *for* the entire scientific community and more-than-humans in general. In short and by way of acknowledging my own lack of expertise or even intellectual ignorance, I have saved this most critical and perhaps contentious issue for last and to end this book, in the hope for better theory and explanation in future geographies of the Anthropocene.

11    See chapter 2 on posthumanism work. For a posthumanist approach to the question and politics of the Anthropocene, see Bennett (2010), Holbraad and Pedersen (2017), and Lorimer (2020). In human geography, Adams (2021: p. 1594) recently incorporates human agency and adaptive capacity in rethinking socio-ecological system resilience and responses to environmental change: 'the construction of adaptive capacity as the agency to choose and drive the course of climate change adaptation, via the influences of developments in the theory of the social–ecological system and human development in particular, makes possible transformative forms of adaptive change absent from earlier cultural ecological models. This sense of agency is a powerful part of the appeal of the discourse that distinguishes it from the top-down technocracy of biophysical risk management and the attention to structural challenges in the contextual vulnerability approach'.

12    In Black geographies, Kathryn Yusoff (2018) has argued for the notion of 'Black Anthropocenes' that fundamentally questions the racialized blindness and material politics in the so-called scientific study of the Anthropocene, such that 'geology is a racialized optic razed on the earth' (p.14). To her, 'If the Anthropocene proclaims a sudden concern with the exposures of environmental harm to white liberal communities, it does so in the wake of histories in which these harms have been knowingly exported to black and brown communities under the rubric of civilization, progress, modernization, and capitalism. The Anthropocene might seem to offer a dystopic future that laments the end of the world, but imperialism and ongoing (settler) colonialisms have been ending worlds for as long as they have been in existence. The Anthropocene as a politically infused geology and scientific/popular discourse is just now noticing the extinction it has chosen to continually overlook in the making of its modernity and freedom' (Yusoff, 2018: p. xiii).

13    Claiming the powers of affirmation, Braidotti (2011: p. 298) concludes that 'Against the general lethargy, the rhetoric of selfish genes and possessive individualism, on the one hand, and the dominant ideology of melancholic lament, on the other, hope rests with an affirmative ethics of sustainable futures. A deep and careless generosity, the ethics of nonprofit at an ontological level. Why should one pursue this project? For no reason at all. Reason has nothing to do with this. Let's just do it for the hell of it – to be worthy of our times while resisting the times and for love of the world'.

# References

Abbott, Andrew (2001), *Time Matters: On Theory and Method*, Chicago, IL: University of Chicago Press.

Abbott, Andrew (2016), *Processual Sociology*, Chicago, IL: University of Chicago Press.

Abrahamsson, Sebastian, Bertoni, Filippo, Mol, Annemarie, and Martin, Rebeca Ibáñez (2015), 'Living with omega-3: new materialism and enduring concerns', *Environment and Planning D: Society and Space*, Vol.33(1), pp.4–19.

Adams, Sophie (2021), 'The pragmatic holism of social–ecological systems theory: explaining adaptive capacity in a changing climate', *Progress in Human Geography*, Vol.45(6), pp.1580–1600.

Adams-Hutcheson, Gail and Smith, Paula (2020), 'Skin, sweat and materiality: feminist geographies of emotion and affect', in Anindita Datta, Peter Hopkins, Lynda Johnston, Elizabeth Olson, and Joseli Maria Silva (eds.), *Routledge Handbook of Gender and Feminist Geographies*, London: Routledge, pp.80–90.

Adey, Peter (2012), 'How to engage? Assemblage as ethos/ethos as assemblage', *Dialogues in Human Geography*, Vol.2(2), pp.198–201.

Agarwal, Renu, Bajada, Christopher, Green, Roy, and Skellern, Katrina (eds.) (2022), *The Routledge Companion to Global Value Chains*, London: Routledge.

Agnew, John A. (2011), 'Space and place', in John A. Agnew and David N. Livingstone (eds.), *The SAGE Handbook of Geographical Knowledge*, London: Sage, pp.316–330.

Agnew, John A. and Livingstone, David N. (eds.) (2011), *The SAGE Handbook of Geographical Knowledge*, London: Sage.

Ahmed, Sara (1998), *Differences That Matter: Feminist Theory and Postmodernism*, Cambridge: Cambridge University Press.

Ahmed, Sara (2015 [2004]), *Cultural Politics of Emotion*, Second Edition, New York: Routledge.

Ahmed, Sara (2017), *Living a Feminist Life*, Durham, NC: Duke University Press.

*Theory and Explanation in Geography*, First Edition. Henry Wai-chung Yeung.
© 2024 John Wiley & Sons Ltd. Published 2024 by John Wiley & Sons Ltd.

Ahmed, Waquar (2010), 'Neoliberalism, corporations, and power: Enron in India', *Annals of the Association of American Geographers*, Vol.100(3), pp.621–639.

Aitken, Stuart and Valentine, Gill (eds.) (2015a), *Approaches to Human Geography*, Second Edition, London: Sage.

Aitken, Stuart and Valentine, Gill (2015b), 'Ways of knowing and ways of doing geographic research', in Stuart Aitken and Gill Valentine (eds.), *Approaches to Human Geography*, Second Edition, London: Sage, pp.1–13.

Alami, Ilias and Dixon, Adam D. (2020), 'The strange geographies of the "new state capitalism"', *Political Geography*, Vol.82. https://doi.org/10.1016/j.polgeo.2020.102237.

Alami, Ilias and Dixon, Adam D. (2023), 'Uneven and combined state capitalism', *Environment and Planning A*, Vol.55(1), pp.72–99.

Allen, Douglas, Lawhon, Mary, and Pierce, Joseph (2019), 'Placing race: on the resonance of place with black geographies', *Progress in Human Geography*, Vol.43(6), pp.1001–1019.

Allen, John (1983), 'In search of a method: Hegel, Marx and realism', *Radical Philosophy*, Vol.35, pp.26–33.

Allen, John (1987), 'Realism as method (Review Essay on Sayer's 'Method in Social Science')', *Antipode*, Vol.19(2), pp.231–240.

Allen, John (1999), 'Spatial assemblages of power: from domination to empowerment', in Doreen Massey, John Allen, and Philip Sarre (eds.), *Human Geography Today*, Cambridge: Polity, pp.194–218.

Allen, John (2003), *Lost Geographies of Power*, Oxford: Blackwell.

Allen, John (2012), 'A more than relational geography?', *Dialogues in Human Geography*, Vol.2(2), pp.190–193.

Allen, John (2016), *Topologies of Power: Beyond Territory and Networks*, London: Routledge.

Allen, John (2020), 'Power's quiet reach and why it should exercise us', *Space and Polity*, Vol.24(3), pp.408–413.

Allen, John and Cochrane, Allan (2010), 'Assemblages of state power: topological shifts in the organisation of government and politics', *Antipode*, Vol.42(5), pp.1071–1089.

Alvesson, Mats, Gabriel, Yiannis, and Paulsen, Roland (2017), *Return to Meaning: A Social Science with Something to Say*, Oxford: Oxford University Press.

Amin, Ash (2001a), 'Moving on: institutionalism in economic geography', *Environment and Planning A*, Vol.33(7), pp.1237–1241.

Amin, Ash (2001b), 'Globalization: geographical aspects', in Neil Smelser and Paul B. Baltes (eds.), *International Encyclopedia of the Social and Behavioural Sciences*, Amsterdam: Elsevier Science, pp.6271–6277.

Amin, Ash (2002), 'Spatialities of globalisation', *Environment and Planning A*, Vol.34(3), pp.385–399.

Amin, Ash (2004), 'Regulating economic globalization', *Transactions of the Institute of British Geographers*, Vol.29(2), pp.217–233.

Amin, Ash and Thrift, Nigel (1994), 'Living in the global', in Ash Amin and Nigel Thrift (eds.), *Globalization, Institutions, and Regional Development in Europe*, Oxford: Oxford University Press, pp.1–22.

Amoore, Louise (2020a), *Cloud Ethics: Algorithms and the Attributes of Ourselves and Others*, Durham, NC: Duke University Press.

Amoore, Louise (2020b), 'Merely feminist: politics, partiality, gender, and geography', *Progress in Human Geography*, Epub. https://doi.org/10.1177/0309132520911570.

Amsden, Alice H. (1989), *Asia's Next Giant: South Korea and Late Industrialization*, New York: Oxford University Press.

Amsden, Alice H. (2001), *The Rise of 'The Rest': Challenges to the West From Late-Industrializing Economies*, New York: Oxford University Press.

Amsden, Alice H. (2007), *Escape from Empire: The Developing World's Journey through Heaven and Hell*, Cambridge, MA: MIT Press.

Anderson, Ben (2006), 'Becoming and being hopeful: towards a theory of affect', *Environment and Planning D: Society and Space*, Vol.24(5), pp.733–752.

Anderson, Ben (2009), 'Affective atmospheres', *Emotion, Space and Society*, Vol.2(2), pp.77–81.

Anderson, Ben (2014), *Encountering Affect: Capacities, Apparatuses, Conditions*, Aldershot: Ashgate.

Anderson, Ben (2016), 'Neoliberal affects', *Progress in Human Geography*, Vol.40(6), pp.734–753.

Anderson, Ben (2019), 'Cultural geography II: the force of representations', *Progress in Human Geography*, Vol.43(6), pp.1120–1132.

Anderson, Ben and Harrison, Paul (eds.) (2010a), *Taking-Place: Non-Representational Theories and Geography*, Aldershot: Ashgate.

Anderson, Ben and Harrison, Paul (2010b), 'The promise of non-representational theories', in Ben Anderson and Paul Harrison (eds.), *Taking Place: Non-Representational Theories and Geographies*, Aldershot: Ashgate, pp.1–34.

Anderson, Ben, Kearnes, Matthew, McFarlane, Colin, and Swanton, Dan (2012a), 'On assemblages and geography', *Dialogues in Human Geography*, Vol.2(2), pp.171–189.

Anderson, Ben, Kearnes, Matthew, McFarlane, Colin, and Swanton, Dan (2012b), 'Materialism and the politics of assemblage', *Dialogues in Human Geography*, Vol.2(2), pp.212–215.

Anderson, Ben and McFarlane, Colin (2011), 'Assemblage and geography', *Area*, Vol.43(2), pp.124–127.

Anderson, Ben and Tolia-Kelly, Divya (2004), 'Matter(s) in social and cultural geography', *Geoforum*, Vol.35(6), pp.669–674.

Anderson, Ben and Wylie, John (2009), 'On geography and materiality', *Environment and Planning A*, Vol.41(2), pp.318–335.

Ang, Yuen Yuen (2016), *How China Escaped the Poverty Trap*, Ithaca, NY: Cornell University Press.

Appadurai, Arjun (1996), *Modernity at Large: Cultural Dimensions of Globalization*, Minneapolis, MN: University of Minnesota Press.

Appadurai, Arjun (1999), 'Globalization and the research imagination', *International Social Science Journal*, Vol.51, pp.229–238.

Appadurai, Arjun (2013), *The Future as Cultural Fact: Essays on the Global Condition*, London: Verso.

Ash, James (2015), 'Technology and affect: towards a theory of inorganically organised objects', *Emotion, Space and Society*, Vol.14, pp.84–90.

Ash, James (2020a), 'Flat ontology and geography', *Dialogues in Human Geography*, Vol.10(3), pp.345–361.

Ash, James (2020b), 'Post-phenomenology and space: a geography of comprehension, form and power', *Transactions of the Institute of British Geographers*, Vol.45(1), pp.181–193.

Ash, James (2020c), 'Form and the politics of world', *Dialogues in Human Geography*, Vol.10(3), pp.378–381.

Ash, James and Simpson, Paul (2016), 'Geography and post-phenomenology', *Progress in Human Geography*, Vol.40(1), pp.48–66.

Ash, James and Simpson, Paul (2019), 'Postphenomenology and method: styles for thinking the (non)human', *Geohumanities*, Vol.5(1), pp.139–156.

Bair, Jennifer and Werner, Marion (2011), 'Commodity chains and the uneven geographies of global capitalism: a disarticulations perspective', *Environment and Planning A*, Vol.43(5), pp.988–997.

Barad, Karen (2007), *Meeting the Universe Halfway: Quantum Physics and the Entanglement of Matter and Meaning*, Durham, NC: Duke University Press.

Barnes, Trevor J. (2001), 'Lives lived and lives told: biographies of the quantitative revolution', *Environment and Planning D: Society and Space*, Vol.19(4), pp.409–429.

Barnes, Trevor J. (2011), 'Spatial analysis', in John A. Agnew and David N. Livingstone (eds.), *The SAGE Handbook of Geographical Knowledge*, London: Sage, pp.381–392.

Barnes, Trevor J. (2019), 'The importance of "being various": a commentary on "Moving beyond Anglo-American economic geography"', *International Journal of Urban Sciences*, Vol.23(2), pp.170–176.

Barnes, Trevor J. and Farish, Matthew (2006), 'Between regions: science, militarism, and American geography from world war to Cold War', *Annals of the Association of American Geographers*, Vol.96(4), pp.807–826.

Barnes, Trevor J. and Sheppard, Eric (2010), 'Nothing includes everything.' Towards engaged pluralism in Anglophone economic geography', *Progress in Human Geography*, Vol.34(2), pp.193–214.

Barnett, Clive (1998), 'The cultural turn: fashion or progress in human geography?', *Antipode*, Vol.30(4), pp.379–394.

Barnett, Clive (1999), 'Deconstructing context: exposing Derrida', *Transactions of the Institute of British Geographers*, Vol.24(3), pp.277–293.

Barnett, Clive (2005), 'The consolations of "neoliberalism"', *Geoforum*, Vol.36(1), pp.7–12.

Barnett, Clive (2008), 'Political affects in public space: normative blind-spots in non-representational ontologies', *Transactions of the Institute of British Geographers*, Vol.33(2), pp.186–200.

Barnett, Clive (2015), 'Postcolonialism: powers of representation', in Stuart Aitken and Gill Valentine (eds.), *Approaches to Human Geography*, Second Edition, London: Sage, pp.163–180.

Barrientos, Stephanie (2019), *Gender and Work in Global Value Chains: Capturing the Gains?*, New Delhi: Cambridge University Press.

Barua, Maan (2021), 'Infrastructure and non-human life: a wider ontology', *Progress in Human Geography*, Vol.45(6), pp.1467–1489.

Bathelt, Harald (2006), 'Geographies of production: growth regimes in spatial perspective 3 –towards a relational view of economic action and policy', *Progress in Human Geography*, Vol.30(2), pp.223–236.

Bathelt, Harald and Glückler, Johannes (2003), 'Toward a relational economic geography', *Journal of Economic Geography*, Vol.3(2), pp.117–144.

Bathelt, Harald and Glückler, Johannes (2014), 'Institutional change in economic geography', *Progress in Human Geography*, Vol.38(3), pp.340–363.

Bathelt, Harald, Malmberg, Anders, and Maskell, Peter (2004), 'Clusters and knowledge: local buzz, global pipelines and the process of knowledge creation', *Progress in Human Geography*, Vol.28(1), pp.31–56.

Beach, Derek (2013), 'Taking mechanisms seriously?', *European Political Science*, Vol.12(1), pp.13–15.

Beach, Derek (2021), 'Evidential pluralism and evidence of mechanisms in the social sciences', *Synthese*, Vol.199, pp.8899–8919.

Beach, Derek and Pedersen, Rasmus Brun (2013), *Process-Tracing Methods*, Ann Arbor, MI: University of Michigan Press.

Beach, Derek and Pedersen, Rasmus Brun (2016), *Causal Case Study Methods*, Ann Arbor, MI: University of Michigan Press.

Beach, Derek and Pedersen, Rasmus Brun (2018), 'Selecting appropriate cases when tracing causal mechanisms', *Sociological Methods & Research*, Vol.47(4), pp.837–871.

Beach, Derek and Pedersen, Rasmus Brun (2019), *Process-Tracing Methods*, Second Edition, Ann Arbor, MI: University of Michigan Press.

Beaverstock, Jonathan V., Smith, Richrad G., and Taylor, Peter J. (2000), 'World-city network: a new metageography?', *Annals of the Association of American Geographers*, Vol.90(1), pp.123–134.

Bechtel, William and Abrahamsen, Adele (2005), 'Explanation: a mechanist alternative', *Studies in History and Philosophy of Science Part C*, Vol.36(2), pp.421–441.

Behuria, Pritish (2020), 'The domestic political economy of upgrading in global value chains', *Review of International Political Economy*, Vol.27(2), pp.348–376.

Bengtsson, Bo and Hertting, Nils (2014), 'Generalization by mechanism: thin rationality and ideal-type analysis in case study research', *Philosophy of the Social Sciences*, Vol.44(6), pp.707–732.

Bennett, Andrew (2014), 'The mother of all isms: causal mechanisms and structured pluralism in international relations theory', *European Journal of International Relations*, Vol.9(3), pp.459–481.

Bennett, Andrew and Checkel, Jeffrey T. (eds.) (2015), *Process Tracing: From Metaphor to Analytic Tool*, Cambridge: Cambridge University Press.

Bennett, Jane (2004), 'The force of things: steps towards an ecology of matter', *Political Theory*, Vol.32(3), pp.347–372.

Bennett, Jane (2010), *Vibrant Matter: A Political Ecology of Things*, Durham, NC: Duke University Press.

Bergson, Henri (1910), *Time and Free Will: An Essay on the Immediate Data of Consciousness*, Trans. Frank Lubecki Pogson, London: Allen and Unwin.

Bhabha, Homi (2004 [1994]), *The Location of Culture*, London: Routledge.

Bhaskar, Roy (1975), *A Realist Theory of Science*, Leeds: Leeds Books.

Bhaskar, Roy (1979), *The Possibility of Naturalism: A Philosophical Critique of the Contemporary Human Sciences*, Brighton: Harvester.

Bhaskar, Roy (1986), *Scientific Realism and Human Emancipation*, London: Verso.

Bhaskar, Roy (1989), *Reclaiming Reality: A Critical Introduction to Contemporary Philosophy*, London: Verso.

Bhaskar, Roy (2008 [1993]), *Dialectic: The Pulse of Freedom*, With a New Introduction, London: Routledge.

Bhaskar, Roy (2009 [1986]), *Scientific Realism and Human Emancipation*, Second Edition, London: Routledge.

Bhaskar, Roy (2010), *The Formation of Critical Realism: A Personal Perspective*, with Mervyn Hartwig, London: Routledge.

Bhaskar, Roy (2016), *Enlightened Common Sense: The Philosophy of Critical Realism*, ed. Mervyn Hartwig, London: Routledge.

Bingham, Nick (1996), 'Object-ions: from technological determinism towards geographies of relations', *Environment and Planning D: Society and Space*, Vol.14(6), pp.635–657.

Birch, Kean and Siemiatycki, Matti (2016), 'Neoliberalism and the geographies of marketization: the entangling of state and markets', *Progress in Human Geography*, Vol.40(2), pp.177–198.

Bledsoe, Adam (2021), 'Methodological reflections on geographies of blackness', *Progress in Human Geography*, Vol.45(5), pp.1003–1021.

Blunt, Alison and Rose, Gillian (eds.) (1994), *Writing Women and Space: Colonial and Postcolonial Geographies*, New York: Guilford.

Boschma, Ron (2017), 'Relatedness as driver of regional diversification: a research agenda', *Regional Studies*, Vol.51(3), pp.351–364.

Boschma, Ron (2022), 'Global value chains from an evolutionary economic geography perspective: a research agenda', *Area Development and Policy*, Vol.7(2), pp.123–146.

Boschma, Ron A. (2004), 'Competitiveness of regions from an evolutionary perspective', *Regional Studies*, Vol.38(9), pp.1001–1014.

Boschma, Ron, Coenen, Lars, Frenken, Koen, and Truffer, Bernhard (2017), 'Towards a theory of regional diversification', *Regional Studies*, Vol.51(1), pp.31–45.

Boschma, Ron A. and Frenken, Koen (2006), 'Why is economic geography not an evolutionary science? Towards an evolutionary economic geography', *Journal of Economic Geography*, Vol.6(3), pp.273–302.

Bosco, Fernando J. (2015), 'Actor-network theory, networks, and relational geographies', in Stuart Aitken and Gill Valentine (eds.), *Approaches to Human Geography*, Second Edition, London: Sage, pp.150–162.

Bourdieu, Pierre (1988), 'Vive la crise! For heterodoxy in social science', *Theory and Society*, Vol.17(5), pp.773–787.

Bourdieu, Pierre and Wacquant, Loïc J.D. (1992), *An Invitation to Reflexive Sociology*, Chicago, IL: University of Chicago Press.

Bradbury, Hilary and Lichtenstein, Benyamin M. Bergmann (2000), 'Relationality in organizational research: exploring *The Space Between*', *Organization Science*, Vol.11(5), pp.551–564.

Braidotti, Rosi (2011), *Nomadic Theory: The Portable Rosi Braidotti*, New York: Columbia University Press.

Braun, Bruce (2005), 'Writing geographies of hope', *Antipode*, Vol.37(4), pp.834–841.

Brenner, Neil (2001), 'The limits to scale? Methodological reflections on scalar structuration', *Progress in Human Geography*, Vol.25(4), pp.591–614.

Brenner, Neil (2019), *New Urban Spaces: Urban Theory and the Scale Question*, Oxford: Oxford University Press.

Brenner, Neil, Peck, Jamie, and Theodore, Nick (2010), 'Variegated neoliberalization: geographies, modalities, pathways', *Global Networks*, Vol.10(2), pp.182–222.

Breznitz, Dan and Murphree, Michael (2011), *The Run of the Red Queen: Government, Innovation, Globalization, and Economic Growth in China*, New Haven, CT: Yale University Press.

Bridge, Gary (1997), 'Mapping the terrain of time-space compression: power networks in everyday life', *Environment and Planning D: Society and Space*, Vol.15(5), pp.611–626.

Bridge, Gary (2021), 'On pragmatism, assemblage and ANT: assembling reason', *Progress in Human Geography*, Vol.45(3), pp.417–435.

Brigstocke, Julian, Bresnihan, Patrick, Dawney, Leila, and Millner, Naomi (2021), 'Geographies of authority', *Progress in Human Geography*, Vol.45(6), pp.1356–1378.

Bryson, John R. and Vanchan, Vida (2020), 'COVID-19 and alternative: conceptualisations of value and risk in GPN research', *Tijdschrift voor Economische en Sociale Geografie*, Vol.111(3), pp.530–542.

Bunge, Mario (1996), *Finding Philosophy in Social Science*, New Haven, CT: Yale University Press.

Bunge, Mario (1997), 'Mechanisms and explanation', *Philosophy of the Social Sciences*, Vol.27(4), pp.410–465.

Bunge, Mario (2004), 'How does it work? The search for explanatory mechanisms', *Philosophy of the Social Sciences*, Vol.34(2), pp.182–210.

Burt, Ronald S. (1992), *Structural Holes*, Cambridge, MA: Harvard University Press.

Butler, Judith (1988), 'Performative acts and gender constitution: an essay in phenomenology and feminist theory', *Theatre Journal*, Vol.40(4), pp.519–531.

Butler, Judith (1997), *The Psychic Life of Power: Theories in Subjection*, Stanford, CA: Stanford University Press.

Butler, Judith (2006 [1990]), *Gender Trouble: Feminism and the Subversion of Identity*, New York: Routledge.

Butler, Judith (2011 [1993]), *Bodies That Matter: On the Discursive Limits of 'Sex'*, London: Routledge.

Butler, Judith (2015a), *Notes Toward a Performative Theory of Assembly*, Cambridge, MA: Harvard University Press.

Butler, Judith (2015b), *Senses of the Subject*, New York: Fordham University Press.

Callon, Michel (1999) 'On recalling ANT', in John Law and John Hassard (eds.), *Actor Network Theory and After*, Oxford: Blackwell, pp.181–195.

Castree, Noel (2002), 'False antitheses? Marxism, nature and actor-networks', *Antipode*, Vol.34(1), pp.111–146.

Castree, Noel (2008a), 'Neoliberalising nature: the logics of deregulation and reregulation', *Environment and Planning A*, Vol.40(2), pp.131–152.

Castree, Noel (2008b), 'Neoliberalising nature: processes, effects, and evaluations', *Environment and Planning A*, Vol.40(2), pp.153–173.

Chakrabarty, Dipesh (2008 [2000]), *Provincializing Europe: Postcolonial Thought and Historical Difference*, With a new preface, Princeton, NJ: Princeton University Press.

Charnock, Greig and Starosta, Guido (eds.) (2016), *The New International Division of Labour: Global Transformation and Uneven Development*, London: Palgrave Macmillan.

Checkel, Jeffrey T. (2006), 'Tracing causal mechanisms', *International Studies Review*, Vol.8(2), pp.362–370.

Chisholm, Michael (1975), *Human Geography: Evolution or Revolution*, Harmondsworth: Penguin Books.

Christophers, Brett (2015), 'The limits to financialization', *Dialogues in Human Geography*, Vol.5(2), pp.183–200.

Clark, Gordon L., Feldman, Maryann A., Gertler, Meric S., and Wójcik, Dariusz (eds.) (2018), *The New Oxford Handbook of Economic Geography*, Oxford: Oxford University Press.

Clayton, Philip and Davies, Paul (eds.) (2006), *The Re-Emergence of Emergence: The Emergentist Hypothesis From Science to Religion*, Oxford: Oxford University Press.

Clegg, Stewart R. and Haugaard, Martin (eds.), (2009), *The Sage Handbook of Power*, London: Sage.

Clifford, Nicholas, Holloway, Sarah L., Rice, Stephen P., and Valentine, Gill (eds.) (2009), *Key Concepts in Geography*, Second Edition, London: Sage.

Cloke, Paul, Cook, Ian, Crang, Philip, Goodwin, Mark, Painter, Joe, and Philo, Chris (2004), *Practising Human Geography*, London: Sage.

Cockayne, Daniel G., Ruez, Derek, and Secor, Anna (2017), 'Between ontology and representation: locating Gilles Deleuze's "difference-in-itself" in and for geographical thought', *Progress in Human Geography*, Vol.41(5), pp.580–599.

Coe, Neil, Dicken, Peter, and Hess, Martin (2008), 'Global production networks: realizing the potential', *Journal of Economic Geography*, Vol.8(3), pp.271–295.

Coe, Neil, Dicken, Peter, Hess, Martin, and Yeung, Henry Wai-chung (2010), 'Making connections: global production networks and world city networks', *Global Networks*, Vol.10(1), pp.138–149.

Coe, Neil, Hess, Martin, Yeung, Henry Wai-chung, Dicken, Peter, and Henderson, Jeffrey (2004), '"Globalizing" regional development: a global production networks perspective', *Transactions of the Institute of British Geographers*, Vol.29(4), pp.468–484.

Coe, Neil M. (2021), *Advanced Introduction to Global Production Networks*, Cheltenham: Edward Elgar.

Coe, Neil M. and Yeung, Henry Wai-chung (2015), *Global Production Networks: Theorizing Economic Development in an Interconnected World*, Oxford: Oxford University Press.

Coe, Neil M. and Yeung, Henry Wai-chung (2019), 'Global production networks: mapping recent conceptual developments', *Journal of Economic Geography*, Vol.19(4), pp.775–801.

Coleman, James S. (1986), 'Social theory, social research, and a theory of action', *American Journal of Sociology*, Vol.91(6), pp.1309–1335.

Coleman, James S. (1990), *Foundations of Social Theory*, Cambridge, MA: Harvard University Press.

Collier, Andrew (1994), *Critical Realism: An Introduction to Roy Bhaskar's Philosophy*, London: Verso.

Colls, Rachel (2012), 'Feminism, bodily difference and non-representational geographies', *Transactions of the Institute of British Geographers*, Vol.37(3), pp.430–445.

Connell, Raewyn (2007), *Southern Theory: The Global Dynamics of Knowledge in Social Science*, Cambridge: Polity.

Connolly, William E. (2005), *Pluralism*, Durham, NC: Duke University Press.

Cooke, Philip N. and Morgan, Kevin (1993), 'The network paradigm: new departures in corporate and regional development', *Environment and Planning D: Society and Space*, Vol.11(5), pp.543–564.

Cooke, Philip N. and Morgan, Kevin (1998), *The Associational Economy: Firms, Regions, and Innovation*, Oxford: Oxford University Press.

Corbridge, Stuart (1993), 'Marxisms, modernities and moralities: development praxis and the claims of distant strangers', *Environment and Planning D: Society and Space*, Vol.11(4), pp.449–472.

Cosgrove, Denis (1984), *Social Formation and Symbolic Landscape*, London: Croom Helm.

Cosgrove, Denis and Daniels, Stephen (eds.) (1988), *The Iconography of Landscape*, Cambridge: Cambridge University Press.

Cosgrove, Denis and Jackson, Peter (1987), 'New directions in cultural geography', *Area*, Vol.19(2), pp.95–101.

Country, Bawaka, Wright, Sarah, Suchet-Pearson, Sandie, Lloyd, Kate, Burarrwanga, Laklak, Ganambarr, Ritjilili, Ganambarr-Stubbs, Merrkiyawuy, Ganambarr, Banbapuy, Maymuru, Djawundil, and Sweeney, Jill (2016), 'Co-becoming Bawaka: towards a relational understanding of place/space', *Progress in Human Geography*, Vol.40(4), pp.455–475.

Cox, Kevin R. (1998), 'Spaces of dependence, spaces of engagement and the politics of scale, or: looking for local politics', *Political Geography*, Vol.17(1), pp.1–23.

Cox, Kevin R. (2004), 'Globalization and the politics of local and regional development: the question of convergence', *Transactions of the Institute of British Geographers*, Vol.29(2), pp.179–194.

Cox, Kevin R. (2013a), 'Notes on a brief encounter: critical realism, historical materialism and human geography', *Dialogues in Human Geography*, Vol.3(1), pp.3–21.

Cox, Kevin R. (2013b), 'The continuing relevance of old Debates', *Dialogues in Human Geography*, Vol.3(1), pp.49–55.

Cox, Kevin R. (2014), *Making Human Geography*, New York: Guilford.

Cox, Kevin R. (2021), *Advance Introduction to Marxism and Human Geography*, Cheltenham: Edward Elgar.

Cox, Kevin R. and Evenhuis, Emil (2020), 'Theorising in urban and regional studies: negotiating generalisation and particularity', *Cambridge Journal of Regions, Economy and Society*, Vol.13(3), pp.425–442.

Craggs, Ruth and Neate, Hannah (2017), 'Post-colonial careering and urban policy mobility: between Britain and Nigeria, 1945–1990', *Transactions of the Institute of British Geographers*, Vol.42(1), pp.44–57.

Craggs, Ruth and Neate, Hannah (2020), 'What happens if we start from Nigeria? Diversifying histories of geography', *Annals of the American Association of Geographers*, Vol.110(3), pp.899–916.

Craig, David and Porter, Douglas (2006), *Development Beyond Neoliberalism? Governance, Poverty Reduction and Political Economy*, London: Routledge.

Craver, Carl F. and Darden, Lindley (2013), *In Search of Mechanisms: Discoveries Across the Life Sciences*, Chicago, IL: University of Chicago Press.

Cresswell, Tim (2006), *On the Move: Mobility in the Modern Western World*, New York: Routledge.

Cresswell, Tim (2010), 'New cultural geography – an unfinished project?', *Cultural Geography*, Vol.17(2), pp.169–174.

Cresswell, Tim (2013), *Geographic Thought: A Critical Introduction*, Chichester: Wiley-Blackwell.

Curley, Andrew and Smith, Sarah (2020), 'Against colonial grounds: geography on Indigenous lands', *Dialogues in Human Geography*, Vol.10(1), pp.37–40.

Danermark, Berth, Ekstrom, Mats, and Karlsson, Jan ch. (2019), *Explaining Society: Critical Realism in the Social Sciences*, Second Edition, London: Routledge.

Datta, Anindita, Hopkins, Peter, Johnston, Lynda, Olson, Elizabeth, and Silva, Joseli Maria (eds.) (2020), *Routledge Handbook of Gender and Feminist Geographies*, London: Routledge.

Dean, Kathryn, Joseph, Jonathan, and Norrie, Alan (eds.) (2005), 'Special issue on "Critical realism today"', *New Formations: A Journal of Culture, Theory and Politics*, Vol.56, pp.7–161.

Decoteau, Claire Laurier (2018), 'Conjunctures and assemblages: approaches to multicausal explanation in the human sciences', in Timothy Rutzou and George Steinmetz (eds.), *Critical Realism, History, and Philosophy in the Social Sciences*, Bingley: Emerald, pp.89–118.

DeLanda, Manuel (2006), *A New Philosophy of Society: Assemblage Theory and Social Complexity*, London: Continuum.

DeLanda, Manuel (2016), *Assemblage Theory*, Edinburgh: Edinburgh University Press.

DeLanda, Manuel and Harman, Graham (2017), *The Rise of Realism*, Cambridge: Polity.

Deleuze, Gilles (1991 [1953]), *Empiricism and Subjectivity: An Essay on Hume's Theory of Human Nature*, Trans. Constantin V. Boundas, New York: Columbia University Press.

Deleuze, Gilles (1994 [1968]), *Difference and Repetition*, New York: Columbia University Press.

Deleuze, Gilles and Guattari, Félix (1987 [1980]), *A Thousand Plateaus: Capitalism and Schizophrenia*, Minneapolis, MN: University of Minnesota Press.

Deleuze, Gilles and Parnet, Claire (2002 [1977]), *Dialogues II*, Trans. Hugh Tomlinson and Barbara Habberjam, New York: Columbia University Press.

Demeritt, David (2005), 'Hybrid Geographies, relational ontologies and situated knowledges', *Antipode*, Vol.37(4), pp.818–823.

Demeulenaere, Pierre (ed.) (2011), *Analytical Sociology and Social Mechanisms*, Cambridge: Cambridge University Press.

Deng, Ping, Delios, Andrew, and Peng, Mike W. (2020), 'A geographic relational perspective on the internationalization of emerging market firms', *Journal of International Business Studies*, Vol.51(1), pp.50–71.

Dewsbury, John-David, Harrison, Paul, Rose, Mitch, and Wylie, John (2002), 'Enacting geographies', *Geoforum*, Vol.33(4), pp.437–440.

Dicken, Peter (1986), *Global Shift: Industrial Change in a Turbulent World*, London: Harper & Row.

Dicken, Peter (1994), 'Global-local tensions: firms and states in the global space-economy', *Economic Geography*, Vol.70(2), pp.101–128.

Dicken, Peter (2004), 'Geographers and "globalization": (yet) another missed boat?', *Transactions of the Institute of British Geographers*, Vol.29(1), pp.5–26.

Dicken, Peter (2015), *Global Shift: Mapping the Changing Contours of the World Economy*, Seventh Edition, London: Sage.

Dicken, Peter, Kelly, Philip, Olds, Kris, and Yeung, Henry Wai-chung (2001), 'Chains and networks, territories and scales: towards an analytical framework for the global economy', *Global Networks*, Vol.1(2), pp.89–112.

Dicken, Peter, Peck, Jamie, and Tickell, Adam (1997) 'Unpacking the global', in Roger Lee and Jane Wills (eds.), *Geographies of Economies*, London: Arnold, pp.158–166.

Dicken, Peter and Thrift, Nigel (1992), 'The organization of production and the production of organization', *Transactions of the Institute of British Geographer*, Vol.17(3), pp.279–291.

Dittmer, Jason (2014), 'Geopolitical assemblages and complexity', *Progress in Human Geography*, Vol.38(3), pp.385–401.

Dixon, Deborah P. and Jones III, John Paul (2015), 'Feminist geographies of difference, relation, and construction', in Stuart Aitken and Gill Valentine (eds.), *Approaches to Human Geography*, Second Edition, London: Sage, pp.49–63.

Doel, Marcus (1996), 'A hundred thousand lines of flight: a machinic introduction to the nomad thought and scrumpled geography of Gilles Deleuze and Félix Guattari', *Environment and Planning D: Society and Space*, Vol.14(4), pp.421–439.

Doel, Marcus (1999), *Poststructuralist Geographies: The Diabolical Art of Spatial Science*, Edinburgh: University of Edinburgh Press.

Doel, Marcus A. (2004) 'Post-structuralist geographies: the essential selection', in Paul Cloke, Phil Crang, and Mark Goodwin (eds.), *Envisioning Human Geographies*, London: Arnold, pp.146–171.

Donati, Pierpaolo (2010), *Relational Sociology: A New Paradigm for the Social Sciences*, London: Routledge.

Donati, Pierpaolo and Archer, Margaret S. (2015), *The Relational Subject*, Cambridge: Cambridge University Press.

Doucette, Jamie (2020), 'Political will and human geography: non-representational, post-political, and Gramscian geographies', *Progress in Human Geography*, Vol.44(2), pp.315–332.

Dowler, Lorraine, Cuomo, Dana, and Laliberte, Nicole (2014), 'Challenging "The Penn State Way": a feminist response to institutional violence in higher education', *Gender, Place and Culture*, Vol.21(3), pp.387–394.

Driver, Felix (2001), *Geography Militant: Cultures of Exploration and Empire*, Oxford: Blackwell.

Dufty-Jones, Rae and Gibson, Chris (2022), 'Making space to write 'care-fully': engaged responses to the institutional politics of research writing', *Progress in Human Geography*, Vol.46(2), pp.339–358.

Dyer, Jeffrey H. and Singh, Harbir (1998), 'The relational view: cooperative strategy and sources of interorganizational competitive advantage', *Academy of Management Review*, Vol.23(4), pp.660–679.

Eagleton, Terry (1996), *The Illusions of Postmodernism*, Oxford: Blackwell.

Eagleton, Terry (2004), *After Theory*, London: Penguin.

Ebbensgaard, Casper Laing and Edensor, Tim (2021), 'Walking with light and the discontinuous experience of urban change', *Transactions of the Institute of British Geographers*, Vol.46(2), pp.378–391.

Edensor, Tim (2011), 'Entangled agencies, material networks and repair in a building assemblage: the mutable stone of St Ann's Church, Manchester', *Transactions of the Institute of British Geographers*, Vol.36(2), pp.238–252.

Edwards, Paul K., O'Mahoney, Joe, and Vincent, Steve (eds.) (2014), *Studying Organizations Using Critical Realism: A Practical Guide*, Oxford: Oxford University Press.

Elden, Stuart (2001), *Mapping the Present: Heidegger, Foucault and the Project of a Spatial History*, London: Continuum.

Elden, Stuart (2003), 'Review of *Poststructuralist Geographies: The Diabolical Art of Spatial Science* by Marcus Doel', *Political Geography*, Vol.22(2), pp.238–240.

Elden, Stuart (2004), *Understanding Henri Lefebvre: Theory and the Possible*, London: Continuum.

Elden, Stuart (2017), *Foucault's Last Decade*, Cambridge: Polity.

Elder-Vass, Dave (2005), 'Emergence and the realist account of cause', *Journal of Critical Realism*, Vol.4(2), pp.315–338.

Elder-Vass, Dave (2008), 'Searching for realism, structure and agency in actor network theory', *British Journal of Sociology*, Vol.59(3), pp.455–473.

Elder-Vass, Dave (2010), *The Causal Powers of Social Structures: Emergence, Structure and Agency*, Cambridge: Cambridge University Press.

Elder-Vass, Dave (2012), *The Reality of Social Construction*, Cambridge: Cambridge University Press.

Elder-Vass, Dave (2022), 'Critical realism', in Gerald Delanty and Stephen P. Turner (eds.), *Routledge International Handbook of Contemporary Social and Political Theory*, Second Edition, London: Routledge. Chapter 19.

Elster, Jon (1989), *Nuts and Bolts for the Social Sciences*, Cambridge: Cambridge University Press.

Elster, Jon (1999), *Alchemies of the Mind: Rationality and the Emotions*, Cambridge: Cambridge University Press.

Elster, Jon (2015), *Explaining Social Behaviour: More Nuts and Bolts for the Social Sciences*, Second Edition, Cambridge: Cambridge University Press.

Emirbayer, Mustafa (1997), 'Manifesto for a relational sociology', *American Journal of Sociology*, Vol.103(2), pp.281–317.

Engelmann, Sasha and McCormack, Derek P. (2021), 'Elemental worlds: specificities, exposures, alchemies', *Progress in Human Geography*, Vol.45(6), pp.1419–1439.

England, Kim (1994), 'Getting personal: reflexivity, positionality, and feminist research', *The Professional Geographer*, Vol.46(1), pp.80–89.

England, Kim, Dyck, Isabel, Ortega-Alcázar, Iliana, and Raven-Ellison, Menah (2020), 'Care, health and migration', in Anindita Datta, Peter Hopkins, Lynda Johnston, Elizabeth Olson, and Joseli Maria Silva (eds.), *Routledge Handbook of Gender and Feminist Geographies*, London: Routledge, pp.336–346.

England, Kim and Ward, Kevin (eds.) (2007), *Neoliberalization: States, Networks, People*, Oxford: Blackwell.

Ettlinger, Nancy (2003), 'Cultural economic geography and a relational and microspace approach to trusts, rationalities, networks, and change in collaborative workplaces', *Journal of Economic Geography*, Vol.3(2), pp.145–171.

Evans, Peter (1995), *Embedded Autonomy: States and Industrial Transformation*, Princeton, NJ: Princeton University Press.

Fairclough, Norman, Jessop, Bob, and Sayer, Andrew (2003) 'Critical realism and semiosis', in Jonathan Joseph and John Michael Roberts (eds.), *Realism, Discourse and Deconstruction*, London: Routledge, pp.23–42.

Falleti, Tulia G. and Lynch, Julia F. (2009), 'Context and causal mechanisms in political analysis', *Comparative Political Studies*, Vol.42(9), pp.1143–1166.

Faria, Caroline and Mollett, Sharlene (2020), '"We didn't have time to sit still and be scared": a postcolonial feminist geographic reading of "An other geography"', *Dialogues in Human Geography*, Vol.10(1), pp.23–29.

Faulconbridge, James R. (2012), 'Economic geographies of power: methodological challenges and interdisciplinary analytical possibilities', *Progress in Human Geography*, Vol.36(6), pp.735–757.

Featherstone, Mike and Lash, Scott (1995), 'Globalization, modernity and the spatialization of social theory', in Mike Featherstone, Scott Lash, and Roland Robertson (eds.), *Global Modernities*, London: Sage, pp.1–24.

Ferguson, James (2010), 'The uses of neoliberalism', *Antipode*, Vol.41(S1), pp.166–184.

Ferraris, Maurizio (2014 [2012]), *Manifesto of New Realism*, Trans. Sarah De Sanctis, Albany, NY: SUNY Press.

Ferraris, Maurizio (2015), *Introduction to New Realism*, London: Bloomsbury.

Fleetwood, Steve and Ackroyd, Stephen (eds.) (2004), *Critical Realist Applications in Organisation and Management Studies*, London: Routledge.

Fligstein, Neil (2021), *The Banks Did It: An Anatomy of the Financial Crisis*, Cambridge, MA: Harvard University Press.

Foucault, Michel (1975), *Discipline and Punish: The Birth of the Prison*, Trans. Alan Sheridan, New York: Vintage Books.

Foucault, Michel (1977), 'Intellectuals and power: a conversation between Michel Foucault and Gilles Deleuze', in Donald F. Bouchard and Sherry Simon (trans.), *Language, Counter-Memory, Practice: Selected Essays and Interviews*, Ithaca, NY: Cornell University Press, pp.205–217.

Foucault, Michel (1988 [1977]), 'Confinement, psychiatry, prison', in Lawrence D. Kritzman (ed.), Alan Sheridan and others (trans.), *Politics, Philosophy, Culture: Interviews and Other Writings, 1977–1984*, New York: Routledge, pp.178–210.

Foucault, Michel (1988 [1980]), 'The masked philosopher', in Lawrence D. Kritzman (ed.), Alan Sheridan and others (trans.), *Politics, Philosophy, Culture: Interviews and Other Writings, 1977–1984*, New York: Routledge, pp.323–330.

Foucault, Michel (2001), *Power: Essential Works of Foucault, 1954–1984*, Vol.3, ed. James D. Faubion, New York: The New Press.

Foucault, Michel (2002 [1969]), *The Archaeology of Knowledge*, London: Routledge.

Frangenheim, Alexandra, Trippl, Michaela, and Chlebna, Camilla (2020), 'Beyond the *single path view*: interpath dynamics in regional contexts', *Economic Geography*, Vol.96(1), pp.31–51.

Frank, Andre Gunder (1998), *ReORIENT: Global Economy in the Asian Age*, Berkeley, CA: University of California Press.

Frenken, Koen and Boschma, Ron A. (2007), 'A theoretical framework for evolutionary economic geography: industrial dynamics and urban growth as a branching process', *Journal of Economic Geography*, Vol.7(5), pp.635–649.

Friedman, Thomas L. (1999), *The Lexus and the Olive Tree*, New York: HarperCollins.

Friedman, Thomas L. (2005), *The World Is Flat: A Brief History of the Twenty-first Century*, New York: HarperCollins.

Fröbel, Folker, Heinrichs, Jurgen, and Kreye, Otto (1980), *The New International Division of Labour*, Cambridge: Cambridge University Press.

Fu, Wenying and Lim, Kean Fan (2022), 'The constitutive role of state structures in strategic coupling: on the formation and evolution of Sino-German production networks in Jieyang, China', *Economic Geography*, Vol.98(1), pp.25–48.

Fuller, Crispian (2022), 'Time for change: corporate conventions, space–time and uneven development', *Progress in Human Geography*, Vol.46(2), pp.441–462.

Fuller, Douglas B. (2016), *Paper Tigers, Hidden Dragons: Firms and the Political Economy of China's Technological Development*, Oxford: Oxford University Press.

Fumerton, Richard (2018), 'Reasoning to the best explanation', in Kevin McCain and Ted Poston (eds.), *Best Explanations: New Essays on Inference to the Best Explanation*, Oxford: Oxford University Press, pp.65–79.

Gabriel, Markus (2015), *Fields of Sense: A New Realist Ontology*, Edinburgh: Edinburgh University Press.

Gallagher, Michael (2016), 'Sound as affect: difference, power and spatiality', *Emotion, Space and Society*, Vol.20, pp.42–48.

Gambetta, Diego (1998), 'Concatenations of mechanisms', in Peter Hedström and Richard Swedberg (eds.), *Social Mechanisms: An Analytical Approach to Social Theory*, Cambridge: Cambridge University Press, pp.102–124.

Garcia, Tristan (2014), *Form and Object: A Treatise on Things*, Trans. Mark Allan Ohm and Jon Cogburn, Edinburgh: Edinburgh University Press.

García-Ramon, Maria-Dolors (2003), 'Globalization and international geography: the questions of languages and scholarly traditions', *Progress in Human Geography*, Vol.27(1), pp.1–5.

Garson, Justin (2013), 'The functional sense of mechanism', *Philosophy of Science*, Vol.80(3), pp.317–333.

Garson, Justin (2018), 'Mechanisms, phenomena, and functions', in Stuart Glennan and Phyllis Illari (eds.), *The Routledge Handbook of Mechanisms and Mechanical Philosophy*, London: Routledge, pp.104–115.

Gereffi, Gary (2018), *Global Value Chains and Development: Redefining the Contours of 21ˢᵗ Century Capitalism*, New Delhi: Cambridge University Press.

Gereffi, Gary, Humphrey, John, and Sturgeon, Timothy (2005), 'The governance of global value chains', *Review of International Political Economy*, Vol.12(1), pp.78–104.

Gerring, John (2005), 'Causation: a unified framework for the social sciences', *Journal of Theoretical Politics*, Vol.17(2), pp.163–198.

Gerring, John (2008), 'The mechanismic worldview: thinking inside the box', *British Journal of Political Science*, Vol.38(1), pp.161–179.

Gerring, John (2010), 'Causal mechanisms: yes, but...', *Comparative Political Studies*, Vol.43(11), pp.1499–1526.

Gerring, John (2012), *Social Science Methodology: A Unified Framework*, Second Edition, Cambridge: Cambridge University Press.

Gibson-Graham, J.K. (2006 [1996]), *The End of Capitalism (As We Knew It): A Feminist Critique of Political Economy*, Minneapolis, MN: University of Minnesota Press.

Gibson-Graham, J.K. (2008), 'Diverse economies: performative practices for "other worlds"', *Progress in Human Geography*, Vol.32(5), pp.613–632.

Gibson-Graham, J.K. (2011), 'A feminist project of belonging for the Anthropocene', *Gender, Place, and Culture*, Vol.18(1), pp.1–21.

Gibson-Graham, J. K. (2020), 'Reading for difference in the archives of tropical geography: imagining an(other) economic geography for beyond the Anthropocene', *Antipode*, Vol.52(1), pp.12–35.

Gibson-Graham, J. K., Cameron, Jenny, and Healy, Stephen (2013), *Take Back the Economy: An Ethical Guide for Transforming Our Communities*, Minneapolis, MN: University of Minnesota Press.

Giddens, Anthony (1984), *The Constitution of Society: Outline of the Theory of Structuration*, Cambridge: Polity Press.

Gilmore, Ruth W. (2002), 'Fatal couplings of power and difference: notes on racism and geography', *Professional Geographer*, Vol.54(1), pp.15–24.

Glennan, Stuart (2002), 'Rethinking mechanistic explanation', *Philosophy of Science*, Vol.69(S3), pp.S342–S353.

Glennan, Stuart (2017), *The New Mechanical Philosophy*, Oxford: Oxford University Press.

Glennan, Stuart and Illari, Phyllis (eds.) (2018a), *The Routledge Handbook of Mechanisms and Mechanical Philosophy*, London: Routledge.

Glennan, Stuart and Illari, Phyllis (2018b), 'Introduction: mechanisms and mechanical philosophies', in Stuart Glennan and Phyllis Illari (eds.), *The Routledge Handbook of Mechanisms and Mechanical Philosophy*, London: Routledge, pp.1–10.

Glennan, Stuart and Illari, Phyllis (2018c), 'Varieties of mechanisms', in Stuart Glennan and Phyllis Illari (eds.), *The Routledge Handbook of Mechanisms and Mechanical Philosophy*, London: Routledge, pp.91–103.

Glückler, Johannes and Panitz, Robert (2021), 'Unleashing the potential of relational research: a meta-analysis of network studies in human geography', *Progress in Human Geography*, Vol.45(6), pp.1531–1557.

Goertz, Gary (2017), *Multimethod Research, Causal Mechanisms, And Case Studies*, Princeton, NJ: Princeton University Press.

Gong, Huiwen and Hassink, Robert (2020), 'Context sensitivity and economic-geographic (re) theorising', *Cambridge Journal of Regions, Economy and Society*, Vol.13(3), pp.475–490.

Gorski, Philip S. (2013), 'What is critical realism? And why should you care?', *Contemporary Sociology*, Vol.42(5), pp.658–670.

Gorski, Philip S. (2015), 'Causal mechanisms: lessons from the life sciences', in Margaret S. Archer (ed.), *Generative Mechanisms Transforming the Social Order*, Cham: Springer, pp.27–48.

Gorski, Philip S. (2018), 'After positivism: critical realism and historical sociology', in Timothy Rutzou and George Steinmetz (eds.), *Critical Realism, History, and Philosophy in the Social Sciences*, Bingley: Emerald, pp.23–45.

Grabher, Gernot (2009), 'Yet another turn? The evolutionary project in economic geography', *Economic Geography*, Vol.85(2), pp.119–127.

Graham, Stephen (1998), 'The end of geography or the explosion of place? Conceptualizing space, place and information technology', *Progress in Human Geography*, Vol.22(2), pp.165–185.

Granovetter, Mark (1985), 'Economic action and social structure: the problem of embeddedness', *American Journal of Sociology*, Vol.91(3), pp.481–510.

Granovetter, Mark (2017), *Society and Economy: Framework and Principles*, Cambridge, MA: Harvard University Press.

Green, Jeremy and Lavery, Scott (2018), 'After neoliberalisation? Monetary indiscipline, crisis and the state', *Transactions of the Institute of British Geographers*, Vol.43(1), pp.79–94.

Gregory, Derek (1978), *Ideology, Science and Human Geography*, London: Hutchinson.

Gregory, Derek (1994), *Geographical Imaginations*, Cambridge, MA: Basil Blackwell.

Gregory, Derek (2004), *The Colonial Present: Afghanistan, Palestine, Iraq*, Oxford: Blackwell.

Gregory, Derek and Urry, John (eds.) (1985), *Social Relations and Spatial Structures*, London: Macmillan.

Groff, Ruth (2004), *Critical Realism, Post-Positivism and the Possibility of Knowledge*, London: Routledge.

Groff, Ruth (ed.) (2008), *Revitalizing Causality: Realism about Causality in Philosophy and Social Science*, London: Routledge.

Groff, Ruth (2017), 'Causal mechanisms and the philosophy of causation', *Journal for the Theory of Social Behaviour*, Vol.47(3), pp.286–305.

Groff, Ruth (2019), 'Sublating the free will problematic: powers, agency and causal determination', *Synthese*, Vol.196(1), pp.179–200.

Groff, Ruth and Greco, John (eds.) (2013), *Powers and Capacities in Philosophy: The New Aristotelianism*, London: Routledge.

Gross, Neil (2009), 'A pragmatist theory of social mechanisms', *American Sociological Review*, Vol.74(3), pp.358–379.

Gross, Neil (2018), 'The structure of causal chains', *Sociological Theory*, Vol.36(4), pp.343–367.

Grosz, Elizabeth A. (1994), *Volatile Bodies: Towards a Corporal Feminism*, Bloomington, IN: Indiana University Press.

Grosz, Elizabeth A. (2017), *The Incorporeal: Ontology, Ethics, and the Limits of Materialism*, New York: Columbia University Press.

Gulati, Ranjay (2007), *Managing Network Resources: Alliances, Affiliations, and Other Relational Assets*, Oxford: Oxford University Press.

Gunnarsson, Lena, Dy, Angela Martinez, and van Ingen, Michiel (eds.) (2016), 'Special issue on "Critical realism, gender and feminism"', *Journal of Critical Realism*, Vol.15(5), pp.433–549.

Haberly, Daniel and Wójcik, Dariusz (2022), *Sticky Power: Global Financial Networks in the World Economy*, Oxford: Oxford University Press.

Habermas, Jürgen (1972), *Knowledge and Human Interests*, London: Heinemann.

Hacking, Ian (1999), *The Social Construction of What?* Cambridge, MA: Harvard University Press.

Haggard, Stephan (1990), *Pathways from the Periphery: The Politics of Growth in the Newly Industrializing Countries*, Ithaca, NY: Cornell University Press.

Haggard, Stephan (2018), *Developmental States*, Cambridge Elements in the Politics of Development, Cambridge: Cambridge University Press.

Häkli, Jouni (2020), 'What can flat ontology teach the legislator?', *Dialogues in Human Geography*, Vol.10(3), pp.370–373.

Hall, Peter A. and Soskice, David (eds.) (2001), *Varieties of Capitalism: The Institutional Foundations of Comparative Advantage*, Oxford: Oxford University Press.

Hall, Sarah (2018), *Global Finance: Places, Spaces and People*, London: Sage.

Hallaq, Wael B. (2018), *Restating Orientalism: A Critique of Modern Knowledge*, New York: Columbia University Press.

Hamilton, Gary G. and Kao, Cheng-Shu (2018), *Making Money: How Taiwanese Industrialists Embraced the Global Economy*, Stanford, CA: Stanford University Press.

Hamilton-Hart, Natasha and Yeung, Henry Wai-chung (2021), 'Institutions under pressure: East Asian states, global markets and national firms', *Review of International Political Economy*, Vol.28(1), pp.11–35.

Hancké, Bob (ed.) (2009), *Debating Varieties of Capitalism: A Reader*, Oxford: Oxford University Press.

Hannah, Matthew G. (2019), *Direction and Socio-Spatial Theory: A Political Economy of Oriented Practice*, London: Routledge.

Haraway, Donna J. (1988), 'Situated knowledges: the science question in feminism and the privilege of partial perspective', *Feminist Studies*, Vol.14(3), pp.575–599.

Haraway, Donna J. (1991), *Simians, Cyborgs, and Women: The Reinvention of Nature*, London: Free Association Books.

Haraway, Donna J. (2016), *Staying with the Trouble: Making Kin in the Chthulucene*, Durham, NC: Duke University Press.

Harding, Sandra (1986), *The Science Question in Feminism*, Ithaca, NY: Cornell University Press.

Harding, Sandra (1991), *Whose Science? Whose Knowledge? Thinking from Women's Lives*, Ithaca, NY: Cornell University Press.

Harding, Sandra (2008), *Sciences From Below: Feminisms, Postcolonialities, and Modernities*, Durham, NC: Duke University Press.

Harman, Graham (2008), 'DeLanda's ontology: assemblage and realism', *Continental Philosophy Review*, Vol.41, pp.367–383.

Harman, Graham (2010), *Towards Speculative Realism: Essays and Lectures*, Hants: Zero Books.

Harman, Graham (2016), *Immaterialism: Objects and Social Theory*, Cambridge: Polity.

Harman, Graham (2017), *Object-Oriented Ontology: A New Theory of Everything*, London: Penguin.

Harman, Graham (2018), *Speculative Realism: An Introduction*, Cambridge: Polity.

Harney, Liam, McCurry, Jenny, Scott, James, and Wills, Jane (2016), 'Developing "process pragmatism" to underpin engaged research in human geography', *Progress in Human Geography*, Vol.40(3), pp.316–333.

Harré, Rom (1970), *The Principles of Scientific Thinking*, London: Macmillan.

Harré, Rom (1972), *The Philosophies of Science*, Oxford: Oxford University Press.

Harré, Rom (1985 [1972]), *The Philosophies of Science*, Second Edition, Oxford: Oxford University Press.

Harré, Rom (1986), *Varieties of Realism: A Rationale for the Natural Sciences*, Oxford: Basil Blackwell.

Harris, Jack Laurie (2021), 'Rethinking cluster evolution: actors, institutional configurations, and new path development', *Progress in Human Geography*, Vol.45(3), pp.436–454.

Harrison, Paul (2002), 'The Caesura: remarks on Wittgenstein's interruption of theory, or, why practices elude explanation', *Geoforum*, Vol.33(4), pp.487–503.

Harrison, Paul (2015), 'Poststructuralist theories', in Stuart Aitken and Gill Valentine (eds.), *Approaches to Human Geography*, Second Edition, London: Sage, pp.132–145.

Hart, Gillian (2018), 'Relational comparison revisited: Marxist postcolonial geographies in practice', *Progress in Human Geography*, Vol.42(3), pp.371–394.

Harvey, David (1969), *Explanation in Geography*, London: Edward Arnold.

Harvey, David (1973), *Social Justice and the City*, London: Edward Arnold.

Harvey, David (1982), *The Limits to Capital*, Oxford: Basil Blackwell.

Harvey, David (1985), *The Urbanisation of Capital*, Oxford: Basil Blackwell.

Harvey, David (1987), 'Three myths in search of a reality in urban studies', *Environment and Planning A*, Vol.5(4), pp.367–376.

Harvey, David (1989), *The Condition of Postmodernity: An Enquiry into the Origins of Cultural Change*, Oxford: Basil Blackwell.

Harvey, David (1996), *Justice, Nature and the Geography of Difference*, Oxford: Basil Blackwell.

Harvey, David (2005), *A Brief History of Neoliberalism*, New York: Oxford University Press.

Harvey, David (2006a [1982]), *The Limits to Capital*, New Edition, London: Verso.

Harvey, David (2006b), 'Neo-liberalism as creative destruction', *Geografiska Annaler B*, Vol.88(2), pp.145–158.

Harvey, David (2006c), *Spaces of Global Capitalism: Towards A Theory of Uneven Geographical Development*, London: Verso.

Harvey, David (2014), *Seventeen Contradictions and the End of Capitalism*, New York: Oxford University Press.

Harvey, David (2017), *Marx, Capital, and the Madness of Economic Reason*, New York: Oxford University Press.

Hassink, Robert (2007), 'It's the language, stupid! On emotions, strategies and consequences related to the use of one language to describe and explain a diverse world', *Environment and Planning A*, Vol.39(6), pp.1282–1287.

Hassink, Robert, Gong, Huiwen, and Marques, Pedro (2019a), 'Moving beyond Anglo-American economic geography', *International Journal of Urban Sciences*, Vol.23(2), pp.149–169.

Hassink, Robert, Isaksen, Arne, and Trippl, Michaela (2019b), 'Towards a comprehensive understanding of new regional industrial path development', *Regional Studies*, Vol.53(11), pp.1636–1645.

Hassink, Robert, Klaerding, Claudia, and Marques, Pedro (2014), 'Advancing evolutionary economic geography by engaged pluralism', *Regional Studies*, Vol.48(7), pp.1295–1307.

Hayles, N. Katherine (1999), *How We Became Posthuman: Virtual Bodies in Cybernetics, Literature, and Informatics*, Chicago, IL: University of Chicago Press.

Hayles, N. Katherine (2017), *Unthought: The Power of the Cognitive Nonconscious*, Chicago, IL: University of Chicago Press.

Hedström, Peter (2005), *Dissecting the Social: On the Principles of Analytical Sociology*, New York: Cambridge University Press.

Hedström, Peter and Swedberg, Richard (1996), 'Social mechanisms', *Acta Sociologica*, Vol.39(3), pp.281–308.

Hedström, Peter and Swedberg, Richard (eds.) (1998a), *Social Mechanisms: An Analytical Approach to Social Theory*, Cambridge: Cambridge University Press.

Hedström, Peter and Swedberg, Richard (1998b), 'Social mechanisms: an introductory essay', in Peter Hedström and Richard Swedberg (eds.), *Social Mechanisms: An Analytical Approach to Social Theory*, Cambridge: Cambridge University Press, pp.1–31.

Hedström, Peter and Udéhn, Lars (2009), 'Analytical sociology and theories of the middle range', in Peter Bearman and Peter Hedström (eds.), *The Oxford Handbook of Analytical Sociology*, Oxford: Oxford University Press, pp.25–49.

Hedström, Peter and Wittrock, Björn (eds.) (2009), *Frontiers of Sociology*, Leiden: Brill.

Hedström, Peter and Ylikoski, Petri (2010), 'Causal mechanisms in the social sciences', *Annual Review of Sociology*, Vol.36, pp.49–67.

Hempel, Carl (1942), 'The function of general laws in history', *Journal of Philosophy*, Vol.39(2), pp.35–48.

Hempel, Carl (1965), *Aspects of Scientific Explanation*, New York: The Free Press.

Henderson, George and Sheppard, Eric (2015), 'Marx and the spirit of Marx', in Stuart Aitken and Gill Valentine (eds.), *Approaches to Human Geography*, Second Edition, London: Sage, pp.64–78.

Henderson, Jeffrey, Dicken, Peter, Hess, Martin, Coe, Neil, and Yeung, Henry Wai-chung (2002), 'Global production networks and the analysis of economic development', *Review of International Political Economy*, Vol.9(3), pp.436–464.

Henderson, Jeffrey and Hooper, Mike (2021), 'China and European innovation: corporate takeovers and their consequences', *Development and Change*, Vol.52(5), pp.1090–1121.

Hendrikse, Reijer, Van Meeteren, Michiel, and Bassens, David (2020), 'Strategic coupling between finance, technology and the state: cultivating a Fintech ecosystem for incumbent finance', *Environment and Planning A: Economy and Space*, Vol.52(8), pp.1516–1538.

Henry, Nick, Angus, Tim, and Jenkins, Mark (2021), 'Motorsport Valley revisited: cluster evolution, strategic cluster coupling and resilience', *European Urban and Regional Studies*, Vol.28(4), pp.466–486.

Hepach, Maximilian Gregor (2021), 'Entangled phenomenologies: reassessing (post-) phenomenology's promise for human geography', *Progress in Human Geography*, Vol.45(5), pp.1278–1294.

Herod, Andrew (2010), *Scale*, London: Routledge.

Hess, Martin (2004), '"Spatial" relationships? Towards a reconceptualization of embeddedness', *Progress in Human Geography*, Vol.28(2), pp.165–186.

Hess, Martin (2021), 'Global production networks: the state, power and politics', in Florence Palpacuer and Alistair Smith (eds.), *Rethinking Value Chains: Tackling the Challenges of Global Capitalism*, Bristol: Policy Press, pp.17–35.

Holbraad, Martin and Pedersen, Morten Axel (2017), *The Ontological Turn: An Anthropological Exposition*, Cambridge: Cambridge University Press.

Honig, Bonnie (2021), *A Feminist Theory of Refusal*, Cambridge, MA: Harvard University Press.

Horner, Rory (2014), 'Strategic decoupling, recoupling and global production networks: India's pharmaceutical industry', *Journal of Economic Geography*, Vol.14(6), pp.1117–1140.

Horner, Rory (2017), 'Beyond facilitator? State roles in global value chains and global production networks', *Geography Compass*, Vol.11(2), p. e12307.

Horner, Rory (2020), 'Towards a new paradigm of global development? Beyond the limits of international development', *Progress in Human Geography*, Vol.44(3), pp.415–436.

Hsing, You-tien (2010), *The Great Urban Transformation: Politics of Land and Property in China*, Oxford: Oxford University Press.

Huang, Chin-Hao (2022), *Power, Restraint, and China's Rise*, New York: Columbia University Press.

Huang, Yasheng (2008), *Capitalism with Chinese Characteristics: Entrepreneurship and the State*, New York: Cambridge University Press.

Hubbard, Phil (2011), 'The city', in John A. Agnew and David N. Livingstone (eds.), *The SAGE Handbook of Geographical Knowledge*, London: Sage, pp.549–562.

Hubbard, Phil, Kitchin, Rob, Bartley, B., and Fuller, D. (2002), *Thinking Geographically: Space, Theory, and Contemporary Human Geography*, London: Continuum.

Hudson, Ray (1999), 'The learning economy, the learning firm and the learning region: a sympathetic critique of the limits to learning', *European Urban and Regional Studies*, Vol.6(1), pp.59–72.

Hudson, Ray (2003), 'Fuzzy concepts and sloppy thinking: reflections on recent developments in critical regional studies', *Regional Studies*, Vol.37(6/7), pp.741–746.

Huggins, Robert and Thompson, Piers (2014), 'A network-based view of regional growth', *Journal of Economic Geography*, Vol.14(3), pp.511–545.

Illari, Phyllis McKay and Russo, Federica (2014), *Causality: Philosophical Theory Meets Scientific Practice*, Oxford: Oxford University Press.

Illari, Phyllis McKay, Russo, Federica, and Williamson, Jon (eds.) (2011), *Causality in the Sciences*, Oxford: Oxford University Press.

Ioannou, Stefanos and Wójcik, Dariusz (2019), 'On financialization and its future', *Environment and Planning A: Economy and Space*, Vol.51(1), pp.263–271.

Jackson, Peter (2000), 'Rematerializing social and cultural geography', *Social & Cultural Geography*, Vol.1(1), pp.9–14.

Jacobs, Jane (1996), *Edge of Empire: Postcolonialism and the City*, London: Routledge.

James, Al, Bradshaw, Michael, and Coe, Neil M. (2018), 'Sustaining economic geography? Business and management schools and the UK's economic geography diaspora', *Environment and Planning A*, Vol.50(6), pp.1147–1170.

Jazeel, Tariq (2016), 'Between area and discipline: progress, knowledge production and the geographies of Geography', *Progress in Human Geography*, Vol.40(5), pp.649–667.

Jazeel, Tariq (2019), *Postcolonialism*, London: Routledge.

Jazeel, Tariq and Legg, Stephen (eds.) (2019), *Subaltern Geographies: Subaltern Studies, Space and the Geographical Imagination*, Athens, GA: University of Georgia Press.

Jessop, Bob (1999), 'Some critical reflections on globalization and its illogic(s)', in Kris Olds, Peter Dicken, Philip Kelly, Lily Kong, and Henry Wai-chung Yeung (eds.), *Globalisation and the Asia Pacific: Contested Territories*, London: Routledge, pp.19–38.

Jessop, Bob (2001), 'Institutional re(turns) and the strategic-relational approach', *Environment and Planning A*, Vol.33(7), pp.1213–1235.

Jessop, Bob, Brenner, Neil, and Jones, Martin (2008), 'Theorizing socio-spatial relations', *Environment and Planning D: Society and Space*, Vol.26(3), pp.389–401.

Johnson, Chalmers (1982), *MITI and the Japanese Economic Miracle*, Stanford, CA: Stanford University Press.

Johnston, Lynda (2019), *Transforming Gender, Sex and Place: Gender Variant Geographies*, London: Routledge.

Johnston, Lynda, Datta, Anindita, Hopkins, Peter, Silva, Joseli Maria, and Olson, Elizabeth (2020), 'Introduction: establishing, placing, engaging and doing feminist geographies', in Anindita Datta, Peter Hopkins, Lynda Johnston, Elizabeth Olson, and Joseli Maria Silva (eds.), *Routledge Handbook of Gender and Feminist Geographies*, London: Routledge, pp.1–14.

Johnston, Ron J. and Sidaway, James D. (2016), *Geography and Geographers: Anglo-American Human Geography since 1945*, Seventh edition, London: Routledge.

Jones, John Paul, III, Woodward, Keith, and Marston, Sallie A. (2007), 'Situating flatness', *Transactions of the Institute of British Geographers*, Vol.32(2), pp.264–276.

Joronen, Mikko and Häkli, Jouni (2017), 'Politicizing ontology', *Progress in Human Geography*, Vol.41(5), pp.561–579.

Kaidesoja, Tuukka (2013a), *Naturalizing Critical Realist Social Ontology*, London: Routledge.

Kaidesoja, Tuukka (2013b), 'Overcoming the biases of microfoundationalism: social mechanisms and collective agents', *Philosophy of the Social Sciences*, Vol.43(3), pp.301–322.

Kaidesoja, Tuukka Juhani (2019a), 'Building middle-range theories from case studies', *Studies in History and Philosophy of Science*, Vol.78(1), pp.23–31.

Kaidesoja, Tuukka Juhani (2019b), 'A dynamic and multifunctional account of middle-range theories', *British Journal of Sociology*, Vol.70(4), pp.1469–1489.

Kaier, Marie I. (2018), 'The components and boundaries of mechanisms', in Stuart Glennan and Phyllis Illari (eds.), *The Routledge Handbook of Mechanisms and Mechanical Philosophy*, London: Routledge, pp.116–130.

Kalleberg, Arne L., Hewison, Kevin, and Shin, Kwang-Yeong (2021), *Precarious Asia: Global Capitalism and Work in Japan, South Korea, and Indonesia*, Stanford, CA: Stanford University Press.

Kalter, Frank and Kroneberg, Clemens (2014), 'Between mechanism talk and mechanism cult: new emphases in explanatory sociology and empirical research', *KZfSS Kölner Zeitschrift für Soziologie und Sozialpsychologie*, Vol.66(1), pp.91–115.

Kano, Liena (2018), 'Global value chain governance: a relational perspective', *Journal of International Business Studies*, Vol.49(6), pp.684–705.

Kano, Liena, Tsang, Eric W.K., and Yeung, Henry Wai-chung (2020), 'Global value chains: a review of a multidisciplinary literature', *Journal of International Business Studies*, Vol.51(4), pp.577–622.

Katz, Cindi (1996), 'Towards minor theory', *Environment and Planning D: Society and Space*, Vol.14(4), pp.487–499.

Katz, Cindi (2004), *Growing Up Global: Economic Restructuring and Children's Everyday Lives*, Minneapolis, MN: University of Minnesota Press.

Katz, Cindi (2017), 'Revisiting minor theory', *Environment and Planning D: Society and Space*, Vol.35(4), pp.596–599.

Kaul, Nitasha (2002), 'A critical "post" to critical realism', *Cambridge Journal of Economics*, Vol.26(6), pp.709–726.

Khalifa, Kareem, Millson, Jared, and Risjord, Mark (2018), 'Inference to the best explanation: fundamentalism's failures', in Kevin McCain and Ted Poston (eds.), *Best Explanations: New Essays on Inference to the Best Explanation*, Oxford: Oxford University Press, pp.80–96.

Kilduff, Martin and Tsai, Wenpin (2003), *Social Networks and Organizations*, London: Sage.

Kincaid, Harold (ed.) (2012), *Oxford Handbook of the Philosophy of Social Science*, Oxford: Oxford University Press.

Kindon, Sarah, Pain, Rachel, and Kesby, Mike (2007), *Participatory Action Research Approaches and Methods: Connecting People, Participation and Place*, New York: Routledge.

Kingsbury, Paul and Pile, Steve (eds.) (2014a), *Psychoanalytic Geographies*, Eldershot: Ashgate.

Kingsbury, Paul and Pile, Steve (2014b), 'Introduction: the unconscious, transference, drives, repetition and other things tied to geography', in Paul Kingsbury and Steve Pile (eds.), *Psychoanalytic Geographies*, Eldershot: Ashgate, pp.1–38.

Kinkaid, Eden (2019), '"Rights of nature" in translation: assemblage geographies, boundary objects, and translocal social movements', *Transactions of the Institute of British Geographers*, Vol.44(3), pp.555–570.

Kinkaid, Eden (2020), 'Can assemblage think difference? A feminist critique of assemblage geographies', *Progress in Human Geography*, Vol.44(3), pp.457–472.

Kinkaid, Eden (2021), 'Is post-phenomenology a critical geography? Subjectivity and difference in post-phenomenological geographies', *Progress in Human Geography*, Vol.45(2), pp.298–316.

Kinkaid, Eden and Nelson, Lise (2020), 'On the subject of performativity: Judith Butler's influence in geography', in Anindita Datta, Peter Hopkins, Lynda Johnston, Elizabeth Olson, and Joseli Maria Silva (eds.), *Routledge Handbook of Gender and Feminist Geographies*, London: Routledge, pp.92–101.

Kinpaisby, Mrs (2008), 'Taking stock of participatory geographies: envisioning the communiversity', *Transactions of the Institute of British Geographers*, Vol.33(3), pp.292–299.

Kitching, John (2018), 'Critical realism as a supporting philosophy for entrepreneurship and small business studies', in Alain Fayolle, Stratos Ramoglou, Mine Karatas-Ozkan, and Katerina Nicolopoulou (eds.), *Philosophical Reflexivity and Entrepreneurship Research*, London: Routledge, pp.92–107.

Knoke, David and Yang, Song (2020), *Social Network Analysis*, Third Edition, London: Sage.

Kofman, Eleonore and Raghuram, Parvati (2015), *Gendered Migration and Global Social Reproduction*, New York: Palgrave Macmillan.

Kofman, Eleonore and Raghuram, Parvati (2020), 'Geographies of gendered migration: place as difference and connection', in Anindita Datta, Peter Hopkins, Lynda Johnston, Elizabeth Olson, and Joseli Maria Silva (eds.), *Routledge Handbook of Gender and Feminist Geographies*, London: Routledge, pp.244–253.

Kohli, Atul (2004), *State-Directed Development: Political Power and Industrialization in the Global Periphery*, Cambridge: Cambridge University Press.

Kritzman, Lawrence D. (1988), 'Introduction: Foucault and the politics of experience' in Lawrence D. Kritzman (ed.), *Michel Foucault – Politics, Philosophy, Culture: Interviews and Other Writings, 1977–1984*, New York: Routledge, pp. ix–xxv.

Larner, Wendy (2009), 'Neoliberalism, mike moore, and the WTO', *Environment and Planning A*, Vol.41(7), pp.1576–1593.

Latham, Alan and McCormack, Derek P. (2004), 'Moving cities: rethinking the materialities of urban geographies', *Progress in Human Geography*, Vol.28(6), pp.701–724.

Latour, Bruno (1987), *Science in Action: How to Follow Scientists and Engineers Through Society*, Cambridge, MA: Harvard University Press.

Latour, Bruno (1988), 'The politics of explanation: an alternative', in Steve Woolgar (ed.), *Knowledge and Reflexivity: New Frontiers in the Sociology of Knowledge*, London: Sage, pp.155–177.

Latour, Bruno (1990), 'Technology is society made durable', *The Sociological Review*, Vol.38(S1), pp.103–131.

Latour, Bruno (1991), 'Technology is society made durable', in John Law (ed.), *A Sociology of Monsters: Essays on Power, Technology and Domination*, London: Routledge, pp.103–131.

Latour, Bruno (1993), *We Have Never Been Modern*, Trans. Catherine Porter, Cambridge, MA: Harvard University Press.

Latour, Bruno (1994), 'On technical mediation – philosophy, sociology, genealogy', *Common Knowledge*, Vol.4(1), pp.29–64.

Latour, Bruno (1996), 'On actor-network theory: a few clarifications', *Soziale Welt*, Vol.47(4), pp.369–381.

Latour, Bruno (1999), 'On recalling ANT', *The Sociological Review*, Vol.47(S1), pp.15–25.

Latour, Bruno (2005), *Reassembling the Social: An Introduction to Actor-Network-Theory*, Oxford: Oxford University Press.

Latour, Bruno (2013), *An Inquiry into Modes of Existence: An Anthropology of the Moderns*, Trans. Catherine Porter, Cambridge, MA: Harvard University Press.

Latour, Bruno (2017), 'On actor-network theory. A few clarifications, plus more than a few complications', *Philosophical Literary Journal Logos*, Vol.27(1), pp.173–197.

Law, John (1999), 'After ANT: complexity, naming and topology', *The Sociological Review*, Vol.47(S1), pp.1–14.

Law, John (2009), 'Actor-network theory and material semiotics', in Barry Turner (ed.), *The New Blackwell Companion to Social Theory*, Oxford: Blackwell, pp.141–158.

Lawson, Tony (2003), *Reorienting Economics*, London: Routledge.

Lawson, Tony (2015), *Essays on the Nature and State of Modern Economics*, London: Routledge.

Lawson, Victoria (2007), 'Geographies of care and responsibility', *Annals of the Association of American Geographers*, Vol.97(1), pp.1–11.

Leamer, Edward E. (2007), 'A flat world, a level playing field, a small world after all, or none of the above? A review of Thomas L. Friedman's *The World is Flat*', *Journal of Economic Literature*, Vol.45(1), pp.83–126.

Lee, Roger, Castree, Noel, Kitchin, Rob, Lawson, Vicky, Paasi, Anssi, Philo, Chris, Radcliffe, Sarah, Roberts, Susan M., and Withers, Charles (eds.) (2014), *The SAGE Handbook of Human Geography*, London: Sage.

Lefebvre, Henri (1991 [1974]), *The Production of Space*, Oxford: Blackwell.

Ley, David and Samuels, Marwyn S. (eds.) (1978), *Humanistic Geography: Prospects and Problems*, London: Croom Helm.

Leys, Ruth (2017), *The Ascent of Affect: Genealogy and Critique*, Chicago, IL: University of Chicago Press.

Leyshon, Andrew (2021), 'Economic geography I: uneven development, "left behind places" and "levelling up" in a time of crisis', *Progress in Human Geography*, Vol.45(6), pp.1678–1691.

Lim, Kean Fan (2014), 'Socialism with Chinese characteristics: uneven development, variegated neoliberalization and the dialectical differentiation of state spatiality', *Progress in Human Geography*, Vol.38(2), pp.221–247.

Lim, Kean Fan (2018), 'Strategic coupling, state capitalism, and the shifting dynamics of global production networks', *Geography Compass*, Vol.12(11). https://doi.org/10.1111/gec3.12406.

Lim, Kean Fan (2019), *On Shifting Foundations: State Rescaling, Policy Experimentation and Economic Restructuring in Post-1949 China*, Chichester: Wiley.

Lin, George C.S. (2009), *Developing China: Land, Politics and Social Conditions*, London: Routledge.

Linder, Benjamin (2022), 'Sensing scalarity: towards a humanistic approach to scale', *Progress in Human Geography*, Vol.46(1), pp.67–85.

Linz, Jess and Secor, Anna J. (2021), 'Undoing mastery: with ambivalence?', *Dialogues in Human Geography*, Vol.11(1), pp.108–111.

Lipton, Peter (2004 [1991]), *Inference to the Best Explanation*, Second Edition, London: Routledge.

Little, Daniel (1991), *Varieties of Social Explanation: An Introduction to the Philosophy of Social Science*, Boulder, CO: Westview Press.

Little, Daniel (2011), 'Causal mechanisms in the social realm', in Phyllis McKay Illari, Federica Russo, and Jon Williamson (eds.), *Causality in the Sciences*, Oxford: Oxford University Press, pp.273–295.

Little, Daniel (2016), *New Directions in the Philosophy of Social Science*, Lanham, MD: Rowman & Littlefield.

Little, Daniel (2018), 'Disaggregating historical explanation: the move to social mechanisms', in Stuart Glennan and Phyllis Illari (eds.), *The Routledge Handbook of Mechanisms and Mechanical Philosophy*, London: Routledge, pp.413–422.

Liu, Weidong (2019), *The Belt and Road Initiative: A Pathway Towards Inclusive Globalization*, London: Routledge.

Liu, Yi (2017), 'The dynamics of local upgrading in globalising latecomer regions: a geographical investigation', *Regional Studies*, Vol.51(6), pp.880–893.

Livingstone, David N. (1992), *The Geographical Tradition: Episodes in the History of a Contested Enterprise*, Oxford: Blackwell.

Locke, John (1975 [1690]), *An Essay Concerning Human Understanding*, Oxford: Oxford University Press.

Lorimer, Jamie (2012), 'Multinatural geographies for the Anthropocene', *Progress in Human Geography*, Vol.36(5), pp.593–612.

Lorimer, Jamie (2020), *The Probiotic Planet: Using Life to Manage Life*, Minneapolis, MN: University of Minnesota Press.

Lukes, Steven (ed.) (1986), *Power*, Oxford: Blackwell.

Lury, Celia (2021), *Problem Spaces: How and Why Methodology Matters*, Cambridge: Polity.

Maccarini, Andrea, Morandi, Emmanuele, and Prandini, Riccardo (eds.) (2011), *Sociological Realism*, London: Routledge.

MacFarlane, Key (2017), 'A thousand CEOs: relational thought, processual space, and Deleuzian ontology in human geography and strategic management', *Progress in Human Geography*, Vol.41(3), pp.299–320.

Machamer, Peter, Darden, Lindley, and Craver, Carl F. (2000), 'Thinking about mechanisms', *Philosophy of Science*, Vol.67(1), pp.1–25.

MacKenzie, Donald A. (2009), *Material Markets: How Economic Agents Are Constructed*, Oxford: Oxford University Press.

MacKenzie, Donald (2021), *Trading at the Speed of Light: How Ultrafast Algorithms Are Transforming Financial Markets*, Princeton, NJ: Princeton University Press.

MacKinnon, Danny (2011), 'Reconstructing scale: towards a new scalar politics', *Progress in Human Geography*, Vol.35(1), pp.21–36.

MacKinnon, Danny (2012), 'Beyond strategic coupling: reassessing the firm-region nexus in global production networks', *Journal of Economic Geography*, Vol.12(1), pp.227–245.

MacLeavy, Julie, Fannin, Maria, and Larner, Wendy (2021), 'Feminism and futurity: geographies of resistance, resilience and reworking', *Progress in Human Geography*, Vol.45(6), pp.1558–1579.

Mahoney, James (2001), 'Beyond correlational analysis: recent innovations in theory and method', *Sociological Forum*, Vol.16(3), pp.575–593.

Mahoney, James (2008), 'Towards a unified theory of causality', *Comparative Political Studies*, Vol.41(4/5), pp.412–436.

Mäki, Uskali, Marchionni, Caterina, Oinas, Päivi, and Sayer, Andrew (eds.) (2004), 'Essay symposium: scientific realism, geography and economics', *Environment and Planning A*, Vol.36(10), pp.1717–1789.

Malpas, Jeff (2018), *Place and Experience: A Philosophical Topography*, Second Edition, London: Routledge.

Manicas, Peter T. (2006), *A Realist Philosophy of Social Science: Explanation and Understanding*, Cambridge: Cambridge University Press.

Manning, Erin (2016), *The Minor Gesture*, Durham, NC: Duke University Press.

Manzo, Gianluca (ed.) (2014), *Analytical Sociology: Actions and Networks*, Chichester: Wiley.

Manzo, Gianluca (ed.) (2021), *Research Handbook on Analytical Sociology*, Cheltenham: Edward Elgar.

Markusen, Ann (1999), 'Fuzzy concepts, scanty evidence, policy distance: the case for rigor and policy relevance in critical regional studies', *Regional Studies*, Vol.33(9), pp.869–884.

Markusen, Ann (2003), 'On conceptualization, evidence and impact: a response to Hudson, Lagendijk and Peck', *Regional Studies*, Vol.37(6/7), pp.747–751.

Marston, Sallie A. (2000), 'The social construction of scale', *Progress in Human Geography*, Vol.24(2), pp.219–241.

Marston, Sallie A., Jones, John Paul, III, and Woodward, Keith (2005), 'Human geography without scale', *Transactions of the Institute of British Geographers*, Vol.30(4), pp.416–432.

Martin, Ron (2010), 'Roepke Lecture in economic geography—rethinking regional path dependence: beyond lock-in to evolution', *Economic Geography*, Vol.86(1), pp.1–27.

Martin, Ron (2012), 'Regional economic resilience, hysteresis and recessionary shocks', *Journal of Economic Geography*, Vol.12(1), pp.1–32.

Martin, Ron (2018), 'Is British economic geography in decline?', *Environment and Planning A*, Vol.50(7), pp.1503–1509.

Martin, Ron and Sunley, Peter (2006), 'Path dependence and regional economic evolution', *Journal of Economic Geography*, Vol.6(4), pp.395–437.

Martin, Ron and Sunley, Peter (2015), 'On the notion of regional economic resilience: conceptualization and explanation', *Journal of Economic Geography*, Vol.15(1), pp.1–42.

Massey, Doreen (1973), 'Towards a critique of industrial location theory', *Antipode*, Vol.5(3), pp.33–39.

Massey, Doreen (1979), 'In what sense a regional problem?', *Regional Studies*, Vol.13(2), pp.233–243.

Massey, Doreen (1984), *Spatial Divisions of Labour: Social Structures and the Geography of Production*, London: Macmillan.

Massey, Doreen (1991), 'A global sense of place', *Marxism Today*, June, pp.24–29.

Massey, Doreen (1993), 'Power-geometry and a progressive sense of place', in Jon Bird, Barry Curtis, Tim Putnam, George Robertson, and Lisa Tickner (eds.), *Mapping the Futures: Local Cultures and Global Change*, London: Routledge, pp.59–69.

Massey, Doreen (1995), *Spatial Divisions of Labour: Social Structures and the Geography of Production*, Second Edition, New York: Routledge.

Massey, Doreen (2001), 'Geography on the agenda', *Progress in Human Geography*, Vol.25(1), pp.5–17.

Massey, Doreen (2004), 'Geographies of responsibility', *Geografiska Annaler*, Vol.86(1), pp.5–18.

Massey, Doreen (2005), *For Space*, London: Sage.

Massey, Doreen (2007), *World City*, Cambridge: Polity.

Massey, Doreen, Allen, John, and Sarre, Philip (eds.) (1999), *Human Geography Today*, Cambridge: Polity.

Massumi, Brian (2002), *Parables of the Virtual: Movement, Affect, Sensation*, Durham, NC: Duke University Press.

Massumi, Brian (2015), *Politics of Affect*, Cambridge: Polity.

Mayhew, Robert J. (2011), 'Geography's genealogies', in John A. Agnew and David N. Livingstone (eds.), *The SAGE Handbook of Geographical Knowledge*, London: Sage, pp.21–38.

Mayntz, Renate (2004), 'Mechanisms in the analysis of social macro-phenomena', *Philosophy of the Social Sciences*, Vol.34(2), pp.237–259.

McAdam, Doug, Tarrow, Sidney, and Tilly, Charles (2001), *Dynamics of Contention*, Cambridge: Cambridge University Press.

McCain, Kevin and Poston, Ted (eds.) (2018), *Best Explanations: New Essays on Inference to the Best Explanation*, Oxford: Oxford University Press.

McCormack, Derek P. (2003), 'An event of geographical ethics in spaces of affect', *Transaction of the Institute of British Geographers*, Vol.28(4), pp.488–507.

McCormack, Derek P. (2012), 'Geography and abstraction: towards an affirmative critique', *Progress in Human Geography*, Vol.36(6), pp.715–734.

McCormack, Derek P. (2017), 'The circumstances of post-phenomenological life worlds', *Transactions of the Institute of British Geographers*, Vol.42(1), pp.2–13.

McCormack, Derek (2018), *Atmospheric Things: On the Allure of Elemental Envelopment*, Durham, NC: Duke University Press.

McCormack, Derek (2020), 'Forms of comprehension', *Dialogues in Human Geography*, Vol.10(3), pp.366–369.

McDowell, Linda (1995), 'Understanding diversity: the problem of/for "theory"', in Ron J. Johnston, Peter J. Taylor, and Michael J. Watts (eds.), *Geographies of Global Change: Remapping the World in the Late-Twentieth Century*, Oxford: Blackwell, pp.280–294.

McDowell, Linda (2004), 'Work, workfare, work/life balance and an ethic of care', *Progress in Human Geography*, Vol.28(2), pp.145–163.

McFarlane, Colin (2009), 'Translocal assemblages: space, power and social movements', *Geoforum*, Vol.40(4), pp.561–567.

McGrath, Siobhán (2018), 'Dis/articulations and the interrogation of development in GPN research', *Progress in Human Geography*, Vol.42(4), pp.509–528.

McKittrick, Katherine (2006), *Demonic Grounds: Black Women and the Cartographies of Struggle*, Minneapolis, MN: University of Minnesota Press.

McKittrick, Katherine and Woods, Clyde Adrian (eds.) (2007), *Black Geographies and the Politics of Place*, Cambridge, MA: South End Press.

Meillassoux, Quentin (2008), *After Finitude: An Essay on the Necessity of Contingency*, Trans. Ray Brassier, London: Continuum.

Merriman, Peter, Jones, Martin, Olsson, Gunnar, Sheppard, Eric, Thrift, Nigel J., and Tuan, Yi-Fu (2012), 'Space and spatiality in theory', *Dialogues in Human Geography*, Vol.2(1), pp.3–22.

Merton, Robert K. (1968 [1949]), *Social Theory and Social Structure*, Revised Edition, New York: Free Press.

Meulbroek, Chris, Peck, Jamie, and Zhang, Jun (2023), 'Bayspeak: narrating China's Greater Bay Area', *Journal of Contemporary Asia*, Vol.53(1), pp.95–123.

Mitchell, Katharyne and Elwood, Sarah (2012), 'Mapping children's politics: The promise of articulation and the limits of nonrepresentational theory', *Environment and Planning D: Society and Space*, Vol.30(5), pp.788–804.

Mittelman, James H. (2000), *The Globalization Syndrome: Transformation and Resistance*, Princeton, NJ: Princeton University Press.

Mol, Annemarie (2010), 'Actor-network theory: sensitive terms and enduring tensions', *Kölner Zeitschrift für Soziologie und Sozialpsychologie. Sonderheft*, Vol.50(1), pp.253–269.

Mollett, Sharlene and Faria, Caroline (2018), 'The spatialities of intersectional thinking: fashioning feminist geographic futures', *Gender, Place & Culture*, Vol.25(4), pp.565–577.

Moore, Adam (2008), 'Rethinking scale as a geographical category: from analysis to practice', *Progress in Human Geography*, Vol.32(2), pp.203–226.

Morgan, Jamie (2015), 'Seeing the potential of realism in economics', *Philosophy of the Social Sciences*, Vol.45(2), pp.176–201.

Morgan, Kevin (1997), 'The learning region: institutions, innovation and regional renewal', *Regional Studies*, Vol.31(5), pp.491–503.

Moss, Pamela and Donovan, Courtney (eds.) (2017), *Writing Intimacy into Feminist Geography*, London: Routledge.

Müller, Martin (2021), 'Worlding geography: from linguistic privilege to decolonial anywheres', *Progress in Human Geography*, Vol.45(6), pp.1440–1466.

Müller, Martin and Schurr, Carolin (2016), 'Assemblage thinking and actor-network theory: conjunctions, disjunctions, cross-fertilisations', *Transactions of the Institute of British Geographers*, Vol.41(3), pp.217–229.

Mumford, Stephen and Anjum, Rani Lill (2011), *Getting Causes from Powers*, Oxford: Oxford University Press.

Murdoch, Jonathan (1995), 'Actor-networks and the evolution of economic forms: combining description and explanation in theories of regulation, flexible specialization, and networks', *Environment and Planning A*, Vol.27(5), pp.731–757.

Murdoch, Jonathan (1997a), 'Towards a geography of heterogeneous associations', *Progress in Human Geography*, Vol.21(3), pp.321–337.

Murdoch, Jonathan (1997b), 'Inhuman/nonhuman/human: actor-network theory and the prospects for a nondualistic and symmetrical perspective on nature and society', *Environment and Planning D: Society and Space*, Vol.15(6), pp.731–756.

Murdoch, Jonathan (2006), *Post-Structuralist Geography: A Guide to Relational Space*, London: Sage.

Nagar, Richa, Lawson, Vicky, McDowell, Linda, and Hanson, Susan (2002), 'Locating globalization: feminist (re)readings of the subjects and spaces of globalization', *Economic Geography*, Vol.78(3), pp.257–284.

Narayanan, Nipesh Palat (2021), 'Southern theory without a north: city conceptualization as the theoretical metropolis', *Annals of the American Association of Geographers*, Vol.111(4), pp.989–1001.

Naughton, Barry and Tsai, Kellee S. (eds.) (2015), *State Capitalism, Institutional Adaptation, and the Chinese Miracle*, Cambridge: Cambridge University Press.

Nee, Victor and Opper, Sonja (2012), *Capitalism From Below: Markets and Institutional Change in China*, Cambridge, MA: Harvard University Press.

Neilson, Jeff and Pritchard, Bill (2009), *Value Chain Struggles: Institutions and Governance in the Plantation Districts of South India*, Oxford: Wiley-Blackwell.

Neilson, Jeffrey, Pritchard, Bill, and Yeung, Henry Wai-chung (2014), 'Global value chains and global production networks in the changing international political economy', *Review of International Political Economy*, Vol.21(1), pp.1–8.

Nem Singh, Jewellord T. and Ovadia, Jesse Salah (eds.) (2019), *Developmental States Beyond East Asia*, London: Routledge.

Nielsen, Peter (2002), 'Reflections on critical realism in political economy', *Cambridge Journal of Economics*, Vol.26(6), pp.727–738.

Noble, Safiya Umoja (2018), *Algorithms of Oppression: How Search Engines Reinforce Racism*, New York: New York University Press.

Norris, William J. (2016), *Chinese Economic Statecraft: Commercial Actors, Grand Strategy, and State Control*, Ithaca, NY: Cornell University Press.

Noxolo, Pat (2022), 'Geographies of race and ethnicity 1: black geographies', *Progress in human geography*, Vol.46(5), pp.1232–1240.

Nussbaum, Martha Craven (2000), *Women and Human Development: The Capabilities Approach*, New York: Cambridge University Press.

O'Boyle, Brian and McDonough, Terrence (2011), 'Critical realism, Marxism and the critique of neoclassical economics', *Capital & Class*, Vol.35(1), pp.3–22.

O'Brien, Richard (1992), *Global Financial Integration: The End of Geography*, New York: Council on Foreign Relations Press.

O'Dowd, Liam (2010), 'From a 'borderless world' to a 'world of borders': 'bringing history back in'', *Environment and Planning D: Society and Space*, Vol.28(6), pp.1031–1050.

Oberhauser, Ann M., Fluri, Jennifer L., Whitson, Risa, and Mollett, Sharlene (2018), *Feminist Spaces: Gender and Geography in a Global Context*, London: Routledge.

Ohmae, Kenichi (1990), *The Borderless World: Power and Strategy in the Interlinked Economy*, London: Collins.

Ohmae, Kenichi (1995), *The End of the Nation State: The Rise of Regional Economies*, London: HarperCollins.

Olds, Kris and Yeung, Henry Wai-chung (1999), '(Re)shaping "Chinese" business networks in a globalising era', *Environment and Planning D: Society and Space*, Vol.17(5), pp.535–555.

Ong, Aihwa (2006), *Neoliberalism as Exception: Mutations in Citizenship and Sovereignty*, Durham, NC: Duke University Press.

Ornston, Darius (2018), *Good Governance Gone Bad – How Nordic Adaptability Leads to Excess*, Ithaca, NY: Cornell University Press.

Oswin, Natalie (2008), 'Critical geographies and the uses of sexuality: deconstructing queer space', *Progress in Human Geography*, Vol.32(1), pp.89–104.

Oswin, Natalie (2020), 'An other geography', *Dialogues in human geography*, Vol.10(1), pp.9–18.

Ouma, Stefan (2015), *Assembling Export Markets. The Making and Unmaking of Global Market Connections in West Africa*, Oxford: Wiley-Blackwell.

Pain, Rachel, Rezwana, Nahid, and Sahdan, Zuriatunfadzliah (2020), 'Trauma, gender and space: insights from Bangladesh, Malaysia and the UK', in Anindita Datta, Peter Hopkins, Lynda Johnston, Elizabeth Olson, and Joseli Maria Silva (eds.), *Routledge Handbook of Gender and Feminist Geographies*, London: Routledge, pp.287–296.

Park, Bae-Gyoon, Hill, Richard Child, and Saito, Asato (eds.) (2012), *Locating Neoliberalism in East Asia: Neoliberalizing Spaces in Developmental States*, Oxford: Wiley-Blackwell.

Pearl, Judea (2009 [2000]), *Causality: Models, Reasoning and Inference*, Second Edition, Cambridge: Cambridge University Press.

Peck, Jamie A. (2002), 'Political economies of scale: scalar politics, fast policy, and neoliberal workfare', *Economic Geography*, Vol.78(3), pp.331–360.

Peck, Jamie A. (2003), 'Fuzzy old world: a response to Markusen', *Regional Studies*, Vol.37(6/7), pp.729–740.

Peck, Jamie A. (2010), *Constructions of Neoliberal Reason*, Oxford: Oxford University Press.

Peck, Jamie A. (2013), 'Explaining (with) neoliberalism', *Territory, Politics, Governance*, Vol.1(2), pp.132–157.

Peck, Jamie (2015), 'Cities beyond compare?', *Regional Studies*, Vol.49(1), pp.160–182.

Peck, Jamie (2016), 'Macroeconomic geographies', *Area Development and Policy*, Vol.1(3), pp.305–322.

Peck, Jamie (2021), 'On capitalism's cusp', *Area Development and Policy*, Vol.6(1), pp.1–30.

Peck, Jamie (2023), *Variegated Economies*, New York: Oxford University Press.

Peck, Jamie A. and Theodore, Nikolas (2007), 'Variegated capitalism', *Progress in Human Geography*, Vol.31(6), pp.731–772.

Peck, Jamie A. and Theodore, Nikolas (2015), *Fast Policy: Experimental Statecraft at the Thresholds of Neoliberalism*, Minneapolis, MN: University of Minnesota Press.

Peck, Jamie A., Theodore, Nikolas, and Brenner, Neil (2010), 'Postneoliberalism and its malcontents', *Antipode*, Vol.41(S1), pp.94–116.

Peck, Jamie A. and Tickell, Adam T. (2002), 'Neoliberalizing space', *Antipode*, Vol.34(3), pp.380–404.

Peck, Jamie, Werner, Marion, and Jones, Martin (2023), 'A dialogue on uneven development: a distinctly regional problem', *Regional Studies*, Vol.57(7), pp.1392–1403.

Peck, Jamie, Werner, Marion, Lave, Rebecca, and Christophers, Brett (2018), 'Out of place: Doreen Massey, radical geographer', in Marion Werner, Jamie Peck, Rebecca Lave, and Brett Christophers (eds.), *Doreen Massey: Critical Dialogues*, Newcastle upon Tyne: Agenda Publishing, pp.1–38.

Peck, Jamie A. and Zhang, Jun (2013), 'A variety of capitalism... with Chinese characteristics?', *Journal of Economic Geography*, Vol.13(3), pp.357–396.

Peet, Richard (1991), *Global Capitalism: Theories of Societal Development*, London: Routledge.

Phelps, Nicholas A., Atienza, Miguel, and Arias, Martin (2018), 'An invitation to the dark side of economic geography', *Environment and Planning A*, Vol.50(1), pp.236–244.

Philo, Chris (2012), 'A "new Foucault" with lively implications – or "the crawfish advances sideways"', *Transactions of the Institute of British Geographers*, Vol.37(4), pp.496–514.

Phipps, Alison (2014), *The Politics of the Body: Gender in a Neoliberal and Neoconservative Age*, Chichester: Wiley.

Phipps, Alison and Young, Isabel (2015), 'Neoliberalisation and "lad cultures" in higher education', *Sociology*, Vol.49(2), pp.305–322.

Pickles, John and Smith, Adrian (2016), *Articulations of Capital: Global Production Networks and Regional Transformations*, Oxford: Wiley-Blackwell.

Pike, Andy, MacKinnon, Danny, Cumbers, Andrew, Dawley, Stuart, and McMaster, Robert (2016), 'Doing evolution in economic geography', *Economic Geography*, Vol.92(2), pp.123–144.

Pike, Andy and Pollard, Jane (2010), 'Economic geographies of financialization', *Economic Geography*, Vol.86(1), pp.29–51.

Pile, Steve (2010), 'Emotions and affect in recent human geography', *Transactions of the Institute of British Geographers*, Vol.35(1), pp.5–20.

Pile, Steve (2021), *Bodies, Affects, Politics: The Clash of Bodily Regimes*, Chichester: Wiley.

Polanyi, Karl (1944), *The Great Transformation: The Political and Economic Origins of Our Time*, New York: Holt Rinehart.

Ponte, Stefano, Gereffi, Gary, and Raj-Reichert, Gale (eds.) (2019), *Handbook on Global Value Chains*, Cheltenham: Edward Elgar.

Popke, E. Jeffrey (2003), 'Poststructuralist ethics: subjectivity, responsibility and the space of community', *Progress in Human Geography*, Vol.27(3), pp.298–316.

Porpora, Douglas (2015), *Reconstructing Sociology: The Critical Realist Approach*, Cambridge: Cambridge University Press.

Posthuma, Anne and Nathan, Dev (2011), *Labour in Global Production Networks in India*, Oxford: Oxford University Press.

Potter, Rob (2001), 'Geography and development: "core and periphery"?', *Area*, Vol.33(4), pp.422–427.

Povinelli, Elizabeth A. (2011), *Economies of Abandonment: Social Belonging and Endurance in Late liberalism*, Durham, NC: Duke University Press.

Povinelli, Elizabeth A. (2016), *Geontologies: A Requiem to Late Liberalism*, Durham, NC: Duke University Press.

Pow, Choon-Piew (2015), 'Urban dystopia and epistemologies of hope', *Progress in Human Geography*, Vol.39(4), pp.464–485.

Pozzoni, Gianluca and Kaidesoja, Tuukka (2021), 'Context in mechanism-based explanation', *Philosophy of the Social Sciences*, Vol.51(6), pp.523–554.

Pratt, Andy C. (1991), 'Reflections on critical realism and geography', *Antipode*, Vol.23(2), pp.248–255.

Pratt, Andy C. (1995), 'Putting critical realism to work: the practical implications for geographical research', *Progress in Human Geography*, Vol.19(1), pp.61–74.

Pratt, Andy C. (2009), 'Critical realism/critical realist geographies', in Rob Kitchen and Nigel Thrift (eds.), *International Encyclopedia of Human Geography*, Vol.2. Oxford: Elsevier, pp.379–384.

Pratt, Andy C. (2013), '"… the point is to change it": critical realism and human geography', *Dialogues in Human Geography*, Vol.3(1), pp.26–29.

Pratt, Geraldine and Rosner, Victoria (eds.) (2012a), *The Global and the Intimate: Feminism in Our Time*, New York: Columbia University Press.

Pratt, Geraldine and Rosner, Victoria (2012b), 'Introduction: the global and the intimate', in Geraldine Pratt and Victoria Rosner (eds.), *The Global and the Intimate: Feminism in Our Time*, New York: Columbia University Press, pp.1–27.

Price, Patricia L. (2010), 'At the crossroads: critical race theory and critical geographies of race', *Progress in Human Geography*, Vol.34(2), pp.147–174.

Ptolemy (2000), *Ptolemy's Geography: An Annotated Translation of the Theoretical Chapters*, Trans. J. Lennart Berggren and Alexander Jones, Princeton, NJ: Princeton University Press.

Puar, Jasbir K. (2017), *The Right to Maim: Debility, Capacity, Disability*, Durham, NC: Duke University Press.

Puar, Jasbir K. (2017 [2007]), *Terrorist Assemblages: Homonationalism in Queer Times*, 10th Anniversary Expanded Edition, Durham, NC: Duke University Press.

Radcliffe, Sarah A. (2015), *Dilemmas of Difference: Indigenous Women and the Limits of Postcolonial Development Policy*, Durham, NC: Duke University Press.

Radcliffe, Sarah A. (2017), 'Decolonising geographical knowledges', *Transactions of the Institute of British Geographers*, Vol.42(3), pp.329–333.

Ramoglou, Stratos and Tsang, Eric W.K. (2016), 'A realist perspective of entrepreneurship: opportunities as propensities', *Academy of Management Review*, Vol.41(3), pp.410–434.

Ramoglou, Stratos and Tsang, Eric W.K. (2017), 'In defense of common sense in entrepreneurship theory: beyond philosophical extremities and linguistic abuses', *Academy of Management Review*, Vol.42(4), pp.736–744.

Reiss, Julian (2007), 'Do we need mechanisms in the social sciences?', *Philosophy of the Social Sciences*, Vol.37(2), pp.163–184.

Reiss, Julian (2015), *Causation, Evidence, and Inference*, London: Routledge.

Resch, Robert Paul (1992), *Althusser and the Renewal of Marxist Social Theory*, Berkeley, CA: University of California Press.

Reskin, Barbara F. (2003), 'Including mechanisms in our models of ascriptive inequality', *American Sociological Review*, Vol.68(1), pp.1–21.

Rinard, Susanna (2018), 'External world skepticism and inference to the best explanation', in Kevin McCain and Ted Poston (eds.), *Best Explanations: New Essays on Inference to the Best Explanation*, Oxford: Oxford University Press, pp.203–216.

Roberts, John Michael (2001), 'Realistic spatial abstraction? Marxist observations of a claim within critical realist geography', *Progress in Human Geography*, Vol.25(4), pp.545–568.

Roberts, Tom (2014), 'From things to events: Whitehead and the materiality of process', *Environment and Planning D: Society and Space*, Vol.32(6), pp.968–983.

Roberts, Tom (2019), 'Resituating post-phenomenological geographies: Deleuze, relations and the limits of objects', *Transactions of the Institute of British Geographers*, Vol.44(3), pp.542–554.

Roberts, Tom and Dewsbury, John-David (2021), 'Vital aspirations for geography in an era of negativity: valuing life differently with Deleuze', *Progress in Human Geography*, Vol.45(6), pp.1512–1530.

Robinson, Jennifer (2006), *Ordinary Cities: Between Modernity and Development*, London: Routledge.

Robinson, Jennifer (2016), 'Thinking cities through elsewhere: comparative tactics for a more global urban studies', *Progress in human geography*, Vol.40(1), pp.3–29.

Rodríguez-Pose, Andrés (2004), 'On English as a vehicle to preserve geographical diversity', *Progress in Human Geography*, Vol.28(1), pp.1–4.

Rose, Gillian (1993), *Feminism and Geography: The Limits of Geographical Knowledge*, Minneapolis, MN: University of Minnesota Press.

Rose, Gillian (1997), 'Situating knowledges: positionality, reflexivities and other tactics', *Progress in Human Geography*, Vol.21(3), pp.305–320.

Rosenman, Emily, Loomis, Jessa, and Kay, Kelly (2020), 'Diversity, representation, and the limits of engaged pluralism in (economic) geography', *Progress in Human Geography*, Vol.44(3), pp.510–533.

Roux, Sophie (2018), 'From the mechanical philosophy to early modern mechanisms', in Stuart Glennan and Phyllis Illari (eds.), *The Routledge Handbook of Mechanisms and Mechanical Philosophy*, London: Routledge, pp.26–45.

Roy, Ananya (2009), 'The 21st century metropolis: new geographies of theory', *Regional Studies*, Vol.43(6), pp.819–830.

Roy, Ananya (2020), '"The shadow of her wings": respectability politics and the self-narration of geography', *Dialogues in Human Geography*, Vol.10(1), pp.19–22.

Roy, Ananya, Wright, Willie J., Al-Bulushi, Yousuf, and Bledsoe, Adam (2020), '"A world of many Souths": (anti) Blackness and historical difference in conversation with Ananya Roy', *Urban Geography*, Vol.41(6), pp.920–935.

Ruez, Derek and Cockayne, Daniel (2021), 'Feeling otherwise: ambivalent affects and the politics of critique in geography', *Dialogues in Human Geography*, Vol.11(1), pp.88–107.

Runhardt, Rosa W. (2015), 'Evidence for causal mechanisms in social science: recommendations from Woodward's manipulability theory of causation', *Philosophy of Science*, Vol.82(5), pp.1296–1307.

Rutzou, Timothy (2017), 'Finding Bhaskar in all the wrong places? Causation, process, and structure in Bhaskar and Deleuze', *Journal for the Theory of Social Behaviour*, Vol.47(4), pp.402–417.

Rutzou, Timothy and Elder-Vass, Dave (2019), 'On assemblages and things: fluidity, stability, causation stories, and formation stories', *Sociological Theory*, Vol.37(4), pp.401–424.

Rutzou, Timothy and Steinmetz, George (eds.) (2018), *Critical Realism, History, and Philosophy in the Social Sciences*, Bingley, UK: Emerald Publishing.

Ruwanpura, Kanchana N. (2022), *Garments Without Guilt?: Global Labour Justice and Ethical Codes in Sri Lankan Apparels*, Cambridge: Cambridge University Press.

Sack, Robert David (1980), *Conceptions of Space in Social Thought*, London: Macmillan.

Said, Edward W. (2003 [1978]), *Orientalism: Western Conceptions of the Orient*, Harmondsworth: Penguin.

Salmon, Wesley C. (1984), *Scientific Explanation and the Causal Structure of the World*, Princeton, NJ: Princeton University Press.

Salmon, Wesley C. (1989), *Four Decades of Scientific Explanation*, Minneapolis, MN: University of Minnesota Press.

Salmon, Wesley C. (1998), *Causality and Explanation*, Oxford: Oxford University Press.

Sassen, Saskia (1991), *The Global City: New York, London, Tokyo*, Princeton, NJ: Princeton University Press.

Sassen, Saskia (1996), *Losing Control? Sovereignty in an Age of Globalization*, New York: Columbia University Press.

Sassen, Saskia (2007), 'Introduction: deciphering the global', in Saskia Sassen (ed.), *Deciphering the Global: Its Scales, Spaces and Subjects*, New York: Routledge, pp.1–18.

Saxenian, AnnaLee (2006), *The New Argonauts: Regional Advantage in a Global Economy*, Cambridge, MA: Harvard University Press.

Sayer, Andrew (1979), 'Epistemology and conceptions of people and nature in geography', *Geoforum*, Vol.10(1), pp.19–44.

Sayer, Andrew (1981), 'Abstraction: a realist interpretation', *Radical Philosophy*, Vol.28, pp.6–15.

Sayer, Andrew (1982a), 'Explanation in economic geography: abstraction versus generalization', *Progress in Human Geography*, Vol.6(1), pp.68–88.

Sayer, Andrew (1982b), 'Explaining manufacturing shift: a reply to Keeble', *Environment and Planning A*, Vol.14(1), pp.119–125.

Sayer, Andrew (1984), *Method in Social Science: A Realist Approach*, London: Hutchinson.

Sayer, Andrew (1985), 'Industry and space: a sympathetic critique of radical research', *Environment and Planning D: Society and Space*, Vol.3(1), pp.3–29.

Sayer, Andrew (1992), *Method in Social Science: A Realist Approach*, Second Edition, London: Routledge.

Sayer, Andrew (1995), *Radical Political Economy: A Critique*, Oxford: Basil Blackwell.

Sayer, Andrew (2000), *Realism and Social Science*, London: Sage.

Sayer, Andrew (2001), 'For a critical cultural political economy', *Antipode*, Vol.33(4), pp.687–708.

Sayer, Andrew (2004), 'Seeking the geographies of power: review of *Lost Geographies of Power* by John Allen', *Economy and Society*, Vol.33(2), pp.255–270.

Sayer, Andrew (2010 [1992/1984]), *Method in Social Science: A Realist Approach*, Revised Second Edition, London: Routledge.

Sayer, Andrew (2015), 'Realism as a basis for knowing the world', in Stuart Aitken and Gill Valentine (eds.), *Approaches to Human Geography*, Second Edition, London: Sage, pp.106–116.

Sayer, Andrew (2018), 'Ontology and the politics of space', in Marion Werner, Jamie Peck, Rebecca Lave, and Brett Christophers (eds.), *Doreen Massey: Critical Dialogues*, Newcastle upon Tyne: Agenda Publishing, pp.103–112.

Sayer, Andrew and Storper, Michael (1997), 'Ethics unbound: for a normative turn in social theory', *Environment and Planning D: Society and Space*, Vol.15(1), pp.1–17.

Schatzki, Theodore (2002), *The Site of the Social: A Philosophical Account of the Constitution of Social Life and Change*, University Park, PA: The Pennsylvania State University Press.

Schatzki, Theodore (2019), *Social Change in A Material World: How Activity and Material Processes Dynamize Practices*, New York: Routledge.

Scott, Allen J. (1988), *New Industrial Spaces: Flexible Production, Organisation and Regional Development in North America and Western Europe*, London: Pion.

Scott, Allen J. (1998), *Regions and the World Economy: The Coming Shape of Global Production, Competition and Political Order*, Oxford: Oxford University Press.

Scott, Allen J. (2012), *A World in Emergence: Cities and Regions in the 21st Century*, Cheltenham: Edward Elgar.

Scott, Allen J. and Storper, Michael (2015), 'The nature of cities: the scope and limits of urban theory', *International Journal of Urban and Regional Research*, Vol.39(1), pp.1–16.

Scott, Joan Wallach (2019), *Knowledge, Power, and Academic Freedom*, New York: Columbia University Press.

Seamon, David (2015), 'Lived emplacement and the locality of being: a return to humanistic geography?', in Stuart Aitken and Gill Valentine (eds.), *Approaches to Human Geography*, Second Edition, London: Sage, pp.35–48.

Shannon, Jerry, Hankins, Katherine B., Shelton, Taylor, Bosse, Amber J., Scott, Dorris, Block, Daniel, Fischer, Heather et al. (2021), 'Community geography: toward a disciplinary framework', *Progress in Human Geography*, Vol.45(5), pp.1147–1168.

Sharp, Joanne P. (2009), *Geographies of Postcolonialism: Spaces of Power and Representation*, London: Sage.

Sharp, Joanne P. (2011), 'Gender', in John A. Agnew and David N. Livingstone (eds.), *The SAGE Handbook of Geographical Knowledge*, London: Sage, pp.430–440.

Shaviro, Steven (2014), *The Universe of Things: On Speculative Realism*, Minneapolis, MN: University of Minnesota Press.

Sheppard, Eric (2002), 'The spaces and times of globalization: place, scale, networks, and positionality', *Economic Geography*, Vol.78(3), pp.307–330.

Sheppard, Eric (2008), 'Geographic dialectics?', *Environment and Planning A*, Vol.40(11), pp.2603–2612.

Sheppard, Eric (2011), 'Geographical political economy', *Journal of Economic Geography*, Vol.11(2), pp.319–331.

Sheppard, Eric (2016), *Limits to Globalization: The Disruptive Geographies of Capitalist Development*, Oxford: Oxford University Press.

Sheppard, Eric and Barnes, Trevor J. (1990), *The Capitalist Space Economy: Geographical Analysis after Ricardo, Marx and Sraffa*, London: Unwin Hyman.

Shirk, Susan (1993), *The Political Logic of Economic Reform in China*, Berkeley, CA: University of California Press.

Sidaway, James D. (2000), 'Postcolonial geographies: an exploratory essay', *Progress in Human Geography*, Vol.24(4), pp.591–612.

Sidaway, James D. (2022), 'Psychogeography: walking through strategy, nature and narrative', *Progress in Human Geography*, Vol.46(2), pp.549–574.

Sil, Rudra and Katzenstein, Peter J. (2010), 'Analytic eclecticism in the study of world politics: reconfiguring problems and mechanisms across research traditions', *Perspectives on Politics*, Vol.8(2), pp.411–431.

Simonsen, Kirsten (2010), 'Encountering O/other bodies: practice, emotion and ethics', in Ben Anderson and Paul Harrison (eds.), *Taking-Place: Non-Representational Theories and Geography*, Eldershot: Ashgate, pp.221–240.

Simonsen, Kirsten (2013), 'In quest of a new humanism: embodiment, experience and phenomenology as critical geography', *Progress in Human Geography*, Vol.37(1), pp.10–26.

Simonsen, Kirsten and Koefoed, Lasse (2020), *Geographies of Embodiment: Critical Phenomenology and the World of Strangers*, London: Sage.

Simpson, Paul (2021), *Non-Representational Theory*, London: Routledge.

Slater, David (1992), 'On the borders of social theory: learning from other regions', *Environment and Planning D: Society and Space*, Vol.10(3), pp.307–327.

Slater, David (1993), 'The geopolitical imagination and the enframing of development theory', *Transactions of the Institute of British Geographers*, Vol.18(4), pp.419–437.

Slater, David (1999), 'Situating geopolitical representations: inside/outside and the power of imperial interventions', in Doreen Massey, John Allen, and Philip Sarre (eds.), *Human Geography Today*, Cambridge: Polity, pp.62–84.

Slater, David (2002), 'Other domains of democratic theory: space, power and the politics of democratization', *Environment and Planning D: Society and Space*, Vol.20(3), pp.255–276.

Slater, David (2004), *Geopolitics and the Post-Colonial: Rethinking North–South Relations*, Oxford: Blackwell.

Smith, Adrian (2015), 'The state, institutional frameworks and the dynamics of capital in global production networks', *Progress in Human Geography*, Vol.39(3), pp.290–315.

Smith, Neil (1984), *Uneven Development: Nature, Capital and the Production of Space*, Oxford: Basil Blackwell.

Smith, Neil (2004), *The Endgame of Globalization*, London: Routledge.

Soja, Edward (1989), *Postmodern Geographies: The Reassertion of Space in Critical Social Theory*, London: Verso.

Sparke, Matthew (2013), *Introducing Globalization: Ties, Tensions, and Uneven Integration*, Oxford: Wiley-Blackwell.

Sparrow, Tom (2014), *The End of Phenomenology: Metaphysics and the New Realism*, Edinburgh: Edinburgh University Press.

Spivak, Gayatri Chakravorty (1988), 'Can the Subaltern speak?', in Cary Nelson and Lawrence Grossberg (eds.), *Marxism and the Interpretation of Culture*, Basingstoke: Macmillan, pp.271–313.

Spivak, Gayatri Chakravorty (1999), *A Critique of Postcolonial Reason: Towards a History of the Vanishing Present*, Cambridge, MA: Harvard University Press.

Spivak, Gayatri Chakravorty (2012), *An Aesthetic Education in the Era of Globalization*, Cambridge, MA: Harvard University Press.

Springer, Simon, Birch, Kean, and MacLeavy, Julie (eds.) (2016), *The Handbook of Neoliberalism*, London: Routledge.

Stewart, Kathleen C. (2007), *Ordinary Affects*, Durham, NC: Duke University Press.

Stiglitz, Joseph (2002), *Globalization and its Discontents*, London: Penguin.

Stiglitz, Joseph (2006), *Making Globalization Work*, New York: W.W. Norton.

Stiglitz, Joseph (2017), *Globalization and its Discontents Revisited: Anti-Globalization in the Era of Trump*, London: Penguin.

Stinchcombe, Arthur L. (1991), 'The conditions of fruitfulness of theorizing about mechanisms in social science', *Philosophy of the Social Sciences*, Vol.21(3), pp.367–388.

Storper, Michael (1997), *The Regional World: Territorial Development in a Global Economy*, New York: Guilford Press.

Storper, Michael (2001), 'The poverty of radical theory today: from the false promises of Marxism to the mirage of the cultural turn', *International Journal of Urban and Regional Research*, Vol.25(1), pp.155–179.

Storper, Michael (2009), 'Roepke lecture in economic geography – regional context and global trade', *Economic Geography*, Vol.85(1), pp.1–21.

Storper, Michael (2013), *Keys to the City: How Economics, Institutions, Social Interaction, and Politics Shape Development*, Princeton, NJ: Princeton University Press.

Storper, Michael and Walker, Richard (1989), *The Capitalist Imperative: Territory, Technology and Industrial Growth*, Oxford: Basil Blackwell.

Strabo of Amasia (1917–1932), *Geography*, Trans. Horace L. Jones, 8 Volumes, Cambridge, MA: Harvard University Press.

Strauss, Kendra (2019), 'Process, mechanism and the project of economic geography', *Dialogues in Human Geography*, Vol.9(3), pp.256–261.

Sun, Yutao and Grimes, Seamus (2017), *China and Global Value Chains: Globalization and the Information and Communications Technology Sector*, London: Routledge.

Sundberg, Juanita (2014), 'Decolonizing posthumanist geographies', *Cultural Geographies*, Vol.21(1), pp.33–47.

Sunley, Peter (1996), 'Context in economic geography: the relevance of pragmatism', *Progress in Human Geography*, Vol.20(3), pp.338–355.

Sunley, Peter (2008), 'Relational economic geography: a partial understanding or a new paradigm?', *Economic Geography*, Vol.84(1), pp.1–26.

Swedberg, Richard (2014), *The Art of Social Theory*, Princeton, NJ: Princeton University Press.

Swyngedouw, Erik A. (1997), 'Neither global nor local: 'glocalization' and the politics of scale', in Kevin R. Cox (ed.), *Spaces of Globalization: Reasserting the Power of the Local*, New York: Guilford, pp.137–166.

Tan, Yeling (2021), *Disaggregating China, Inc.: State Strategies in the Liberal Economic Order*, Ithaca, NY: Cornell University Press.

Tavory, Iddo and Timmermans, Stefan (2014), *Abductive Analysis: Theorizing Qualitative Research*, Chicago, IL: University of Chicago Press.

Taylor, Peter J. (2007), 'Problematizing city/state relations: towards a geohistorical understanding of contemporary globalization', *Transactions of the Institute of British Geographers*, Vol.32(2), pp.133–150.

Taylor, Peter J., Watts, Michael J., and Johnston, Ron J. (2001), 'Geography/globalization', *GaWC Research Bulletin*, Vol.41, Department of Geography, Loughborough University.

Teixeira, Tiago R.A. (2022), 'Global production networks and the uneven development of regional training systems: conceptualizing an approach and proposing a research agenda', *Progress in Human Geography*, Vol.46(2), pp.507–526.

Thévenot, Laurent (2001), 'Organized complexity: conventions of coordination and the composition of economic arrangements', *European Journal of Social Theory*, Vol.4(4), pp.405–425.

Thrift, Nigel (1986), 'Little games and big stories: accounting for the practices of personality and politics in the 1945 general election', in Keith Hoggart and Eleonore Kofman (eds.), *Politics, Geography and Social Stratification*, London: Croom Helm, pp.90–155.

Thrift, Nigel (1996), *Spatial Formations*, London: Sage.

Thrift, Nigel (2000), 'Afterwords', *Environment and Planning D: Society and Space*, Vol.18(2), pp.213–255.

Thrift, Nigel (2003), 'The might of "might": how social power is being refigured', in Jamie Peck and Henry Wai-chung Yeung (eds.), *Remaking the Global Economy: Economic-Geographical Perspectives*, London: Sage, pp.130–144.

Thrift, Nigel (2004), 'Intensities of feeling: towards a spatial politics of affect', *Geografiska Annaler: Series B, Human Geography*, Vol.86(1), pp.57–78.

Thrift, Nigel J. (2007), *Non-Representational Theory: Space, Politics, Affect*, London: Routledge.

Thrift, Nigel (2021), *Killer Cities*, London: Sage.

Thrift, Nigel and Dewsbury, John-David (2000), 'Dead geography – And how to make them live', *Environment and Planning D: Society and Space*, Vol.18(4), pp.411–432.

Thrift, Nigel and Olds, Kris (1996), 'Refiguring the economic in economic geography', *Progress in Human Geography*, Vol.20(3), pp.311–337.

Tilly, Charles (2001), 'Mechanisms in political processes', *Annual Review of Political Science*, Vol.4, pp.21–41.

Tilly, Charles (2004), 'Social boundary mechanisms', *Philosophy of the Social Sciences*, Vol.34(2), pp.211–236.

Tolia-Kelly, Divya P. (2006), 'Affect – an ethnocentric encounter? Exploring the "universalist" imperative or emotional/affectual geographies', *Area*, Vol.38(2), pp.213–217.

Tolia-Kelly, Divya P. (2013), 'The geographies of cultural geography III: material geographies, vibrant matters and risking surface geographies', *Progress in Human Geography*, Vol.37(1), pp.153–160.

Tomaney, John (2013), 'Parochialism – a defence', *Progress in Human Geography*, Vol.37(5), pp.658–672.

Tsang, Eric W.K. (2014), 'Case studies and generalization in information systems research: a critical realist perspective', *Journal of Strategic Information Systems*, Vol.23(2), pp.174–186.

Tsang, Eric W.K. (2022), *Explaining Management Phenomena: A Philosophical Treatise*, New York: Cambridge University Press.

Tsang, Eric W.K. and Kwan, Kai-Man (1999), 'Replication and theory development in organizational science: a critical realist perspective', *Academy of Management Review*, Vol.24(4), pp.759–780.

Tuan, Yi-Fu (1977), *Space and Place: The Perspective of Experience*, Minneapolis, MN: University of Minnesota Press.

Tuck, Eve and Yang, K. Wayne (2012), 'Decolonization is not a metaphor', *Decolonization: Indigeneity, Education and Society*, Vol.1(1), pp.1–40.

Unwin, Tim (2011), 'The role of geography and geographers in policy and government departments', in John A. Agnew and David N. Livingstone (eds.), *The SAGE Handbook of Geographical Knowledge*, London: Sage, pp.271–284.

van Ingen, Michiel, Grohmann, Steph, and Gunnarsson, Lena (eds.) (2020), *Critical Realism, Feminism, and Gender: A Reader*, London: Routledge.

Van Meeteren, Michiel (2019), 'On geography's skewed transnationalization, anglophone hegemony, and qualified optimism toward an engaged pluralist future; a reply to Hassink, Gong and Marques', *International Journal of Urban Sciences*, Vol.23(2), pp.181–190.

Van Meeteren, Michiel, Bassens, David, and Derudder, Ben (2016a), 'Doing global urban studies: on the need for engaged pluralism, frame switching, and methodological cross-fertilization', *Dialogues in Human Geography*, Vol.6(3), pp.296–301.

Van Meeteren, Michiel, Derudder, Ben, and Bassens, David (2016b), 'Can the straw man speak? An engagement with postcolonial critiques of "global cities research"', *Dialogues in Human Geography*, Vol.6(3), pp.247–267.

Varró, Krisztina (2015), 'Making (more) sense of political-economic geographies of continuity and change: dialoguing across ontological divides', *Progress in Human Geography*, Vol.39(1), pp.26–46.

Venugopal, Rajesh (2015), 'Neoliberalism as concept', *Economy and Society*, Vol.44(2), pp.165–187.

Volkoff, Olga and Strong, Diane M. (2013), 'Critical realism and affordances: theorizing IT-associated organizational change processes', *MIS Quarterly*, Vol.37(3), pp.819–834.

Wade, Robert (1990), *Governing the Market: Economic Theory and the Role of Government in East Asian Industrialization*, Princeton, NJ: Princeton University Press.

Walker, Richard and Storper, Michael (1981), 'Capital and industrial location', *Progress in Human Geography*, Vol.5(4), pp.473–509.

Wan, Poe Yu-ze (2016), *Reframing the Social: Emergentist Systemism and Social Theory*, London: Routledge.

Weber, Erik (2007), 'Social mechanisms, causal inference, and the policy relevance of social science', *Philosophy of the Social Sciences*, Vol.37(3), pp.348–359.

Weheliye, Alexander G. (2014), *Habeas Viscus: Racializing Assemblages, Biopolitics, and Black Feminist Theories of the Human*, Durham, NC: Duke University Press.

Weller, Nicholas and Barnes, Jeb (2014), *Finding Pathways: Mixed-Method Research for Studying Causal Mechanisms*, Cambridge: Cambridge University Press.

Weller, Sally and O'Neill, Phillip (2014), 'An argument with neoliberalism: Australia's place in a global imaginary', *Dialogues in Human Geography*, Vol.4(2), pp.105–130.

Werner, Marion (2021), 'Geographies of production II: thinking through the state', *Progress in Human Geography*, Vol.45(1), pp.178–189.

Whatmore, Sarah (1997), 'Dissecting the autonomous self: hybrid cartographies for a relational ethics', *Environment and Planning D: Society and Space*, Vol.15(1), pp.37–53.

Whatmore, Sarah (2002), *Hybrid Geographies: Natures, Cultures, Spaces*, London: Sage.

Whatmore, Sarah (2005), 'Hybrid Geographies: author's responses and reflections', *Antipode*, Vol.37(4), pp.842–845.

Whitehead, Alfred North (1929), *Process and Reality. An Essay in Cosmology. Gifford Lectures Delivered in the University of Edinburgh During the Session 1927–1928*, Cambridge: Cambridge University Press.

Whiteside, Heather (2019), 'Is, ought and being careful what you wish for', *Dialogues in Human Geography*, Vol.9(3), pp.267–272.

Whiteside, Heather, Alami, Ilias, Dixon, Adam D., and Peck, Jamie (2023), 'Making space for the new state capitalism', *Environment and Planning A: Economy and Space*, Vol.55(1), pp.63–71.

Whittaker, D. Hugh, Sturgeon, Timothy, Okita, Toshie, and Zhu, Tianbiao (2020), *Compressed Development: Time and Timing in Economic and Social Development*, Oxford: Oxford University Press.

Wilkinson, Eleanor and Lim, Jason (2021), 'Life from the fragments: ambivalence, critique, and minoritarian affect', *Dialogues in Human Geography*, Vol.11(1), pp.112–116.

Wilson, Helen F. (2017), 'On geography and encounter: bodies, borders, and difference', *Progress in Human Geography*, Vol.41(4), pp.451–471.

Woods, Michael, Fois, Francesca, Heley, Jesse, Jones, Laura, Onyeahialam, Anthonia, Saville, Samantha, and Welsh, Marc (2021), 'Assemblage, place and globalisation', *Transactions of the Institute of British Geographers*, Vol.46(2), pp.284–298.

Woodward, James (2002), 'What is a mechanism? A counterfactual account', *Philosophy of Science*, Vol.69(S3), pp.S366–S377.

Woodward, James (2003), *Making Things Happen. A Theory of Causal Explanation*, Oxford: Oxford University Press.

Wright, John (2018), *An Epistemic Foundation for Scientific Realism: Defending Realism Without Inference to the Best Explanation*, Cham: Springer.

Wright, Sarah (2015), 'More-than-human, emergent belongings: a weak theory approach', *Progress in Human Geography*, Vol.39(4), pp.391–411.

Wu, Di (2022), 'Forging connections: the role of "boundary spanners" in globalising clusters and shaping cluster evolution', *Progress in Human Geography*, Vol.46(2), pp.484–506.

Wu, Fulong (2008), 'China's great transformation: neoliberalization as establishing a market society', *Geoforum*, Vol.39(3), pp.1093–1096.

Wu, Fulong (2010), 'How neoliberal is China's reform? The origins of change during transition', *Eurasian Geography and Economics*, Vol.51(5), pp.619–631.

Wu, Fulong (2018), 'Planning centrality, market instruments: governing Chinese urban transformation under state entrepreneurialism', *Urban Studies*, Vol.55(7), pp.1383–1399.

Wylie, John (2005), 'A single day's walking: narrating self and landscape on the South West Coast Path', *Transactions of the Institute of British Geographers*, Vol.30(2), pp.234–247.

Xing, Yuqing (2021), *Decoding China's Export Miracle: A Global Value Chain Analysis*, Singapore: World Scientific.

Yang, Dali (2004), *Remaking the Chinese Leviathan: Market Transition and the Politics of Governance in China*, Stanford, CA: Stanford University Press.

Yang, Mayfair Mei-Hui (1994), *Gifts, Favors and Banquets: The Art of Social Relationships in China*, Ithaca, NY: Cornell University Press.

Yeung, Henry Wai-chung (1994), 'Critical reviews of geographical perspectives on business organisations and the organisation of production: towards a network approach', *Progress in Human Geography*, Vol.18(4), pp.460–490.

Yeung, Henry Wai-chung (1997), 'Critical realism and realist research in human geography: a method or a philosophy in search of a method?', *Progress in Human Geography*, Vol.21(1), pp.51–74.

Yeung, Henry Wai-chung (1998a), *Transnational Corporations and Business Networks: Hong Kong Firms in the ASEAN Region*, London: Routledge.

Yeung, Henry Wai-chung (1998b), 'Capital, state and space: contesting the borderless world', *Transactions of the Institute of British Geographers*, Vol.23(3), pp.291–309.

Yeung, Henry Wai-chung (2001), 'Redressing the geographical bias in social science knowledge', *Environment and Planning A*, Vol.33(1), pp.1–9.

Yeung, Henry Wai-chung (2003), 'Practicing new economic geographies: a methodological examination', *Annals of the Association of American Geographers*, Vol.93(2), pp.442–462.

Yeung, Henry Wai-chung (2005), 'Rethinking relational economic geography', *Transactions of the Institute of British Geographers*, Vol.30(1), pp.37–51.

Yeung, Henry Wai-chung (2007), 'Remaking economic geography: insights from East Asia', *Economic Geography*, Vol.83(4), pp.339–348.

Yeung, Henry Wai-chung (2008), '*Review of World City by Doreen Massey*', RGS-IBG Economic Geography Research Group Book Reviews, https://egrg.org/2008-reviews, accessed on 18 October 2021.

Yeung, Henry Wai-chung (2009a), 'Globalization – Economic', in Rob Kitchin et al. (eds.), *International Encyclopedia of Human Geography*, Oxford: Elsevier, pp.581–586.

Yeung, Henry Wai-chung (2009b), 'Regional development and the competitive dynamics of global production networks: an East Asian perspective', *Regional Studies*, Vol.43(3), pp.325–351.

Yeung, Henry Wai-chung (2012), 'East Asian capitalisms and economic geographies', in Trevor Barnes, Jamie Peck, and Eric Sheppard (eds.), *The Wiley-Blackwell Companion to Economic Geography*, Oxford: Wiley-Blackwell, pp.116–129.

Yeung, Henry Wai-chung (2014), 'Governing the market in a globalizing era: developmental states, global production networks, and inter-firm dynamics in East Asia', *Review of International Political Economy*, Vol.21(1), pp.70–101.

Yeung, Henry Wai-chung (2015), 'Regional development in the global economy: a dynamic perspective of strategic coupling in global production networks', *Regional Science Policy & Practice*, Vol.7(1), pp.1–23.

Yeung, Henry Wai-chung (2016), *Strategic Coupling: East Asian Industrial Transformation in the New Global Economy*, Cornell Studies in Political Economy Series, Ithaca, NY: Cornell University Press.

Yeung, Henry Wai-chung (2018), 'The logic of production networks', in Gordon L. Clark, Maryann P. Feldman, Meric S. Gertler, and Dariusz Wójcik (eds.), *The New Oxford Handbook of Economic Geography*, Oxford: Oxford University Press, pp.382–406.

Yeung, Henry Wai-chung (2019a), 'Rethinking mechanism and process in the geographical analysis of uneven development', *Dialogues in Human Geography*, Vol.9(3), pp.226–255.

Yeung, Henry Wai-chung (2019b), 'What kind of theory for what kind of human geography?', *Dialogues in Human Geography*, Vol.9(3), pp.283–292.

Yeung, Henry Wai-chung (2019c), 'Alice Amsden', in David Simon (ed.), *Key Thinkers on Development*, Second Edition, London: Routledge, pp.30–36.

Yeung, Henry Wai-chung (2021a), 'Regional worlds: from related variety in regional diversification to strategic coupling in global production networks', *Regional Studies*, Vol.55(6), pp.989–1010.

Yeung, Henry Wai-chung (2021b), 'The trouble with global production networks', *Environment and Planning A: Economy and Space*, Vol.53(2), pp.428–438.

Yeung, Henry Wai-chung (2022), *Interconnected Worlds: Global Electronics and Production Networks in East Asia*, Innovation and Technology in the World Economy Series, Stanford, CA: Stanford University Press.

Yeung, Henry Wai-chung (2023), 'Troubling economic geography: new directions in the post-pandemic world', *Transactions of the Institute of British Geographers*, Vol.48.

Yeung, Henry Wai-chung and Coe, Neil M. (2015), 'Toward a dynamic theory of global production networks', *Economic Geography*, Vol.91(1), pp.29–58.

Yeung, Henry Wai-chung and Lin, George C.S. (2003), 'Theorizing economic geographies of Asia', *Economic Geography*, Vol.79(2), pp.107–128.

Yeung, Henry Wai-chung and Peck, Jamie (2003), 'Making global connections: a geographer's perspective', in Jamie Peck and Henry Wai-chung Yeung (eds.), *Remaking the Global Economy: Economic-Geographical Perspectives*, London: Sage, pp.3–23.

Ylikoski, Petri (2011), 'Social mechanisms and explanatory relevance', in Pierre Demeulenaere (ed.), *Analytical Sociology and Social Mechanisms*, Cambridge: Cambridge University Press, pp.154–172.

Ylikoski, Petri (2012), 'Micro, macro, and mechanisms', in Harold Kincaid (ed.), *Oxford Handbook of the Philosophy of Social Science*, Oxford: Oxford University Press, pp.21–45.

Ylikoski, Petri (2018), 'Social mechanisms', in Stuart Glennan and Phyllis Illari (eds.), *The Routledge Handbook of Mechanisms and Mechanical Philosophy*, London: Routledge, pp.401–412.

Ylikoski, Petri and Kuorikoski, Jaakko (2010), 'Dissecting explanatory power', *Philosophical Studies*, Vol.148(2), pp.201–219.

Yusoff, Kathryn (2013), 'Geologic life: prehistory, climate, futures in the Anthropocene', *Environment and Planning D: Society and Space*, Vol.31(5), pp.779–795.

Yusoff, Kathryn (2018), *A Billion Black Anthropocenes or None*, Minneapolis, MN: University of Minnesota Press.

Zhang, Jun and Peck, Jamie (2016), 'Variegated capitalism, Chinese style: regional models, multi-scalar constructions', *Regional Studies*, Vol.50(1), pp.52–78.

Zhou, Yu, Lin, George C.S., and Zhang, Jun (2019), 'Urban China through the lens of neoliberalism: is a conceptual twist enough?', *Urban Studies*, Vol.56(1), pp.33–43.

Zukauskaite, Elena, Trippl, Michaela, and Plechero, Monica (2017), 'Institutional thickness revisited', *Economic Geography*, Vol.93(4), pp.325–345.

Zürn, Michael and Checkel, Jeffrey T. (2005), 'Getting socialized to build bridges: constructivism and rationalism, Europe and the nation-state', *International Organization*, Vol.59(4), pp.1045–1079.

# Index

*Theory and Explanation in Geography*, First Edition. Henry Wai-chung Yeung.
© 2024 John Wiley & Sons Ltd. Published 2024 by John Wiley & Sons Ltd.

Printed and bound by CPI Group (UK) Ltd, Croydon, CR0 4YY

15/09/2023

08115986-0001